KAROOLA

WWI. No. 1 AUSTRALIAN HOSPITAL SHIP

The story of Medical Service, Official War History,
and the Diaries and Letters of Rex Sargent
who served on the Hospital Ship 'Karoola' as a
Medical Orderly and Pathologist from 1917-1919

By Rhonda Dolzan
(nee Sargent)

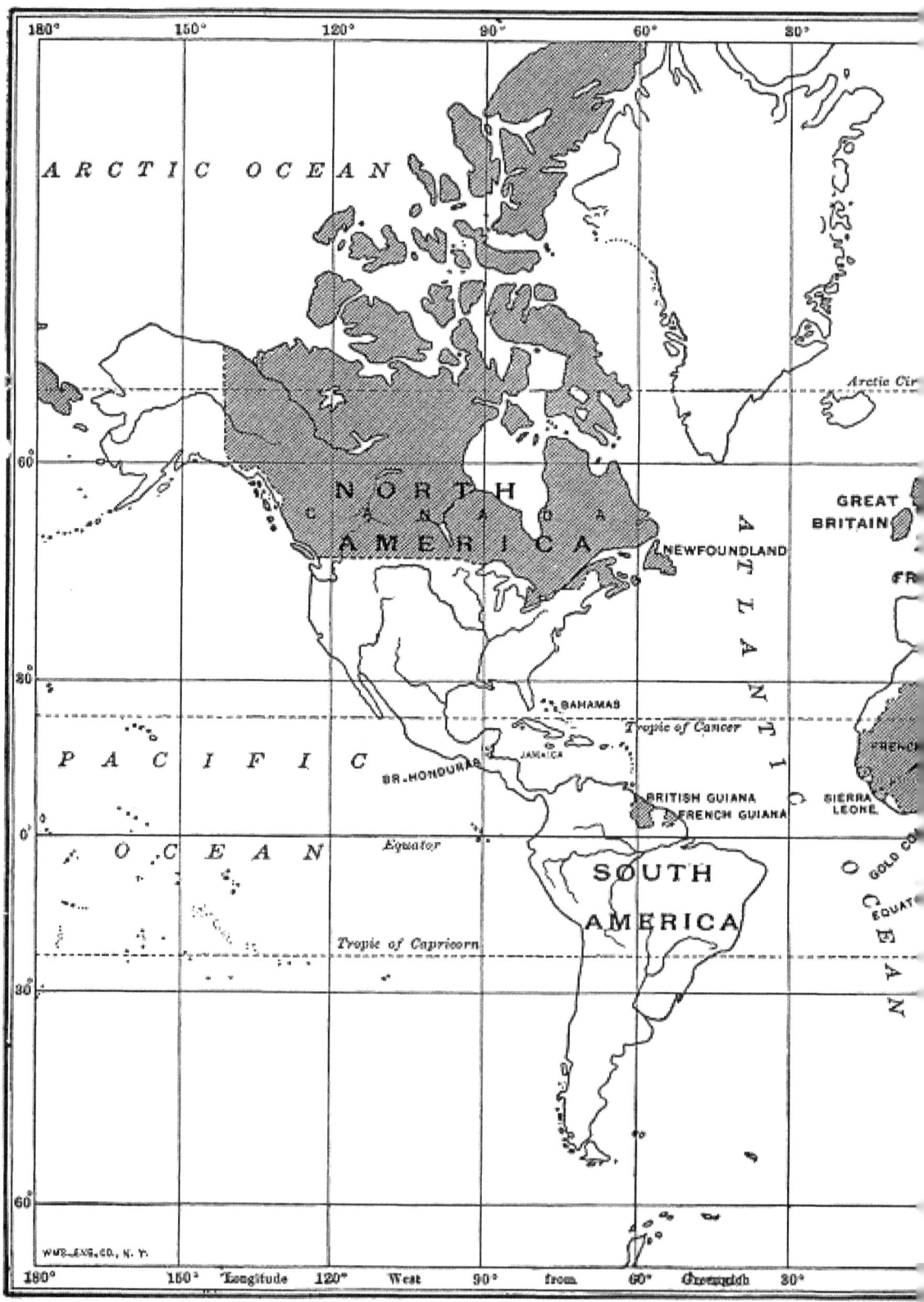

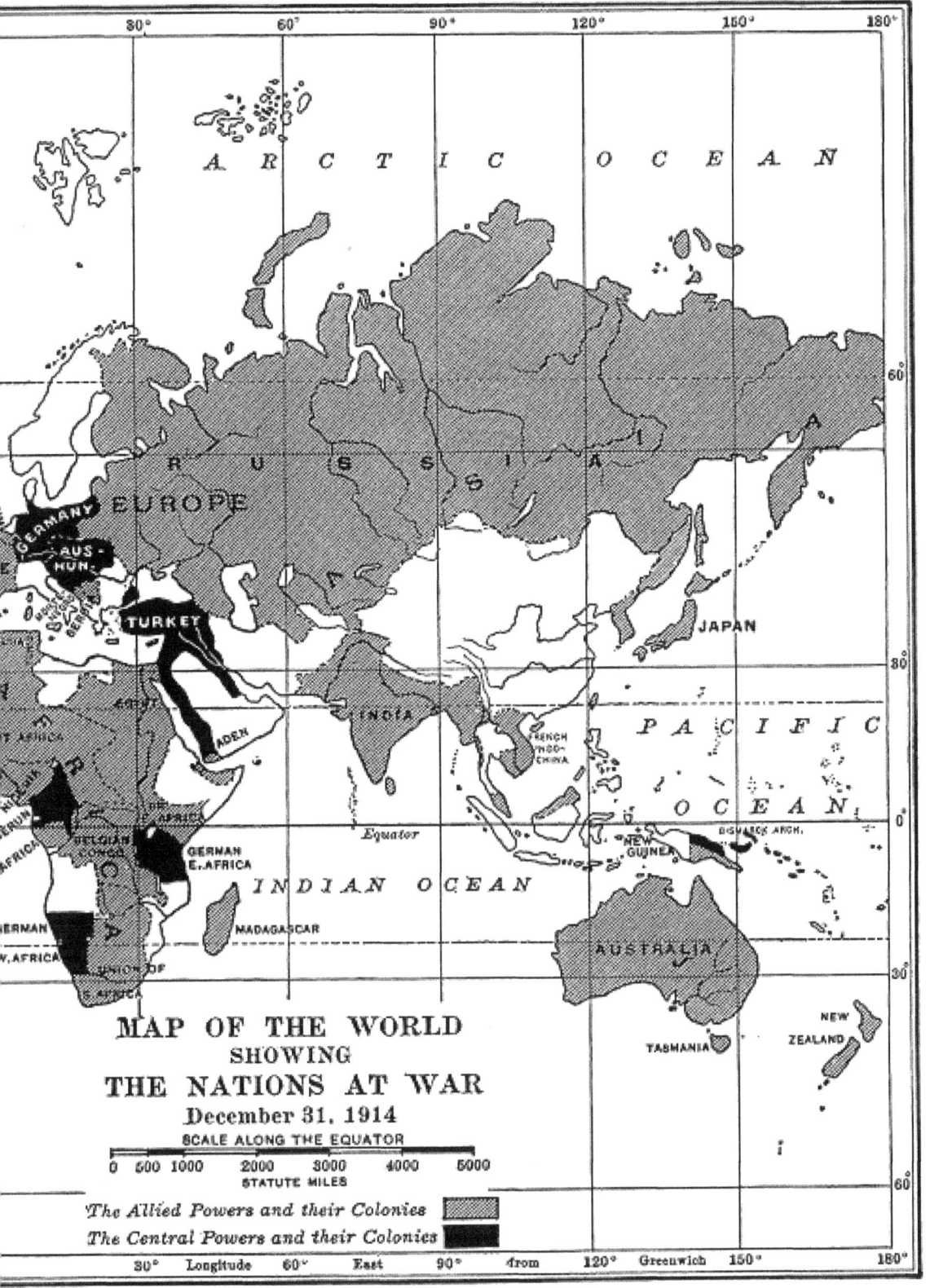

MAP OF THE WORLD
SHOWING
THE NATIONS AT WAR
December 31, 1914

The Allied Powers and their Colonies
The Central Powers and their Colonies

© Copyright Rhonda Dolzan 2015

Published by and copies available from:
Rhonda Dolzan
rdolzan@adam.com.au

ISBN: 978-1-7644207-1-6

Designed by:
Openbook Howden
www.openbookhowden.com.au

23699

HISTORY OF "KAROOLA"

McIlwraith McEacharn Limited. 1909-1937.

Built:	1909 by Harland & Wolff, Belfast
Tonnage:	7,391 gross/4,324 net
Dimensions:	437 x 56 ft/135.5 x 17 m
Service speed:	15 knots
Engines:	Quadruple expansion
Propulsion:	Twin screws

McIlwraith McEacharn had long been a minor force in passenger trading along the Australian coast, operating cargo ships fitted with rather austere accommodation, and they were not considered serious competition by the well established passenger lines.

All this changed in 1909 when they introduced 'KAROOLA'. The vessel was launched on the 10th March 1909, and left Britain on 29th July for Australia, stopping at Durban on the 24th August before arriving in Melbourne on the 11th September.

The new liner caused an immediate sensation in shipping circles, being the first coastal liner to top seven thousand tons, and of a much more modern appearance than previous coastal liners. After a week spent fitting out in Melbourne, 'KAROOLA' steamed on to Sydney arriving on the 20th September, and she sailed from that port on the 25th September on her maiden coastal voyage to Fremantle.

The accommodation was of a very high standard, being divided into 144 first class, 156 second class, and 130 third class. There were many who considered the vessel too large and luxurious for the coastal trade, but within a very short space of time 'KAROOLA' was the most successful ship on the coast, and other companies were forced to build larger ships themselves in order to compete. 'KAROOLA' was used only on the Fremantle service, and managed to retain a faithful following even when newer and larger ships arrived.

During the thirties 'KAROOLA' was occasionally taken off the regular service to make cruises to Queensland and the South Pacific, and in September 1935 she was taken off the Fremantle service and transferred to the east coast route from Melbourne to Cairns.

In May 1936 the new liner 'KANIMBLA' arrived in Australia, entering service on the tenth of the month, and on the 19th May 'KAROOLA' was laid up in Sydney.

Ten months later the vessel was sold to Z.F.Yih Shipping Co, who took delivery of 'KAROOLA' in Sydney on the 25th March 1937. The new owners were from Shanghai, and stated they intended to operate the ship on the coast of China, and after leaving Sydney 'KAROOLA' went to Java to load a cargo of scrap iron, which she took to Shanghai. Whether the new owners really had meant to use the ship is not known, as shortly after arriving in Shanghai, 'KAROOLA' was broken up.

WAR SERVICE WWI

During May 1915 'KAROOLA' was requisitioned by the British Government and converted into a troop-ship at Sydney, being allocated the number A63. She carried a contingent of troops to Egypt, and then proceeded to Britain, where she was converted into a hospital ship at Southampton with funds raised by public subscription in Australia. This work was completed early in September 1915, and left on her initial voyage as a hospital ship on the 9th of that month. This was a short trip to Alexandria and back, and showed many minor defects in the general arrangements which would cause much inconvenience on a longer trip, and these were rectified on return to England. At Southampton a steam laundry was fitted, and other alterations undertaken, on its completion the ship left for Australia on 19th October 1915.

An incident of the return trip from Alexandria was the rescue on the Spanish coast of 29 passengers from the 'HIGHLAND WARRIOR', a British ship bound from London to Buenos Aires.

During the Great War the 'KAROOLA' No. 1 Hospital Ship travelled extensively between Australia and Britain, to Egypt and eastern Mediterranean.

No other country had ever before such a distance to carry their grievously wounded, and taking into consideration the fact that the ship had to load up with necessary foods and supplies for such long voyages at their home ports, only taking coal, water, fresh fruit and vegetables at the various ports of call, it was meritorious service of devotion on behalf of our Australian wounded, and in keeping with the world deeds performed on the Western front, in Egypt and Palestine.

How these brave soldiers longed to see their beloved homeland again. The 'Karoola' bought home the wounded, the grievously ill, the blind, the mentally ill, and the limbless. For some the long trip home from the battlefield had taken many months, and despite the loving care for their physical, mental and spiritual welfare from a dedicated staff of Surgeons, Nursing Sisters, and trained Medical Orderlies, some died at sea and were committed to the deep.

On the 6th May, 1919 the ship left Plymouth on her voyage back to Australia with the last patients from various English hospitals.

When 'KAROOLA' arrived in Sydney on the 27th June, 1919 she was released from Government service and taken to Cockatoo Dock where work began on refitting the liner for commercial service, and she left Sydney on the 11th October on her first trip to Fremantle.

Because of war losses and sales, McIlwraith, McEacharn were now the major company in the trade to the west, having both 'KAROOLA' and 'KATOOMBA' on the route, and it was not until the motor ships 'MANUNDA' and 'WESTRALIA' came into service in 1929 that their position was challenged.

'Karoola', WWI. No.1 Australian Hospital Ship

DR. REX SARGENT

Dr. Rex Sargent was a remarkable man. He left school in his early teens, and worked for the Savings Bank of S.A. at Pt Pirie and Mt Barker from about 1908 until early in W.W.I.

He enlisted in the A.I.F., and stated training March 1917 at the Mitcham Camp with the 13/32, and transferred to A.M.C. for training as a Medical Orderly at the Keswick Army Hospital. He joined the A.A.M.C. staff on the first Australian Hospital Ship 'Karoola' on the 11th September 1917 as a Medical Orderly, and later was an assistant Pathologist as well.

Coming from a long family line of Doctors, and this with his medical experiences during the war made him realize he also wanted to be a Doctor. He spent two years matriculating, and then went to Adelaide University where he completed the full medical course in 1929. He trained at the Royal Adelaide Hospital, and it was here that he met his future wife, Aileen Besley.

He was on the medical staff on the Repatriation General Hospital, Keswick, in the years 1930-32, worked at the Glenside Mental Asylum and held positions as Medical Superintendent at Kalgoorlie and Fremantle, Western Australia. In 1935 he was Acting Superintendent at the Broken Hill Hospital, and after this he took up practice at Berri and Barmera, where he spent the next 15 years. He was the only doctor in this area for some time, and at one stage he took over the Berri practice as well. During this period he married Aileen Besley (then a Matron).

During WWII with the rank of Lieutenant he was part time officer at the prison hospital at Barmera. There were four blocks, and he was in charge of 'Loveday'. After this he was ill for 6 months from overwork, and sold the practice in 1951.

On returning to Adelaide he had a practice in the Bank of N.S.W building in Adelaide for a short while.

When Dr Lynn went to England, he relieved him for 12 months as Acting Superintendent at Northfield Infectious Diseases Hospital. The Polio epidemic was on at this time. During the years 1952-53 he was Poliomyelitis Medical Officer in the Department of Public Health, and in 1954 was appointed Medical Superintendent of the Infectious Diseases Hospital at the Northfield Wards of the Royal Adelaide Hospital. He was there until he reached retirement age and had to leave.

His last few years of active medical work after retirement were spent with the Government Health Department, where he visited country school children. He was especially interested in the work of the school medical service, and in the welfare of children. The human side of medicine appealed to him strongly, and his guidance to anxious parents was a greatly appreciated characteristic. His wide medical experience, together with his sound judgement and manliness, made him a splendid doctor.

During his student years, he spent much time, especially in the long vacations, in heavy physical work. He worked for a time at the Broken Hill Mines and also on the construction of the Gorge Road in the hills. He had several periods of work on the Harbours Board 'Conqueror', when that little vessel was engaged on lighthouse duties about the South Australian coast. He always enjoyed hard work, and his love of the sea was a lifelong passion.

Also when a medical student he took up land at Myponga, and set about growing a plantation of pines. A few years later, he took another adjoining property and began farming activities on a small scale. Any spare time from his medical work he devoted mainly to supervising the work on his farm, and doing most of the heavy work himself. He was of sturdy physical build.

In all his wide range of activities Rex made a host of friends, and he retained these friendships to the end.

The above in part was in Dr Rex Sargent's Obituary by Dr. A.R. Southwood placed in The Medical Journal of Australia dated October 15, 1966. I have added additional history of his life.

Rhonda Dolzan (nee) Sargent (niece).

Ralph Sargent

Amos and Laura Sargent

Ada Sargent

Rex Sargent 1912

Vere Sargent

Colin Sargent

Rene Bailey (nee Sargent)

Laura Sargent

FOREWORD

I knew my Uncle Dr Rex Sargent very well, seeing him throughout my life when visiting or staying with my Grandparents and Aunties at 141 Swain Avenue, Toorak Gardens, South Australia, at his home, family functions, but also later when I went with him and Aunty Aileen on a number of occasions to their farms at Myponga. I loved it there, and yearn for those times still. I went there many times with my children after Uncle's death, until it was eventually sold. As a young person I also went with him to stay at Barmera when he was a Doctor there.

Where ever we went, there was always the inevitable stops visiting the many people he knew along the way at numerous farms. It seemed to me as a young child, that we were never going to get to where we were going, but I understood even then how respected he was. He had such an interest in the working man, and on our way in the country if he saw a farmer not far from the road, he always stopped to have a chat. He was like that. I remember when I started work at Goode, Durrant and Murray a wholesale firm in Grenfell Street, Adelaide, one man hearing my name came and asked me if the Doctor was a relative and on hearing he was my Uncle, told me he owed his life to him. This in early days was a common occurrence, and Nurses hearing who I was, told me he was so gentle and caring with patients at the Northfield Infections disease hospital.

I was the recipient of many of the family photos, and memorabilia as I was so intensely interested in the family history from a very young age. I treasured all that I was given, and am pleased to say that nowadays, more and more of our family are interested in our heritage.

I decided many years ago to copy Uncles diaries. I had to do a hand written copy first because the diaries were becoming faded in places with time, and due to Uncle having to water down the ink to make it last over the longer voyages. The writing was so small in some places I found it necessary to use a magnifying glass. He often stuck pieces of paper into the centre that went further out, and then folded them back to fit into the size of the diary. Eventually I typed it all so that others can appreciate this piece of history.

Karoola as Hospita Ship

I have visited the Research Centre at the Australia War Memorial in Canberra, ATC for any information on my subject as well as visiting Maritime Museums in Brisbane, Victoria, Adelaide and Perth and State Libraries.

I would like to apologise for any spelling errors of place names or people. I was able to find some places on Google, but some may now have a different name or no longer exist.

It has been almost 100 years since my Uncle wrote these diaries. I have completed all this work to not only honour my Uncle, but also all the Doctors, Nurses, Medical Orderlies, and Crew who gave their all to the grievously wounded WWI Soldiers while serving on the Hospital Ship, Karoola.

Rhonda Dolzan (nee Sargent) 2014.

Rex Sargent   *Karoola in peacetime*

Rex Sargent in peacetime

Rex's Diaries

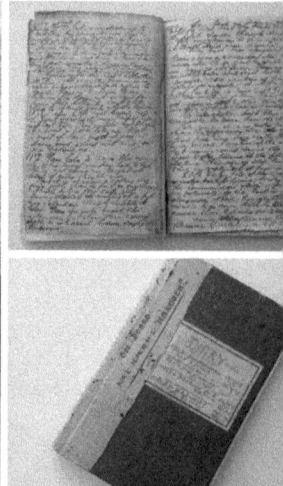

Sisters

Officers

Staff

Diary One

MARCH, 1917

5th Monday
Started Mitcham Camp, Adelaide. South Australia.

Leave granted, attended evening concert.
Saw bank chaps, and wrote Edgar.
Struck with many facilities for soldiers e.g. Y.M.C.A., other Institutions and their respective advantages.

6th Tuesday
Physically also dentally examined, and put down for C.Coy.
Inoculated, and vaccinated at 4.20pm.
Went to Miss Felsteads concert in evening, and in company with other celebrated artists, the entertainment was of a high order and much enjoyed.
Received part of issue i.e. Kit. Getting used to hard boards.

7th Wednesday
Light duties (24 hours).

8th Thursday
First instruction – squad drill.

9th Friday
Orderlies for the day. Oliver and myself.
Private parades, and squad drill.
Went through Battalion and Coy, drill on ceremonial parades. Instructors decent.

10th Saturday
Dental parade.
Swabbing huts.
Weekend leave at 12 o'clock.

11th Sunday
Leave.

12th Monday
Arrived from home at 6.30am in time for morning parade.
Vac-inspection and drill, offered a job in C. Coy office.

13th Tuesday
Route march to Belair, via Devils Elbow, and ord drill.
Obtained leave to attend accountancy class but found Mr Calvin's office closed.
Presumably night changed.

14th Wednesday
Week-night leave.

15th Thursday
Paraded for Dental treatment.
Made sure of A.M.C.

16th Friday
Dental.

17th Saturday
Granted general leave for Pat's day. (St. Patrick Bank Holiday, Ireland).

18th Sunday
Weekend leave. Harvest thanksgiving at Finsbury Church.

19th March
Second inoculation.
Informed that no top plate required.
Anticipate transfer 20/3/17.

20th Tuesday
Wrote Mr. Cocks.
Transferred to the 13/32, expecting to leave on April 9th, 1917.
Long leave granted to some.
Attended Mr. Calvin's class, being leave tonight.

21st Wednesday
Parade and Private drill.
Attended S.S.'KATOOMBA' orchestral party, and Alberton Cheer-up combined concert, very good and much enjoyed.

22nd Thursday
Transferred to A.M.C. from 13/32. First lecture 'Bleeding'.

23rd Friday
Evening Moving Pictures 'Why Britain went to War'.

24th Saturday
Weekend leave.

25th Sunday
Made small donation to Finsbury Baptist Church Building Fund.

26th Monday
Route march in evening, and concert.

27th Tuesday
General week- night leave.

28th Wednesday
Concert in evening after short route march by Returned Anzac 'Booz-up'.

29th Thursday
Getting more accustomed to A.M.C. chaps. Jock Gillies decent fellow, found that he had passed thro' second at Sem 4 Lewis.

31st Saturday
Scrubbing every Saturday morning of huts and lockers etc.

APRIL, 1917

1st Sunday
Easter Services.
Weekend leave. Went with father to Central Methodist Mission in afternoon, and in evening to Aunt's son and Kentown.

2nd Monday
Detailed to Cook House (Hospital).
Drill in morning by Sgt from Keswick, and short route march in evening to Torrens Park by Booz-up, via old track. Sampled figs at rear of premises for second time.

3rd Tuesday
Mr. Calvin's class in evening.

6th Friday
Easter leave from 1pm to 12pm, 9/4/17.

7th Saturday
Went per motorcycle to 'Old Spot' with father re fruit trees. Stayed evening at Quinlavens.

10th Tuesday
Received uniform.
Detailed as Drs. Assistant, also S.C.O. Staff at A.M.C.'s office.

14th Saturday
Weekend leave took father per motorcycle to Walsh's.

16th Monday
Detailed to Army Pay Corps as Corporal's Assistant.
Wrote Mrs. Hyne.
Attended lecture by Camp Comdt, to A.M.C. in evening, very good. Re Gallipoli and France. (Dressing Stations etc.)

17th Tuesday
Heard that very likely go to Keswick 1/5/17.
Wrote Bert Liddle.

18th Wednesday
Lecture by Lt. Col. Hill on bones.

19th Thursday
Lecture by Lt. Col. Hill on the Head, showing model etc., of face, eyes, ears, nose etc.

20th Friday
Went to Pvte. Collivers to tea at Parkside, being his birthday.

21st Saturday
Weekend leave, rode motorcycle home.

22nd Sunday
Went with father for walk from Adelaide via Tusmore to Burnside to Waterfall Gully, up to Eagle on Hill Hotel, and back to Glen Osmond via Mt. Barker road, thence to Fullarton train for Adelaide. Most enjoyable outing, day superb and scenery perfect. Time in walking only 2.20pm to 8.15pm.

23rd Monday
Leave till 9.30am, so stayed home until this morning. Leave pass granted, anticipating trip to Mt. Barker.
Wrote Miss Hodge, and Mrs. Kemp re socks, also B. Brock.

24th Tuesday
Leave changed to Wednesday on account of Anzac procession that day.

25th Wednesday
Anzac Day.
Entrained at Mitcham at 8.15am. Marched procession thro' Adelaide.
Went to Aunt's son for afternoon after dismiss.
Had dinner behind Cheer-up Hut.

26th Thursday
Les Dunstone's third Degree at Emulation Norwood, but unable to get away in time to attend. Also same for Jock Gilles at Sema 4.
Attended Miss Felstead's concert in evening at camp after Col. Hills lecture, 'Bones' or (Skeleton).

27th Friday
Arranged with Sgt. Green (Pay Sgt.) to get off in afternoon. Went home and arranged with father to go to Mt. Barker next day.

28th Saturday
Being Drs. assistant during 7-8am, arranged with R. Dunstone to take my place. Caught train at Mitcham for Mt. Barker, and met father on board. Stayed at Grays. Saw many friends, and invited by Weads to stay there next visit. Went for motor drive with Mr. Smith Sunday, in afternoon, and drove father to Bridgewater at night in Miss Rundle's turn out. Came home myself on 8.45am Victor Harbor express to Adelaide on Monday, arrived 11am having obtained leave.

29th Sunday
We had most enjoyable weather during stay at Mt. Barker, father quite contented, and promised to visit Mrs. Gray again.

30th Monday
Stretcher drill in readiness for Keswick training.

MAY, 1917

1st Tuesday
Stretcher drill in morning. **Transferred to Keswick** in afternoon, per charge Cpl. Renney R.S.

2nd Wednesday
Detailed to No. 14 Ward.
Two spinal cases Q.M.S. Chapman, and Pvte. Jas Sprague, an old Pt. Pirie boy. These two very ill, latter having been laid up for 22 months. Fine fellow, and gives an idea of suffering wrought by the war-makers.

3rd Thursday
Sprague very low. Number of wounded men with various troubles sleep in No. 14 to be boarded tomorrow. Chapman transferred to Ward 13.

4th Friday
Sprague unconscious. Morphia gives sleep so weary his body. Treated for bed-sores each time changed over, although unconscious of any pain attaching to them, being paralyzed below bottom of Dorsal Vertebrae.

5th Saturday
6.30am. Sprague still unconscious, recognizes his mother about 9am, reported to be very ill. Met Birtles, now Sgt. from Pirie who came to see him, he was present at time of Sprague's wounding.

6th Sunday
On weekend leave

7th Monday
Returned to duty. Sprague died 11.30am Sunday, funeral left hospital 3pm (Military funeral).

8th Tuesday
Owing to no patients left in 14, transferred temporarily to Ward 7. (Surgical in charge Sister Stacey).

9th Wednesday
Get a few hints from Sister Stacey re dressings etc. Twelve men in ward.

10th Thursday
So far things satisfactory. Picking up ideas and ways, also organization of ward. On with Pvte. Colliver.

11th Friday
Had letter from Miss Mortimer re Sprague and his mother, also letter from the Misses Hodge.

12th Saturday
Given several dressings to do, and complimented on effort.
Rain and hail the record in Adelaide, very large hail, parade ground like a snowfield.

13th Sunday
Wrote to Mrs. Mac.
On duty, saw three operations performed by Dr. Poulton.

14th Monday
Went to Aunts, night leave.

15th Tuesday
Worked 6-8pm, off afternoon 2-5pm.
Went to Mitcham Camp, and received money for gun from Oliver, four pounds.

16th Wednesday
Visited Hays evening. Walker family away at Victor Harbor.
Sent 10/6 to Les Walkom re lodge fees.

17th Thursday
Sent 15/- to Perry for balance owing on gun as due.
Leopold Installation, unable to attend after arranging with Mr. Ewens, owing to lengthily lecture on hemorrhage by Dr. Cpt. Dawkins.

19th Saturday
Weekend leave, took Vere (*younger sister*) to Waterfall Gully. Very wet and foggy.

20th Sunday
Went with father and mother to Hams, took Colin (*very young brother*) whose behavior was creditable.

21st Monday
Rode bike to Keswick – first thing fire piquet 89.

22nd Tuesday
Discovered that Pvte. George (suffering from French feet), is one of old A. Coy, in 10th A.I.R., and knows Butlers well, also that Sgt. Moller is an old boy at Shipping Office at Pt. Adelaide when I was young.
Young Messner a relative of Barbers (*mother's maiden name Barber*) of Sandy Creek.

23rd Wednesday
Sister Stanley, a Miss Stanley from Williamstown, related to Messner, and Barbers of Sandy Creek.
Transferred to Ward 6. Medical Sister O'Brien in charge, fine woman.

24th Thursday
Sister Macklin also transferred from Ward 7. Ptve. Dunn most serious case suffering from Spinal Myelitis received thro' drinking milk in Egypt. Way back Queenslander station hand.

27th Sunday
Home Sunday night 6-11pm.

28th Monday
New scheme started at Keswick for stretcher drill.
Went for candidate for Corporal.
Wrote Edgar and Miss Mortimer.

29th Tuesday
Went up for exam in Squad drill, and First Aid theory. Six went up. Kilmartin, Burgess, and two Neighbour Bros.

30th Wednesday
Signs of fracture. Pain. Loss of power. Swelling. Deformity. Mobility. Irregularity. Crepitus.

31st Thursday
Heard the 'Sly Dinkum Oil' that made Corporal. Half hope this is not so, would like to see Kilmartin or Neighbour get same.

JUNE, 1917

1st Friday
On Routine Orders that Mitchell and I **received N.C.O. as Corporal from 1/6/17.** Detailed to Wards 10 and 11, assisted for time being by Sgt. Gillain.

2nd Saturday
Leave. Went home from 1pm Saturday to 11pm Sunday.

4th Monday
First day on wards in charge by myself. Not doing badly first go off. Went out to see Bert Liddle but not home, met stranger. Name P. Fitzgerald.

5th Tuesday
Very busy.

6th Wednesday
Got stripes and cross from Mitcham.

7th Thursday
Sister Holdgrave sewed same on for me. On night duty in charge of Barracks.

8th Friday
Went with Bert Liddle and brother to pictures, 'Great Expectations'. Not good enough for Dickens.

9th Saturday
Home for afternoon.
Sister Bryant sewed on stripes on Great Coat.

10th Sunday
Saw four operations. Hernia. Vericoscele. Amputated foot, and break of elbow joint. Wards 7 and 9.

11th Monday
Two operations in my own Ward 10. H. Johns and Hanop. Bending joints under anesthetic. To Aunt's son in evening.

12th Tuesday
Met Sister from Pt. Pirie Hospital

14th Thursday
Went to Outer Harbor. Saw 300 Sisters depart for Salonika. Many from Eastern States. Said goodbye to Sisters Macklin and Stacey.

15th Friday
Poor old Dunn very ill in no. 6, and suffering very much. Capt. Verco advises Peritonitis.

16th Saturday
Home for weekend after wasting three hours Saturday afternoon in hospital pending inspection by Gen. Logg.

17th Sunday
Played at Bible Class with mother as requested by Bob Simpson.

20th Wednesday
Pte. Penfound A.A.M.C. died under anesthetic. Subscribed to wreath.

22nd Friday
Operation Hamilton's leg. Much puss, and two bones removed.

23rd Saturday
Went to Outer Harbor to see troops depart for the front. February and March recruits of A.A.M.C., and 13/32, 7/43, 12/48 departed.

26th Tuesday
Nankivell to take over Wards 10 and 11.

28th Thursday
Operation on Harvey, removed bone from anus wound in buttocks.

30th Saturday
Finished topping tree.
Night duty as N.C.O. 6pm.

JULY, 1917

1st Sunday
Night duty not too bad.

2nd Monday
Went home and cut down trunk of tree.

3rd Tuesday
Received letter from Edgar.

4th Wednesday
Wrote Bill and Mrs. Bishop.

5th Thursday
Received letter and invitation from Mt. Barker Cheer-up and Welcome Home Society. Had photo taken at Ronas.

7th Saturday
Saw Mrs. Bishop and Mary. Had afternoon tea at Arcadia. Proceeded to Mt. Barker at invitation of Cheer-up and Welcome Home Society. Caught Melbourne express at 4pm. Alighted at Mt. Barker junction, and got a lift by cab. Had good evening, and presented with pocket book. Three returned soldiers were present and Fry, Stephenson and myself departing guests. Saw old friends. Slept at Grays. Mr. Bishop drove me to Junction to catch 8.24am Sunday.

8th Sunday
Melbourne express to town arrived in Adelaide at 10.5am, and walked home, could not wait for train. Mother and father presented me with the promised gold watch chain. Ada, Vere a lovely frame for picture, Renie a cake and chocolate, and Ralphy, a khaki handkerchief. *(brother and his three sisters)*.
Returned to duty 6pm.

10th Tuesday
Received proofs of photos.
Went to Aunt Ada, and she well satisfied with them. Chose side face for picture.

11th Wednesday
Went to Aunt's son, did a little odd job or two.

12th Thursday and 13th Friday
Night duty. Hospital nearly empty, making room for fresh batch to arrive from 'RUNIC' after furlough.

14th Saturday
Went home and tried to root out stump of tree. A big contract.

15th Sunday
Went home in the morning, slept in and had a good rest.
Duty at 6pm. Hospital very quiet.

16th Monday
Wrote Allchurch.
Went to see the Misses Hodge.
Hospital busier, on account being filled up with patients finishing furlough.

17th Tuesday
Went to Misses Hodge. Made arrangements for Wednesday week.

18th Wednesday
Wrote Bill Brockelbank.

19th Thursday
Bought wristlet watch two pounds, five shillings from Shepps.

20th Friday
Received photos, and took same to Aunt Ada.
Called on Walkers for ½ hour.

21st Saturday
Went home, and helped father to complete sawing tree.

22nd Sunday
Went home, and with father and Vere went to Semaphore.

23rd Monday
Went to Aunt's son.
Still on night duty, and no notification as to when to remove off.

24th Tuesday
Saw Wynn at Blackwood from No.5. Went to Blackwood to Treloar's home, and to Mr. Craigies in evening. Had a nice evening, and presented with a pair of socks. Dunstone and Colliver present. Wrote Bert Liddle re motorbike.

25th Wednesday
Paid visit to Hams in afternoon, and to Miss Hodges in evening where I met Miss Smith again. Address no. 2 Park Terrace.

28th Saturday
Went home.

29th Sunday
Stayed at Keswick.

30th Monday
Went home, and did last evening on night duty.

31st Tuesday
Went to Aunt's son during afternoon, and stayed for evening.

AUGUST, 1917

1st Wednesday
Took over charge Wards 5 and 6 (Capt. Hamilton).
May reinforcements A.A.M.C. split in two. Colliver, Dunstone and Dumas left for Melbourne by express.

3rd Friday
Night on duty at orderly office till 10.15pm.

4th Saturday
Caught 12.35pm to Blackwood, but found no coach waiting to convey me to Kangarilla. Saw Jack Treloar at his home and had dinner. Did not wait for Williams motor, so borrowed Treloar's bike, and rode out to Coromandel and Kangarilla over the old road. Saw them all well out there, took one hour to ride over. Had a good time and came back, and caught 8.15am train at Blackwood, and arrived at Keswick at 9am on Monday. Never forget what a very beautiful morning this was, absolutely superb.

5th Sunday
At Edgars.

6th Monday
Arrived camp 9am and went on duty, my old boys went back to Mitcham. They didn't hooray some?
Visited Hayes in evening.

7th Tuesday
Cyril Maude from Grumpy gave concert in Rec. Hall at Keswick, very good.

8th Wednesday
Went to Mr. Goldsmiths for evening, and had a good time. Presented by Mrs. G. with socks, face-washer, handkerchief, very nice presents indeed.

9th Thursday
W.O. on furlough. Sgt. Smith relieving.

10th Friday
Father, Vere and I went to Adelaide to hear Adelaide Orchestra. Had a most enjoyable time, and was much taken with Miss Chaplins playing of violin.

11th Saturday
Stayed on weekend duty.

12th Sunday
Father came to Keswick, and we had a good look round. Went home with him, and attended church in evening.

14th Tuesday
Lecture, did not go out.

15th Wednesday
Went to Aunt's son for evening.

16th Thursday
Went to see Reeves in evening. Had a nice time, and chat re old times.

17th Friday
Stayed in barracks, having attended lecture.

18th Saturday
Home for weekend. Raining so could do nothing. Father had planted trees in front of house in Glengyle Street. (*his home*).

19th Sunday
Father and I went for walk down to Rosewater via Torrens Road, and returned home via Junction Road. Had a very enjoyable afternoon. Many beautiful sky larks about, everything fresh.

20th Monday
Went to Torrensville Lodge with Sgt. Page. Met Mr. Beaumont, and had a dashed good time.

21st Tuesday
Lecture, stayed in camp.

22nd Wednesday
Went home for evening.

23rd Thursday
Went to Aunt's son for evening.

24th Friday
Went to Hams with the girls, our promised visit. Got off from lecture.

25th Saturday
Went to see famous Mc Ewen, Hypnotist. Reckons he's a Scotchman, I don't think so.

26th Sunday
Off at 1pm. Went home, and with father went to see poor old Uncle George, who was very unwell, says he has one foot in grave.

27th Monday
Heard that July reinforcements would soon be leaving Keswick for Mitcham.
Went out to Hays in evening, and had a good game of table bowls 21-13 (15-10) our game.

28th Tuesday
To St. Andrews with Higg. Also promised Scotty Wiltshire. Had a jolly good time at St. Andrews. Page also went.

29th Wednesday
Went home for evening, and noticed an invitation to mother and father to attend a farewell to me to be given at Church by Bible Class.

30th Thursday
Went out to Aunt's son for evening.

31st Friday
Mothers birthday.
Went to Aunt Adas for evening. Making good use of all available nights as going to Mitcham on Monday is confirmed.

SEPTEMBER, 1917

2nd Sunday
Now hear that N.C.O's going to Mitcham on Tuesday.
Went home for dinner. Father and I went for a walk.
Called on Uncle Josiah, and arranged with Torey on Sunday week for a trip to Millbrook.

3rd Monday
Caught 5.25pm train from Adelaide, and went to Mt. Barker. Saw Mrs. Gray, and arranged to stay there for night.
Attended Installation, and met Bros. Rankine, Bros. Colgate, Add.Lewis. Had a real good time. Caught 7.50am train Tuesday morning having obtained permission from Mitcham to do so i.e., report later than supposed to.

4th Tuesday
Reported 10am, took twelve men to No. 15 A.G.H. North Adelaide, and bought back twenty to Mitcham.
News this that Mitchell, Nankivell, Treloar, Smith and self to go to Sydney by next Mondays train **to join 'KAROOLA' to form part and parcel of staff.**
All delighted at time at prospects of being together, and being with so many Sisters whom we knew at Keswick, who had departed for Melbourne just previously.

5th Wednesday
Wired Bill to the effect of leaving. Handed long leave pass at 5pm. When I went home found wire from Bill stating that he would be down to see me off. Delighted to hear same.

6th Thursday

Bill came down from Pirie by morning train.
Went to see Siebert dentist. Capt. Arnolds advice.
Went to Keswick and said goodbye to all, and went home and found Bill in bed, having missed him somehow in Adelaide Station.
Arranged with Andy Ledger to have motor cleaned.
Saw Mr. Hendry and other friends.

7th Friday

Walked with Bill cross-country to Rosewater to see Jim Mitchell. Not home so went to see Rev. J. Hughes. Had dinner there. Saw Bice Tenell, Cornishes at Fire Station. Went straight to town, met father at Harris Scarfes at 3pm. Got fountain pen from Coles. Father bought me leather waistcoat. Bill and I went to pictures, and later had photos taken together in shop next to Tiv Pictures. Bill presented me with a pipe.
Had letters from Mrs. Mac and Mrs. Simpson.

8th Saturday

Told Friday night that train left 7.10am in morning. However as no train, we were seriously delayed. Bill jumped on bike, and caught Pirie train at Nth. Adelaide. Got bike myself afterwards, and brought back to Woodville. Saw all bank folk, Mrs. Goldsmith, Aunties, Walkers and Aunt Ada.
Missed last train by 5mins, thinking it left 11.20pm, and had to walk from Hindmarsh as caught train to there.

9th Sunday

Last day.
Saw to say goodbye Mrs. Butler, James family, and Uncle Josiah.
Went to church in evening to see friends. Promised Mrs. Bradshaw and Densley, also L. Harman I would write. After church too late to go and see poor old Uncle George.
Had motor cleaned by Andy Ledger and called for same.

10th Monday
(Left Adelaide to travel to Melbourne for war service on No.1 Australia Hospital Ship 'KAROOLA'.)

Reported Mitcham at 10am. Received remainder of rig-out. Proceeded to Adelaide by 3pm train. There met father, Ada, Mrs. Goldsmith, Aunt's son, Aunt Ada, Jock, Mrs. Fry. Recipient of many presents. All boys had plenty of delicacies on train. Sisters looked us up at intervals. Had good fun, up till 10.30pm when all turned in. Some of us slept pretty well. Party on board Cpl. Scetheway, Nankivell, Mitchell, Pens, Rundle, Messner, Treloar, Smith, Holden, and several old Keswick Sisters.

11th Tuesday

Arrived Melbourne 10am, time half hour before Adelaide time at Spencer Street Station, took another train to Melbourne, thence to Pt. Melbourne. **Saw old 'KAROLLA'. Looked OK in new paint.** Boarded her after awhile. Issued with mattress etc., after kit inspection. Given afternoon off from 3-12pm. Had a good look around Melbourne, principal streets. Went to "A Tale of Two Cities' picture in evening, which was very good indeed. Met Rundle and Messner, and went back to ship by train. Arrived back 11.15pm. and went to bed, put in Ward E4, most comfortable and in best part of ship.

12th Wednesday

Up at 9am. Good tucker. Cleaned a few parts, after parading on boat deck. Left pier at 2pm, bound for Albany to coal. Heard that she would have to dock on voyage. Rained a good deal. All greatly disappointed to see that Sisters Kennedy, Conaine, Goode and Manning were amongst crowd on pier, and after all were not going with us. Glasses came in very handy to watch sights going thro' 'Heads'. Three search lights playing on us. Saw pretty scenery, and was impressed with apparent beautiful peace and quietness of Queenscliff and Yatala on our left. Did several constitutionals up and down deck and turned in.

13th Thursday
Given No. 18980.

At sea. Nothing much doing. Every boy in S.A. crowd except self feeling very groggy. Most were actually sick. My duty very light. Detailed to Ward D1. Good old ocean swell on.

14th Friday

Quiet day at sea. Passed steamer bound inwards. Bit calmer. Some of the boys a bit better. Jock Treloar worst of all (slept on deck last night).
Had lobster for tea. Sisters tell us they were ill (from sea sickness).

15th Saturday

Nothing very exciting, detailed to boats, for boat drill in near future. All except Smith and Treloar quite recovered. Very comfortable. Learn from Engineer that we are to dock at Simons Bay at Durban.
Coming up windy towards evening, feel propellers racing. Issued with Putties. Hear that we had to replace as reinforcements, the men who came off boat as Malarial fever cases, caught at Sierra Leone.

16th Sunday

Half day off. Church parade put off, but held in evening by Salvation Army officer on poop deck.
Had a good sing song and solo by Nankivell. Still blowing.

17th Monday

Arrived Albany 12.30pm. Melbourne time 2.30pm, difference two hours. Memory served well. Remembered old sights on approaching. Still beautiful, clean and rugged. Started coaling. Nearly all went ashore. Mark, Mitch and self climbed over Mounts Melville and Clarence. Good views. Atmosphere very bracing, had a good appetite for tea at boarding house.
Went to Rev. Brays house, and had most pleasant evening. Caught 10 o'clock boat back to ship.

18th Tuesday

Wrote mother, B. Brock, Edgar, Sister Hamp, Uncle Charlie. Finished coaling, left at 1pm and headed out to sea. Still some familiar old sights. Stiff breeze coming up. Regret not being able to go to Brays again, anticipated getting leave, but no luck. First evening prayer meeting.

19th Wednesday
The Commonwealth left well behind.
A trifle choppy again. Some of the boys ill. Issued with white shoes.
First of a series of lectures by Major. Holmes-a-Court. Shifted to A.M.C. quarters.

20th Thursday
Rose early after sleeping on well deck. Most perfect day. Sea as calm as could possibly be. Like a mill pond, surface unbroken. Saw a large shark a little distance from boat. Many jelly fish in water. Sea like ' Reckitts Blue ' and glittering, very sunny. Everybody well and happy. Second lecture by Major on' Fevers', cause and precautions.
Travelled 319 miles in 24 hours.

21st Friday
Little rough at sea. Wind right behind us. Traveled 314 miles for 24 hours up to 12 noon. Threw bottle out to sea, all names enclosed with message. Three days sail from Albany bound for Durban (about 1,000 miles out).
Lecture. Raining. First guard posted 4pm. Not allowed to sleep on well deck in Hammocks without permission. Had to unpack again.

22nd Saturday
News by Wireless of riot in Melbourne. Nothing else very startling.
Beautiful sea, quite blue. Rained heavily last night. (Dental examined).

23rd Sunday
Divine Service 11.30am by O.C., at 7.30pm by Nankivell and Snow.
Sea again very beautiful. Nice fresh breeze. Treloar pretty ill again. Rough in afternoon.

24th Monday
Treloar better. Ships time 2pm, Melbourne time 6pm – four hours.
Sea very blue and sun drowsy. 287 miles for 24 hours – average 11-8 knots.

25th Tuesday
Mounted to guard. 11pm-1am. Slept in guard quarters.
299 miles up to 12 noon.

26th Wednesday
Sea exceptionally calm again. Water very blue. Saw school of whales, about five in number. On guard 7-9am and 3-5pm. Two hours on and six off.
317 miles average speed 13 knots. Address in evening by Pvte. Clark on eight years experience as Gaol Chaplain in N.S.W. Saw peculiar, wavering and moving light, like a large star, rising and falling, which finally disappeared, just before turning in.

27th Thursday
Detailed to Mess deck, fairly arduous first day. Nice breeze blowing, blue waves, white-crested. Dipping a good deal towards evening.
Through kindness of officer on Bridge and thro' Sister Hicks, S.A. boys received consignment of apples.

28th Friday
Heavy head wind, sea running pretty high. Mileage 270 average speed 11-1 knots. Detailed to No. 4 Hatch removing stores for a day. More oranges from officer. Boat Station Call.

29th Saturday
Jimmie Smith's birthday, opened his box brought from home, Sweets, Almonds, Nuts etc, very nice. Packed by his wife.

30th Sunday
Time on ship 11-40pm. Melbourne 6pm, difference 2hours-20minutes, clock is altered about 20-25 minutes daily. Church in evening.
317 miles. Boat deck in afternoon 2-3pm. Learn from Purser that 'RUNIC' just behind about two days sail. Issued with tropical uniform.

OCTOBER, 1917

1st Monday
Called at 4am to attend Pvte. Westlake. Appendicitis supposed. Promised afternoon off, but not relieved. On mess deck from tea time last night.
Day not sunny and sea perfect.
305 miles. Received pay and pay books.

2nd Tuesday
Finish 'Five Years Of My Life' by Capt. Dreyfus. Detailed to Doctor for trip to England when patients taken on board. Hear that crew trying to get vessel into Durban by 6pm Wednesday as 6 o'clock Port. Very large Albatross following. Jack Treloar been in hospital for nearly a week.

3rd Wednesday
Day rather sultry. Ship slowed down to very slow pace to kill time. Passed a tramp steamer bound from Durban. Half holiday.
Lesson by W.O. on 'Soft stretcher and lifting patients'. Lesson by Sisters on bed making on boat deck 2-4pm, where Hockey match was played.
Lightning at night illuminating sky to very large extent.

4th Thursday
Rained very heavily last night. First thing saw land, beautiful sunrise and glasses very useful. Saw several ships in leeway, and found about 8-9 when tied alongside waiting for wharf space. Arrived Durban 7am. Saw whaling boats, lighthouse on bluff etc. Started to coal with Zulu labour. Wireless Station, expansive country and ranges.

Went ashore 2pm. Went in Rick-sha to Zoo with Mitch. Met Nankivell and had a good look round. Saw Sisters, and all had photos taken. Caught tram (two deckers, electric) to P.O. thence to beach, watched breakers, went to Baths, and had a much enjoyed swim. Beach most beautiful. Residential houses and restaurants, also large Hotels on promenade. Residential houses also on road to Zoo. Fell in at tram terminus at 5.50 (those on guard came back to ship). Half hour guard, 7-7.30pm. Guard also 12-1am.

Ship coaling all night. Durban most beautiful and clean, tropical looking place.

5th Friday

Worked in Wards till 11.15am, then granted leave to go ashore till 3.30pm. Marched to tram sheds and dismissed. Went to Town Hall and posted letters (26). Nankivell took photo of Town Hall and P.O. Went to beach for swim but no surf, tide out. Then had dinner and took a tram to Umbilo leaving Berea on right. Struck with vegetation and undergrowth. Saw many Monkeys from tram, which scampered away on our approach. Bought book of views and posted to Mother. Took glasses and had a good look at the harbour as we almost went round. 20.25 vessels in port.

Sailed 5pm, followed by Jap boat which crossed over our track, and went in another direction. We headed due south, could see Southern Cross. Natives received 2/6 for twelve hours shift all night work. Four Sth. African A.M.C. left staff. Wrote Mother.

6th Saturday

Ship heading S. by S.W. travelled 235 miles up to noon.
Very heavy swell on. Jack Treloar in hospital again with sea-sickness. Slept in Ward D1 last night as detailed. Supposed to be about 30 miles from land. Brought six naval men as patients from East Africa embarked at Durban.

7th Sunday

Church parade at 11am. Equipment inspection at 11.45am. Use of boat deck at 2-4pm. Reckon to get in Cape Town by noon on the morrow. Cape Town another 6 o'clock port. Passed three vessels outward bound from Cape Town.

8th Monday

About 10am land in sight. Very high ranges at first appearance. Arrived at 12noon. Started arranging all beds with sheets, mattresses, coverings, blankets, pillows, laid in dock. (*Capetown was a hospital base for receiving sick and wounded English soldiers from Mesopotamia and German East Africa. They were given compliment of patients awaiting transfer to English hospitals*).

Noted dark greeny colours of water, and break-water. Eleven ships in port, could see Table Mountain. Hout Bay. Twelve Apostles, and Lions Head when approaching, also noted the large bay lighthouse, and pier on the left side. Got leave at 6-11pm. Went in old Brougham to the town, gave chap 6d ea, wanted 1/-. Went to Main Street P.O. posted letter to Nick. Had look round, and hired a motor-car to Camps Bay, six of us, most beautiful, roads super. Stude-car. Had supper at Alexanders, nice fish. Noted the fine buildings, Mansions, House Chambers. Had a look over pier (concrete), and caught motor-car back to the docks. Many A.M.C. intoxicated. Turned in at 12pm. Coaled 200 tons in bags.

Note from diary Cpl. C.R. Mortimer AWM.

> Had to carry a mattress, two blankets, two pillows for each cot. Sheets and pillow cases were also provided. The cots had to be made up before embarkation. Officers inspected the ship, praise was given to the C.O. for the neat appearance of the wards, and the ship generally.

9th Tuesday

Embarking of patients put off till tomorrow. Still preparing wards. Cloth of mist on Table Mountain. Light rain at intervals, leave 3-11pm.

Went in Brougham to town, wanted to charge 1/- each, but 6d given him again. Sister sent cablegram by East Extension. Jumped on car to Camp Bay, and did round route thro'

DURBAN

Rickshaw stand

Zulu horse

Main Street

Native policeman

Town hall

Type of Coolie

Coaling in progress

Devil's Dance

Zulu coal lumper

Scramblers for pennies

Surfing ocean beach

'Karoola', WWI. No.1 Australian Hospital Ship

CAPE TOWN

Cecil Rhodes monument

The Table Cloth

Triumphal Arch

Pilot ship

Macedonia Aux Cruiser

Doing Devils Peak

On Devils Peak

Entering harbour 'Table Bay'

'Party' Hout Bay Hotel

Ronde Busch

Houses of parliament

Dutch cottage Muizenberg

Kloof Neck round Lions Head. Noted silver trees there, and heavy surf on beach, also was heavy on line, smashing tram post. Conductor considerate, slowed down at intervals to show view. Noted Jews houses. Had a glorious ride for 1/-. Had tea and caught tram, got out to see Cecil Rhodes house. Beautiful avenues of trees, and very quiet with rugged mountains behind. Walked back a little way. Saw Railway Station. Other tram altitude 700ft above sea level. Our Sisters went right thro Cecil Rhodes house and garden. At present occupied by Premier, but he away on active service. Nankivell went on 37mile motor trip and had a good time (thro Hout Bay). Wrote Mother, and Aunt's son.

10th Wednesday

Started embarking patients at 11am. Came by train 400 men, 30 officers. Some mental and 16 T.B., who came to our ward and had dinner. 'MACEDONIA' left noon. Saw the masts of a small barque, the fastest sailing vessel overseas in the world. Large Japanese vessel in dry dock.

We left at 2pm, and met a heavy ocean swell as ever, as out of the breakwater shelter. Ship pts E. by N. Our patients decent fellows. Smithy and I manage very well. Slept in night men's hammocks, rather cold, and not much rest. Great many men from Mesopotamia and India. Just come from Wynberg Military Hospital. Jimmy sick. Our Ward T.B. patients. Reveille 5.30am from now onwards.

As written in the official history of The No. 1 Hospital Ship Karoola by Lt.Col. T.G. Wilson, Australian, Army, Medical Corp. AWM Canberra.

SYSTEM OF EMBARKATION

'Immediately particulars of the cases to be embarked are available, the wards are divided into sections, i.e. medical, surgical, spinal, tubercular, mental, isolation, convalescent, etc., according to their suitability for the treatment of the different classes of cases.

The commanding officer, adjutant, or other medical officer conducting the embarkation takes up a position at the top of the gangway, sees each individual patient as he is carried, or walks on to the ship, and allots him to a ward according to his disability.

A clerk takes up a position close to the embarkation officer, with a sheet with the bed numbers consecutively stamped under each ward, and with a small box in the pigeon holes of which are tally-cards for the respective wards, one stamped for each bed. A tally-card is attached to the clothing of each patient embarked for the information of the stretcher bearers, so that there will be no delay in taking the patient to the ward allotted, and as an authority for the Ward N.C.O. to admit the patient. As each tally-card is issued it is scored off the tabulated sheet. Any information the officer conducting the embarkation might require (i.e. the total number of patients embarked, the available accommodation in any particular ward, etc., can be readily supplied. It is practically impossible, no matter how great the rush of patients, to miss a patient, for no one is admitted to a ward without a tally-card: should one arrive at a ward without a tally, he is kept under observation, and the Ward N.C.O. immediately reports to the embarkation officer.

The ship is fitted with two lifts - one forward and one aft - for embarking and disembarking, and, apart from the special cases, arrangements are made, as far as possible, for patients to be alternately allotted to the forward and aft wards. This prevents any congestion and greatly facilitates embarkation.

Should it be necessary (as in the case of a short and rush voyage as made on two occasions to the Syrian Coast) to embark at both ends, on account of a large number of patients (practically double the accommodation) having to be taken on board, a similar system is followed at each end.

As regards the stretcher bearing work, the usual procedure is for the shore stretcher bearers to deliver the patients on the ship, and for the ship's staff to bear the patients thence to the wards.

Strict accuracy is absolutely essential with embarkation, and as the returns are called for by the shore embarkation authorities and the ship-owner's representative on board within a very short space of time after embarkation is completed, a system had to be devised whereby a patient cannot possibly be missed, more especially as experience has shown over and again that the rolls and figures supplied by the shore officials were incorrect.

The above system has been found a very good one in practice.

Upon receipt of instructions detailing the number of patients and time they are to be embarked, the Quartermaster notifies the Chief Steward as to the number of respective diets required and the time they are to be ready. The Chief Steward makes the necessary arrangements for having diets ready so that patients may be fed as soon as possible after embarkation.'

Note from diary Cpl. C.R.Mortimer AWM
Last on board were mental cases. The worst placed in padded cells, and the others in that part of E4 ward (during his time on ship).

11th Thursday
Good day at sea. Our deck and ward looking pretty good towards evening. Had afternoon off 2-5pm, and had a short nap. One patient's sister lives at Launceston in Cornwall. Had an interesting chat with him. Says Larrrick (St.Peth Road) Lesant, and Larnston as they pronounce it, are situated closely together. (*Sargent family came from these areas*). Sister Barry in charge of ward. Mitch on night duty D1, and Nank sick and off duty.

12th Friday
Mitch says passed ship during night. Smith off from 2-5pm. One patient suffering pain over cardiac region. (Scotch boy). Mental patients, Officers and men given airing and sunning in enclosure. Speed 13.4 knots. Slept on deck aft promenade. Sister Romaine in ward in afternoon and previous evening. Awnings erected over decks. Plenty of Phosphorous in sea at night.

13th Saturday
Jack Treloar much better since on night duty. Beautiful day at sea.
Learn that an old man named Hammond lives at Launceston, about 90 years of age, must look him up. Bristol about 10-12 miles from Launceston.
Average speed 13.4 knots.

14th Sunday
Our sick patient feeling better. Church service at 11.30am. Many patients turned up. Chap. Capt. Burrows from Capetown took service on 'Courage'.

Mitch lost another 'Austr.' and caught culprit red-handed. All ranks previously cautioned on a/c petty thefts. Other accusations followed. Waiting further developments as I lost several small articles some time ago.

Mileage 317. Average speed 13.1.

15th Monday
Quiet day. Sick patient showing symptoms of Typhoid. Learn that about two days sail from St. Helena. Passed a large steamer.

Person found guilty of petty theft. (Placed under open arrest last night), and awarded punishment C.B. 21 days.

16th Tuesday
Saw flying fish, flying and diving into water. First lot. Sea again very blue. Getting warm and trifle sultry. 317 miles.

17th Wednesday
Pay day. Very calm day. Saw large fish not far from ship. Some say a small whale, others a large shark. 302 miles.

18th Thursday
Passed a large steamer, which first seemed to cross in front of us when some distance away, then headed N.W. bound apparently for New York. Passed over Equator at 6pm. First issue of lime juice. Still heading North. Very warm and scarcely any breeze.

19th Friday
Tropical uniforms much appreciated this weather. Shedding perspiration.
About 7pm. large bright star nearly in crescent of new moon. Attracted much attention as rest of sky dark. Star moved into moon.

20th Saturday
Started Quinine anti Malaria. Sea like blue glass. Scarcely a ripple on it. About 60-80 miles from Sierra-Leone according to chart. Little swallow unconcernedly settled and rested on docking bridge amongst night hammocks, took no notice of us.

21st Sunday
Lords Supper 7am. and Divine Service 11.20am and 7.30pm.
Passed Bijouga Island at 12 noon. Large number of porpoise seen early in morning, some jumping high out of water. More swallows, and larger birds following ship. Passed steamer during last night.

22nd Monday
Sighted Dakar at 7am, noted large rocks left of entrance, also that low lying country. Scarcely any hills about. Any rises at all were mostly of rock. Met by Pilot boat which proceeded us into harbour. Had to pass between two Forts and a break in a long mine chain. Anchored in leeway, many natives in canoes came alongside and dived for pennies. About 20 vessels in port, two French cruises, one British four funnels, 'KING ALBERT', later moved thro' wonderful break-water, tied to wharf by stern, and anchored by bow. By use of glasses, struck with large buildings, and fine wharfage. Looked O.K. from where we were. Parade called in evening, and warned against Malaria. No leave ashore and staff advised to sleep down decks. Natives still diving etc. Very glad of our 'refuse', and even when thrown in the salt water, was eagerly grabbed and eaten.

23rd Tuesday

All patient Officers, ships Staff Officers, and Sisters granted leave (immune from Malaria). Quiet day.

Very irksome, no leave, especially when told by French Shore Authority that he had informed Col. that we may go on shore.

Noticed about eight laden vessels gone. British Cruiser also went out at 7am. Suppose act as convoy to ships. Hope to catch them up. Finished coaling and water by 5pm. On duty till 9pm. Finished up, and borrowed stewards rig out (disguised), jumped aboard ships boat and got ashore. Had a look round the town. Noted the type of restaurants. Met others disguised also, got aboard at 11.30pm, (after having had a bit of fun) in safety, and spent a wretched night under decks (close and muggy), no fresh air.

Had a chat with Frenchman, 27 years in Dakar. He says no Malaria at all. Rumoured amongst us that only six whites on shore had escaped it, a fallacy according to him. Bought postcards, and he advised me what places to see. Saw market and Government House, also large square garden in center of town. Native guards posted around Forts.

24th Wednesday

Up at 5.30am, is hot and stuffy, and feeling rotten. No rest. Take all risks of Malaria in future, and sleep out on deck. Sailed at 7am preceded by French steamer, which we soon caught up and passed. Had another good look at Island Fort, and noted heavy mist everywhere. Headed north and passed large lighthouse on high hill on our right. Sea calm and blue. Two little birds alighted on board, one was glad of bread and water after capture, resembles a small Jay.

25th Thursday

Our patients very buoyant now bound for old England. Hear that Col. finds out that some of staff had been ashore. Dakar also a mail port. Fresh troops arrived with black troops on board, and population 5-6,000 Frenchmen.

All emergency lights in case of submarine hung up. About 5pm. caught up and passed 'KING ALBERT' acting as convoy to nine steamers bound for England. Sight most impressive and stately.

26th Friday

Sea beautiful and calm. Seem to be steering a zigzag course.
Lime juice finished. Weather very much cooler.

27th Saturday

Notified by parade notices that no cameras to be used in event friendly or enemy warship coming alongside. Ward men complimented by Col. during inspection on thoroughness, and cleanliness of ward. He stated never looked as well or nice before.

28th Sunday

Passed wreckage which first thought to be a submarine, as mast just showing above water. In danger zone proper. Tommy soldiers do their light duties very willingly, and efficiently. Fond of concerts. Hold same nearly every night up deck. Never seem to tire of songs and ditties. Australian talent appreciated at the organized concert held a few evenings previous.

29th Monday
Mental patients Officers very decent chaps. Had an interesting chat with one, a very gentlemanly fellow. Has sane moments. Very pitiable, as most of these cases caused thro' V.D.

30th Tuesday
Had likeness of Jimmy and self, and group of our patients taken.
Sea with us. 300 miles.

31st Wednesday
Opposite Bay of Biscay. Sea very rough, but ship riding splendidly. Passed a tramp steamer steering a zigzag course and signaling to us. She was rolling and tossing a good deal.

NOVEMBER, 1917

1st Thursday
Bristol Channel. Lands' End lights sighted at 7pm. Foggy and damp all day. Later another light on opposite side. 10pm ship takes two or three very sharp and sudden turns almost within her own length. A dark object distinctly seen astern in mist. Presumably a patrol boat or trawler advising course to take.
Soundings showing sandy bottom and 30 fathoms of water taken at 5pm.
10.30pm, light misty rain and heavy fog. Sea fairly calm. Can scarcely realize that this is old England, the world's greatest Empire at War. Patients enthused at idea of a last seeing shore lights of their motherland.

2nd Friday
At 1am ran into a sand bank and stuck fast. All were awakened by rattle and shaking of ship thro' engines reversed. Leaning to angle of nearly 40 degrees. Thick fog. Off again 3.30am. See breakers notifying shallowness of water. Tide out. Boats on Port side lowered. Lean to starboard great strain of ship. Continual bumping, tough work in engine room. Proceeded slowly. Met by Pilot early morning. Passed many ships at Barry. Passed Cardiff. Channel narrowing. Fog horns on shore blowing. Anchored a little distance from Avonmouth. Noted farms on shore and hedge fences, thatch roofed farm houses. Very pretty. Waiting for tide in morning as delayed previous high water by grounding. Still foggy. 36ft rise and fall of tide.

A.W.M. Official report of T.G. Wilson. Lieut. Colonel. A.A.M.C. concerning the running aground in the Gulf of Bristol.

"The routine for patients in cases of emergency was posted in each ward and the ward N.C.Os were responsible that they knew what portion of the deck those able to walk and shift for themselves were to go to. Boat stations were held regularly with patients on board, all cot cases being excluded, and a certain number of walking patients warned as stretcher cases in order to get the orderlies accustomed to their duties. Certain orderlies were assigned to work the lifts, others to police the decks and so on and every preparation made for emergencies, which fortunately for us never occurred – except once when we ran aground in the Gulf of Bristol and the boat had such a list that it was impossible to get down to the wards without crawling, and if the ship had not righted itself the loss would have been appalling. It often strikes one how impossible it is to prepare beforehand for every emergency."

DAKAR

French cruiser

Harbour

Treed Avenue

Street scene

Overlooking bay

Street scene

Divers for coins

3rd Saturday

Avonmouth – Bristol, 6 miles in train. 40 mins journey is bus. Proceeded at high tide to Avonmouth, 9am tide running fast. Passed pretty buildings and country on starboard side. Entered the docks. Several ships in dry dock, fine wharves. Got all wards clear of patients. Disembarked at 12.30pm. Shook hands with all our men on station in hospital train. Two trains left station. Waiting since Thursday night. Leave at 3.30pm. Proceeded to Bristol by motor- bus. Had exciting trip. Many side slips on slippery road. Passed thro' Clifton Downs, Oak trees beautiful, landscape beautiful en route. Had a hurried look over part of city. Nearly all in darkness. Find strictness on food supplies. Back to ship by train. Reported back by 7pm. Ship left for Liverpool at 8pm. Good tide, and dock gates open. This arrangement interferes with plans somewhat as anticipated going to Shepton Mallet in Somerset and Launceston in Cornwall from Bristol. Fog horn resembling mooing of cow as proceeding down Channel. Bristol is a big city. Large steamer there on Avon. Sisters and some Officers gone on leave. Beautiful shades and colours on leaves of trees en route.

4th Sunday

The best day experience for some time. Ship clear of Officers, Sisters and patients. Passed Holyhead, Holy Island, and Anglesea very close to land. Sun quite warm, air fresh and embracing. Fish species of birds following ship. Some feeding casually on ship. On boat bridge 2-4pm. Steamer stopped at 8pm. for awhile. Hear we are to dock at Birkenhead. Coast rugged in places. Two church services held by Pvte. Snow. Mitch fearing Bronchitis, feeling previous symptoms. Very little work all day, bar inspection at 10.30am. Mitch detailed to laundry. Noted large lighthouses on shore, also on Holy Island. Noticed small steamers running to Ireland. Took on Pilot at 8pm, and went ahead. Very foggy indeed. When ship finally came to stop could scarcely see either side of stream. Many ferry boats crossing and re crossing. Dropped anchor at 9pm. Waiting word from Headquarters O.C. to London from Avonmouth re leave.

5th Monday

Up early. Now notice many ships in harbour. Two American passenger steamers painted in such a way to deceive submarines. Tide very fast. Ferry boats carrying workers. Notice spacious wharves and large buildings nearby on Liverpool side. Large P.& O. steamer came out of docks at 2pm, in control of seven tugs, four after and three forehead. We then went in passing naval cruisers, destroyers, and other naval craft. Noticed many manufacturing establishments on docks. Passed through bridges, saw handling coal bunkering steamer by elevating truck at a time of 10 tons each. At first the wharfingers called out thro' megaphone that they knew nothing nor heard anything of us, but we finally pulled up at a clear wharf, near large buildings resembling mills. Canal goes on for some distance further. Other naval boats in channel outside also. Our present locality called 'Poulton'. No news yet of leave, and staff not allowed off ship for evening.

Notes from diary of Cpl. C.R.Mortimer, who served on 'Karoola' AWM.

'At Liverpool they had apparatus something like the usual coal barge, provision being made for small trucks to pass underneath where the coal was stored. These trucks were connected on either side to belts so arranged that the truck always in the same position when ascending loaded with coal, or descending empty on their way to be refilled, a hole in the barge allowed the coal to gradually keep on the move into the trucks as they passed underneath. They then proceeded still in an upright position, until they came to a shute, the lower end of which had previously been placed through the side of the ship leading into one of the bunkers. After upsetting their contents the truck would travel round to be refilled.

It was one continual stream of coal until the bunker was filled. Very efficient!'

6th Tuesday

Nothing doing all morning. Waiting advice re leave. Word through. Got off ship at 2pm. Went from Birkenhead to Liverpool. Mitch and I had a look round ferry piers. St. Georges Hall, (Court of Assizes) 195 years of age, and historical, fine specimen of Greek masonry. Interior very magnificent. Second largest organ in U.K., large granite pillars all round walls. All Government buildings very dowdy with dirt and age. Law sessions on at St. Georges. Invited to attend next Monday to view ceremony of morning opening. Saw printing of Liverpool 'Echo'. Wonderful. Caught 5.20 train L.& N.W. to London. Great speed, arrived 10.15pm, could not see much owing to darkness. Got out at Euston Station and in tube Elect Railway proceeded further. Walked up Tottenham Court Road to Shakespeare Hut, so called because on sight of Memorial to be erected to Shakespeare's memory. First opened by N.Z., many Zealanders put up here. Fine apartments and every facility for soldiers and conveniences. People very sociable and obliging. 300 staff of voluntary assistants. Fare moderate. No sugar, and requested to be easy with bread, which is darker in colour than ours. Had supper, turned in and had a good night. Arranged with Corp. in charge to visit Old Curiosity Shop before tour in morning.

7th Wednesday

Paid visit to 'Old Curiosity'. Thoughts ran wild for a bit. Opened by elderly lady and sells curios. Booked fares for drag trip thro' city 4/- no extras. Nank, Mitch, Rundle and self together with strangers from various Huts on board. Went first to The Strand, and all along the way our guide explained things to us, so many that cannot enter here. Passed Admiralty, War office, place of Charles I's death opposite old Kings Palace. Places visited A.I.F. and war chest quarters for soldiers on leave, Tower of London (needing a month proper to investigate), St. Pauls, Trafalgar Square, Thames Embankment, Westminster Abbey, (feeding of pigeons), 'Royal Stables', bought photo of 'Chapman' a black thoroughbred, Belgian Sire used for stud purposes. Beautiful stables, too good for horses, pity some humans could not fare as well, stagecoach gilded with gold leaf four and a half tons. 174 horses in stables. Harness superb. Walked back to Trafalgar square, back to Stock Exchange, looked up McIlwraith Mc Eacharn's office for letters, arranged to call again in morning. Poor Nank receives word at Horseferry Road of his brother's death in France. Very sad at this time. He hoped to be able to see him on leave. Fine concert in hut in evening, Y.M.C.A. Control Quarters, fine building, and furnished well.

8th Thursday

Up early – out to Brockelbanks, and ? Park, Bills sister-in-law, and two children putting up with their troubles very bravely, as Mr. Brock at the front gave me message for Bill re his mother. Had no time to go ? well Hill, but saw result of air-raid by Zeppelins on cottages near Brock's house. Jumped on tram, and proceeded to Madame Tussaud's. Well worthwhile. Met lady from Manchester who was a great help and informative in looking round. Noted with interest the old cabs used by Napoleon at Waterloo, Moscow, and St. Helena and many, many other things belonging to the great soldier. This took up all morning.

In afternoon with party from the Hut, went to Guild Hall to witness the investiture of the new Worshipful Lord Mayor of London, a Cornishman. With Naval officer from Destroyer went to G.P.O., and enquired for letters. Went to part of service in St. Pauls Cathedral, then to Royal Stock Exchange around the Bank of England. Back thro' the Strand to Somerset House, but too late to make any enquiries re people at Launceston.

In evening went to Alpam? Theatre and saw 'Round the Map', very good staging, beautiful. Had free tickets (tickets from Soldiers Buffet, Vic St.) to 10/6 seats. Lost the others in the crowd. Had to find my way back to Hut on my own, took some little time to find it too. Surprised to see girls, who before war were innocent, out on streets waiting for late men.

9th Friday

Called early and packed everything for return journey to Liverpool. Caught a tube for Euston. Had a sandwich and hot coffee there with 'Sugar', train left at 6.50am. At a good rattle passed thro' some magnificent looking country. Hardly creditable that so much open country near such a vastly congested place like London, 30x40 miles in area (all suburbs). Noted the large groves of trees, canals, and horses pulling barges and punts up them at Stratford. Crewe Station a large place, and terminus for Manchester.

Arrived Liverpool on time 12.30pm. Went in ferry to Birkenhead, caught tram and reported to ship at 2pm. Given local leave till next day 2pm. Had a look round docks. Many ships with all sorts of complaints laid up. Torpedoed broken backs, bent plates etc. Our own ship on dry dock, beautiful shape. Saw Russian Destroyers, 17year old models, 26 knots, being repaired. Costing 3,500 pounds each to repair. Crew not allowed on board as several times mysterious occurrences happened delaying machinery, delaying their putting out.

Nine months already in docks. Engineer on contract showed us over Grayson's Works. Big morning. Went to Liverpool in evening to pictures and slept on board.

10th Saturday

Up early, and proceeded to Camel-Lairds. Found we could not possibly get in either thro' repair yards nor new yards without a very special permit from the manager. These restrictions only been in force for last two months, now no Ranks of any kind allowed in, and rightly so. Disappointed all the same, but recommended to apply in writing to Works manager. Arranged at Ranks Flour Mills to look over them at a later date. Saw all over large American oil tank steamer, recently submarined for second time. Three men killed, damage done in engine room remarkable. Hole in side ten yards square. All engines smashed completely up – everything uprooted from floor to ceiling. Big cranes taking cylinders out. Three men killed in engine room, engines aft.

Saw small schoolboys playing brass band, quite wonderful, splendid music. Some scarcely big enough to carry instruments. Perfect day, yesterday drizzle. Reported on board for duty. Guard 12.30am to 4pm on the 11th. Father's birthday. Trust he has received electric fan O.K. as my present arranged between myself and Uncle Jock before leaving.

11th Sunday

Did guard 12.30a – 4.00am, an absolute farce, no duty detailed (some have a sleep instead). Leave at 2pm. Went out to Sefton Park, and found it very pretty spot. Saw old English garden at Thornton Park (close by). Road near by that King Rufus used to ride over on way to forest and hunting grounds. Ranthorne, an old English family over all property round there, family history 400 years. Lakes, menageries etc., beautiful ducks and other birds on lake. Noted the large and commodious palm house. Went to Central Hall, Lime St (Methodist Mission) in evening, and much enjoyed the service.

12th Monday

Obtained a certificate as to our being bona-fides A.I.F. men aboard Aust. 'Karoola', in order to try and get into Camel-Laird dock yards. For a trial presented this, and found would have to present to Admiralty office, Water Street, Liverpool and obtain a permit, but informed would be very lucky if even then could have the luck. Went round the docks, saw mine-layer on slips, also a life-boat driven by suction. Inspected the big grain ship lately submarined. Engines blown to smithereens. Salvage ship alongside pumping water out. Shifting grain (oats), this used in distilleries (whisky). Taskar firemen killed. Two not yet brought out as buried by debris. Saw diver clearing gates of a dry dock, very interesting. Received pass for further three days. Mitch stayed behind, Nank to London. I caught 4.20 train to Manchester, arrived 6pm (stopping every station). Housed at Y.M.C.A., Piccadilly. Went to Hippodrome and witnessed 'Where is the Chicken'. Beautiful building.

13th Tuesday

Met Ptve. Roberts at Y.M.C.A. hut, and together went thro' Manchester Art Gallery, very fine collection (in Mosely Streeet). In afternoon went to 'Bellevue'. Inspected Zool-gardens. These kept by a millionaire. Quite out of season now and nothing doing. Plenty of provision made for amusements and pastimes. Dancing hall, skating etc. Flower houses and lot of houses for botanical purposes. Also a small museum. Went to pictures in evening, 'A Nations Awakening', not up to much. Afterwards went for a walk out Blackley way (a suburb). Weather very foggy, could not see across street till 2pm, dark again 5pm, very short time to look round. Note that the largest Stock Exchange room in U.K., is to be built, work already started. Beds at 'Khaki Hotel Club' 6d. Margarine used instead of butter, a good substitute, no sugar. Went to Reference Library in Piccadilly, a very commodious building with a huge supply of books, past and present. Boys arrived midnight train being escorted to various hospitals in ambulances. Others going back to London, and thence to France, collect at Y.M.C.A., have a snooze around fire, and catch very early train.

14th Wednesday

Went out to Trafford Bridge and dock works, stations, good sheds etc., on a very extensive scale. Large steamers from New York in. Mersey looks very dirty. Very many advertisements to effect ship by canal docks all over Manchester. Morning very cold and damp, enjoyed a good dinner at vegetarian café. Had a look right thro' Town Hall by a very courteous deacon. Everything interesting. All stairways a different marble. Saw main hall now used for recruiting purposes, beautiful cedar and tiled floors everywhere. Ascended largest tower, 285ft high, 182 steps to dock. Wonderful architecture, bell eight and a half tons. Saw mechanism of clock, sixteen foot across dial, each minute space nine inches. Could not see far for smoke and fog. Saw over Stock Exchange and alterations being made, massive columns removed and fresh stone placed by large overhead crane, to be largest hall in U.K., supported by four pillars only.

Saw Rylands Library. More impressed with this, than any other up to date. Stone and all oak floors, simply marvelous. Building alone cost half million, add very valuable land and over 1,000.000, solid bound leather books, subscription ? second in U.K., boasts of having only copies in existence of certain books printed.

Went to Manchester Cathedral and shown over by priest. Many ancient and historical things, too many to mention. Building 1421. Wonderful brass work. Went to evening pictures 'Civilization'.

15th Thursday

Went out to Openshaw. Obtained permission from Armstrong Whitworth Limited to go thro' their munitions works if in Manchester again. Caught 12.30pm. train at Victoria Station. Train late, reached Liverpool 7.30pm. Caught tube Mersey Railway and reported to ship. Got evening leave 6-12pm. Went to Shakespeare Theatre and saw 'Diplomacy', fine indeed.

Met a native of – student at University. Address in front page, good fellow and very clever, a B.A., and medical student. Ships address, West Float, Birkenhead. (Received letters from Mrs. Hyne, Mrs. Gray 12 inst).

LONDON

Resolution and defiance

Tower bridge London

Kings State Coach and famous creams

Old curiosity shop

Tower of London

16th Friday

Had to wait round re more leave before the Colonel came on board. Handed leave passes and warrants for further four days B section. Had a look round the 'Great City', and saw shells being taken from beneath oats in hold, and went to Liverpool. Made enquiries at Admiralty, looked thro' Colonial Buildings, Water Street. Had brief look at Dock Board buildings. Met Nank at 6pm, made enquiries Belfast Shipping Co. Caught boat at Docks, left ll.45pm for Ireland. Passed big docks. Our boat soon steaming 17-18 knots. Turned in third class amidst plenteous Irishmen, and soldiers on leave taking trip to land of shamrock. Plenty stout and stuff, also tobacco smoke. Atmosphere as heavy as paint, but being dog-tired slept like a brick. Boat bound for Cork torpedoed previous night. Some speculation.

17th Saturday

Woke early and found a few intoxicated. Quite a rush on the bar where Stout was sold. Had shave etc., under difficulties, my large razor being broken across blade. On deck – sighted coast of Ireland and of islands hereabouts. Passed Whitehead and snug looking town on our right. Hills and fields looking O.K. Foggy so could not see far. Noted the large ships at entrance to Belfast, further up the huge ship building yards. Many ships both war boats and otherwise under course of construction, and some nearing completion. Noted Harland and Wolfe's yards on left.

Arrived alongside wharf 11.30am. There met by lady who directed us to Soldier's Buffet. On walking to this place pestered by begging youngsters. Satisfy one and there were more. Seem to take a fancy to 'Aussies'. Found ladies at Buffet exceptionally kind and large hearted. All Ulster of course. Directed and accompanied by a run-a-way sailor from 'H.M.AUX' cruiser to – station. Caught train 12.30pm for Portrush. Notice that a number of towns begin with a 'Bally', such as 'Ballymorley' etc. Country very beautiful en route, and weather continuing fine, other passengers very obliging, instructive, and kind to us. Country fairly level. When nearing Portrush could see Londonderry Hills in distance – 40 miles.

Arrived Portrush 3pm. Went to Londonderry Hotel, and hired motor car for Giant's Causeway for 9/- as no electric trams running (out of season). Pretty little town, and very clean. Nice substantial residences and roads. Passed Bush Mills en route noted for 'Whiskey and Fish', a real Irish Valley, then Lord Mc Naughton's property. Met by guide at hotel in G. Causeway, and proceed on foot to beach. Many objects of interest shown us all. (See post cards and information on back), but most interested in Amphitheatre and Giant's Organ, columns 40ft height of basalt rock. Had a look at Dunluce Castle on return journey. Had to find our way in dark for history see P.C. Very interesting old place. Just missed by hair breath 6.30pm train for Belfast, so hired car again and caught in Coleraine, arrived Belfast 9pm. Had supper buffet, sorry to leave these people as kind to us.

18th Sunday

Arrived Dublin 5am. Had a short look round, noted the havoc wrought by Sinn Feiners, P.O., and other buildings, also their Head Quarters 'Liberty Hall' leveled to the ground by small gun-boat by bombardment near bridge. Went to Soldiers and Sailors Rest. Had wash and clean-up, met by Boy Scouts and escorted there. Afterwards had a look at lofty monument. Staircase to top so expected to have a good look round, but not opened till 10am. Walked along river (splendidly banked by solid stone wall, beautifully built). Some of houses in streets very dirty, small, and dilapidated. Caught train at Kings Bridge Station 9.30am. Very comfortable train. Few demonstrations by Sinn Feiners en route for Killarney such as band, drum and fife, flying their colours and decorated by badge, white, yellow and green. At Emily Station they were on platform, in formation and did drill splendidly. Evidently there to meet a visitor. Several walked up and down train boo-hooing passenger soldiers, but no notice taken of them.

Country down this way denotes grazing, farms small. Plenty of peat bogs, small plantations of trees, all hedge fences. Changed trains at M?low, this a very pretty place. Given trip by R.T.O re Sinn Fein element at Killarney, and advised to stay at Shamrock Hotel. Reached Killarney 5.30pm., and on station experience most dreadful jostling possible by various hotel keepers, and public house stewards for our patronage. My coat was taken etc. etc., pamphlets pushed into our hands, and a fight was only just avoided between two of them. Went to Shamrock Hotel however on jaunting car, after argument as to prices, fees etc., for trips next day, and coming finally to an understanding went to bed. Many begging youngsters about.

19th Monday

Up at 6am. Had early breakfast, and started out on trip for lakes in carriage. Big burly Irishman the driver, very witty but hard to understand, talked fast and typically Irish tongue. Passed up road near Earl of Kennare's property. Hedge consisting of various shrubs, and creepers very beautiful. Told plenty of game. Hares, rabbits and foxes about, especially in Earl's property, but that no trespassing allowed. Further on came to Kate Kearney's Cottage. Here bought postcards, and small cup of deer horn. Noted peat fire burning. Engaged ponies for ride of six miles to Lake at 3/6d ea.

Came to entrance of Gap of Dunloe. This very wild and rugged. Noted sheep and goats on sides of mountains, jumping from rock to rock. Ponies seem to know road, when to canter, trot or walk. Crossed several bridges, old and rustic. Called at Arbutus Cottage and noted beautiful inlaid work of Arbutus wood in handkerchief boxes, writing desks, gave address for any order in future as promised Vere a present of a handkerchief box before leaving. Called at various cottages in Dunloe Valley. Noted the beautiful speckled reddish brown colouring due to moss covering rocks on hills peculiar in the autumn season. Plenty of Holly about. Black Valley very beautiful as mists lifting. Left ponies at Tower in property owned by Canadian gentleman. Jumped in boat which was waiting and started off thro' Upper Lake. Boatman typically Irish and very servile. Then entered river passing Eagles Head and saw Deer (Buck), and two pine on bank. Shot rapids under old weir bridge. Noted the lovely spot of Island and Forc Mountain on right. Trees of various kinds and shades growing here.

Passed thro' Middle Lake noting the large Colleen Bawn Rock in front. Reached Lower Lakes 55-7 miles in area, and by far the prettiest. Many small islands here all bearing different names and bearing different traditional history. Saw ? Rock, and Honeycomb Rock. Trees around the Lower Lake very plentiful and magnificent, being all natural growth. Alighted not far from Ross Castle doing 15 miles by boat. There met by carriage from hotel, drove to castle and went up tower. Many wild birds en route. Castle epoch history Cromwell's time. Drove home, amidst glorious scenery, passing Earl of Kenmare's property and 'Flower Pot', large trees encircled by stone built up around its trunk height of 6-7ft.

Arrived hotel, had dinner, and caught train for capital 3pm. Bridge from Middle to Lower Lake' Brickeen', dating 1815. Water 70-360 ft deep, fish, trout, salmon and carp, these plentiful. Fishermen hold licenses. Many cattle in Black Valley. Sheep, English cross-bred, very hardy and suitable for conditions, dark faces and points, very shaggy, not unlike 'shrops'. Arrived 8.30pm Dublin. Walked to West Wall Station G.W.R. passed underground and waited for **Str. 'Scotia'** sail 9.40pm for Holyhead. At Soldiers Buffet, same thro' all Ireland, these willing workers, very kind and courteous.

20th Tuesday

The **'Scotia'** 12.30am traveling 20 knots, a fine two funneled boat. Slept out on deck, midst Tommy soldiers, some bound from, and some going back to France having been on leave to Ireland from France because route ordinarily closed week-ends. Very cold however. Reached Holyhead about 1.30-1.45am. Had a good look over dock, noted the ships, cattle passages, women ? ships from Ireland with cattle, poultry, butter etc. Large railway station, junction Manchester, Liverpool, and London. Posted P.C. to Ada. Started off for Liverpool 3am, thro' Dallington and Chester arriving 6.50am at Lime Street. Reported at 'Karoola' 8am, and had breakfast.

Detailed to meet Capt. Southwood at 6pm at Woodside Station, from Liverpool G.W.R.& Y. & L.R. joint station. Took afternoon off and went with Crofty thro' portion of the 'Royal' Liver buildings – magnificently furnished. Liverpool Club rooms. Also thro' Cunard and Pacific Coy. offices, not equaled by any offices for grandeur yet seen. Also the Dock board offices, finest mercantile offices in Europe. Exquisite building, and luxuriously lined and paneled with oak and cedar. Saw destroyer 'BRISK' mined in Irish Sea being rebuilt in Docks, bow blown right away.

Letter from mother dated 17/9/17. Met Nank in evening and had a stroll round. Referred to Reference Library for information re Dunluce Castle etc. a small peninsula. No authentic history beyond facts that the English held it in the 15th century, and successively in hands of Mc Quillan, Mac Donnell families, later being driven out in 1584 after nine months siege by Sir John Perrott.

21st Wednesday
Caught 11.35pm train at Exchange Station L. & Y. Railway and had a day at Manchester. Arranged to go thro' Rylander Cotton Mills on next visit.

Mr. Pillion. Daca Twist, 100 Portland Street. Caught open show car and with kind permission of secretary at Armstrong Whitworth Limited, went thro' their munitions works. Space does not allow enumeration. Steel wire for 12inch naval gun. 179 miles, weight 70 tons (i.e. gun), cost 12,000 pounds. Noted rolling of 6 inch armour plate 9x9, cost 2,000 pounds. Simply play with big guns there.

22nd Thursday
With Crofty and Nank, took a walk along esplanade to Seacombe. Noted fine Municipal Hall there and steps leading to it. Then on to New Brighton. Inspected buildings round, but not allowed up New Brighton tower, 621 feet above sea level. Shops on top. Against 'War Precautions Act' to go up. Building very massive. Fine esplanade houses, mostly of business men. Big baths there. Beautiful paths and roads, no vehicles allowed on them, embarked by brick wall. Sand every year comes over portion of esplanade, blown there by wind from shore of river. Took tram to Wallesley Village, and by Wirral Railway – Mersey Railway had an evening in Liverpool. Went to Mr. Hudson's house, 16 Cambridge Street. Not home, at Masonic.

23rd Friday
Detailed to night duty. Wards E1-3. Mitchell D1. Up to 2pm preparing wards with bed gear etc., then turned in for duty @ 9pm till 7am. Others on leave 5-11.30pm. Best day and evening yet during our stay in Liverpool.

24th Saturday
Left docks 3am for Mersey. Shifted up or down on several occasions. Everything quiet all day. Day duty men still preparing wards for 2pm embarkation tomorrow.

IRELAND

Old bridge beyond 'Kate Karney's' cottage

Ancient Bricken Bridge

Watching mountain goats, Killarney

Carriage Killarney

Killarney

Meeting of the waters

Echo Point 'Gap of Dunloe'

Dunluce Castle

Arbutus Cottage

Giants Causeway

Killarney sheep

25th Sunday
Up and down stream. Embarked patients 4pm, and stayed alongside wharf all night. Wire cable-cutting apparatus affixed in docks to be tested. Sailed at 12.30pm. Busy.

Note from diary Cpl C.R. Mortimer AWM.
Two cutters were placed one on either side of the front of ship. Shaped something like a cigar, each one provided with an ingenious device for sawing through cable holding the two mines together, the wash off the ship being expected to send them clear off the ship.

26th Monday
Very bad night. Many of patients suffering from sea-sickness. Mitchell ill, and I had to work in D1 from 4am. Hear that this the worst boat load of patients leaving England.

27th Tuesday
Still rough at sea. Patient in E3, heart very bad in consequence of gas at front, died 6pm. One of mine-sweeping drum arrangements lost. Many of staff ill.

28th Wednesday
Patient buried at sea 1pm. Last post sounded. Engines stopped. Very impressing. Poor fellow now lying beneath billows of Atlantic after nearly reaching home.

29th Thursday
Superb night at sea. Fit well with day on trip from Avonmouth to Liverpool. Wrote C.S.M., Lower North Wales.

30th Friday
Still busy, but nothing special. Noticed the beautiful sunrise.

December

1st Saturday
Poor old Pvte. Daniels pretty low, and not expected to last very long. Four sons at front. Were all together – two killed, he stayed on with remainder until obliged to leave.

2nd Sunday
Church services. Pay day, 6 pounds two shillings.

3rd Monday
Glorious day at sea. Warm sun and cool breeze. All taking quinine, (Malaria). Busy night.

4th Tuesday
Warm.

5th Wednesday
Arrived Dakar 8.30am. Remember the various points of interest on approaching and entering. Sea a bit too choppy for natives in canoes to come out. Started coaling. Flag dipped to us from British steamer. Many British ships in port, evidently waiting a convoy, 34 vessels –altogether. Experiencing a great yearning to go ashore, but no leave granted.

6th Thursday
Left Dakar 2.30pm. Nice breeze at sea. Deceased patient Ptve. Driar buried at sea 9pm, ceremony most impressing. Died of Cerebro Abscess, and spreading Meningitis. Post mortem held during the day.

7th Friday
Poor old Daniels died 8.57pm of Carcinoma in abdomen according to P.M. Much missed during night on duty. Most patient man, and easily satisfied, and of no trouble. Saw very large school of porpoises.

8th Saturday
Daniels buried at sea mid-day. Another tremendous school of Porpoise, shooting and jumping high out of water just before burial.
328 miles. Making good headway 2-4am every morning especially.

9th Sunday
Church services. Saw large ship in full sail on South Africa side.

10th Monday
Suspected Chicken Pox. Isolated.
Passed an English Hospital Ship during night, also a convoy of nine vessels bound for Britain. Could see Hospital Ship distinctly as all green lights were on, others were in darkness, but ship's Officer gave us this information.

Note from diary of Cpl. C.R. Mortimer AWM.
Karoola's funnel had a large red cross fixed on either side, the principle being electric globes in a cross and covered with red glass. These were taken down and red crosses painted on either side when a ship went very close to being rammed by another boat in the Irish Sea. This boat came on to us in a fog early one morning and seeing the red light tried to cross over, as he thought, to his right side and just grazed along the side of our boat. As we had the red light on either side, it was a breach of the rules of navigation, and was altered during one of our trips to Alexandria.

11th Tuesday
Getting along splendidly with patients, found some very fine chaps. How very different all are tho' to the poor submissive and meek little Tommy, who is overridden and cowered by 'discipline', ours do not know the word in the true sense and feel their independence.

12th Wednesday
Everybody remarking on the wonderfully smooth passage. Old hands say that no previous trip equals this both from and back to Australia.

13th Thursday
Large sailing ship 6-7 miles from us. Not many sails up. An Officer taken to D3 ward. Chicken Pox and isolated.

14th Friday
Another case isolated. Wrote Miss Wittaker in Belfast. Weather continues beautifully cool.

15th Saturday
Pay day. To call at Cape Town by wireless message summons. Durban first intended.

16th Sunday
Very quiet day. Sea beautiful.

17th Monday
Arrived off and anchored in Cape Town Bay 8pm, just too late to get in.
Davies (Ammunition worker) died 10pm. His sufferings from malignant growth bottom jaw, being terrible. His is considered a happy relief.
An English hospital ship in port, all walking patients on home leave.

18th Tuesday
Got leave Capetown 2—8pm. Received letter from Mother dated November 10th. Went ashore with Mitch. Caught Wynberg car, and came back to Cecil Rhodes. Saw zoo and walked to memorial. Went on top and had look round, noted the beautiful flowers up gully from Cecil Rhodes house, chased squirrels there being many about, and attracting our attention by falling shells etc., and cones from pine trees. Walk was beautiful, came on to tram line again, amongst plantation oaks. Monument in beautiful spot with large high and steep mountain behind. Supposed to be erected in spot where Rhodes planned his great plans.

After arriving back in Cape Town, had a walk up pier and up tower for good look round. Noted magnificent cloud descending down gully, like a huge cloth between Lions Head and Table Mountain. Poor old Davies body taken ashore. The poor old chaps wish before leaving England that he did not want to be buried at sea. His wish co-incidentally complied with. Davies body taken ashore to be buried at Rhone Busch Cemetery. Intend having a look at it next visit.

19th Wednesday
Crofty in (hot) water owing to challenging the ships Captain's identity at gangway last night. Left Cape Town 6pm. Patients had leave again, but we none. A glorious day, and fine to be ashore. Sea a bit rough, and causing a lurch or two and pitching a good deal. This is similar to our leaving last time for England.

20th Thursday
Sea pretty rough still, a roll now and a heavy one. Things movable shifted during night.

21st Friday
Sea calm again, beautiful blue. Dvr. Penny from D1 ward died about 9pm.

22nd Saturday
Penny committed to the deep. More convinced that Sgt. Carr, one of our blind boys is a splendid chap, and I am much struck with his fine qualities – formally a stock and station agent. Very plucky outlook on life.

23rd Sunday
Church services. Beautiful day at sea. Our old friends the Albatross following us again, also the small black bird which flies like the former. My thoughts as I lie in my old hammock wander back to my dear father, and reminiscences follow of this season of the year during earlier periods of my life. What happy golden days of my youth.

24th Monday
A little dull first thing. Christmas carol singers visited wards before 9 o'clock. Padre, three Sisters, a couple of crew and several of A.M.C. staff, amongst whom was Nankivell. His solos much appreciated. Tried to smooth path between night Sister and one of the blind boy patients. She having threatened to report him if seen smoking down convalescent wards again, as it is dangerous to do so. He takes exception to be threatened, but misunderstands I think. The other blind boys do not agree with him, a fine lot of chaps and very reasonable.

25th Tuesday
Day again beautiful. Splendid Christmas weather. Nice spread for Christmas day at tea-time, poultry, jellies, fruit and nuts. Mess deck ornamented with Union Jack and Signaling flags. Patients also provided with a little cheer.

26th Wednesday
All anxious to get home again. Learn that we are far south in order to get fine weather, and smoother passage in consideration of patients. Supposed combat (boxing) Harris and Westlake does not come off. A piece of poetry composed at Westlake's expense stating that he won in talk, and also Harris disqualified for hitting below belt, having picked up Westlake and spanked him on the bare posterior.

27th Thursday
Beautiful clear sky and shiny silvery moon, which shows up gorgeously on the calm sea. Seems that line of light of moon shows as far as the horizon.

28th Friday
Slept very little. Beautiful night, full moon, pretty effect on water. Hausman or Hansman E3 died 2.45pm. Post mortem same afternoon, and buried at 9pm. Happy release for this poor man, who was suffering from a Lymphatic disease. Very sad indeed to have passed away when so near home.

29th Saturday
Large school of whales very close to ship, so the day boys tell us. Discovered Pvte. Sandercock in E3, a fine chap who was in 50th Battalion with many Pt. Pirie boys of my acquaintance. Near Frank Bulbeck my predecessor at Mt. Barker Branch at time of his death. Told me all about him. Died a hero and gentleman, admired and respected by all his acquaintances. Has news of? to be appreciated by Reeves family, gave him their address.

30th Sunday

Services. Rained in morning. Early dawn 4am now. Had Calabash pipe presented me by W.O. Bay.

31st Monday

Our poor old Gnr. Swanson, my favourite patient died 7.15pm. Tumor of bladder. Absolutely the bravest man I met to bear up with suffering. Tumor finally perforated bowel. A fine big fellow, blacksmith by trade from N.S.W.
His manliness gained the respect of other patients.

JANUARY, 1918

1st Tuesday

A bit of a flare up by a few in keeping with New Years Eve.
Swanson after a Post mortem committed to the deep at 1pm. His address C/- Mrs. Mary Swanson, McIntosh Street, Gordon (Sydney) N.S.W.

ORDERLIES DUTIES AND DAILY ROUTINE

The day after embarkation work of storing the patients kit would commence, a ticket with his name, company, ward and cot number was fastened to his kit, bags and carried down to the pack store. The place set apart in the store for his gear was marked with a similar number, so it was an easy matter to get his things if required. When all of this was completed, and everything working smoothly, arrangements were made for half the staff to go off duty at 2pm, until 4pm. Those remaining would carry patients either to the top deck to enjoy fresh air, and the company of their mates, or to the x/ray room or for an operation. Cot patients had to be carried again down to their wards before preparing for tea. It was a continual round of stretcher bearing up and down stairs. The Orderlies on duty all afternoon would be relieved at 6pm when he would have his own tea, have a shave, and very often either take part in some entertainment on behalf of a cot patient, or relieve someone who had volunteered to assist. The afternoon he was off duty from 2 till 4pm, he would have a shave, take his soiled clothes to the laundry, as clothes had to be smart and clean. There was also letter writing, and notes in the diary to do, so that his time was fully occupied from 6am till 9pm.

The cots in most of the wards were arranged so that they could be rigidly fixed or allowed to swing in harmony with the motion of the ship. The exception being in the place set apart for Orderlies known as the steerage aft and the wards forward where the patients most advanced in convalescence were lodged. In both places cots were double tiered and fixed. In the latter patients spent most of their time in deck chairs provided by Red Cross, only going down to meals and to sleep. In the tropics they were allowed to sleep on deck, provided they had a life belt for a pillow. Of all the patients allowed out on deck during good weather, many were wonderfully improved by rest, sunshine and improved diet by the time they reached home.

There was a Barber shop, and dry canteen where tobacco, cigarettes, cool drinks, tin fruits, tin fish etc, could b purchased for a reasonable price.

Orderlies other than attending patients generally, was to have all patients washed by the time the day duty staff relieved them by 6am (started 9pm night before).

The parade was at 6am, when the N.C.O would march their staff down to their various wards. Some of the staff would proceed to clean down the bed boards as it was necessary that they should be cleaned up ready for breakfast to be served up to them. Others attended the patients while the remainder prepared for breakfast. Knives, forks and spoons had to be placed on each bedboard of those confined to their cots and tables prepared for those able to sit up. Plates had to be placed in a hotpress to warm, and the bread cut and buttered. By the time these duties were performed they went to the gallery to draw the food for breakfast. This usually consisted of porridge, chops, sausages, steak, stew, or eggs and bacon, differing from day to day. Orderlies divided the meal hour between them, half going to their meal while the patients were having theirs, and the rest went to theirs while those who went away first were doing the washing up. From the breakfast to inspection time it was hard going. On the stroke of 10am, the inspection would commence. The buglar came to the door of each ward, and blow the 'G', Orderlies sprang to attention. The O.C. accompanied by Officers came along, and as he was out to find fault, would detect dirt and defects here and there as he went from ward to ward. He carried an electric torch and flashed it behind baths and all likely places. After inspection cot patients were served with biscuits, cocoa, tea or beef tea contributed also by the Red Cross. The dinner consisted of soup, hot joints, vegetables and puddings and sometimes fish. At 4pm tea, cocoa and biscuits or bread and butter were given to cot patients. The evening meal consisted of rabbit, fish, stew or cold joints, potatoes, fruit, fresh or tinned, pickles or tomato sauce. Again at 8pm, coffee, biscuits and cheese were given round.

Diary 1.
Arrivals and Departures 1917

Left Mitcham	10th September
Arrived Melbourne	11th
Left "	12th
Arrived Albany	17th
Left "	18th
Arrived Durban	4th October
Left "	5th
Arrived Capetown	8th
Left "	10th
Arrived Dakar	22nd
Left "	24th
Arrived Avonmouth	2nd November
Left "	3rd 8pm.
Arrived Mersey Birkenhead Liverpool	4th
Left Liverpool	26th 9pm.
Arrived Dakar	5th December
Left "	6th
Arrived Capetown	17th
Left "	18th

The following written on last pages of Diary 1.

I shall pass thro' this world but once,
any good thing therefore that I can do or any kindness that I can show to any living creature,
let me do it now, let me not defer or neglect it,
for I shall not pass this way again. CARLYLE.

Battalion National Anthem – Tune "What a friend we have in Jesus".

Only just one more Reveille
   Only one more night parade,
Only one more kit inspection,
   Then we're marching home again!
When we get our civil clothes on,
   O'h! how happy we shall be!
When this gory war is over,
   No more soldiering for me!

Compliments will then be fewer,
   Guards, fatigues, will be no more.
Will be spooning with the wenches,
   As we did in days of yore,
N.C.O's will then be navies,
   Privates own their motor cars,
No more 'Sir-ing' and saluting,
   No more tea in two pound jars!

No more marching, no more doubling,
   In the dewy morn in haste,
No more pushing blooming barrows,
   On the range at Crannock Chase,
No more 'Smarter, men! Now Smarter!'
   No more bread like 'Granite Rocks',
No more rising at five-thirty,
   Or 'Lights Out', at 10 o'clock.

No more asking, when w'ere marching,
   Please, sir, may we ha a --- drink?
Or, because we drop a shovel,
   No more 'Shun-ing' as you we're-ing',
No working for a bob a day,
   When next the Country has a war on,
We'll find a job that brings more pay!

People told us, when we listed,
   Fame, and medals we should win,
But the fame is in the guard room,
   And the medal made of tin!
When we've finished with the ?
   At the Palace we shall sing,
The Battalion National Anthem,
   Twice a night, God save the King.

Printed Abroad. Copied from a Tommy Soldier bound from Mesopotamia embarked at Capetown 10/10/1917.

Diary Two

JANUARY, 1918

2nd Wednesday
Days rather cold. W.A. boys full of anticipation re disembarkation. Hear that nearly all farmers in Wagin District are Sth. Australians.

3rd Thursday
Still a bit cold and sea choppy, but the good ship stands up to it. Expect to dawdle outside so as to reach Fremantle at dawn.

4th Friday
Sighted Rottnest Island, lighthouse (third largest in the world) at 2.30am, scented the beautiful gum leaves off the land, wind blowing our way.

Tied up at 8am, passed 'KAROOLA's' sister ship 'KATOOMBA' at wharf. Her bugler rendered patriotic airs on cornet 'My little grey home in the West', and 'Home sweet home.' Very impressive to see poor blind boys, (one Jimmy James and 'old Dad') looking into sky, and not able to appreciate the scene. Military Band present.

Put in for extended leave 2-6pm, granted, saw Mr. Westlake and family at gates on wharf. Went to see Uncle Charles and had good fortune to see Alf and Dave at the yard too. Saw Greta at Melbourne S.S. Co, and Alan at railway goods sheds. No time to go to Beaconsfield to see Aunt Grace. Hear that Rollo is still doing O.K. at front. Had a good walk round with Charles and a talk about his trip to England. Treated me as usual (i.e.good). Learn from Uncle Dave that his wife is in S.A.

Left at 7.30pm. Noticed old familiar sights, and light houses by which we steered. P.S. Charlie gave me a little history of Fremantle as he knew it twenty years ago. Walked to old landmark at rear of town, where an excellent view of Fremantle was obtainable and Cottesloe, also Garden Island, Rottnest out to sea. Rottnest previously used for German internment camp, only two farmers on Garden Island. Just imagine this place with its big street dotted round with tents in days of 'Golden West'. Trust that father will pay his long promised visit now that Great Western Railway completed. (Transcontinental). Remembered very vividly some of the places in Fremantle. (A Jap cruiser in port nine years ago).

5th Saturday
Glorious day. Passed steamer bound for Fremantle. Lovely sea, saw coast line all day.

6th Sunday
Church services. Shady and windy day.
Hear S.A. boys have to go on to Sydney.
Hear that Capt. Harrop, Military dentist at Mitcham was killed from a fall from his horse.
Entered Aust. Bight and remarkably smooth (usually a fear to travellers here).

7th Monday
Good sea. More Albatross now following.
Very quiet night work now.

8th Tuesday
Slept in open and sunburnt to a chip. Considerable uneasiness from leg as far as ankle.
Beautiful day and sea good.
Many talking of home now.

9th Wednesday
Good sea on, very blowy during night. Passed Otway lighthouse 2am.

10th Thursday
Arrived Melbourne 1pm, after sighting heads 8am. Good wind blowing Pt. Philip, A.U.S.N. boat just ahead and proceeding up Yarra.
Disembarked Melbourne, Adelaide, Tasmanian, patients 3pm. Left again 6pm, and wind threatened a gale for outside. At dusk noticed many flashlights and beacons and lighthouses suggesting difficult navigation born out by many twists and turns of our ship. Sea calm on reaching heads.

11th Friday
Sea good and blue. Passed Wilson's Promontory and a splendid sight. Saw lighthouse and ranges, and ravages of a fire along them evidently some time ago, in way of all dead trees. Big Collins Street our passage, noted Little Collins Street, also islands to Tasmania, whence came the theory that Tasmania once linked up with mainland. Followed coast for some miles. At 9pm. caught and passed large steamer, but it followed till 5am (12th) then turned back, and headed for Melbourne. We hear of minefield round Gabo way.

12th Saturday
Good night, changing of addresses with patients etc. Poor chaps longest voyagers of all. Very eager to get on land again.

13th Sunday
Many kind invitations from patients.
Passed Coogee and Bondi lights at about 2.30am. Passed into Heads, and reached this glorious Sydney harbour at 6am, saw old Port Mc Quarie and many other interesting points and views explained to us by Sydney boys. Anchored till 8am. As soon as remaining patients discharged got leave. Had to use a slipper to right foot, borrowed puttie stockings from Sgt. Biggs and found them most useful. Got in ferry for Tooronga Park. This is a fine Zoo, and promises to be a splendid place when completed. Got in tram from there for the Spit Road. Changed cars at Mosman, crossed over in punt to next car and went to Manly. This is a delightful place, with its houses close to front of beach and avenues of pines. Enjoyed a good surf bathe and returned to Circular Quay by half hour ferry.

14th Monday
Saw old troopship 'KYARRA' at anchor. Went out to Bondi, and Coogee via Bondi Junction, much enjoyed the trip, but all were of opinion that Bondi beach superior, but not to Manly of course. Had a good look round city in afternoon, went to top of Commonwealth Bank building. Changed our English money there. A glorious building right throughout. Over to Manly in afternoon, and enjoyed a good surf bathe. Every facility afforded in sheds.

15th Tuesday
Got an early start. Had another look round the city. Saw the Town Hall, and its famous organ (largest in the world) in George Street. Went to wharf (Circular Quay), but too late to go to Lane Cove.

Interviewed Col. re leaving by train for home, but he flatly refused the idea. Reported to ship at 3pm, and got extended leave till midnight. Went to Museum and noted with particular interest old nautical instruments of Capt. Cook, and old curios dredged from Thames. Had a look thro' Botanical Gardens on our way back to ship. These are well laid out. Went out to Gordan to see the Swanson family re their deceased son. My visit much appreciated, and asked to stay there next visit. Poor old lady much grieved, and expected boy home till two days previous to arrival of ship, even had invitation tickets to social to be given by town in honour of the occasion. Gordon on north shoreline, train leaves Milsons Point (very pretty and good view of harbour). Gordon reminds me of Blackwood. How the poor boy must have looked forward to getting back to his home, amongst that beautiful timbered country. Nice springs just here near the house.

16th Wednesday
Finished coaling and left Sydney 11am. Passed sister ship **'KATOOMBA'** just coming in again. She travelled from W.A. in good time.

Heard about the wreck of the DUNBAR at Sydney Heads. Captain had a wager as to time in doing his trip, and tried to steer ship thro' the Gap thinking that it was the opening to the harbour.

Sea seems inclined to be a bit rough later on. Coast in sight for a few miles, but steering pretty far south.

17th Thursday
Good old storm on, doing about four knots. Raining.

18th Friday
Sea calmer and doing good speed. Mitch says he saw shark following at stern. Anxious about our time in getting in so as to catch Melbourne Express to Adelaide. Arrived at Heads at noon just off Admiralty Pier, 3pm. Anchored. Alongside at 4.20. Handed passes 4.25, ran to gates and caught taxi. Made a dash for train but missed it by three minutes, our time home now to be limited. All very disappointed. Stayed at Victoria Coffee Palace, four of us in a very small room. Went to Vaudeville in evening. Slept on floor owing to scarcity of room.

Group of soldiers and sisters on ship

Bowling green Perth

Japanese ship taken over by British

Karoola coming into Melbourne from Sydney

SS 'Beltana' camouflaged

River Swan at Perth

Crew and sisters on top of ship

'Karoola', WWI. No.1 Australian Hospital Ship

19th Saturday
Went to A.I.F. Head Quarters, St. Kilda Road and obtained full warrant passes home. Went to St. Kilda per tram to St. Kilda Place, very dead. Went into baths and had a good dip, had a look round city for awhile. Caught the express in good time.
Met Mrs. Treloar on Blackwood Station, and handed Jack's letter to her. Spent a wearisome night.

20th Sunday
Glad back in our own state once again. Arrived Adelaide 10am. Noticed Mitcham Camp looks same as usual. Fortunately Mitch's friend at station to meet us otherwise a walk home.

Arrived home just after 11am. Mother and girls at church. Gave my dear father a surprise. Informed me that he should have come to Melbourne next day had I not come home. Caught him in bath. Gave Mother and girls a beautiful surprise, altho' Uncle Dave had informed them from West that I had called in to see him. Found them all well, and little Colin now walking and looking a strong little chap, a dear little fellow, a good head and all proud of him. Dear Mother quite concerned about my old leg, but nearly better now. Went out to Aunties with father, all well except Aunt Ada, who was there laid up sick. Saw our bonny garden, and dear fathers handwork, trellis now completed and a thorough job as usual. Hear with regret of the loss of our dear old cow. Night warm so slept on verandah. So endeth the history of first voyage on Active Service.

Monday 21st
Regretfully remember that have to depart again today. Saw Mr. Densly and Clive Bailey. Dear father came home midday. All home and pleased with little presents of mine. Pleased to see the electric fan going, and much appreciated by father after work on hot days. Parting a hard job Ada, Vere, Aunts Minnie and Ana Ham at Adelaide Station. Recipient of delicacies. nuts etc., from my dear Mother. Ref? big cake etc., which had been made for me. Not a bad journey.

22nd Tuesday
Arrived ship in good time. S.A. Sisters also aboard train. Duties commenced by carrying sundries on board, leave in evening, but we four had no guard duty. Went ashore nevertheless. Good day and cool.

23rd Wednesday
Sailed at 2.30pm. Small crowd on wharf to bid farewell, reached Heads at 6pm. and headed for sea. Hear we are to go only a short trip this time, but a very large supply of stores aboard. Now have a new O.C. Lt. Col. McIntosh. Capt. McShane and Capt. Burrell left ship, the latter a good fellow and will be missed. Could have had another day at home after all.

24th Thursday
Good sea. Passed one of the small steamers of Howard Smith line yesterday evening about dusk. On dispensary duty at Red Cross store.

Note from Official Report from Lt. Col. T.G. Wilson AWM.
> The equipment of the Hospital Ship as a Hospital was all that one wished for, thanks largely to the generosity of the Australian Red Cross who provided all sorts of extra equipment for the wards, operating theatre and other departments besides making provision regularly for extras on the voyage in the way of food, games,

gramophones, pyjamas, socks and other necessaries. The only complaint I ever had from the Red Cross was that I did not requisition for enough but I always worked on the principle that if I could get supplies from Government sources, it was not a fair thing to ask the Red Cross to supply them, and I always kept a check upon Red Cross supplies exactly as on those obtained from Ordnance.

25th Friday
Sports committee meeting held at 8pm., but no new members elected as yet.
Better feeling and happier amongst the staff themselves since new O.C. came on board.

26th Saturday
Half holiday.
Tournament in deck quoits played. Put shelf in locker, giving more room.

27th Sunday
Church services. O.C. Morning parade, no work. O.C. does not believe in work on Sunday until absolute occasion. Up on boat deck till 4pm.
Saw land, supposed to be off Albany.

28th Monday
Passed Leeuwin during night. Six hours run from there to Cape Naturalist thence eight hours to Fremantle. Sighted Rottnest about 2pm, also passed steamer going east. Overseas boat, about a mile off. Went into port 7.30pm, got leave 8 – midnight, but as we anchored in harbour, no boat available till one and half hours to take us off. McIlwraith's motor boat at last took us off. Uncle Charlie not home, but met him coming out of pictures with Uncle Alf. Spent a pleasant one and a half hours. Charlie came to barrier, caught 12 o'clock boat back. Our ship looked O.K. with all lights on.

29th Tuesday
Got further leave 11am – 3pm. Went to Uncles yard again, the other boys went to Perth. Afterwards had dinner with him. Saw Uncle Dave at his yard. Told me of his intention in giving up business shortly, and taking up quieter occupations perhaps in S.A. again. Saw Uncle Jim also, first time I remember. Hear that Winnie and her husband now living in Fremantle.

Sailed at 6pm. Wrote to Ralphie, father and mother. Beautiful sunset, turned round Rottnest. Air good and mild, grand sleeping out. Evening tints on blue water with red retiring sun seem to remind one of the 'Golden West'.

30th Wednesday
Good day. Choppy in afternoon. Good old Australia once again out of sight.
Our choir under leadership of Pens held their first practice. Promises to turn out well. Three Officers members.

31st Thursday
Slept out on deck as usual on starboard side, but washed out by a big sea coming over port, and floating on deck round steering house to us, our mattresses completely swamped. Started with Crofty and Mitchell to acquire art of Sema 4 signalling.

FEBRUARY, 1918

1st Friday
Good many flying fish about, also number of porpoise.
Detailed to F2, Mess deck for duty.

2nd Saturday
Half holiday.
Noted many dolphins followed by numerous black birds about a mile from ship. Beguiled time in playing deck quoits. In morning sailed into a sea of 'blue-bottles'. Remember the one off Manly of which bathers were careful to avoid.

3rd Sunday
Remember old date 3/2/12. First parting of home to go to Pt. Pirie.
Church services – boat deck 2-4pm, our choir under leadership of Pens to assist. My thoughts travel back to father on this grey dull morning for a Sabbath walk thro' our paddocks. Overheard a conversation re the hypocrites of S.A. boys who do not play games on Sundays. Very amusing.

5th Tuesday
Grand concert by 'Karoolacean' concert party. O.C., Chairman and all staff on ship present. Alphabet and sending of Sema 4 now learnt pretty well. Hear by wireless of serious strikes – labour in Germany.

6th Wednesday
Euchre tournament by those interested in evening.

7th Thursday
Sea beautiful. Blue and crisp.
Getting better at Semaphore.

8th Friday
Detailed to staff – Mess deck.

10th Sunday
Services. Games on boat deck 2-4pm.
Poor Messner received a nasty blow just beneath right eye when fielding in cricket thro' batman letting bat go flying from his hand. Very painful for a time. Numerous birds now following ship

11th Monday
Doing good mileage 337.

12th Tuesday
A fancy dress ball held during evening. No apparent preparation during preceding days, but when all participants assembled, many surprises were in store. The get-ups considering the limited material and time taken, were marvellous. Boat deck decorated

with flags. Prizes given to J. Rundle (Bride) for best impersonation, and Croft for best sustained character. (Two S.A. Fordham, Lucifer) also a prize for myself dressed as a 'Manly Life Saver'.

13th Wednesday

Arrived Capetown 5.30pm (15 days run) handed passes 6.30pm., clock put on an hour so 7.30 – 11pm. Went by handsome to city, and saw 'Remnant' in Opera House which was very much enjoyed. Had to leave before quite finished. Caught motor car for ship. ps. During morning at Colonels request, time off to have photos taken of Ball party in rig-outs.

14th Thursday

Went ashore 10am, first to Information Bureau and received booklet etc. Went to Camps Bay, had swim and afternoon tea at Pagoda. Went thro' Pinery, and climbed to 'Kloof' thence halfway in prohibited area up Lions Head. Caught tram back. Fairly warm climbing, but beautiful breeze from sea later. Reported at 6.30pm. and went on guard.

P.S. In morning obtained permit from City Engineer to explore top of Table Mountain. Given continuous passes to 22/2/18. Expecting to have a fairly long stay. Rumoured that we are to leave Saturday. 'H.S. GILFORD CASTLE' in port again, but went to sea during afternoon on German East run.

15th Friday

'DUNLUCE CASTLE' arrived 6pm. 435 patients on board, a fine big ship. Signalled Sema 4 to a chap on board, told us that food was poor and scanty, mainly subsisting on bread and Irish butter. Had a good voyage out, took 20 days.

Went on leave 6.30pm. Had a most interesting walk thro' Government Avenue and into Municipal Park and Gardens, these very beautiful and something about them which suggests tropical life. Came back past hotel on right side, cutting thro' lane at rear of Government House, thence to Adderley Street. Saw many nice and quaint buildings. View of mountain at top of avenue very impressive as it was covered with a very dense white cloth. Afterwards went to Pier Head, but no concert as we expected, so movies instead. Some munitions workers from the 'BELTANA' were there also.

16th Saturday

To go back to Australia today, so all plans re running about cancelled.

Started Embarkation at 10am. Went on board 'DUNLUCE CASTLE', (hospital ship) but not over struck with cleanliness or tidiness of the wards etc. Our boys glad to pay 1/- a box for matches. All complain of scarcity of food.

Off duty at 2pm. Went to bed, and started night duty at 9pm. Quiet night, patients seem used to ship life, great contrast to early stages of last trip from England. Passed Hospital ship at midnight apparently bound for Capetown.

17th Sunday

R.C. Padre on board. Services as usual.
Patients all seemed satisfied with their new ship, both regards housing, comfort and meals. (Hear that Mitchell and I considered picked men). On good terms with our W.O. who decides duties.

18th Monday
Ran across a long line of yellow substance in water, looking very much like rust.
Met A.M.C stretcher bearer Ptve. Decorated D.C.M. and M.M., a fine fellow. Enjoys this ship, and appreciates our work.

19th Tuesday
Passed over a sea of 'blue-bottles' again.

20th Wednesday
Beautiful sea.
In evening concert by patients and staff. Nank and Croft also Pens (S.A's encored and items much enjoyed).
Remember sight in moonlight. Came during concert of one legged hero with crutches, as ship tossed up and down, standing near rigging.
Had very interesting chat with Pvte. Quamley V.C. re our duty to country, women (especially our Mothers) sisters and children. Very kind, courteous and frank fellow indeed.
Rained heavily during night.

21st Thursday
Hear of the water spout witnessed by our boys on the 'DUNLUCE CASTLE' coming thro' the tropics.

Ptve. Quamley V.C. of Southhead, Batt. Art., promised me his battery and set for Morse signalling. Promised to interview his friends at home on my behalf in desirous of joining Sig. Corp., attached to ARTILLERY.

22nd Friday
Met Ptve. Stevens a work-mate of Uncle Jocks at Municipal Tramways Trust, a stretcher bearer suffering severely from shell-shock.

A storm coming up, remember the most remarkable sight an hour after sundown of such vivid chain lightening, that sky every few moments lighted up pink similar to a sunset, all linings of clouds distinctly seen.

23rd Saturday
Sea rough and ship rolling considerably during night. Albatross seem to like this weather and many following. 314 miles.

24th Sunday
Church services well attended.

25th Monday
Read book by Rolf Rolderwood. "The Modern Buccaneer', lent me by George Talbot, who knows personally some of the characters in the Islands and brother of H. Telfer in Sydney.

26th Tuesday
Engines noisy owing to rush of steam thro' leaky packing of cylinder.

27th Wednesday
Beautiful sea, absolutely unbroken.

28th Thursday
A lovely swell, but sea unbroken.
A few cot cases brought on deck to enjoy the glorious sunshine.

MARCH, 1918

1st Friday
Hear of Castle liner Hospital Ship sunk in Bristol Channel.

3rd Sunday
Lads expectant and excited as lights on Rottnest are sighted and more so when Fremantle glimmers come into view. Dropped anchor to go in at 8am in morning. No Pilot required (Morse message from shore).

4th Monday
Weighed anchor and proceeded into port first thing. The same Military Band on the wharf. Leave at noon – 4pm for night staff. Went to Uncles and saw the four of them again. Gave Charlie Boer Tobacco. Received several letters from home. Mother, Ada and Vere, Mrs. Mac and Walter, also Jack Treloar, left at 8pm. Round Rottnest. Work with Navel Base proceeding at ..... Island near there.

5th Tuesday
At sunset passed a steamer turning into Albany. Seem to be hugging the coast here for not so near last trip. Could distinctly see the Baytop Rocks eastern entrance to Albany. Hear that S.A. boys to get off ship in Melbourne.

6th Wednesday
A perfect day at sea, the old Bight again very friendly.
Poor Gibson suffering from Nephritis in D1. Mitch's patient died 4.50pm. and buried by R.C. Padre at 9pm. A follower of the sea, and had sailed this water many times before. Very sad that after being away over three years, he was not permitted when so near to reach his home in Brisbane.

7th Thursday
At 6pm. Passed a three mast Barque. Will never forget this sight, for she was the picture of grace and elegance, being only three miles from us. After passing us gave her number and name. All sails were up, and proceeding at our pace. It was a beautiful sight as she seemed on the horizon to us, to watch her disappear with the red glowering set of the sun in front of her.

8th Friday
Leave list up, have to report back in Melbourne on 19th. This makes up for very short leave last time.
Good old wind last night.

10th Sunday
Arrived Melbourne 10am and disembarked patients, no special Hospital train to Adelaide. Capt. Southwood fixes us with a ride over on train on duty.

Had meals at Y.M.C.A. down St. Kilda drive. Stayed at Victoria Coffee palace for night.

11th Monday
With Mitch went to have a look at Public Library and Museum. Library dome beautiful, note many shelves of books on walls high up, and Silky Oak fittings. Went to H.Q. and made sure of our passes home and caught train which left 3pm. With 55 S.A. wounded. A happy family of S.A.'s, all our Sisters except Sally and Ransome on board.
Met Mr. Beresford at Federal and hear of poor Aunt Ada's death.

12th Tuesday
Arrived Adelaide at 9.45am. At Bacchus Marsh, Ballarat, Murray Bridge, patients brought flowers and dainties by hospitable people. Mitch and I carried few patients on stretchers to Ambulances on Adelaide Station. Afterwards Messner sent to Keswick to report our names off duty by P.M.O. Went to Kindernans? with Mitch's Aunt, and had refreshment, then out to Aunt's son deeming this better account of their recent bereavement. Aunt Ada's death a sad blow to them. Got home in time for tea, all surprised to see me. Aunt Emily there. Going back to W.A. next Thursday. Little Colin not very well. All others O.K.

13th Wednesday
Day at home. Hear that Mitcham Camp to be only a receiving base shortly. Keswick Hospital staffed with home-service except a few A.I.P. A.M.C. to be shortly replaced, all units going to Melbourne unattached and sent away as drafts required. A.M.C. to collapse at Mitcham apparently. Good old days passing.
Sent out to Aunt son's and Hams and together with Renie went with Mr. Hall in car for a trip past Magill and back along Morialta, a very enjoyable time, good outing. Garden looking simply beautiful.

14th Thursday
On Father's bike took a ride to Pt. Adelaide and made arrangements with Percy for hire of his horse and trap for trip with Father to Millbrook. In afternoon went out to Keswick Hospital and saw many of the old staff and some old 'Karoola' patients, who were very pleased to see me.

In evening went out to Goldsmiths and Hams. Found all well. Poor little Ralph injured by collision with a trap whilst riding on a bike with another boy going to their Scout meeting, thro' horse shying. Nasty bruise on left chest and carried two chains on end of shaft held there by his shirt which was torn to shreds. Very fortunate indeed to have escaped with his life. Suffered a good deal of pain during night.

15th Friday
Went out to Mitcham Camp. Met Sgt. Black, Sgts. McKinnon and Penny, old privates at Keswick, also Scetheway and Jack Treloar. They doing nothing, and heard nothing at what is to become of them. Promised Mr. McHoney? to write. Young Goldsmith in Light Horse and likes it. His people a good deal concerned about his leaving.

Fathers half day off so went home, and went with him to see Uncle Josiah whom we found well and in good spirits. Aunt's son came during the afternoon. Poor old soul. First time for about ten weeks owing to Aunt Ada's illness. Most A.M.C. at Mitcham out in hills bivouacking. (Lucky beggars).

16th Saturday
Father went to Percys and brought horse and trap. Dear Mother prepared a good and well packed hamper for our trip (long promised) to Millbrook, took Ralphie. Went via Modbury, Teatree Gully and Inglewood. Day beautiful and fresh for travelling. Tied up and housed horse in stables of old Millbrook Hotel. Workmen and reservoir batching there (to be pulled down after completion of weir). Made tea there and had lunch in paddock. Much enjoyed. Bank 50ft wide on top, tower 86ft high. Reservoir to hold four billion gallons. 40 bullocks and 140 horses on job. Water to 15ft above chimney of Hotel. Came back and went to Chain of Ponds, and not far on Williamstown road found tunnel where artesian supply was struck. Tunnel 12ft high, 6 wide, beautiful concrete work, returned home via Houghton, and Payneham to Adelaide. Noted new deviation road Inglewood to Chain of Ponds.

17th Sunday
Harvest Thanksgiving at church. Went to see poor old Uncle George. Just celebrated his 97th birthday, and proud of statements in paper about him. Promised to go to his old Native Village if going to England again. Not feeling very well. Uncle and Aunt at church to hear Rev. Morris at Brompton re his altercation with Rev. Schafer at Ovingham caused thro' stating his views re conscription contrary to Methodist Conference ruling. Much interest roused thro' same. Went to see Mrs. Butler in afternoon. Clive and ? at home. Attended church in evening, service by Mr. Adcock. Met many old friends.

18th March
Said goodbye to dear Father. He wanted to take afternoon off, but advised him not to do so. Went to see Mrs. Densley, Mrs. Bradshaw, and Mrs. James, old friends. Dear Mother feels my going away keenly. Aunt, Miss Cath Ham, Ada, Vere, (*his 2 younger sisters*) and Mrs. Goldsmith at Adelaide Station to see me off. Before train went, went to Bank, and had my Bankbook made up. Saw most of heads. Keswick refused us warrants, so boarded train without ticket and took chance, as we think this treatment unfair.

19th Tuesday
Train conductor accepted our unused warrants from Melbourne (issue) as temporary tickets on understanding that we see Passenger Supt in Melbourne. Spent not a bad night on train and genial company in way of fellow travellers. One a sheep grazier from South East in S.A., near land of Murrays in which Styles implicated in public scandal re R. Soldiers Repatriation (settling soldiers on land scheme). Passenger Supt., informs us he will have to claim from Military authorities in same way as usual. Probably our pay books will be debited with the amounts later on. Reported ship 3pm. and obtained further leave. Went moonlight excursion in Hydreia from Pt. Melbourne with Messner. Went over to Williamstown during afternoon and had a look round dockyards (laying slips there on which a 5,000 ton ship to be built). Saw dry dock and French vessel loading wheat from a huge stack.

20th Wednesday
Over to Williamstown again to see beach and gardens which I had previously missed. Gardens very beautiful indeed, beds of flowers quite a treat and perfectly arranged. Noted the large goldfish in ponds, also four guns 1854 made by Sir Wm. Armstrong and Co. Newc. On Tyne, now Armstrong Whitworth and Co. Ltd., (huge guns for Crimea). Evening went to 'Within the Law', and much enjoyed same.

21st Thursday

On guard from 3pm yesterday, and nothing exciting. Large transport, 'EURIPEDES' arrived with 1,600 men from England, great crowd at barrier to meet the men. Motor cars in lines two and half lengths of Admiralty Pier to take the boys for a ride. Off guard 3pm. and saw procession through Swanson Street. Rather straggly, as all motors, some closely following others far behind and causing gaps. Bought accountancy books at Coles. Went to Lunar Park with Crofty and Smith. Scenic Railway much enjoyed, had a ride home in motor car, a good finish up.

22nd Friday

Young Giles Holders successor and I had a good look round wharves and Melbourne dock. Several large steamers in (two Jap boats) an English transport cattle ship and others (coastal steamers). Had invitation to Gas Coys. works by Supt., to look round, no time, but next time if opportunity offers.

23rd Saturday

Left Melbourne 11am, destiny Egypt rumoured. Expect to get to Fremantle Friday afternoon. Saw old spot (The Rip), where 'AUSTRALIA' P.& O. mail steamer was wrecked.

24th Sunday

Services – use of boat deck 2-4pm.

25th Monday

An orchestra in full formed up. Myself playing second violin. Good practice, as only time I have touched a violin since leaving home.

26th Tuesday

Passed thro' a sea of 'Blue Bottles' again. The sea a perfect unbroken mass of blue, so blue, that anything thrown overboard seems to be magnified.

27th Wednesday

Passed the 'NOORINGA' first thing this morning. Sea a bit choppy and we have a list on. Bottle overboard.

28th Thursday

Steaming slowly. Admiralty orders to go slowly to arrive Fremantle Friday afternoon.

29th Friday (Good Friday)

Sighted Rottnest 1pm., and arrived at Fremantle wharf 5pm. Leave 6-12. Anchored at buoy, and taken on shore by motor launch. Posted letter to Mother. With Mitch went round to Uncle Charlie's yard. All went to Her Majesties pictures in evening, afterwards a walk to North Fremantle over Tramway Bridge and back via railway. Very cool and nice round the Swan River. Uncle points out intended alterations to bridge and extension of wharves on both sides.

30th Saturday
Further leave 9am-3pm. Went to Uncles. Saw Alf and he informs me that Aunt Em and Uncle Dave were home on previous evening, also he himself was there. Caught 11 train with Chas and went to Subiaco, thence by tram to Perth. Got out at Hay Street and went thro' Kings Gardens – past Parliament House. Day very muggy and close, threatened heavy rain during morning, walked back near Swan Brewery via track on banks of the Swan. Noted tropical plants such as Bananas and Chinese bamboos. Walked down Hay Street thence Barrack Street. Good buildings and clean. Had dinner. Had a look at new P.O. Went round station down the famous 'Rowe Street' and back over Horseshoe Bridge, caught 2pm. train back and arrived Fremantle 2.45p. Fremantle much cooler than Perth, noticeable as soon as arrived.

Left at 4.45pm, and ship heading N.W. (bound for Colombo?) Sunset absolutely beautiful, no pen can describe, only minds-eye realise as a mental picture is taken. Lightning prolific, flashing four or five places almost at once, reflection behind clouds accounting for it. This a phenomenon, long streaks of chain lightning is rosy hue of sky, waters blue and our wake red thro' reflection of sun, then north salmon streaks of colour lighting up horizon in a most wonderful way. Looking back we see our old track to Africa.

31st Sunday
Church services.
ps. on Saturday Donawa receives a telegram conveying news of poor Harris' death from Ethmoiditis. Telegram of sympathy sent by ships staff to relative.

APRIL, 1918

1st Monday
Everybody keenly interested in the battle of all battles now raging in France on the Somme. Australians taking a very important strenuous part. ('poor old Ossies').

2nd Tuesday
Orchestra in conjunction with choir hold a practice for tomorrow evening when hymns are to be rendered, and memorial service in memory of late Pvte. Harris.
Down on Mess deck doing puttying work.

3rd Wednesday
Wireless news of Lloyd Georges appeal for further reinforcements from the Dominions for upkeep of their armies in the field. Things seem to be taking a serious turn at front. Lloyd George says 'war only just begun'. Strange that such startling news should come thro' as we pass the renowned Cocos Islands where German Cruiser 'EMDEN' sank by Australian cruiser 'SYDNEY', Australia's really 1st big stride into naval warfare, to be later on a great historical event. Memorial service to Ptve. Harris held in evening, very successful solo by Nank, choir assisted by orchestra. Col, chairman, references made by Ptve. Snow in his address very fitting and creditably to our late comrade. Last post sounded, but old ship thumps, forges ahead in quiet sea as if nothing happened.

4th Thursday
Passed Cocos at 11am, 25 miles distance, so could not see it. Would like to see old 'EMDEN'. Days pretty hot now under decks, but cool breeze blowing today. Progressive Euchre Tournament held tonight. Average: 142 knots, good travelling.

5th Friday
Rather warm. Working down decks.

6th Saturday
Debate on Prohibition held in E5 at 7.30pm. Affirmative, Leader – Roberts, Nankivell, Croft and Snow. Negative, Leader – Mc?, Donowa, Mc Queen, Cuthbertson. Adjudicator – Chas. Clark. Result in favour of negative 25 points – 14 affirmative. To most people's mind queer judgement. Lively interest by all taken in proceedings and much animated discussion time for leaders, 5 mins other 3, not nearly sufficient, responses 3.
Cricket match Corporals v Rest of staff played during afternoon

7th Sunday
Heavy showers last night, all sleeping on deck had to shift.
Services as usual. Cricket match on boat deck, same teams as yesterday, win for Corporals at 11.45am.

Sighted a large sailing ship on horizon going in diagonal direction to us, passed her bows at 12.45 at ¾ mile distance, full sail set, could read name painted on side distinctly as 'HIPPILOS-CHILE', a neutral vessel.

Service in evening by Chas. Clarke. Singing assisted by choir and orchestra.
Heavy tropical showers during day.

8th Monday
Water phosphorescent. See propeller very distinctly at night. Expect to get to Ceylon by daylight tomorrow.

9th Tuesday
Up at 5am. Saw 3 lights at Colombo, 2 beacons, light house flashes of 3 in groups every few seconds. A launch met us at 5.30am, and gave us instructions, proceeded on and passed 4 mine sweepers in pairs coming out, on our port side. Passed thro' breakwater (2 openings), supposed to be best in the world, wonderful construction. Capable of keeping water inside in spite of Monsoon and outside (see photo). Anchored mid-stream. Water boats and coal barges towed by launches to ships side. O.C. went ashore to see about leave, leave 11am – midnight. Launch to hold 40 came alongside, but most went off in skiffs. Native mixed breeds, but intelligent, and clean looking. Rather on the small build. As soon as we reached end of pier, were pestered by natives who were so insistent that to speak strongly, and sternly was only way to get them off.

Posted our letters at P.O. Led by unassuming guide in spectacles whose recommendations on paper by other Australian soldiers was good. This man is not a 'bummer' like so many of his breed. Went round to Y.M.C.A. and met a Mr. Soul, a thoroughly English gentleman, lately living in Australia. He arranged a 'Gharry' for us, for a trip to Mt. Leoinia (7 miles). Hire a vehicle 10/-. Mr. Soul arranged for a guide soldier in Barracks to come with us, found him very useful. Passed along beach to Galle Face Hotel, then turned over railway line, and thro' long straight street. House and gardens magnificent places. Thro' native shops, purchases King Cocoa nuts, Bananas. Beautiful to notice blue, surging sea, thro' lanes from the road, behind the palms. Saw native boys climbing cocoa nut trees en route. Went to hotel and beach. Saw Catamaran coming in with fish, and native market places where disposed of by auction.

Had a swim, look thro' Buddhist Temple, old compound of Boer prisoner camp. Well, wash-troughs etc., also saw native women making lace. Plenty of 'bummers' up that way. Hotel a magnificent place. Drove back through Cinnamon Gardens, Reservoir and Mosque.

Had supper at Y.M.C.A. At Y.M. had picture show on brought from Bombay.
In evening purchased walking stick and model of Catamaran originally wanted 4 rupees for same, but begged me to give him 1 rupee at finish, (this at Bristol Hotel). Went later and had a look thro' Army and Navy stores, and Croft bought a large model of Catamaran. Came back to ship by rowing boat. Ten large vessels in port.

10th Wednesday
Left at 7am. Hear that 'VENUS' and 'SUVA', two English gun boats recently operating in Red Sea in bombarding coastal towns, sent out here to search for reported submarine. Met some of their crew. A large interned Dutch steamer in port. A very large boat 'WILTSHIRE' arrived as we were leaving. Passed a vessel outward bound just before dark.

11th Thursday
Heading N.W. Plenty of long yellow streaks in water. A very large whale seen by Nank. Beautiful sunset. Later passed two vessels (out), one signalled to us by Morse. Passed another an hour later. Plenty of ships in these parts.
Passed Minikoi Island at about 10 miles. Noticed large light-house and palm trees, say natives a fine big race of men. Judge size of Island, about size of Rottnest Island.

12th Friday
Sgts. Cabin's papered and ready for fumigation. Passed two more large vessels.

13th Saturday
Paper scraped off cabins during morning.
Lime juice issue very nice and acceptable this weather.

14th Sunday
Church services. Passed Suqotra Island tonight at 11pm. Could not see it. Disappointed, as we had been looking out some time for it. During day can be seen for 5 or 6 hours. Cannibals supposed to exist on island.

15th Monday
Caught up and passed two large steamers, and met another going in opposite direction to us. Also passed 3 Dhows (large native rigged sailing vessels). Last flying French flag. Passed 4 miles from her and could plainly see all on board. Nineteen members of crew counted altogether.

16th Tuesday
Testing of Compasses by steering erratic courses for a few minutes. While watching these manoeuvres, a huge fish leaped high out of the water. It resembled an immense garfish. Presumed it to be a swordfish as they inhabit these waters. At 5.30 when signalling, I had to stop on a/c passing steamer. Five passed today. More Dhows seen.

At dusk noticed lighthouse ahead. At dark noticed a starboard light of a ship moving some distance away. Later noticed Morse signals being given out. 'Lowering a boat to you, stand by', and a few minutes afterwards the hull of an Auxiliary Cruiser loomed

COLOMBO

Colombo Wagon

A big load

Watering

Erecting new telegraph poles

A street corner

On the road to 'Kandy'

Coaling

Harbour

Bridge over canal

Car with three soldiers (Rex in front)

'Karoola', WWI. No.1 Australian Hospital Ship

up. A boat rowed by 6 men with an officer came alongside. Meantime the cruiser stood by and put up a white light. These watchdogs who protect British interests abroad. Something weird in the experience, and interesting to think of. After inspection we proceeded on our way and the other disappeared in the darkness. At midnight saw 2 lighthouses, supposed to be "Dirio Island'.

17th Wednesday

Passed 4 very large vessels again today at 10am. Came to the 'Brothers', a group of Islands in the Red Sea on our starboard. (omitted) at 5am on waking up early, saw a lighthouse flashing. This was an island not more than 200-300 yards from us. Keeper here has to be hauled up to base of lighthouse. Island rose sheer up out of water, on port side land also, with a big mountain from the sea-passage about ½ mile wide. Supposed to be 'Hells Gates'. More islands were passed at 12.30pm, and by aid of glasses, nothing absolutely growing on them, but seemed of rocky formation. All groups were fairly high and supplied with lighthouse to each group e.g. (small drawing of lighthouse). Not nearly so hot as two days sail before Colombo.

18th Thursday

Nice cool breeze blowing today. Mail for Egypt, England and Europe to be posted by 12 noon 19/4/18. Passed a hospital ship at 8am, some distance off. Dipped flag to us. Presumably a Castle Liner. Fine sight.

19th Friday

At 12.30pm. passed a large lighthouse built by the P. & O. Coy. At 5.30pm. passed islands on Port, known as 'The Brothers'. High, all to be seen. Very barren. A little later saw a big clear light flashing. Could see the lighthouse itself and rock on which built altho' dusk. Very cool in evening, and plenty of wind on deck.

20th Saturday

Mitch on night duty, says we passed thro' straights of Gabel at 1am. On waking up found ourselves well in Gulf of Sinai. Passage gradually narrowing. A large shark seen very close to ship. Shore rugged, barren and hilly, lighthouses at various places along both sides. Arrived off Suez and Pt. Tewfik and dropped anchor at 1.30pm. Noticed twenty steamers in port, mostly British, the 'LOYALTY' here. An Indian Hospital Ship presented by a Prince in India. By glasses see on opposite shore the old Light-horse Camp with trees behind, and buildings of matting in front. Large and steep mountain chain on left side going south from Suez. All desiring to go to Cairo handed in names and day. Parade at night, hear that those can go on leave till Wednesday next at midnight, others local leave only till 9.30pm. daily. By order all lights out on ship.

21st Sunday

Leave granted 8.30am. After a short look about Pt. Tewfik and canal, caught 11am. train for Cairo, other lads, sisters and officers on board. Had to travel 3rd class, carriage not decorative or seats (to hold 2) of plush, but nevertheless fairly comfortable.

Passed thro' Suez. (a small scale to what we R to C). Railway line all way to Ismalia follow closely to canal. Train average speed 10-15 miles per hour. After passing thro' long stretches of absolute desert, we see the wonderful transformation of the Nile irrigation scheme. This by the fresh water canal which also runs about parallel with ships canal. Noticed the large vessels passing up and down. Most irrigation here done by water-wheel, drawn by native cow or donkey, other places watered by opening sluice gate.

Several camps passed, Indian, Aust, English, Camel Corps., Donkey Corps., etc. At one of small stations, party of Austs., get on board. Happy, rowdy, knowing lot, plenty of argument with collectors re fare etc. They at fishing camp near Ismalia, 2/3 fish for hospital and other camps, 1/3 for themselves. Natives wash clothes, bathe, drink from creek, also swim and wash their animals in it.

Met Capt. Benson at Ismalia and heard news of his staff whom we knew at Keswick very well. Had a snack at Y.M.C.A. here. Rest of journey thro' good, well watered and cultivated country. Many labourers in fields with donkeys, camels, oxen. Country very flat, many canals. Barley, potatoes, lucerne or clover grown on a very large scale. Irrigation extensive, for we could not see the edge of this country like that prior to Ismailia. Broad gage line. Several very large towns en-route ie., Tel-el-Kabir and Zagasia. Noticed old Cairo in distance on our left, the place we hear so much of.

Noticed large spires in many places showing Citadel and Mosque. Cairo fairly large station, apparently much traffic judging by rolling stock and vehicles. On alighting, pestered by dozens of dragomen, but followed two English Tommies to Anzac Hostel. Had tea, brushed up etc., and had a look round the city till 11.30pm. My impressions were many as I watched and noticed native ways and customs in this place. Turned in at Marquee and slept well.

Omitted:- Caught tram earlier in evening for Luner Park at Heliopolis 1/2 hour ride for 1/2 piastre. Good many soldiers there, many from the old Heliop Hospital now Aerial School for Tommies. No. 4 A.G.H. moved to Pt. Said. Shops close fairly early, so not very much light. Cool however.

22nd Monday

Started the day off early. Had breakfast 5 piastres. Strolled about till 9am, and arranged to go on a trip with guide arranged by Y.M.C.A.

Boarded a tram and travelled thro' native quarters, which were closely confined, dingy, smelly and dirty. Got out before Sultan Hassan's Mosque. Climbed steps and proceeded under the archway passage to body of Mosque, in centre of place stands a holy fountain, where worshippers wash their face, hands and feet 7 times. Floor in place where worship is carried out, this which resembles a courtyard, is paved with large marble tiles. Here, Mohammedans squat down, rich in front, poor behind.

Ascended the stairway of stone leading to pulpit, on right of this is a large heavy door made entirely of gold and silver, with beautiful inlay of patterns worked upon it. This door has bars before it for protection. Noted niche for visitors facing Mecca, led thro' door on left of pulpit, here found a very large room, with a large dome overhead, beautifully gilded and patterns like wonder? worked upon it. Hassan's tomb in centre of floor, various large windows on each side of walls enabling Hassan to see at a glance any and every part of Cairo. Noted large stand like so (small drawing) for holding the Koran. Noted also the holes in wall outside made by cannon balls from Napoleons' cannon, and a ball still remaining in one (1788).

Came out and just had an outside glance of the new Mosque right opposite both Mosques, built of the polished outside casing of the Giza Pyramids, Cheops and Chefren. Proceeded to Citadel. Noted garrison of British troops beneath. This place has a wonderful courtyard affair, holy fountain in centre with numerous pillars and niche like domes all the way round. Here we had to don canvas slippers over our boots. Went inside Citadel proper and what a sight to behold. In centre and above a huge dome not unlike St. Pauls, entirely supported by four pillars of beautiful Alabaster. Smaller columns were also fixed in the walls, the floor is beautifully carpeted with Turkish carpet, hanging above was four or five enormous chandeliers with brilliant hangings. On one side a niche facing Mecca for visitors and pulpit. Above and around is a gallery used by the

Harem at worship. Above again, another used for lights, numbering in all over 2,000. These light especially in month of July, and those in domes could be seen for many miles, and all Mohammedans supposed to turn to Mecca and pray at that time. Citadel built by son of Sultan Hassan, and copied from one in Constantinople. The Mamelanks, then a governing body in Egypt at a banquet given at completion of same, the Mamelanks, being intoxicated were asked to proceed thro' a door leading to a yard outside. As each stepped over the threshold, his throat was cut by Hassan's son. Thus the power passed over to him. His tomb is in a transept in the Citadel. We were led outside and shown their burial places. When the foul deed was done, the leader of the Mamelanks came up to the Citadel. He was immediately tried to be captured, but being on horseback and having no other means of escape, leaped his horse over the wall with iron railing on top. Horse hoof mark there, now supposed to be in evidence of same. Horse was killed, but he ran away unhurt until shot down at a distance. Large columns of Alabaster outside building also, but damaged by weather and Aust. soldiers, I obtained a sample.

Came back to tram and visited the spot (tombs) of Royalty, and under same roof the tombs of Mamelanks mentioned. What treasure here buried with Kings and Queens. What about that also is Caliphs tombs and pyramids, some since ransacked by Arabs. Very poor quarters, here many requests for 'Buckshee', a word taught apparently to kids when first born. Spent remainder of evening in the worst part of Cairo with other S.A.'s. A very deep well nearby.

P.S. Noted the very large bronze clock in the Sultan Hassan's Mosque presented to him by a French Royalty after his visit to Egypt.

23rd Tuesday

Having made arrangements previous evening with guide for a trip this day with his brother, bathed, breakfast, and ready to start at 8am. First visited old Cairo. Went to old Coptic Church enclosed by a high, solid wall. All around the church and inside the wall were the rottenest holes of houses imaginable. Plenty of 'Backsheesites' too. Noted the great massive Sycamore door thro' the wall with the old key of wood.

Passing to the church, we found inside a priest reading from the Bible to a listener, who was nodding his head as if greatly interested. About 2/3rds distance down hall is a partition, and in enclosure at back is where the women worship. 'Backshees' had to be given to woman and child squatting on floor. This church built over the Crypt of Jesus where he lay hidden. We saw this on descending steps, also Josephs' well. Passing out we noticed the new Coptic Church, a very large and much cleaner looking building. One can scarcely realize that this is the Holy ground we read of, in ancient times.

We crossed over the road by which we had come and again came amongst dirty hovels of all descriptions. Came to the bank of the Nile and crossed in punt to Rhoda Island. Here we were taken thro' a very nice garden and shown the old water gauge of the Nile down a well. Noticed the old house, belonging to one of the Royalty now left neglected. At the back of this place we saw what is supposed to be the place where Moses was found amongst the bulrushes. No bulrushes however, now mark the spot, but a wall with an old wheel used as a device for drawing water for the garden can be seen.

I should have mentioned the fact that before going to Coptic Church our guide took us to the old Omar Mosque, built by Omar 1,200 years ago. The old courtyard arrangement is evidence also, there are 365 pillars of marble right round representing the days of the year. In the yard is the holy font and near it a large sycamore tree is growing. We were shown the good and the bad, man (2 pillars) one straight and the other crooked. Many of the pillars showed signs of decay and were much knocked about. Others were lying on the ground.

We crossed over the Nile, over a very fine bridge, and caught a tram for the Pyramids. Noticed the very fine trees (Austr. gums) en-route, also the beautiful road which runs alongside. We were met by camel owners and donkey boys for mounts to the Pyramids. Saw the very fine hotel the Mena Hotel, also the old Mena Camp where 30,000 men were encamped. Lord Kitcheners name much revered in these parts, saw result of his industry in the beautiful fertile irrigation country, from the bridge onwards. Had a good look at the Sphinx, temple where we bought old Roman money. An old Roman wall nearby surrounds the Sphinx. Noticed the tombs of priests, also well where mummies were found. This all granite, some pieces 19x5x55=19 1/2 tons.

Went back to Cheops and entered the passage and shown round by guide. Had to climb lst of all to reach entrance, lst of all descends, then ascends, the passage 95 ft high. Noted – the idea of building the passage so that vaults could be moved, for foothold shallow holes dug in rock. After much slipping and sliding reached the Queens Chamber then the Kings. Large room, with vault still there, and nearby the place where all jewellery was hidden. Were not permitted to go higher to the 5 chambers where Sons are buried. Exploration and excavation work was carried out on the pyramid by an American engineer whose name is hewn in one of the passages, in some places this passage is only 45 ft high. Very dark and we were obliged to the guide for light of candle. On the ? part of casing still remains. Noted the air vents of pyramid, one cleared by this engineer, but blocked up by sand again now. Noted also the stone quarries some distance away where stone was obtained to build one of them. Met Colonel out there astride a camel, seemed to be enjoying himself. (Sphinx 3733BC).

Came back again and visited the Giza Zoological gardens, very nice and covering 10 acres or so, well laid out and rare animals to be seen. Met Crofty, he went to Pyramids, but we went to Cairo to have a look at the native Bazaar. Starting off from Grand Continental Hotel, Bazaar intensely interesting. Saw silk weavers, brass workers etc. Everything from a needle to an anchor sold in the streets and in the shops, very crowded. Sampled Solomon and Sons shop, prices pretty high, could have spent 3 days with profit here.

Went back to Anzac, had tea and made off to Pyramids again with S.A.'s. Saw Sphinx by moonlight. Went further and shown old wells very deep, tombs of Pharaohs and daughters of Cheops, infested with bats, very interesting tho'. Two excavators at work in vicinity of pyramids before war. American and German. Saw their houses, and heard a little of their doings, private and otherwise, found nice specimens of Alabaster on German work, brought away samples. Climbed Cheops 4612 ft, beautiful by moonlight, and to top of flagstaff (Jim Smith and I) connected with wireless.

Went to house near road below. Saw burial grounds of 300,000 slaves who hewed and placed the limestone for this pyramid, unearthed by American. Carved initials on top of Cheops and found descending much easier. Cheops covers 13 acres of ground. Enjoyed ourselves very much, and experiences long to be remembered. Beautiful houses on road to them of well to-do Egyptians. Going out I saw the fastest pony I have ever seen, left our tram well behind despite our good speed and driven by a wealthy merchant. Turned in pretty tired, and slept well after a good bath.

24th Wednesday

Up early and had a stroll round on my own. Met Jimmie Smith and Crofty, got in a car and alighted at Nile Bridge, walked along a little way and boarded another for RD.EL. PARAG where we caught a steam boat for Barrage, started at 10am – arrived there 11.30. A few well to-do Egyptians on board, and many poorer aft. Barrage very beautiful and consists of 5 locks and part of Irrigation scheme, wonderful bridge, climbed up tower, went thro' gardens and saw two chaps facing Mecca and saying prayers. Several Deltas in the river here. Beautiful gardens, several steam pumps on irrigation area, only

MEMPHIS

Ramises II

Sakhara Abushar pyramid in distance

Canon holes - Mohomet Ali Pasha mosque

Hay transport

Road to sphynx and temples

River Nile

Cheops and the Sphynx

Camel team for racing

Irrigation water wheel Suez

Sphynx and Cheops

'Lily Pond' Nouzha botanical gardens

Cheops pyramid

Suez Aerodrome

'Loyalty' Indian hospital ship

'Wandilla' arriving Beirut at Alexandria as Karoola leaving

'The Steps' pyramid

Parade Suez

ones seen used on all our trips. Hired donkeys and went for a tour round. Tried to enter Arabian village on the donkeys, but donks would not go without boys pushing, who refused to do so. Inhabitants kicked up a great fuss when they noticed us trying to go in. Believe the place out of bounds. Two of our donkey boys suffering from venereal disease, so had to be careful. We learn that often donkeys and also camels carry the germ, so were careful to scrub up well.

Caught 2.15 train from Barrage Village after having one of those sundry arguments with the donkey owner (a usual occurrence), arrived in Cairo after coming on line from Ismailia at Junction Station at 3pm. Jim and Crofty went to hostel by gharry. I walked about and casually strolled to cigarette factory, the scene of a strike for more wages the same morning. A good bit of damage done, all windows were broken, furniture and fittings thrown about. The firm an Armenian and by all accounts a tyrant, paying his men only 9 1/2pts per day, contrary to all other manufacturers. Met Jack McElone and Mullinger watching proceedings. Were eventually invited by the detective of police to inspect the place. Cigarettes, wrappings, tobacco cases and everything strewn about, but repairs already in execution. Most windows replaced. Little sympathy shown to proprietor by police, who were guarding the place. The detective a young fellow speaks English fluently and seems to be an intellectual fellow. Afterwards met a young Egyptian attending the Technical School, and Commerce College in Cairo and conducted by him thro' the bazaar again. There bought a stick for father and had it mounted at brass workers. Very interesting. Afterwards saw an Italian funeral and watched the service at the Cathedral, a funny little incident befell me here, not likely to be forgotten, altho' very harmless quite in itself.

Met the boys at the hostel, and caught the 6.15pm. train. Met at the station by the young Egyptian who gave me his address should I require anything to be sent on from Cairo, in way of purchases etc. He brought my stick, having had it mounted, myself not being able to wait for it. Darkness soon set in. The train full of Tommy, and Austr. soldiers bound for their various camps. Arrived back Pt. Tewfik 12.15am. and found the ship berthed inside the harbour, behind the breakwater.

25th Thursday

A rub up given to wards in the morning, and leave granted till 9pm. Went to Suez, being invited by the Sports Committee of Suez Camp to attend their sports in the afternoon. Went there and much enjoyed the Camel races, packing, unpacking, mounting etc., tug of war, foot races, hurdle races etc. An Austr. and New Zealand Camp. Over the way is the British Aerodrome. Watched the machines flying and saw some wonderful exhibitions by the 'Mad' Major in charge of the Station. Truly wonderful. Got right up to sheds and saw him start off before being asked to leave by the M.P. The flyer just as cool as if having his breakfast, 5 in all went up, but the most wonderful, the scouting plane, 8 cylinders. Mitch went shell hunting along the beach. He found many good specimens, uncommon. Met Sgt. Donohue late of Mt. Barker, and arranged with him to take Simpsons' parcel to England. Sent him tea and sugar as they were short. Walked back to Suez and had a good look round the town, bought cucumbers and a small picture book.

26th Friday

Waiting for 2 trains to arrive from Alexandria ex 'DUNLUCE CASTLE'. First arrived at 4.30 and started embarking. Second 6.30pm. Carriages of train white with crescent sign. All knocked off, and finished by 9.30pm. 733 came in 'DUNLUCE', we took 400 odd, remainder stayed in Alexandria to be sent on later by transport, not many very serious cases.

Shall never forget that beautiful greenie blue water of the anchorage, white beach. Suez with its square buildings behind, oil tanks further and mountains, treeless, rugged and bold, what a picture.

27th Saturday
Very cold early this morning. Put out from Pt. Tewfik at 7am, and anchored in Roadway Sea. Smooth and blue. Makes lovely picture before Pt. Suez. Left after breakfast. We hear patients received good treatment on board 'DUNLUCE CASTLE' this trip, learn that she stayed at Gibraltar 6 days.
Perfect moonlight night and we following up line of light. Detailed to E6 ward.

28th Sunday
Passing a good number of ships. Patients satisfied with food etc. 'DUNLUCE CASTLE' left Avonmouth, conditions much better on board than previous trip. In D1 temporarily.

29th Monday
Red Sea warmer than when we came through first.

30th Tuesday
At about 6.30pm came up to the 1st of the Apostles, and on retiring to bed passed the last of them. Very warm down below. Some of poor mental cases rather troublesome.

MAY, 1918

1st Wednesday
In E5 ward temporarily. Passed thro' Hells' Gates very early this morning. Happened to wake and noticed the old light, at 11.30 passed Perim Island. Three steamers in harbour, a few houses, signal station and lighthouse denote the Naval Station. Just after noticed a large 3 funnelled cruiser some little distance off. A good many vessels passed today. Saw land near Aden later. Noted the high rugged mainland for a good distance after Perim. Warmish.

2nd Thursday
Day very warm. Water smooth as a mill pond. Issue of apples appreciated.
Speed 13.2 knots. Very good for this weather, must be hot for stokers. Usually slow down a bit weather like this.

3rd Friday
Nothing much doing.

4th Saturday
Patients all looking forward to seeing Colombo, for some the second time. Am satisfied that these are really a truly speaking a troopship lot. Very few cot cases, and others are fairly well, comparatively speaking.

5th Sunday

Ptve. Ryan a mental patient since joining the ship expired at 4.30am. Returned originally with gastric ulcers. P.M. held at which Mitch attended (by Capt. Southwood). Patient struggled very violently with staff on night duty just previously. Same thing night before. Buried at sea in afternoon.

6th Monday

The deceased patient suffered awful mental agony in that he suffered excruciating pain in hell for 'millions and millions of years' as he himself said. Burning all over, and prayed for water, fearful to hear his wanderings and imaginations all of which I believe he actually mentally suffered.

Note from Diary Cpl C.R. Mortimer AWM

There were so many mental patients on one voyage that only a certain number were allowed up at one time. One patient with others was due to go downstairs at the time several orderlies were off duty until 4pm. One fine stamp of a man came walking along very erect with real military stride, never varied his stride but like a flash dived between 2 orderlies and over the side. On his way down his body just caught the railing on the gangplank which had not been pulled right up, flicking him onto it. All 2 orderlies had to do was reach over and pluck him back on deck. After that it was one on one when exercising and returning them back to the ward.

Note from Diary L. Schaeffer AWM

A sensation was caused in E5 when a mental case attempted suicide with his pyjama string. Fortunately, Robertson and Johns were to hand, and prevented the tragedy. His struggles were terrific, and there was much confusion amongst the others likewise affected. The poor unfortunate was removed to a padded cell. I hate to write of these men so utterly destroyed.

7th Tuesday

Unexciting.

8th Wednesday

Arrived Colombo 5am, and anchored at berth nearest the pier, about 10-12 ships in port, mostly very large. Beautiful sunrise on the domes of temples on our left, showed up also the palm trees along the beach. Leave – to patients 10am-6pm, – staff divided 10-2pm, and 2-6pm. Infections, disease raging in native quarters, so a piquet party from staff posted in various quarters of town. Mitch and I relieved at bridge leading to road to native Bazaar, taken there in motor car from pier. Whilst there bought 2 ? from chap at army and navy stores. Relieved at 4pm, and leave till 5pm, reported again at Bristol Hotel. Detailed to parade the streets and inform all patients met time of departure of punt for ship. Reported at 6pm, and for remainder of evening visited various places like Grand Oriental Hotel, White Hove, Y.M.C.A. Had to use a little coercion at times to persuade the strays. Other parties had more trouble, some forcibly taken back and owing to giving trouble on ship, were put in the cells. One S.A., Ryan of Artillery fame in Mitcham Camp threatened S.Sgt. Grey of our party. During these rambles bought articles in silk, lace, coconut, pineapples, cigars, and work basket and moonstone brooch. Took note of beautiful building of Nat. Mutual Life Assurance Co. Slight shower in afternoon making atmosphere very muggy.

9th Thursday
Left at 10am. Passed the old 'SUVA' and 'VENUS' still lying in port, and as soon as we reached the breakwater started to rise and fall with the ocean swell. Noticed a few catamarans swamped, also the large waves as they smashed up against the solid great breakwater. Men put into clink last night, tried before the O.C. and mostly admonished. Two more of staff sick, Nank in hospital and Mitchell in bed.

10th Friday
Fresher today, a nice breeze blowing. Heavy downpour this morning. Sea choppy.
Just before leaving yesterday, a barge loaded with pineapples, oranges (green), and paw-paw came alongside. After being put on board, the troops asked to help themselves, as storage room in ship limited. Everybody absolutely full of bananas. Never more sick of them in my life. Only wish I could get several large bunches home, but would ripen too quickly. A green bunch given me as a trialer. At every meal bananas, and at all spots of ceiling are hanging large bunch for anybody who cares to take them. Mr. V. Soul visited the ship just before leaving, and we hear that the fruit from Y.M.C.A., and Red Cross combined.

11th Saturday
Muggy day. Never perspired more. Wringing wet all day.
Capt. Kneebone (RAMC) of Woodville taken on board at Colombo with baggage.
On one month's furlough dating from arrival in Austr. Stayed at the Galle Facie Hotel. Previously reported killed at Rehif? of Townsend in Mesopotamia.

12th Sunday
This Major Chaplain on board the laziest man I have known for some time. Refused to take the service this morning 'too hot boys' is his excuse. At other times also he refuses Sunday evening services after our requests, so good old Dad Snow after working all day cheerfully comes forward. The former almost too tired to issue Red Cross comforts his ? duty.

13th Monday
Water absolutely unbroken, but a big swell on, which is scarcely noticeable to the eye from the ship, but we rising and falling and dipping very considerably.

14th Tuesday
Passed Cocos Island 15 miles off at 4pm. Could see palm trees quite plainly, long, flat, low lying island.

15th Wednesday
Hear that a good number of staff applying for transfer this voyage.

16th Thursday
Waiting patiently for home letters at Freemantle.

17th Friday
Cool enough today, enjoyable weather 290 miles. Inspection by ship's Captain, R.A.M.C. Capt. of Day.

18th Saturday
A perfect day. Days very short now. Dark at 6.30am, and dark at 6pm.

19th Sunday
Services. Sighted Rottnest 8.30pm. Good Old Austr., once again. Anticipate a treat in receiving my letters.

20th Monday
Arrived 1am, and steamed right into moorings. Disembarked at 9am, and took on water only. No leave granted to any rank during the day. Band on wharf rendered good music. Left again at 4pm, and judging by the wind, a good blow outside. Received 8 beautiful letters from home.

21st Tuesday
A nice, fresh stiff breeze blowing, sea crowded with white horses and we steering anything but a straight level course. Informed on parade that all intended applications for transfer must be in by 6pm today. Already 19 or 20 sent in. This invited so that they may have time to deal with each one before reaching Melbourne.

22nd Wednesday
Mother states in letters that Adelaide has been experiencing really warm weather right up to middle of May. Received 4 snaps from home, one of little Colin. Mother writing letters in diary form which is a grand and appreciable idea for me.

23rd Thursday
Bight the roughest we have seen it.

24th Friday
Finished our last practice on instrument with Crofty tonight. Find ourselves just passable, so trouble not in vain.

25th Saturday
Passed Cape Nelson at 10am. Steering gear broken down from Bridge, but worked from helm on docking bridge aft. Big swell on.

26th Sunday
Arrived early and anchored off pier at 8am, proceeded in and berthed in old spot. No other ships in. Disembarking at 9am, and patients met by Automobile Assoc., and Military Band. 11.45 ship left towed by 'FALCON'.
Went to Melbourne by cab, and went to Victoria Coffee Palace, where Mitch had previously booked a room. Had dinner at Y.M.C.A. Smithy and I had a thorough look thro' Zoo Gardens at Royal Park. Y.M.C.A. for tea and strolled around, looked thro' Wirths Hospital where S.A. patients put up for night. Heard Israelites preaching their doctrine. Turned into bed, three slept in 2 beds (pulled them close up together).

27th Monday

Dinner at Y.M.C.A., and a most delightful afternoon, long to be remembered, spent at the Melbourne Botanical Gardens. The best I have seen, absolutely a fresh, dull, livening up day. Caught Hospital train with carriages attached for Ballarat at 5-6pm. Sisters wasted all day at H.Q., trying to get on. We had no trouble, and anticipate little as our passes made out "on leave and on duty". Some of the patients had drink, and one or two were inclined to be quarrelsome.

28th Tuesday

Having slept on floor of Ambulance van, felt fairly refreshed. A lovely day.
Poor little Jacky Rundle burnt eyes, lashes and brows pretty badly, when manipulating the gas jet. Very miserable and eyes puffed and sore.

Arrived Adelaide 10.45pm. Capt. Kneebone's people met him at station. Rundle reported for all of us at Keswick. Caught 11.35 train home, and found Mother knew I was somewhere near home. Aunt Eliza and Lily here. Surprised father at 5.15pm, when he came home.

29th Wednesday

Went out to Aunties in afternoon and found them all well, but Aunt Laura in Sydney. Caught 4pm motor to Kangarilla. Arrived at Edgars just before 6pm, had tea and yarned all night. Nice and fresh up there. Plant progressing and things looking well. Edgar clearing a tidy little profit from his 200-300—fowls, laying steadily and well. Has been extending since my last visit out there.

30th Thursday

Caught 4pm coach to Blackwood. A nice ride and very fresh. Went to Jack Treloar's to tea. He came home a few minutes afterwards. His wife well. Met staying there the young lady who went to America with Frank and Mrs. Cocks. Jack and wife living with her people, in fine big house. Had tea and stayed the night on shake down on floor, (my preference) and slept well, nice spot Blackwood.

31st Friday

Came as far as Mitcham with Jack, and saw some of the old friends. Charley Black going away today as Sgt. in charge of A.M.C. reinforcements and Tenny as Cpl. Hear that Cliff Hawke returning gassed. All future men from Camps going as general reinforcements. Had a good yarn to all. Could not see George Hanks as he at Medical Board at Keswick. Met young Edward from the bank, a Cpl. in Light-horse. He soon going away, also young Goldsmith. A draft of infantry going today also. Dr. Morris in Camp, had a talk with him. A decent old fellow. Mr. Mc Honey, and Sgt. Grear O.K. Later met Mrs. Beasley and her sister. Had forgotten about Jack, so went over with them and met him. Quarter master Sgt. 2nd General Reinforcements U.K., and Jack leaving with them today. He apparently very busy issuing and getting troops ready.

JUNE, 1918

1st Saturday

Stayed home during morning. Took girls up town for the afternoon, and went for a row on the lake from Ern Jolleys to Hackney Bridge. We enjoyed ourselves immensely for the 2 hours. Girls had their try at rowing.

2nd Sunday
Went for stroll thro' paddocks with father and later called on Mrs. Butler whom we found quite well. A glorious day, and are similar to those described by Mother in her letter to me when abroad. She often describes herself as sitting out in back veranda sewing or mending, on days like these.

3rd Monday
Helped father put together his ' Eddie' free wheel and rim tyre, and tube on bike. A perfect day, as later went for a ride he on his, and myself on Mr. Pearson's machine. Went down Junction Road to Pt. Adelaide, Docks, and as far as Freezers on Ocean Steamers wharf. Came back after having a look at all shipping then in Port via wood block - Port Road which is now completed up to Overway Bridge before reaching New Market Hotel.

4th Tuesday
Spent the afternoon at Aunt sons, and did several small jobs for her. Had a good time as usual and well cared for. Rode father's machine, left Aunts at 5.30 and went to Black Forest Station. Caught train there, went to Glenelg and spent evening with Reeves. Miss Maxwell there. Nellie Reeves now Mrs Phillips, son of Mr. Herbert Ph. Had a most pleasant evening, music and chats of old times and faces. Caught 11pm train, alighted at Black Forest and rode home, and turned in by midnight.

5th Wednesday
With Mother who was feeling very fit, walked to Harris's place at Ovingham. Saw old Uncle George, who is as hale and hearty as ever. Had a splendid chat re his old pioneer days. Very interesting and makes one admire and respect our old pioneer forefathers. Later Mother with Aunt Liza went to see old lady Harris and I rode having taken pushbike with me, out to Hams. A pleasant afternoon there, intended paying a visit to Mrs. Goldsmith, but darkness set in and had to get home having no light.

6th Thursday
Called on Mrs. Bradshaw, James and Densley. Found them all well, and good news re Alf Densley so far. He is now in Intelligence Corp, a reasonable risky job. Good luck to good old Alf. Had dinner, and left home midday, proceeded to Keswick for warrant on railway. Met Crofty at H.Q. Having time to spare went to Keswick Hospital. Saw some of old staff, but no patients I knew. Caught Melbourne Express 4.30pm where Cath and Mr. Ham, Vere, Nellie, and Mrs. Reeves, and Miss Maxwell saw me off. Had various nice parcels etc. handed me.

7th Friday
Met old Ptve. Healey at Murray Bridge. He left train at Tailem Bend. He made enough fuss of me goodness knows, a hard living man, and an Irish rouse-about. Been working at Pompoota. At Keswick as a patient, a great worry to poor old Nank. Healey's jaw fixed up eventually by Dean Dawson at Pirie. Arrived Melbourne at 10am after a sleepless night, and reported at ship at 11am, granted further leave till 9am next day. During afternoon had a thorough look over Melbourne Gas Coy. works with Smithy and Mitch. The Supt. a very fine chap who previously asked young Giles and I to come over and have a look round at a previous date. Readily gave his consent again, and we were shown over by a young chemist.

A nice lad and explained everything, spent a most instructional and beneficial afternoon. Had tea at the Y.M., and spent evening at the 'Masquerades' with the other boys.

'SUEVIC' came in with 1,100 troops, and Cliff Hawke amongst them. Saw him on a motor car about starting for procession. Landed biggest cargo in Austr. since the war, 10,000 tons. She has a great engineering history.

8th Saturday

Japanese Cruiser lying berth ahead of us, went out at 8am, and Crofty and I walked along wharf to have a look at her. We have seen her previously in Freemantle, but had just come from Sydney. On guard at 9am for 48 hours, but in afternoon obtained leave from Sgt. Biggs, and Crofty and I had a look in at the Ice Skating Rink, also the Roller. Went to the pictures in Collins Street, a rotten show, came out 9.30, finished up the evening by having a look at this 'famous' Russian, late soldier of Eastern front and in Secret Service of Russian War Office. Good shot and juggles with weapons of all kinds.

9th Sunday

Lt. Luton in charge of guard, so no leave till evening when Smith, Crofty and myself went to Melbourne to hear the Rev. Ruth of Collins Street Baptist Church preach in the auditorium on Catholicism with a small 'C'. We enjoyed the subject immensely. A very able and fluent speaker. The hall simply packed. The evening a series of Sunday night services on subjects of this kind.

10th Monday

Off guard at 9am. Smithy, Crofty, Mitch and self went for a long walk, starting from Houses of Parliament. Went thro' Richmond over the Yarra, north of Sth. Yarra along bank of the river and proceeded to rear of Botanical Gardens. Walked up to near Prahan and down to Albert Park and lake, back to St. Kilda Road, and to Y.M. for dinner. In afternoon went to matinee at Hoyt's Pictures. Met the others afterwards at Y.M. for tea, after making enquiries at various places re Uncle Josiah's ?. Spent evening at 'General Post', a military comedy and much enjoyed the same.

11th Tuesday

All leave expires at 3pm today. Crofty and myself went for the round ride by tramcar, 16 miles for 9d. Starting at Princes Bridge Station in Cable Car, alighted at St. Kilda and had a look over Y.M.C.A. beach hut. Were welcomed by a nice young lady who gave us soup (celery), sandwiches and coffee. Amused ourselves on pianola for ½ hour. A meeting of the Executives that day to consider closing of hut as not used by soldiers sufficiently now to warrant its upkeep.

Boarded the electric tram, thro' Balaklava, Malvern where we changed cars, alighted at Re? to see the famous edifice to the memory of Dr. Springthorpe's wife. The Doctor now at Herefields Hospital. A magnificent construction and well worth the visit. Beats any Egyptian patterns of all I saw. Board the tram again, and at Abbotsford changed cable tram again, came back north of Richmond at rear of Houses of Parliament and near the Treasury Buildings which is near Treasury Gardens. We saw these and walked thro' them when on our walking tour on 10th. We then went to see Sntr. Storey re Crofty's transfer, but he not being in I went to Melbourne to catch the train 2.10pm, where I knew the others were. After a few minutes Crofty came along, having seen Storey who arrived just after I departed. The matter had been fixed up, and a letter was given Croft from Sntr. Pearce, Minister of Defence to Storey, showing plainly that Crofty was at last fixed up. He was highly delighted, and spirits knew no bounds. Myself sorry, for I know I shall miss him.

Reported at 3pm, and found all old hands back with the reinforcements to take the place of those getting transfers. Leave given for evening again at 4.30pm. N.S.W. men doing guard. Crofty and I went to Williamstown by ferry to fulfil our many times broken engagement with Miss Carson, cousin to Sir Edward Carson. We met her on train going to Ballarat, where going home on leave. Crofty had forgotten exact address, but after fishing about, and finally ringing up from a shop, we were guided to the house 'Warreen', not far from the esplanade. Three ladies at the house, a Miss Johnstone, Messes Swan and Carson. The two latter teachers at Williamstown High School. Miss Carson teacher of languages. She is a most interesting and charming personality. Highly educated and extremely witty. Much travelled and knew of many of the places of our visits. Had studies in Germany and France, and many tales re experiences in these countries were interesting. Miss Johnstone has a beautiful Grand piano, and is a very advanced pianist indeed. Play anything at all. Crofty in good form in spite of cold and sang his old pieces of choir boy days altho' not touched since then. This combined with his jubilant spirits over transfer business marked him a hero from the onset.

Came home by the train and caught midnight (drunks' express) for Pt. Melbourne. At gangway Croft told by man on guard a message from the Colonel to pack things and stand by to go off ship by morning. Col. received these instructions from H.Q. where as a true sport he had gone to fix matters for poor old Dad Snow, whose little girl had died whilst he was home. Duty off the ship for one trip was granted the poor old chap. All hearts in sympathy with him. This man admired and respected by all for his moral code and living, preaching, and example to everybody.

12th Wednesday
Left wharf at 11.15am just after the 'MARATHON', (with dummy funnel), arrived from England by way of New York and the Panama. A good many troops on board her. We came away without a few firemen, so stood out in the offing till 2.30pm. They came on board in a motor boat. We also have on board 3 Officers, 1 Sgt., 2 Privates and 1 mental patient from 'SUEVIC' and 'MARATHON' to disembark at W.A. Ordered to close all port holes as we are warned of bad weather outside. As soon as reaching the 'Heads' we began to rise and fall to it as we did last trip.

13th Thursday
Coming up pretty windy and looking squally. Much speculation as to whether we call at Albany or Fremantle. By evening nearly all S.A. laid up with sea-sickness and many of new hands, even some of stewards a bit groggy on it. Detailed to night duty and Tug Wilson to take charge of mental patients.

14th Friday
Wind boisterous and waves very high. Seas dashing themselves against the ship causing us to pitch and toss very considerably. Had views from all parts of the ship as she dashed into the seas. Spray simply blinding. Nank secured some good snaps of high waves. Decks fore and aft continually wet, myself wet through as a huge wave came over stern where I was standing. Even monkey deck splashed. Three of the new lads sick, transferred to Doctor and one in particular looks fearfully ill and wretched.

15th Saturday
Sea somewhat abated this morning. Find we are to call at Fremantle, but will not reach there till about Wednesday morning. Have only been doing 8-9 knots to date. Wind coming up again towards evening. Heavy rain fell at 4.30pm. Harry and Charlie, night steward and baker looked after us particularly well.

16th Sunday
Names of subscribers to Dad Snows Relief Fund taken today. Should raise a good deal according to subscriptions so far. She is a good old ship and looks a magnificent sight as she rises and falls, sometimes gracefully and sometime in a hurry, according to the size and power of the seas. A good old sea boat. Heard an interesting explanation of way things are done regarding passing ships through at Panama by one of the patients.

17th Monday
A bit rough again this morning at about 7.45, saw a huge waterspout at some distance on the W.A. side. Noticed by staff Gray and myself simultaneously. After a while it broke in the centre, and the top part connecting the clouds like a hose, swing about like the bottom tail end of a balloon. Eventually this split in two lengthways. This was quite black, the half above the sea being quite white, and as the upper part shifted along with the clouds so the bottom half altho' parted and disconnected, followed suit by keeping exactly underneath in alignment. Ever since hearing of them from fellows on 'DUNLUCE CASTLE' at Cape town I have been very anxious to witness one and have my wish gratified at last. Sea moderate at evening.

18th Tuesday
Sea calm, lovely fresh breeze at 10.30pm. Sighted Rottnest and passed a ship on our starboard. Arrived Fremantle early morning.

19th Wednesday
Leave at 10.30am. Posted letters and went around to Uncle Charlies. Saw Uncle Alf and on his advice went to Aunt Grace. Altho' curtly received by her, and only admitted after an 'account of myself'. Shown the direction of her house by Aunt Emily. Came back to Aunt Emily, Uncle Dave came home and we had tea. Later went to Palmyra to see Winnie and Bill Toms. They have a nice little home. Had a very pleasant evening. Walked back thro' East Fremantle, and had a look at Uncles new house. Beautiful position and lovely healthy locality not far from Swan and within easy access of sea breeze. Lovely gum trees and quite countrified. Elite locality. Went home with them and came straight back to the ship, and caught ferry at wharf. On duty on gangway for night.

20th Thursday
Left at 7am, and as were lying at moorings quietly slipped our berth. Beautiful day and fresh breeze, a real Fremantle 'doctor'. To do night duty for last night.

21st Friday
Sea calm but big swell. Beautiful sunshine. Slept during morning. At laboratory in afternoon. Staff allotted new duties and on night duty. Saw huge fish a hundred yards from vessel port side. A whale jumped right out of water. Informed this morning that I was to take over laboratory work in L.Cpl. Freeman's stead who has transferred from the ship.

22nd Saturday
Cleaned up in the lab. This should be a great thing for me. Cpt. Southwood sent for me and gave me friendly advice. Saw Capt. Shields later, who has promised to help me, notwithstanding my little knowledge regarding pathology and bacteriology. Had physical jerks before breakfast, now a routine for all staff. Half in mornings, and half in afternoon (alternately). Issued with tropical uniform to new staff and dress ordered for whole staff. Testing blood serums of various members of unit.

23rd Sunday
Started new duties by cleaning up X/ray Dept. S.Sgt. Gray in charge, a fine chap. He and Capt. Southwood wish to help me also in this regard all they can.

24th Monday
Feel it getting warmer now. Nank ill and laid up, seen by doctor.
A lecturette evening. I gave a paper on 'Savings' Banking. King on 'Glass Blowing', and 'Cotten Companies', and others etc. Very instructive.

25th Tuesday
Our Saloon Coffee comes in handy these days, much preferable to issue stuff.

26th Wednesday
Card tournament in evening. Getting the lab ship shape, and sleeping out on forms on promenade deck.

27th Thursday
Concert in evening. Harry Pens 'In Marriage Ceremony of Doreen and her Bloke' from 'Sentimental Bloke', excelled himself. One of the new Sisters played her violin beautifully. Poor old Robbo caused much amusement (at his own expense). During the morning we passed very closely to the 'DEVONSHIRE' Cruiser stern and 4 masts. A fine big ship, and see and wave to chaps standing on her decks. Coffee and new hot bread from the night steward before retiring. A talk with Bertie Deaney re his experiences in the South Sea Islands.

28th Friday
Nearly completed lab, to receive instruction re Sterilizing plant on Monkey Deck. Day warm, but a beautiful breeze during day and evening.

29th Saturday
Concert in evening.

30th Sunday
Our bank balance day, guess the Officers are having a busy time.

JULY, 1918

1st Monday
Many heavy tropical showers, but weather moderately cool.

2nd Tuesday
Another concert in evening. Pens particularly good. S.Sgt. Jaisson gave a good exhibition of disentangling himself from rope tying his hands and body, also got out of box when locked.

3rd Wednesday

Water looking very much shallower. At ?pm we noticed a vessel steaming towards us a goodly speed. We turned sharply towards her and when not far off, stopped our engines. We sent up signals to her, she came quite close and we were allowed to proceed. Heavy rain a little later obscuring partially the shore line which before we could just discern. Passed the 'LOYALTY' going out, 2 funnels, three masts, clipper bow. Steaming at a good pace. She looked majestic, quite close to her. Also 5 other large vessels outward bound. Passed (Bombay Hbr) lightships just before dark and noted the lofty steel framework lighthouses, white and red lights. Signalled for Pilot, and one came on board from ? a dingy. Were further signalled by Morse station as to direction and speed, and finally to anchor near another Hospital Ship. Had a conversation with Col. and Matron re Bombay. Mitch and I met them when at the bow of ship. Bombay brilliantly lighted up along shore. Supposed to be finest harbour in India. Passed an Island with flash light on our starboard before entrance.

4th Thursday

The Hospital Ship 'MADRAS' lying quite close to us. Red Cross steam launch came alongside early. A rough boisterous day and water rough. A big current flowing in this harbour. No one granted leave except Sergeants. A good day wasted, very quiet and monotonous. Heavy showers. A native boat upset by gust of wind some occupants numbering 7 were nearly exhausted by time help was at hand, our motor launch duly rescued them.

5th Friday

Heaved anchor, and proceeded to docks at 7am. Tied alongside wharf for awhile, then through the docks. At entrance were held up by contradicting orders and using our own steam, consequently fouling our own propellers by a rope. Leave granted 9pm - midnight. Wasted an hour, as we were unable to get on shore owing to ships being berthed ½ way and in middle of entrance to dock. Eventually squared native skipper of tug to bring his boat under our stern, and slid down our rope.

Made for P.O, a magnificent building with circular enclosure in middle and brass work on it. All clerks worked in this compound. Met there a stout gentleman in shorts who is Engineer in Charge of constructional works relative to Communication trenches in Mesopotamia. Salary 900 rupees per month. He was trying to get back to Mesopt. having just finished his leave. He took us round to the Railway Station, a most magnificent building, but an awful waste of money. Beautiful granite and marble pillars, all of different shapes and colours in columns and supports. Noted municipal building on our left with its huge tower and minarets. He accompanied us to Y.M.C.A. where we posted our letters. A very fine building and well appointed. From there we visited the famous Taj Mahal Hotel. Had a look right through it. Everything from a needle to an anchor can be bought there, even rail ticket for any part of India. All terraces and passages lined with broken crockery, worked into beautiful patterns. Went to top storey, where a good view of surrounding buildings may be obtained and overlooking the fine palm and fern garden in the yard. Had a look at the sea wall, 6d each for lime drinks at the Taj. One Anna at Y.M.C.A, and other places.

Walked back to car stand, and there parted with our friend who went to his hotel. He was good to us, and kind. Later saw Staff Group Sgt. Chidgey and arranged to go with them on a trip to Malaba Hill by motor.

Changed money at Currency Bank free of exchange. Mitch made some purchases, and we bought our books of views of Bombay. Met Staff Gray at 1pm. We hired a nice car owned by a Parsee. Proceeded via Queens Road where most Govt. buildings are e.g.

Civil Court, University (and Tower) etc. Road beautifully asphalted and running parallel with railway for some distance. Noted several Railway Stations. After travelling for about 2 or 3 miles turned in town-wards, and passed through native quarters and streets. Here all sorts of things resembling the Cairo W?tschke could be seen. We were informed that we were in the famous Grant Road eventually, and sure enough, as was told us on the voyage over and by those who had been there before, was the Wassa? environment, and the poor victims caged behind bars like animals. The dirt and filth of this place is appalling and is by no means improved by the unfortunate chewing the horrible betel nut, and spitting through the cages on to the steps and street outside. In some cases it looked as if this had been going on for years, so thick was it. Woe to those, (the Traffic Slavers), who lead these into such paths and modes of living. Since told that the very back lanes and allies are much worse even than Cairo. Down Grant Road are Japs Chows, and different breeds of natives.

We soon came to a road to entirely different, forming a wonderful contrast to the picture left behind. On either side are planted beautiful big trees which reach each other on top and form a perfect arch. We then came to the Europeans bathing ground on the right, and turning at the junction of the road to the left came opposite to a Temple, with large bathing well in front, nicely decorated on the edge by a decorative stone wall, beautified by pot plants supported by places provided by them. This pool or well cut out of solid rock 30-35ft deep, 120 x 40 ft or thereabouts in area. Took photos here and went to a Parsee Tower of Silence. These situated right on top of Malabar Hill. Rather a steep incline from the main road beneath. Flowers and plants of every shape and hue bordering the roadway.

Gave our permit at 'lodge gate', and were led by guide to the towers or rather gardens surrounding the towers. In this place Vultures dispose of the flesh of dead bodies which are laid in the towers through a door. Altho' nobody is allowed near or inside the towers, even to the exclusion of the mourners, we could plainly see the Vultures about 30 in number waiting for the next 'feed'. One tower is used by the general Parsee, the other is a private concern, and the third for -? Were shown a model of them later. The body is first laid on an iron grating, and when picked of flesh by the birds, taking about 2 hours, the moisture and bone drop to a cavity below where it mixes with lime charcoal, and is drained off and run into the earth by means of 4 subterranean passages thus 'from the earth came and to earth returneth'. Consider by this creed (the most highly educated and richest people of India) to be the most sanitary and proper from a hygienic point of view:- (Rough plan shown)

A good garden there. Our guide courteous. Just below with a huge golden spire on dome is a Hindu Temple. Joining our car we had a good look at the floating or hanging gardens before moving off, and noted the water stored in small Reservoir prior to use in city, originally comes from a huge Reservoir 20 miles up country. Heavy showers of rain fell here. Strolled back and had a panoramic view of Bombay. Red tiled roofs particularly striking. At Malabar the C.S's live (Civil Servants of India). Descending the hill which is steep on this side. Before starting noticed huge Vultures in a palm tree so took snaps. Noticed a native, as though in fearful agony, forming all sorts of contortions of face and body. Some say he was praying, others that he was mentally bereft.

Came back to the city via the esplanade where we noticed numerous fishing boats at sea, and met Queens Road again. Were dropped at P.O. at 4pm, fare 3½ rupees for afternoon. Jimmy sent a cable home, and Mitch, Nank, and myself went for a walk thro' native quarters, past Crawford Market, for the remainder of afternoon to meet Jim Smith at Y.M.C.A. at 6pm. However, we were a bit late in getting back, saw much to interest us, found a message left from Jim to effect that he had gone to Y.W.C.A. to orchestral concert, and would be back to dinner at 8pm.

BOMBAY

Entrance to Mohommedan Temple - Boots must be removed

Railway station 'front view'

A beautiful hospital

Water Police

Cheap rent for the barber

Railway station 'corner view'

Old museum - Now Lady Harding Hospital

Water supply - drinking fountain

Port of Tewfik

Everyday is moving day

Post office

Junction of several streets

Thomas Freeman Hospital

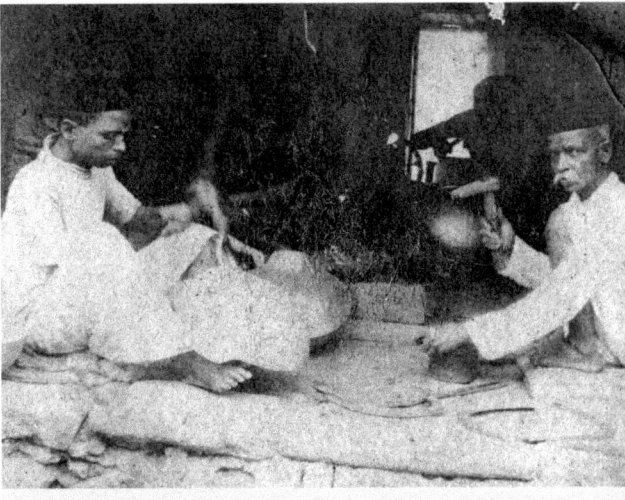
Brass metal workers

'Karoola', WWI. No.1 Australian Hospital Ship

Could not wait so went round to concert and were given a most cordial welcome by the ladies, altho' concert was nearly over, having begun early, they insisted on our staying. Met a fine American lady, a Miss Hall, and Cowdrey. Gave a hearty invitation to come round to Y.W.C.A. again if staying in Bombay, on to she and her sisters flat in Appolo Bunga where they live with two American Lady doctors and one Canadian.

Went to tea at Active Service Hut run by Methodist Church, where we received a most hearty welcome. Met there serving us a Mrs. Walker and her two daughters and the Bombay Supt. of Police people. Mitch and I invited round after and went. Their home near Crawford Market, and a beautiful old English style of building, a Bungalow. In spite of our recent supper, the native servants loaded us with all sorts of goodies. The hall a very large one indeed. Mr. Walker, a big bluff gentleman, holding 30yrs service in India with decorations from King Edward, Delhi Dubha and the German Prince when on visit to India, the latter very much hated owing to his unseemly and unbecoming behaviour. Mr. Walkers' birthday so we were honoured guests. Three English Tommies there also, and one in particular a real hard case. Crackers with contents caused plenty of amusement. Two lady Indian teachers living with them. Both well spoken and courteous. Bombay folk keep late hours and rise late, so as to miss heat of day.

We regretfully left them at 11.45pm to join the ship, much to our sorrow but living in hope of seeing them again tomorrow, and accompanied part of way back by English Tommie by way of P.O. Found that our ship had shifted, and had to walk long way round docks to reach her. Unquestioned on board, and turned in and slept like toffs, only hoping not to strike guard on the morrow. Everybody before going on leave cautioned re overstaying leave. Happily no cause for complaints.

P.S. Saw diver submerge and extricate rope from propeller. Native diver.

6th Saturday

On guard duty till 5pm. Mitch and Jim Smith off during morning, duty to start at 5pm. Mitch intends going round to see the Walkers first thing, and also make arrangements with them to meet me at their house at 5.15pm. Was interested during morning in watching men, women, boys and girl natives loading a steamer near us with wood. All carried 2 or 3 pieces on their heads and kept up a continuous stream all day. A good many arguments amongst the women until stopped by their head Serang. About 15 vessels in Alexandria docks, which is mostly used by hospital ships and transport, six British India boats in. One arrived yesterday with native troops from France. One today with English troops from Bazra. Sassoon Rocks? not far away and apparently very large. Amused myself remainder of afternoon by running people to and from the ship on starboard gangway to wharf by one of ships small boats. A coal hulk lying between us and wharf.

At 5pm made a beeline for Walkers house from rear of docks and through Crawford Market, a large fruit one mostly, but a place where anything eatable live sold in India can be bought. Arranged to meet Walkers at Active Service Hut later where a concert was being given to Tommie soldiers. Altho' asked to come round and sup first and go along with them. Went along to Crawford Market and had a long and interesting look through. The many rich, savoury and spicy smells make one feel bilious, changed 10/- at money changers, received rupees 6, annas 14, costing 10d exchange. Met English lady there with child lately from Hospital. Were in pretty bad way owing to husband's death recently. Bought milk for little girl, and promised to send food from ship in morning if sent for. Arranged to buy 6 egg cups and stand in brass from vendor in market, but arrived back after place had been closed up.

Went on through Silk Market in a different part altogether, guided by an obliging old chap from the fruit market. Passed a beautifully built and imposing Mohammedan

Mosque on the way with large minarets, and brilliantly lighted up. Met a Sydney lady with English Officer in one of the Silk Marts and she chose Indian Silk for me. Vendor wanted more but finally purchased a piece at 2 rupees, 8 annas per yard.

Came back to Crawford after inspecting several shops for Jap tea-sets. Made no purchases in this line, much cheaper in Colombo. Went back to silk places and had a look round and came to Mosque and looked in through doorway at worshippers. Invited by attendant to take my boots off and come in, sat down on steps and did so. Place most beautifully painted and gilded and from an architectural point of view, a magnificently designed place. From the wall hung dozens of dazzling chandeliers, floor beautifully carpeted. Odd persons were performing all sorts of evolutions in prayer facing Mecca. Through portals, on the right on a sort of verandah, one could see the pool where worshippers wash themselves prior to prayer. All colours of light reflected in this made a pretty picture. Went down steps to water's edge and saw people washing face and hands. The mosque soon became full and a priest appeared and service was held in order amidst his chants. Old attendant soon asked for buckshee, put on my boots amidst dozens of curious onlookers. Remember beggar singing as hoarse as could be with musical drum affair as his accompaniment. Drags his head from side to side nearly rubbing his nose against top of it, and made noise like one urging a horse when driving.

Walked to station and waited to see the Madras Express go out at 9.30pm, a big train with huge squealing parting engine. Carriage well fitted up for 1st and 2nd and 3rd better than Cairo tho'. Number of English Officers on board, and Indian soldiers by boat arrival yesterday. Had a good look at marble and granite pillars in station building. At station are hot and cold baths, lunch rooms etc. Caught tram for Active Service Hut. On tram run up against a Parsee, a big dealer in horses from Austr. Great admirer of Australians. Treats with great contempt the Sinn Feinders of Ireland, having been to Belfast himself, and abhors the home rulers of India who he says are influenced by behaviour of Irish. Had a good chat to him and intelligent fellow and gave me his address with the request to write him. Left a written message at Y.W.C.A. for Miss Hall, Cowdrey, and proceeded to Active Service Hut. Met Talbot in Gharry on my way and he came back with me. Saw part of programme which was good, waited for Walkers and said goodbye to them, thanking them for their kindness and hospitality. Wished a bon voyage and safe journey back.

Walked back to Freeman Thomas Hospital, and whistled 'Australia' in front whilst waiting for a car. Watched a Sister (all Aust. Sisters here), she looked up and out of window, noticed two others with heads out of windows upstairs also, who were evidently attracted. Expect poor girls often think of Australia and wish themselves there. Met an English Tommy Sgt. and walked back to dock with him, an interesting chap and on duty at embarkation office at docks. Bought cigars with him, and had nice lime iced drinks. (Very hot and dry). Two of these, and a cup of tea for him cost 2 ½ annas, at Taj Mahal limes 6d each. Turned in pretty tired. All around sheds and wharves at docks, natives lying about asleep everywhere. Poor beggars, no beds some of them I expect. This is characteristic even in Bazaars and markets. Nothing to see vendors sleeping over their goods, and stretched out to it. Some with their legs up on counters, others dozing as they squat amidst their wares.

7th Sunday

Hear of the fever which has been affecting thousands in Bombay. A real epidemic. Day warm. Notices the big B & I boat, 'ROYAL GEORGE', having brought in troops going into dry dock and another trooper B & I going out. Moved to other side of our docks to take in patients, berthed just opposite Alexandria Hospital where native troops are quartered, and Red Cross stores kept. Got a Tommy soldier to post my letter for Mother re photo on rough sea on trip in Bight. English Sisters amongst our patients, and about 130 in all (9 T.B. and about 20 mental), others mostly medical cases, left at 5pm.

Noted the huge hydraulic lifting cranes on wharves and the two storey store and goods cargo sheds. All tile roofed. Waited at gates for awhile just opposite the 'ROYAL GEORGE'. The wharves outside are all of stone, beautifully and solidly built. Alexandria dock opened in 1914. Put out to sea, a nice fresh breeze sprung up. Many ships at anchor in harbour amongst them a hospital ship just out from a berth near us. A ship with beautiful lines, Red Cross painted on top of funnel besides lights on each side. As we steamed away, several Tommies were heard to say "Good bye to that ----- place, hope we will never see it again". Some had been before being returned sick, others had been there for a long time, others had previously been to France.

8th Monday

My birthday, guess they are thinking of it at home. A good steady cool breeze blowing. Expect soon to have hot weather.

9th Tuesday

A good many of staff absent from early morning parade. All these had to report at 8am sick parade. Peculiar tiredness and achy joints, headache, high temperatures, and pain in small of back.

10th Wednesday

More staff sick. Jimmy Smith down to it, felt ill last night and was seen by Doctor. All these patients isolated and instructions to remainder of staff, not to go near or through their ward E5. Crew and returned patients similarly affected. Mitch not too bright and has been lying on deck all day. Capt. Shield and I took specimen blood from several of these chaps for leucocyte count. Showed leucocytosis as many as 15-20,000 per a man.

11th Thursday

More staff sick making about 25 in all. A little discomfiture in routine work naturally. Cases diagnosed as Dengue Fever. Only fluids given, plenty of mist and Alb. and Mag. Sulphur given. Two Sisters on duty, and it was queer to see our boys being blanket bathed and washed by them. No good to me. Most of them are extremely thirsty, breath hot and scorching and perspiring considerably. Jimmy Smith not too good. Had a peculiar turn myself late at night.

12th Friday

Some of new patients discharged, but others going in. Say one feels very ill indeed while fever lasts. Capt. Webb now laid up. Should have mentioned previously that owing to shortage of staff, I have to assist in C1 ward where Sister patients are berthed. Seemed very strange indeed at first and Westlake would persist in saying funny things from the sink hopper. Made things awkward, for several were in bed and feeling sea -sickness terribly.

13th Saturday

Passed the old spot of Aden at 6pm. Heard today that we would have to go in there. Hoped so for I wanted to purchase one of these world renowned baskets. Disappointed however, as we passed right on. One of these Sisters now bound for England, told me of her travels since leaving New Zealand for service in Army. (Now lent to British Govt). Started from N.Z. to Sydney, then to Blighty, via Durban and Cape town calling in at Teneriffe. Service in England, then to Egypt, to Bombay and various ports of India, back to Australia again, and to England via Monte Vides and back to Bombay, up Gulf

(Mesopotamia) seven times on Hospital Ship, thence to ---- in German East for 10 months, and down to CapeTown 9 trips 'GILFORD CASTLE' thence back to Bombay and bound for England again by our ship. A very nice person, has kept a diary all the time, and was particularly careful to keep it written to date while in German East for most people who go there lose their memories for awhile. Whilst in Egypt went to Lemnos and Malta. Nursing our poor boys from Gallipoli, with whom she has very great sympathy and regard indeed. One of the other Sisters, a little Scotchy, a very bright and interesting person. Nearly all English Sisters belong to Territorial Force Nursing Staff (T.F.N.S.)

14th Sunday

Passed Perin at 2am and were held up and inspected by our old friend the cruiser. Hear that we have to call at Abu-Ail lighthouse there being two sick men there, (see notes on 17/4/18 for notes on lighthouse.) When opposite a boat was lowered with 6 crew, Sgt. Biggs and Cpl. Maddison and Col. went to the light. Had previously passed the '----CASTLE' with English troops on board. She passed us again. Thousands of jelly fish in water resembling toad-stools. Water clear as crystal. On mainland on our left we could plainly see the after half of a big steel ship-wreck. Stern was high up out of water and open space for propeller plainly showing. Decks had been taken off or burnt, for stays, and crossbeams could be seen. When our party returned, we were told they had to land on beach at rear and climb up steps in solid rock to house. Brought back pretty shells and coral. Sick men not ill enough to bring away. (Hand drawn picture of lighthouse.)

Guess the first time for many a long day since a big ship pulled up here. More islands later in day. Young Jackie Rundle in hospital today.

15th Monday

Pay day. Had a very interesting chat to a R.A.M.C. Doctor from Mesopotamia. Has had a hard time during his term out there. His head seems affected just occasionally. A common complaint however to campaigners out there. His father a Doctor and he strongly urges me to go to Edinburgh and study for medicine as he himself did. Gave me some most valuable and useful tips. Some of the patients been in many campaigns during the present war. One had been to Gallipoli, Egypt, France and Mesopotamia. Returned once from Mesopotamia and came back in ship hugging the Moroccan coast, Algiers etc., to Alexandria to dodge subs, but were eventually torpedoed, but fortunately not sunk. Others have come to India via the Cape. Durham Light Infantry. Did his term in France and unit, and discharged through head wound. Called up again and did regular army work in India.

16th Tuesday

Posted to E4 ward to duty for morning. Plenty of porpoise racing alongside ship. Saw land on our port just before sunset. Concert tonight. Very good and enjoyed by Tommies, 'Sentimental Bloke' not properly understood by Tommies I guess. Nice breeze today, over whole of ship and over monkey deck. Very nice indeed.

Note from diary Cpl C.R. Mortimer AWM

Various wards were large, airy, and when calm, the portholes were open and wards were nice and cool, electric fans provided to circulate the air.

17th Wednesday

Arrived about 4am, and woke to find ship anchored near old spot. First thing a Dhow boat of 'KANOWNA' boys came over to see us. Westlake's cousin is a Corporal on board, and one of the visitors. 'KANOWNA' arrived 5pm last night. Came via Albany and left about a week before us, so we are much faster. Hear that her operating theatre washed and damaged in Austr. Bight, necessitating repairs and her delay. Also, that we have to take her passengers to arrive at 'WARILDA' at Alexandria. This arrangement upset by our O.C., explaining the poor health at present of most of unit, he contending that they could not stand the work without a spell. So hear we are to be here for at least 12 days, our patients not having left England. Proceeded in to Pt. Tewfik during morning. Our patients still hoping that we may yet take them to England. The Hospital Ship 'LOYALTY' here and 21 other ships of all sizes. Noticed the aeroplanes ascending as of old, natives loading sulphide into a B.I. steamer. Hear that we are to disembark patients in morning. Natives in their Smokeho amused us very much by various antics, and receiving deluges of water from ship when approaching too close for apples and cigarettes. Later they played blind man's bluff, and were clever at listening and dodging both parties being blind-folded. Hospital train arrived and waited for our patients.

19th Friday

Messner in hospital yesterday with fever. O.C. advises all those not properly recovered to stay on board and not have extended leave. Considered to be invalids, hard cheese for them. Disembarked our patients at 7.30am, breakfast at 7. Missed my Doctor friend. Should liked to have bid him bon voyage. Parade at 1pm, and names taken for those going to Cairo, Alexandria and Palestine for the reason as W.O. said, that ships movements were most uncertain as yet, and addresses were required so that immediate summons to ship was possible. Moved out into stream again at 2.30pm, finished all sterilizing at 12.30. Should like Ada (*eldest sister*) to be here and paint this remarkable water colour scene of range on left, white beach, blue water and white tanks standing back from shore, and Suez a little to the right (before commented upon last time we were here.) Noted the 3 funnelled cruiser now lying in canal, 'TOPAZ' 35 knots, and the clipper bows steamer evidently suffering from result of collision, for the nose had been pushed back and went to one side like so much brown paper. No holes noticed however.

20th Saturday

Many inquiries made re our ship to arrive from England with patients for us. No news however, and no likelihood of getting any. Anyhow, leave granted till midnight Thursday. Have all along wished to go to Palestine if opportunity presented itself, otherwise to Cairo and Alexandria. So left ship at 3pm uncertain what to do.

Had to wait for 5 o'clock train to Ismailia, so walked to camp of Suez Motor Boat Corp and made enquiries re trip to Palestine. Hear that it is quite possible, providing one has a movement order. However, I bought a ticket for Kantara and found that Staff Grey, Ash, Nankivell, Rundle, Hayes, Hale, Donowa and Sgt. Biggs, Cottrall, Cpl. Fordham, Westlake and Clark had also done the same, and were going to risk their chance, when I met them on Tewfik Station. We all went together in 2nd class (3rd ticket) to Kantara, first changing at Ismailia. As train did not leave there till 9.30p, Rundle and I got out at Mowaska while Grey went to see his friend in camp close handy. A picture show was being shown of a fight between two champions, and everybody in camp seemed bent towards the pavilion. However, Rundle and I walked towards Tel-el-Kabir to 2nd Aust. Stationary Hospital. He to see his friend Robinson late of Keswick, and I to see Capt Benson, also of Keswick (resides and practises at Alberton) in order to try and obtain a pass from him for Palestine as we hear that this may be done and is effective. However, he was present at sports in Ismailia and R's friend had gone to witness the fight. Other Keswick chaps were there on duty, but we had no time to see them.

Met others at Ismailia, and I walked to the lake where the concert was to be held in hope of seeing Bensen. We found the place near shore of the lake, and much cooler here than on the line (we had been perspiring very, very much). Capt. B. had just departed, but would return shortly. Nearly all Austrs. present, besides men off man-o-war lying in canal. Concert had not yet started, it was being given by lads of A.A.M.C., at 2nd Stationary, but we could wait no longer, so hurried for the train. There is a beautiful avenue of trees from station to lake. Cross over bridge (fresh water creek). Feel that I should like to see it in daylight.

At about 10-10.15 pulled up at Kantara, and intended putting night in there to catch 6.30 train in morning for up the line. Kantara is a bank of canal and a pontoon bridge crosses it. Some of us found it necessary to buy eatables (of a kind) at the Aust. Canteen (eggs-a-cook), others crossed the canal to see what could be done at Y.M.C.A. on other side. I stayed however, and when we returned not being able to obtain beds to station (altho' we had offer to sleep on concert hall stage) would have accepted only heard that a midnight train ran to Palestine, and wished to see what other party would do. We found bridge swing in, so had to walk a distance up the bank to cross in an old flat-bottomed punt. We walked from there to railway station (Kantara East), and met the other party. Train consisted of cattle trucks and others loaded with wagons etc. When asked for our movement orders, handed our leave passes and were blissfully ignorant regarding any other necessity. However, we were referred to the R.T.O., who was most courteous and kind, granting us permission to travel as far as Rafa (120 miles) where this train was to stop and wait for the 6.30am from Kantara. Passengers consisted of English Tommies returning to the line from leave and hospital to duty, also Egyptians belonging to the E.L.C. & E.S.R. Also one or two Austs. on board. Had to doss on the floor, found other occupants most agreeable and sociable. Some of us were tired and soon fell asleep. For my part I unhappily picked a spot where two iron girders were fastened to the bottom and slept about an hour all told. The soot from the engine and sharp blinding sand from the desert was most irritating and uncomfortable, filling ears, eyes, nostrils alike and making ones hair like a cocoa-nut door mat. Beguiled the time by watching out over the desert, for it was a beautiful clear moonlight night. The air became quite cold and damp and was a great contrast to the heat and closeness of atmosphere a few hours previously. After finding at length, a place to put my legs and feet amongst all the others huddled up and slept till arriving at El-Arish at 5.45am.

21st Sunday
This is on the shore of the Mediterranean Sea and is used as a rest camp for British and Indian soldiers alike from up the line. A large canvas city. An Indian Stationary Hospital there, and not 300 yards from water's edge. A beautiful vista as we gazed out over that vast expanse of deep blue water, and back at the white limitless sand, a good picture. There is a canteen where we bought tinned stuff (meat and extracts), biscuits, a few loaves of bread and our bottle filled, some with tea and others with water. Quite a large railway yard, and shed are located here also. We did not have time for a swim worst fortune, but we badly needed it. I might here record that long after we others were awake, Charlie Clark slept on, for he had a comfortable air pillow. I woke him through my laughter, for he was a most disorderly and interesting spectacle to behold. He was no dirtier than the rest of us, but looked eminently worse. My sides fairly ached to see him sleep there, with his head and body rolling from side to side (for it was a rough, rickety ride), and to notice the grime and dirt on his face, and around his brows, and in wrinkles of face, the way he lay showed him off to good advantage and when at length he awoke, he gazed round in bewilderment and surprise, not knowing whether to believe his senses or not, for he thought I was bereft of mine, as I was helpless through laughing and the more so, when he looked so 'doppy'.

Well no wash or shave and nothing to eat as yet, we started for Rafa and when a couple of miles out, we passed through groves and groves of fine big date palms, and several wells. An oasis we were told. The sun now shed a bit of its warmth, but the rest of the trip was interesting for we noticed many hundreds of wild fig trees, navvies working on the line, both Egyptian and Indian. A double line runs right up as far as Gaza, a 4ft.6in gauge. We hear that the British and Austrs. pushed the Turks right back from near Kantara along this line which was originally built by the Turks, but in a light line in the attack on the canal. In some cases 1 to 5 miles of new line and heavier rails were laid by our pioneers and gangs in their big push.

Arrived at Rafa 7.30am. Reported to R.T.O., and obtained permission for Ludd. Here we find no train leaving for Ludd until 2.30 in the afternoon, with the exception of a ration train, and absolutely no passengers allowed on this for carrying ammunition and stores, fires are feared, one or two having happened previously. This is a big place, altho' no British troops there except railway officials and men. An electric light plant is being installed and all rail goods, line and sheds form El-Arish are to be laid down there. We rested in the Rest-tent for awhile and still no wash. A couple of tins of fish were opened and greedily eaten. However, I got restless after awhile so Sgt. Biggs, two others and myself started out for a walk, in the hope of reaching the Mediterranean shore and having a swim which only 'seemed' three or four miles away. The rest of party slept (like sensible fellows). The day was hot, but after a mile or so, found something to interest us, for there on a lonely tufty hill surrounded by trenches and shell holes lies the grave, marked by a solitary wooden cross, and ground bordered with shell stone from the beach, of a Gnr. Mitchell a N. Zealander. The fence was of netting supported by rude wooden posts. A typical Military cemetery cross (hand drawn picture).

We could see others at a distance and had a look at all of them. All N.Z., and killed about March 1917. What thoughts and sentiments passed through my mind as I reflected over these lonely graves, the more so when looking round, the utter desolation and loneliness of the place, the blue sea in the distance, the pure white, merciless sand dunes between, the razor edged lining against their wind- swept tops and the azure sky above. Daresay, their names appeared on some casualty list reported killed at some battle and place, probably given a name. The sorrow and bereavement of the loved one, and wondered if they had a photo or any idea of the grave or surroundings. The utter loneliness makes one feel sad. What a place to live, fight and die in after their beautiful country at home. Picked up Shrapnel shell and pellets not far away and Turkish cartridge case, and kept as mementoes.

We started out for the dunes and reached them in good time, but one or two complained of thirst. However, scaled the first hill found the sand fairly solid at start. Absolutely wind swept clean and not a mark upon them, but a lonely foot track made by a prowling animal of some sort. 1st in circles, then in straight line trots altering to apparently what became a gallop. We walked a goodish distance, along and down the ridges, but one of the party gave in and lay flat down to it. Should liked to have gone on, but were forced to retrace our steps as he seemed unwell.

When on the plane again, slightly altered our course back. Came across a barbed wire enclosure with a sign- board at gate, 'Rafa Cemetery'. These graves are mostly of Englishmen, some of various country regiments and others of Officers in R.F.C., attached to Austr. Squadrons. The biggest and best stone of all was that of an Italian, and had evidently been sent from Italy, for it was all of marble and made attractive by a huge wreath of metal leaves and enamel flowers being placed at foot. The plainest and loneliest of all was a small, painted cross at the head of a mound of earth with this simple inscription 'An unknown Sailor', body found on beach. This too gave room for ruminating thought. On a grave of Crawford, a number of empty cartridge cases were placed, evidently taken from his pouch or rifle, and the whole covered by wire netting. Have one as a memento. On another, a lad from Bucks. I picked up a P.C., a photo of one of its villages with a church standing conspicuously. This particularly interested Biggs, as his sister lives at the village, so has sent her the P.C. and photo of grave with boys name, for her to give to parents if identified. Duly reached the Rest-tent where others still sleeping. We were glad of a drink given us by a Tommy Signalling Corps not far from us.

Went to railway yard, and met an interesting chap from Crewe in Cheshire. Had been chosen for the railway work on account of previous experience. All engines on the line are mostly L. & S.W. Railway. He and I walked over to the market run by desert Arabs and Bedouins about a mile away, and bought melons and tomatoes. Melons good, one 1½ p.t. Bedouins fine looking chaps, but sly and treacherous as in evidenced by the wandering tribes who pimp and spy, and are at enmity and friendship both with our troops in various places. Our chaps much enjoyed the melons, so made another trip and obtained more. Melons grow in desert and are watered by heavy dews at night, which makes sand very damp.

Contrived to get a shave by using water from water bottle. Started aft under similar conditions as before in 6.30 train from Kantara, left at 2.30pm. Tommy soldiers good fellows, eventually arrived at Gaza where double line stops. Here we could purchase cocoa and iced drinks from canteen. Biggs hurried back on the line and obtained a battle affair resembling a bomb, from one of the ruined temples, during British advance. Used for the dome work and arches e.g. (hand drawing). It was at this place that the Turks made such a determined stand, and our forces under Gen. Murray, who really commanded them from Cairo, lost heavily. His name stinks amongst the men at this front, and it was not until Gen. Allenby, late commander of 3rd Division in France took over, and by a clever strategic flank attack on the enemy, that they were dislodged and routed. He is with the men in Palestine all the time. He carries his Union Jack with him, signifying his presence and H.Q. Staff. It is here too that we have apparently passed the Sinai Desert, for the country looks undulating and greener.

We started off again and were held up at Burbeerah where many Frenchmen are encamped. Representatives of all allied countries are to be found up this line. A big Indian Camp also on a hill on the left is in prominence. The country is altogether better and large crops of maize or corn are to be seen. When another train arrived from opposite direction we passed on, it being now dark and about 7.30pm. We reached Ludd at 9.45pm.

A very moonlight night, and orange groves along the line and round the station yard. We alighted and reported to R.T.O., obtained further permission to Jerusalem, and plodded through sand at front of canteen to the dusty road which leads on thro' the village of Ludd, and on to Jaffa. No food, but found a tank of water at Y.M.C.A., had a wash (with soap) under the tap, borrowed a blanket from another tent. Some of us lay in the sand, others on forms in the big marquee tent of Y.M.C. others on stage around the piano. Train does not leave until 9am tomorrow. I changed into shorts, and was glad to get out of boots and socks. Did not sleep much however, altho' pretty tired. Cool as usual towards morning. Night remarkably clear and bright. The others were soon snoring and breathing heavily. Had a pleasant experience in this same deserted and open to-all tent on our way back.

22nd Monday

Up just after break of day, and could distinctly hear the rumble of distant cannon. Washed and before canteen opened strolled round by myself and had a look at another Indian Hospital. Turkish prison camp. A number of Johnnies had been brought in during the stiff stunt up the line a few days previous, together with about 300 Germans, who had been removed to Cairo and Alexandria. Turks looked depressed and poorly dressed. Some very big chaps amongst them. Contained within a high barbed wire fence, other encampments nearby and the Aust. Flying Corp not far distant. Running down the various tracks and roads, wire netting is laid and doubled to facilitate traffic through the sand. A good idea. A great many Ford lorries and ambulances in evidence. Sun pretty warm.

Sudden firing of guns, (anti-aircraft). Could see the smoke in the air after bursting. Johnny in his aeroplane. Hear that he usually makes an attack during the morning, but at a great altitude. One of our planes quickly ascended and gave chase.

Station yards, camps and roads seem to be made in what was once garden for orange trees, and figs grow on side of road and near the tents. Waited until Y.M.C.A. canteen opened and bought cocoa ½ pt pint, and hard rock cakes 1 pt each. Made a satisfactory breakfast anyhow. Visited fruit and vegetable market after. This held on the sand, and goods displayed on boxes etc. Tried a melon which are cheap, and altho' grapes looked tempting dare not buy, for the vendors look abnormally dirty and filthy and fruit covered with swarms of flies.

Met at station at 8.30am, and started off in due time. From here to Junction Station a good decline, and line runs through big cornfields. At next station where gangs of Indians were working, a great many youngsters came to train selling tiny apples, melons, plums and grapes. Even when we threw away the skin of melon, they grabbed it up quickly, fought for it and greedily ate the softer part. Many were diseased, particularly noticeable in the eyes, one kid could scarcely open them, and groped around for anything given him and when the sun got in, when he forgot to shade them in his anxiety to get some of the spoil, he howled piteously with the pain.

From this station we immediately take a big run down hill. It is here that two sets of rail run on same sleepers, the narrow or light one used by the Turks and the new and heavier one of the British. The small one is held as a standby in event of the new not being able to stand the heavy traffic on the original sleepers. The engine and last trucks of train could be seen many times at the one time, so sharp the angles. The line in many places is right on the very edge of steep and precipitous ledges, being cut from the solid rock on the very edge of the hills. How our forces ever shifted the Turks from these mountains and rocky country, no one seems to be able to relate. Many times before reaching here, we were told that this point would strike us, (if we had not been told). Here and there we could see an olive tree and the old familiar Carob or Johns Bread. It was heavy pulling, slow travelling and tiring as I had to stand most of the way, but had the pleasure of looking out.

At Bittir, had time to have a little walk and altho' youngsters were selling figs, and there were fig trees about, no fruit could be found on them except tiny green things. A canteen on station. The hills round here are very steep indeed, and we hear that in the rainy season the earth could soon be washed off, so terraces are built to protect. (Small hand drawing). These are built of loose stones (lime), and earth banked up behind, making a kind of little flat above each terrace. Vines grow plentifully.

Started off again and passed Bethlehem on our right. Olive trees grow plentifully in the valley in these parts. Some of the butts are huge and tops stunted, signifying a great age. We were not long now in sighting Jerusalem the Golden. Arrived there in a very busy railway yard between 2-3 o'clock, about 360 miles from Kantara. Reported P.T.O. who was very nice, but called us fools to coming to such a place as this for leave. Anyhow he may be sick of it, but it was different to us, as later turned out. Had a long hot walk to Y.M.C.A., passed two old Dutch pattern wind mills on right, and German colony on our left. We met a chap on horseback who recognized our colours, and asked for one of our Sgts. recently transferred. Belonged to 1st Light Horse Field Ambulance, and badly wished to get back to Aust. Road long and dusty, passed old Turkish Barracks thence to Main Street and Y.M.C.A. A fine big building. Westlake's brother is to be in charge when alterations finish, for it is being prepared for sleeping accommodation etc. Anyhow were given temporary beds Buckshee, and after ridding ourselves of packs started off for Mount of Olives. Party divided.

Our party passed the Damascus Gate, opposite German Hospice, late German Head Quarters. When reaching end of wall turned to left, stopped there and took photos of Russian Gold Spired Convent, a magnificent edifice, and graves of Mohammedans, in Valley of Johesphat. Walked through olive trees down the valley, and ascended the hill in front where Turks lately had cannon emplaced. Found a small cave in the rocks and fine fern growing inside, procured several samples, walked on higher through a private garden to the road. Met two or three Tommies belonging to the 20th Army Corp. Signallers. They pointed out to us the Valley of Jordan, portion of the river and the old 'Dead Sea'. Whoever should have thought I was permitted to see this. All this to the north. Fighting still going on there. The booming of guns heard. Turks supposed to have 9.2 guns from Goeben there. They had been shelling Ludd day we arrived there, but shells were duds.

Now we saw something we had heard so much about 'the Kaisers Palace', but which was, before the war really a Hospice presented to Jerusalem by Kaiser-Kaiserine now H.Q. of the 20th Army Corps (English). This is on Jericho Road and a little further down from spot we view the Jordan. Guarded, but obtained permission to go inside. Built in spacious grounds, with trees plentifully planted and winding paths, between. Entered by north door. Plenty of Heads about, but found a decent Tommy who showed us round. First of all went to Chapel, where everything without exception was magnificent. A huge organ, immense pictures, with heavy oak frames by great masters. A beautiful alter on ground floor on balcony, two chairs from Berlin. Mosaic work in abundance every pillar ? and otherwise of different pattern and style, tiled floors, and walls decorated in what appears to be chalk scratchings in various colours, making a harmonious whole. Cleverly done. Marble was not wanting along railings.

We ascended the very large tower, square and commodious ascent, not quite finished but has 265 steps, from top a magnificent view is to be had. Especially Jordan Valley and Dead Sea. Visited the Officers dining hall, a very fine apartment indeed. In centre of building is a large courtyard with bronze figures of Kaiser and wife on either side. Here string band plays sometimes, and electric light is fitted up throughout, from our plant. There are at present 6 German Sisters of Mercy living on the premises and they occupy top rooms. They have been doing their work as usual, and unmolested. However, it was found that they have an immense influence with Arabs etc., obtained through issuing food really supplied from English messes. On 26th they are to be sent to Alexandria and Cairo, and an inventory had been taken of every article in the place. All bottom rooms are used as offices etc., and upper as bedrooms for Officers. They are splendidly furnished. The very best timber. These gents live like Lords at this place, and each one seems to have a motorcar to run round in. Asked by guide to come up again tomorrow.

Met others on the hill near the cave, and some of us walked to the Church of the Ascension on Jericho Road. Thence straight down for old church near a very high wall where Christ is said to have wept over the city and predicted its ruin. It was now quite moonlight, and we could easily pick our way to the foot of Mount of Olives and we walked on top of stone wall. When we came to Russian Church, could hear some women wailing and setting up a most mournful cry, and how dismal it sounded on that quiet night. Enough to call back the dead for it was in a graveyard.

We reached the bottom and three of us went to the Virgins tomb, which the R.C.'s hold in such sacredness. Long flights of steps lead downwards to the door. A little old shop is nearby where nuts and grapes are sold and an English Tommy officer and driver were there in a motorcar. He directed us through a large iron gate to a large grave of big olive trees, there we sat and talked during that quiet hour, not far from the groves put there, for the departed thought that when Christ would come again he would manifest himself there, and would call their spirits to him, so they wish to be as near as possible. How we talked, imagined, and went over certain incidents in the Bible relating to this spot. We were seated just below the Mt. of Olives and facing Gethsemane. I fancied I could almost see Christ after he had been betrayed, walking by himself through the trees and praying to God to remove this cup etc., sweating great drops of blood. Afterwards his disciples sleeping, and Jesus delivered into hands of men. I have never experienced feelings such as these. 'He went out and it was night'. This very night with its quietness, light, and state of our minds combined, seemed to draw us into a proper realistic groove. Even after we got up, we went into Gethsemane and saw the old olive tree where Jesus is said to have prayed. Only a small garden, and immediately beneath the Russian church. An old guardian gave us leaves off tree and flowers from borders. A peculiar feeling of reverence and awe seemed to hold me like a spell, and even after passing Stephens Gate, lingered near the old stone wall on road to Jericho, and leading back to Jerusalem and again talked over history recorded in the Sacred Book. Went to Y.M.C.A., found others snoring, remainder of party quickly got into bed, but several times I went to balcony and looked out over those dry hills roundabout and pondered. An experience not to be forgotten.

Every light on the neighbouring hills seemed hallowed and sacred as they twinkled. The song of Arabs only disturbed the peacefulness of everything, but altho' peaceful now, what can history tell regarding tumult, war, destruction, misery, and sadness and the event of all which has meant so much to the world 'calvary', and its happenings. -----Who could have thought I would have been here when reflecting on Rev. French's lecture regarding his visit here, that I should see this for myself. With all past destruction and attacks, in wars not so vast as this, not a stone had been destroyed or displaced today, not a foot of it had been blown by British Canon, and everything is protected by British. None of our troops can enter the Holy City without a pass and an Officer present. Thank God for British reverence. This place isolated as it is, is regarded as all the world to some, and nations have quarrelled over it, and less than a square foot in Bethlehem was the cause of the Crimean War directly. It is regarded so much that denominations Christian and otherwise have striven hard and long for representation on a piece of it. Even the site of the Hospice mentioned e.g. Queen Alex, Victoria, Augusta Hospice, was given by Turks to Kaiser and he in return built that magnificent building on it. Pretty tired when at last I turned in, but mosquitoes were bad. Slept well after a time. Should have mentioned that Sgt. Biggs left us at Ludd and found a friend of his there, later he went to Cairo returning earlier than we. That left us 12 in number and just 12 beds in our room.

23rd Tuesday
Up again very early and two parties started off different ways. Personally went to end of old wall past Damascus Gate, thence down the valley on left. Here the Arab butchers were at work under the olive trees, killing sheep and donkeys for civil consumption. Amongst all their gabble and quarrelling an English soldier (a meat inspector) was working quietly, and decisively, without taking any notice of them whatever, pulling them to pieces, separating one part from another, condemning this piece and putting aside that. An assistant stamped the carcases in various places (P.H.D.) Public Health Dept. He told me that since English took over, management of affairs such as bread baking etc., little or no disease occurred, very frequent previously. Butchers at times put knife between teeth when both hands engaged, otherwise worked in bare feet in slop and blood. Not a single portion of animals wasted, even intestines and contents carefully put aside and prepared in different ways. Girls were on the job doing this also. The sheep and donks throat is cut and allowed to bleed for some time. An incision is made in skin on sheep hind leg, and a fellow with a good stomach, bellow blows into it for all he is worth until knocking the big tail and skin all the time, it swells out very tightly. This helps to separate hide from flesh and assists butcher is skinning very much (small hand drawing) shape of sheep's tail different to any I have seen before. In some cases the sheep are skinned like a rabbit, so that carcase after inspection, is put into the hides again, which resemble bags

two tied together by necks, and slung across donkey and carted off. The carcase of donks is always skinned, the spine broken in the dorsal area and thrown across, and balanced on another donkey. In the thorax portion is placed his head, and in empty abdominal cavity, entrails and other parts are put, and the whole taken into the town. These dear little sheep are like those seen in biblical pictures, and it seems strange that I should see them killed on opposite side of valley to Mt. of Olives. The phrase came into my mind seeing these innocent creatures awaiting their death, 'Like sheep led to the slaughter, yet opened not his mouth'. Christ often referred to sheep himself, and in afternoon I was to see the very place where he was led to the slaughter. A better place is being renovated (a stone building) for the purpose of a slaughter -house in the future.

Met the others, and went back to Y.M.C.A. to meet our guide. However, he and some of the others got an early start, so knowing that they would visit Gethsemane and the Mt. later, we, Nank and I, proposed to go as far as the Virgins' tomb and wait for them. Had a good look at Stephens Gate where the Saint was stoned. It is prettily got up. Protected by an iron gate, a single large room with tiled floor, is subdivided by a glass casement. Therein are various pictures in oil, portraying Stephen being led from what is now known a Sheep's Gate or Gate of the Innocent, to his actual stoning and death. An alter arrangement up far end, decorated by flowers of the everlasting species (bronze and other material). Round the top of the other, some of the bare wall and others on canvas and in frames, are other pictures, the latter evidently from Germany, judging by their markings. More gifts from the Kaiser probably. We now saw the others in Gethsemane, so caught them up. Garden (small hand drawing). In centre is a very deep well, beautiful cool water, and the olive trees, and small borders of shrubs and flowers before mentioned. Hanging in, inside of outer wall are dialogues in glass cases, 12 in number, known as the Stations, depicting scenes where Christ was betrayed, to his nailing on the cross at Calvary. They are splendid workmanship. At rear of gate leading to inner garden is a cross, nails, sop, thorns, old fashioned hammer etc., representative of the things used at time of Cross of Calvary. Grapes are scarce and dear, but bought a few at shop where his scales weights consist of flattened stones, and 1lb is measured out by a stone weighing between ¼ to ½ xx.

Went back to town and had dinner of donkey flesh (so we all reckoned), and miserly other things for 12 ½ pt. Cakes are so sour we cannot possibly eat them xxx (omitted). Retraced the tracks already taken by other chaps before we came upon them. Walked down Valley of Jehovephat through graveyards and past tomb of Absolom. Just a large dome on small thick walls across valley and proceeded uphill alongside wall of old city. Village of Siloam now on the opposite hill, and in the distance further down the valley, is where the pool of Siloam was. Vegetable gardens round about it now.

Walked along to other corner of wall to Zeon Hill. Went into the old building, where excavations are now being made under floor. This has a courtyard, trellis work on top where large vines are hanging and simply loaded with grapes. In one of the porticos in wall surrounding the yard is a heavy marble tablet, standing on the spot where Christ was denied by Peter three times before the cock crew, on the wall is an engraving showing Peter surrounded by accusers of Christ and the cock crowing. Going through a door into another place (at the top of this diary page is written 'Josaphat or Cedron') we find the spot where Christ was questioned and cross-examined by his arrestors, while 'Peter stood without and warmed himself'. Poor Peter. At the rear of this building a fine Coptic Church has been erected.

We went down one of the side lanes near this building and visited the 'Large upper Room' in which Christ and his disciples had their last supper. Great solid pillars support the roof and are of ancient design. The floor is of flagstones, and are stated to be original, but personally I am doubtful, mounting a stone stair case we enter another room, where behind a partition are the tombs of King David and King Solomon.

On walking back to town the old Battlefield of the Philistines, David and Goliath was pointed out. A pebble won the day, but today the modern engines of war hover over the place and over the old city. The aeroplanes of England.

At 2pm, collected at Y.M.C.A., we were lined up and fallen in by Y.M.C.A. Sec., a splendid young fellow, and a Doctor of Divinity by profession. We were taken charge of by a young Tommy Officer and marched through streets to Jaffa Gate. Nearby, and one which we passed through is a very large gate specially made in the old wall for the Kaisers entrance in 1898. We went this way and passed the Sentries, Gen. Allenby's historical, but very quiet entrance to city was made by the old gate, known to the Arabs as Fiend. We halted in front of the Tower of David, an exceedingly old building, large stone at bottom by old builders and finished by smaller ones on top added by more recent builders. It is here that many refugees mainly from Salt receive their food and daily rations. We are told they are very quiet and intelligent people. In front of this tower Gen. Allenby read his proclamation, which promised that every person could pursue his lawful occupation without interruption, and every sacred building, monument, holy spot, shrine, traditional site, endowment, pious bequest or customary place of prayer of whatever form of the great religions of mankind, will be protected according to existing customs and beliefs of those to whose faiths they are sacred. This clearly impressed the populace and even while being read, guns were booming on north and east. Note England's respect and greatness in matters of this kind. The troops were heartily welcomed especially by Jews. Now we were allowed to walk as we pleased, and were cautioned by our splendid guide that we were to go through David St., the main street of the old city, warned to be careful as very slippery. Remarkably so, with our hob-nailed boots over these shiny, smooth cobblestones several of us slipped down nevertheless.

A very narrow street, and resembling parts of Wiitschke in Cairo, small shops, low roofed stalls exhibiting all sort of wares, nuts, vegetables etc. etc., and all kinds of native stuff. Kept by Arabs, Jews, Bedouins and others. The street gradually declines, and every few yards one goes down a single step. Some of the shop entrances, also to some houses resembled rabbit burrows and looking down ended goodness knows where. Seemed to run in vault like fashion in every direction. Would have been interesting to have found out. We visited the place of wailing, which is on east side of wall of the temple area. Here pilgrims make their pilgrimage. Many of them are very poor and constantly wishing to have 'an interest in land' in the Holy Place, a nail is driven into the divisions or mortar of the stone. There are thousands of them, short and long. They think then, though not being able to afford a house or land nearby, they are satisfied with this possession. Many however, have been taken out as curios, mostly by Aust. Soldiers.

Retraced our steps a little and eventually entered into the temple area. This is 35 acres in extent and 1/6th of old Jerusalem area – 210 acres. We first went to Temple of Aksa, but only had a glance in. Was built in early centuries. Noted the huge cedar beams on roof, from trees of Lebanon. This stands directly opposite the Temple of the Rock known to many as the Mosque of Omah. (Which is incorrect, this Mosque in Cairo). Ground between two temples covered with tiles, there is also a fountain where Mohammedans wash. This Mosque for Mohammedans worshippers, and the beautiful patterns carefully worked by the linings in the marble are wonderful. Took our boots off and entered, noticing beforehand the huge dome in centre of building. I had no sooner entered than I was immediately struck by the magnificent beauty of the place. Shall never forget gazing up into that huge dome and noting the mosaic work there, also round the tops of the walls. I could not describe it. The walls lower were even of better pattern in marble. Hanging from the roof are three huge chandeliers. This temple said to be built over part of site of King Solomon's Temple. The carpets on floors best Turkish, and supposed to increase in value instead of depreciating. Certainly they were lovely. The pillars of the temple are enormous and two noticeable more on account of difference of colour to the rest, green are those from Solomon's Temple. Corresponding with size of dome is an enclosure on the floor space. The partition is of iron or steel work of wonderful design and pattern, but really spoilt by the paint that has been daubed upon it, placed there by the early Crusaders. Inside the enclosure is the rock where Abraham led his son Isaac to be offered up as a burnt sacrifice until advised by Angel of the Lord to offer up a goat, he did so on this spot. We taken to basement of rock, where objects of great interest relative to old biblical identities are pointed out, such as for instance, the places or ledges where David and Solomon worshiped God before temple was destroyed by Romans. Mohammed's close by, and above a large hollow in rock said to have been made by him when rising in fervour of prayers and knocking his head. Further inspected the carpets, pillars. There are others about 6 and 7 ft from outside wall, supporting a ceiling, the whole similar to a series of ?, wide, inner (hand drawing) line (hand drawing) of enclosure under domes. Came outside again, and walked to where a chain hangs. Persons on trial for some reason or another, stand beneath the chain with the bottom end clear of their heads, if the chain swings they are telling untruths and are guilty. When our guide (the best I have met by the way), stood beneath in exhibiting to us the ancient custom, the chain swung, he laughed, remarked that he would take back all he had previously told us. His knowledge regarding history of person, people, customs, laws, rights and places, perfectly astound us, this his 266th trip round. Calls for perseverance that. Must be tired of doing it so constantly. He pointed out the Stables of King Solomon. Walked now to south wall and passed the Golden gate. Just near this is where pilgrims worship, and when angels visit (or spirits) of dead they touch or collect the pieces of garment torn by pilgrims from their persons and hung to iron bars and grating, during their prayers. Many strips were hanging as we passed. We now passed through the temple area wall again i.e., lower down south side, having entered at north end. Could plainly see the gilt towers of Russian church on opposite hill above Gethsemane.

(Omitted). In front of Temple of Rock is an archway of marble and stone at top of flight of steps, where it is anticipated that at the last judgement scales for weighing souls will be hung. Next pointed out to us was the Gate of the Innocent, or Sheep's Gate. Came amongst large buildings here, and were led by a French guard to the Church of St. Ann, owned by the French. This is only church which suffered in any way by hands of Turks prior to their evacuation of Jerusalem, about 50,000 pounds in valuables (precious stones and metals) being taken. So called St. Ann after Mother of Virgin Mary. Church is built over spot where the Virgins home stood, and where it is said she was born. A beautiful place inside, and a specially fine and attractive Altar. On the right of this one descends the steps which lead beneath a rock. The primitive church built over this rock used it as a tomb, and is said to be the place where St. Anne was buried. Nothing remains of the old church (which was built like this one over spot of the old house). We are told that a Cavity was found in rock filled with rubbish. Pity it was not left, so the rock is protected by a small mesh of wire netting, from curious fingers. Nearby is a flat ledge supposed to be where body was laid.

Coming out again, we noticed the beautiful painting on the walls of church, I think the best I had seen in Jerusalem. In the space in front of building is a high pillar standing 21 ft in height. A Corinthian column. A garden is also near with old stones with various inscriptions, supposed to be of old church. Several historians have different opinions regarding these particular places (see 'Guide to Holy Land', by D. Meistermaun, Burns and Oates). A very deep well is close handy, and feeling pretty warm lowered the bucket attached to chain and drew water. It was fine, cold and crisp. Just the sort that father would smack his lips after drinking. We now visited a most interesting place brought to earth by the White Fathers after many years of continuous labour and heavy expense. The Pool of Bethesda. One enters a porch prior to entering, where post cards may be bought. The opening to pool has a cave like appearance. A draught comes from it, as cool as any refrigerator, or so it seemed to us that hot day. It was here that the sick man waited for 40 years to try and get near the waters, to be healed when the Angel troubled the waters. Jesus at last succoured him.

It is known that the level of the old city was much lower than that of today. Sometimes it makes one ponder at the various position of things. Calvary for instance, which we know to have been recorded as a hill, but to us seemingly of no greater height than any other place. One must remember however, that Jerusalem has been destroyed no less than 17 times in its history, and what with rubbish and ruins, the surface actually has been raised many feet. Here is a good instance, and one showing plainly the layers of rubbish and ruin. The White Fathers had almost given up in despair the idea of ever proving this pool to be Bethesda, until fortunately sinking a deep and narrow shaft, which we were permitted to gaze down, they found an old and well preserved wall, apparently 2-2.6ft in thickness. This divides the one portion of pool to another, the latter also being found, which proves their claims now. They are awaiting more funds before resuming researches. The top of wall mentioned was 10-12ft, below surface, and all way to top were layers of broken stone, dirt etc.

From here we went to the Pretorium. This is built over site of Court of Trial, where Christ was tried before Pontius Pilate the Roman procurator. In this building which like Church of St. Anne, was inside clean and spotless, and all walls white. We were particularly struck with the beautiful tableaux depicting various scenes of the Stations of the Cross. To our minds they were absolutely perfect. There were also some fine paintings on the walls. Over a portico was a carving in stone, showing Pontius Pilate washing his hands in a bowl, declaring himself free from all responsibility regarding the judgement upon Christ and its future consequences.

From here we walked along the Road to Calvary, and having pointed out to us the various Stations of the Cross beginning at No. 1. At No. 5 we were told that the young man who came to Christ asking what he should do to inherit immortal life, Christ answered, 'Sell all thou hast, and give to the poor, take up thy Cross and follow me', and he went away sorrowing for he had great possessions. It is said that here he noticed our Lord fall from exhaustion through carrying the Cross thus far, as he watched from afar. However, he was requested to take the Cross from Jesus and carry it. Near Station 1, right overhead near the Pretorium, and leading from it is an old archway, but flat on top. It was here that Pontius Pilate had Jesus taken, 'on Exhibition' to the multitude who were all the time crying out, 'Crucify him' when he found no guilt in him. 'Deliver Barabbus' said they. He was taken here, thinking that by sight of him, sympathy for him might be felicitated from the crowd, but of no avail.

We found our way at (hand drawing) length to Calvary. Our guide knocked at a door which was opened by a woman. We ascended the step and walked down a long, wide, airy passageway. Everything appears quite modern here. Part of the old original wall of Jerusalem is here to be seen, and we pass through it to the place where lots were cast for the clothes of Jesus. Magnificent pictures adorn the walls of different Biblical Scenes and Station of the Cross.

Retracing our steps, we notice the elevation with large steps leading up to it. This is Calvary or Golgotha, the place of the Skull. Here many vivid scenes and imaginations flash through the mind. I suppose the place of places in the world I suppose. One thinks that it is hardly a hill, but remembering the gradual heightening of the level of streets due to ruins, we cease to ponder. This place we are told in the Bible is outside the city. Here it is plainly seen that the old wall is between us and Calvary. Judging by the older piece standing. The steps cross over the remainder. We pass by that old wall again and back to the street, and make for the Church of the Holy Sepulchre. This is rather a dilapidated building from the outside, and has a cobblestone paved courtyard in front. We noticed the many pigeons flying about and roosting on wall ledges above front. Running at right angles with the church, and from the two front corners of it, are buildings owned by different Govt's for their Consuls etc. (hand drawing of churches layout).

Herein is to be seen too many things to narrate here. There are 5 churches represented under the one roof, but in different parts of the building. Armenian, Catholic, Greek, Coptic and (left blank). As we enter we see the (left blank) on the tiled floor, in front of the huge dome. This represents (left blank). We notice that the paintings on inside surface, and also the plaster- work of the dome, is in sad need of repair. The question is very naturally asked why it is not repaired by one of the churches represented here? As a matter of fact, other Christian Churches have time and again offered money to effect repairs, but owing to an old Turkish law (which of course was recently in Turkish lands) any church or denomination, building or repairing a roof, the ground or floor space, directly covered by that roof immediately come into the possession of the body who did so. This particular portion of the building being used by all bodies in the whole place, each in turn objects to the other owning the whole spot, so consequence – neglect. Query, why not all contribute part of the cost? Just behind is painted the Holy Sepulchre when our Master was laid after crucifixion, which we are to see more closely later on. We mount a flight of marble stairs, and come out on to a balcony overlooking the spot we have just left. Since we left it, a number of priests are going through a ceremony round the (left blank). One is swinging by a chain a brass bowl (attached) affair, which is smoking from the top. Our friend the guide tells us it is incense. The odour given off permeates the whole place, and I must say that to my sense of smell it is not so very pleasant as I always thought it would be.

We then went to the spot where excavations were made in the year 366 by Queen Helena. Here the Cross of the Crucifixion was found, now stored in Rome we are told. This place runs back to such a distance that we are now not far from the place we saw the steps leading to Golgotha in the other church. Showing that this must have been the spot claimed for it as such. We now come to R.C. portion. Here we see a beautiful figure of the Virgin Mary, mother of Jesus. It is adorned on every available part by beautiful presents of golden articles of adornment, such as bangles and rings, also the most precious stones, set in various things are to be seen, every finger and toe, neck, wrist, head and ankles are decorated. This has been placed there by Pilgrims to the holy spot and are genuine in value.

Now we come to the Sepulchre. This is a huge rock, but does not possess the appearance of one, being lined inside with marble and decorated in different ways on the outside. After going through the incidents related biblically regarding this place, we went inside. It is composed of two chambers and both are luxuriously decorated with marble and precious articles of many kinds. The walls are lined with marble, but personally, and I state the view of many others, I should prefer to see the rock itself, no matter how bare it looked. In the 1st chamber (we notice blast holes), where the Greeks hold a ceremony at regular intervals, a fire is admitted at the one, and by some means flames are allowed to escape through the other. This is symbolical of cleansing by fire when we are 'born again'. Altho' in Christs case he had no guile, we ourselves are to receive purification.

In the inner chamber, Christ's body was laid on a ledge and now covered by marble slabs. Our friend the guide asked us to allow our mind to ruminate over the scenes of old, and the place where we now stood. Added with words of advice from him, a deep atmosphere was created, for up to now most of us had been talking and recalling the old stories etc., and were quite animated with our enthusiasm of interest. We had a look round other parts of the building, and came to a place where the priests previously referred to were praying and chanting hymns in a language foreign to us.

We walked out and passed up a long narrow street again similar to David Street, and came to the wall and passed out at the New Gate. When outside the gate we assembled to have our photos taken with the English officer and our guide, the former by the way, whenever we made a halt, counted us to see that all were present, and if there happened to be a lagger, the whole party had to wait until he put in an appearance, and rightly so, when one thinks of mischief that stragglers have done, which of course is looked upon as a terrible thing by inhabitants of their Holy City.

We were now asked if we should like to see the Gordon Tomb. This is supposed by many to be the real Golgotha or place of the Skull, called 'Gordon's Tomb' by the fact Gen. Gordon himself arrived at the theory. Certainly the rock looks something like a skull for outside appearance, and thither we went going along the road we knew so well by now, proceeding as far as the Damascus Gate, turning past the not completed German Hospice, and meeting a street which runs to the right.

We were admitted to a garden at first and how tempting those hanging grapes were, this hot day. We came to a tomb in a rock. The coffin reminds me of the one in Kings Chamber in Cheops Pyramid in Egypt only not so bulky. The visage of the skull however is quite close to the Jericho road which we had left, this tomb is round further to the left and to the rear, taking us further away from the road and unseen from it. To my mind this seems more like the place where Christ would be buried, not only the surroundings which one imagines in the mind, but we read that Calvary was outside the city. This is where the difference of opinion lies, for it has been proved that many walls existed in Jerusalem at different times owing to its various destructions. As the wall was rebuilt, so it may have been altered in position, sometimes making smaller areas and sometimes larger of the city itself. This may have placed the Sepulchre outside at one time, or in at another.

We have now finished our day with the guide, the others are leg weary and go back to the Y.M.C.A. with him. However, being promised by one of the sentinels at Gate of Military Governors Head Quarters, (late German incomplete hospice already mentioned) permission if I came during day time to go through and inspect the place, I made my way down there. Promisor not there, but Sgt. in charge did not stop me. The place is very solidly built of rough-cast, or rock faced white stone, and three stories high. All rooms are now Officers, and in the corridors of different landings I noticed Arab Bedouins, and others waiting to receive their passports, tickets etc., and making other arrangements for conveyance to various parts of the country. During our occupation, Britain has undertaken to do this, and as one instance, a large motor transport captured from the Turks and Germans, now takes passengers to Jaffa, on the sea coast, at our expense.

Now thought I would like to see that beautiful furniture spoken of in the H.Q. of the 20th Army Corp at Vic, Aug, Alex. Hospice. As I had had nothing to eat or drink for some considerable time, and this place being 1½ miles away and uphill, I pushed on hurriedly. When I got there, I found that all rooms had been taken by visiting Generals, Brigadiers etc., who were attending a concert to be given in the hall that night. I wished to go also, so advised to see the House Commandant at Gate Office re admission. He had gone out for a ride in his car, so took a Cpls. word for it that it would be alright. Tried to find a canteen before concert started, which I eventually did, on top of horse stables originally in use for Hospice. Had nothing I wanted however, a Tommy took pity on me and introduced me to a friend of his in charge of N.C.O's mess. Gave me a tin of Salmon and bread and butter. Made a good repast. This man has had a varied military career during the three years since he joined up. Been to France, Mesopotamia and Palestine. Finished up with a loaf of bread in my pocket and a tin of milk in my shirt. Looked some shape to attend a concert, and literally coated with white dust. Hung about till party arrived, named the Lena Ashwell party. One of the few kept by that great London actress for entertainment of troops on various fronts. These had just come from Egypt. Thought it was never going to start. However, I thought I would be sure of a seat as well in front, but when barrier was lifted and carried along with the rush, (found I would have to stand. Being very tired and having had little sleep up till now, made up my mind to leave early. There were only 8 rows of chairs provided, and 6 of these reserved for Officers. However, the concert started off well, party numbering 4, a pianist, singer, elocutionist, ? or humorist. All were excellent, and although I thought I would go after each item, I stayed on till finished. The audience were in roars with humour of that actor, and personally I was more than infatuated with music of the male pianist. Only Austs. present. The Heads were some Officers, but appeared decent enough.

Walked home in that beautiful moonlight, down the Mt, and up Jericho Road to Y.M.C.A., with my thoughts all to myself. Accosted by nobody, not knowing till next day I should not have been out after 9pm. Found all others sleeping heavily. Turned in at 12 mid – but got up several times to admire that beautiful moonshine and starlight sky. Have seen a book recently published called 'Eastern Stars'. The experience is worthy of a book anyhow and description of the sight.

24th Wednesday

Up again at 5am. Up till now wondering whether I should accept one of the proffered rides by motor transport to either Jericho or Jaffa. However, hearing that others had made arrangements to have a Gharry at basement at 6am. Made up my mind to go with them to Bethlehem. This was to be our last day here, our train leaves at 3pm. Having wired the Col. yesterday for extension of leave and getting a reply same day to effect that none granted, we had to fill in the morning as well as possible. We waited some considerable time for our Gharries, but none came. Sick of this we walked to the stand just opposite Friend Gate or Jaffa Gate. The price being arranged last night at 1 pound per Gharry to hold six. However, when we came to square up, having to pay beforehand, and jumped in Gharries at 6 a piece, the lazy old owners kicked up a fuss when we offered our money. Probably this is why they did not turn up at appointed time. They said their vehicles were only allowed to carry 5 a piece, and wanted 4/- from each of us. Two of us, one from each offered to walk until we got outside the city, but that was of no use, the money part was bothering him. I offered to stay behind, but others would not agree to go unless we all went. So being on box-seat next to driver, he tried to induce me to get off, but I refused thinking perhaps we might bluff him. Anyhow he soon showed his disapproval of our terms, for he got down and promptly began unharnessing the nags and to take them out. This looked pleasant in the main street, for there we all were, stuck up in a Gharry, with no horses, and harness hung on tail-board. I believe I could have knocked him, for he had not only gone back on his word, but had beaten us. We wished to go, so by hiring 3 vehicles, and making 4 a piece and paying about 5/- each, we started off. We treated him with the contempt he deserved after that, and did not forget to prod him occasionally, when we wished to go faster to escape dust of a preceding conveyance, or go slow when we wished to view more closely the sights to be seen. There was luckily a youngster in one of the other Gharries who spoke our lingo well, he told that party what different places were and a little about them, and one of them with a big voice, bowled out loudly to us, and we passed it on to the 3rd party.

We went down the hill past the railway station and yard, and noticed the huge base stores on our right. Here were stores of shells and explosives, dumps, accoutrements of all descriptions, packs trench implements, packs and hosts of other things. These are dumped there when from the line, carriage rifles etc., for repair. Further on we came to a place where 1st Austr. Light Horse were temporarily camped, also a detachment of Imperial Camel Corps. The road forms into a junction at this spot, we keep the one on the left. Road exceedingly dusty. Notice large groves of olive trees on our right, large valleys and undulating country on our left. We come to Rachael's tomb on side of the road. A large place for a tomb, and has a small tower. About another 2 miles brings us to the entrance to the city of Bethlehem. It is plainly built on a hill, and a direct fall straight from a wall and buildings on extreme left of the town. In places, one is reminded of a fortress.

We pulled up at a shop where every curio made in Bethlehem and Jerusalem are to be had. Owner states his prices are dead rock, but later bought things much cheaper at smaller and less 'classy' shops. With our assistant from the shop, we were shown the way to the Church of the Nativity. This appears to be built on the edge of a hill, for on the left of it, and fenced by a strong iron one, a deep valley lies. The chap we had did not know too much about English, but we were singularly fortunate in meeting a Corporal in charge of the guard at the place, who is a churchman and knows the history of Palestine and its old places to the letter. He very kindly consented to take us through and explain things. One has to stoop to get through the doorway, the entrance was made small on account of animals, such as Camels etc., (which seem to relish 'possies' inside) to check their admission. We are inside a lobby about 12ft wide and in length the entire width of the front of the building. To enter the church proper, we pass through another small entrance, over which is to be seen some very ancient writing. This has recently been translated by a visiting Austr. chaplain. It has some reference to the sanctity of the place. The 1st thing that strikes one is the size of the pillars which support the roof. They are of a sombre sort of aromatic colour from about 5-6 ft upwards, to the 5-6 ft level they are Amberish, we are told that pilgrims to the place during their worship, kiss these pillars hence their apparent cleanliness. On top of these pillars just level with the wall of the building, are small crosses cut into the stone and coloured black (small drawing of cross). They are the marks of the old Crusader of the 12th century. Beside the wall on the right side and behind the pillars mentioned, is a rock standing about 4 ft? in height, something like hexagon in shape and lined on the outside with alabaster. The whole place being built in shape of cross, this part representing the vertical lower part. (Small hand drawing of this cross).

We proceed to the end of this and mount some steps, and find ourselves in the area of several chapels, each owned by different sects as in the church of the Holy Sepulchre. At the rear of one and guarded off by a partition is a beautiful and very costly tomb. Of the worshippers, only the priest is allowed to enter and chants to the congregation from there. However, the style of there also gloriously beautiful enough in Eastern eyes, does not suit our taste, it resembles somewhat the royal tombs in old Cairo. In front and not far from it, we descend several steps, and find ourselves in a sort of cave. This is where the Manger lay in which our Lord was born. The Manger itself is now in Rome, this place belonging to the R.C.'s, and marble slab now marks the spot where the Manger was. At the rear, and worked in brass is a representation of the Star of Bethlehem, by this Star in the heavens, the wise men of the east were guided to this spot. For the 1st time I heard that by some means or another, this was really the cause of the beginning of the Crimean War. Over this part a special sentry was posted with fixed bayonet to protect the place. Overhead are numerous brass lamps, embedded with very precious stones. One is a present from a King Louis of France. In it a light is continually burning, fed by palm oil. The rubies and emeralds in this are very beautiful indeed.

We were next led to all sorts of weird places, tombs etc., on the same level, and underground, but all in rock. These were of prophets, saints and the rest. Niches in the alleyway which is dark as pitch, are decorated with beautiful paintings symbolical of or relating to, some incident in the deceased's life, for they are not far from the tombs they refer to. Most of them are protected by a thick, small mesh wire netting. Up till recently no outsider, altho' aware of the existence of a painting in that building on 'brass' canvas. It was shown us, a tapped for our ?ance. Our guide having a good deal of freedom in the place, found this himself, and is proud of the secret he keeps from the Arabs and the rest about the place, also the priests.

Another little thing which interested me very much was a tiny hole in the wall of rock, used by ancient guards over the Holy spot of Manger. Unknowingly we had passed through all these alleyways and passages, light only by tiny tapers which we carried to a spot right in front of the Star of Bethlehem and the Manger. Peeping through this tiny hole, about 6-8 inches through, we could observe the sentry walking up and down on his beat. Retracing our steps we were taken to the Chapel of St. John. This would be about the side of the middle of the Cross, a perfectly clean, white place, possessing one of the best pulpits I have seen. Walking through here were two English Officers being shown round by a priest, who spoke not a word of English. He just pointed things out to them, sometimes spoke in his own tongue, and drew their attention to pretty things. They paid rapt attention to him before us, but were in absolute ignorance as to what he was saying, or what he wished to infer.

We passed down a broad passageway on our way out, and in walls were hanging fine pictures, but the same trouble occurs here as at the Holy Sepulchre. All denominations in the Church own them and neither will undertake to look after them, consequently they are going to rack and ruin. Reached daylight and air once again, and made for the shop where we had left the Gharries, looking meantime into various places at men at work, making curious things. Purchased some. These people excel in ornaments made from Mother of Pearl shell, which comes mostly from the Red Sea and from northern parts of Australia. One of these chaps an old Jew, had a stock of all sorts of old weapons, flint locks, carbines and the rest, which he reckoned had a history, conquests etc. Bought none however. Making a few purchases back at old shop.

We jumped into the Gharries, and one of the drivers turning very sulky when we asked a little lad to jump up and show us round the town, in the bus we gave him nought for a little while. We pulled up at Rachael's tomb going back and had a look at it. Some took photos, and the old Battlefield of David and Goliath being plainly seen from this spot, photos of this were taken also. We drove back by the Hill of Evil Counsel, to the R.T.O.'s office and back to the stand by way which we walked when we first came to Jerusalem.

Had dinner at the Carlton Restaurant, the place of 'Don'ts'. The younger brother took a great fancy to my walking stick, a cane I purchased at Bombay. Reckoned he wanted to have it as a souvenir, and said he would give me a gold ring as one in return. Gave him the cane. These two brothers are refugees from Armenia and are shrewd heads. Great business chaps, gave me all tomato I cared for with the assurance that our meat was not Donk flesh. A vegetable hawker called at the door, while we were having the meal. Brought his old Donk right on to the footpath and unloaded his carrots and trombone things from baskets slung on either side of the animal. While operations were going on, the Donk dropped his head and ears and gazed very intently indeed at the notice board standing on the footpath against the restaurant re 'Carlton Donts'. Don't have your meals here, if you don't appreciate cleanliness. Don't patronize this place if you don't like good food and European dishes etc. Then underneath the menu, the Donk paid particular heed to this, and you could have sworn he was reading the whole thing, his nose about an inch from it and looking hard at it, his head gradually lowering as if reading line by line. Almost human and occupied all our attention. As usual and seemingly indispensable in the class of trade, were several Greek 'Eating houses'.

For the next two hours, I wandered from shop to shop, bargaining etc., but everything is frightfully dear in these parts. Went to a curio makers place and bought a small block of olive wood, he wanted 7 piastres for that, just in the rough and with bark on it. Walked to the station a goodish distance, starting from the Jaffa Gate, past the English Hospital. Dust along road enough to blind one especially when motor-lorries passed. Looked for a canteen near Station but no cool drinks or biscuits to be had. Filled up my leaky water bottle from tanks at Station, very warm. On our train were troops going on leave etc. Mostly Tommies, but in our truck was a young S.A. from Two Wells. We travelled to Ludd together. At canteen tent eat remainder of our fish and had a nice big cup of refreshing cocoa, and had cakes at Y.M.C.A. Nankivell met the Secretary, a Mr. Cameron, a Scotchman, but from S.A. He was in the Home Service at A.M.C. Base at old Exhibition Camp. He knew many chaps we had come in contact when in camp, particularly Skethaway. Being refused many times chances to join the A.I.F. he got his discharge, and determined to get away, joined the Y.M.C.A. and is doing good work at Ludd. Invited us all round to supper before train went. Meanwhile Nank and I set off to try and find the village of Ludd. Gave it up after walking for some time. However much closer we got, we found from all persons enquired of, that it was still 6 miles away. Came back to this supper however, and enjoyed it very much. As much tea and cocoa as we wanted, biscuits and hard cakes. Mr. C gave me a letter for his wife who resides in Lockleys.

Before supper I should have mentioned that we all attended his bi-weekly night service in the same marquee we slept in when going up the line. We Ossies were introduced to the Tommy audience. At the beginning, service took the form of song service. Nank sang a solo and was much appreciated, Clarky played the piano, (our rack for clothes on our previous visit), and preached a sermon. Charlie the ever diplomatic and careful did not appeal to me much, I trust those who did not know him quite as well, did.

Mr. C walked with us to the Station – a perfectly moonlight night. After waiting a long time, a string of trucks, some covered, others with high sides and open, and others like big meat vans rolled into the yard. We immediately mounted and started to settle down. Hear that the train is to run right through without any wait for trains coming in opposite direction. This is now a double line. However, after waiting for awhile for her to move off, we were told by guards to get out as our part was unlinked and had to remain. Narking after all our trouble in cleaning and sweeping with a small boot brush the chaff etc., and heaving it overboard. Missed the others in the commotion, and settled finally in one of the big iron cage trucks. As doors were all open, took preventative measures against rolling out in sleep, for I was tired enough. Swept with a bag, straw, bran, chaff and other rubbish likely to suffocate one when she moved along.

Our old L. & S.W. Railway moved eventually and plunged into the night. The fearful rumbling noise of my bus had no effect and I slept perfectly (for awhile). It wasn't long before someone was tugging at me, and requesting me to shift to another place as the blessed van had to be unlinked here. Found myself at Gaza again, and my word weren't the Tommies disturbed as myself, cursing and chewing raw potatoes a treat. But now the fun was to start as there was no other place available, bar the open high-sided trucks, which everybody had apparently dodged. Well I am a tryer, but when it came to sleeping in that truck I was totally beaten, for to be shaken, bumped, rolled and rocked more than that truck did us, I think is utterly impossible, Kinetic energy all ways. Sleep was out of the question. I have never been jerked about so much in all my life. There seemed to be 6 ins. to spare between the phalanges of the wheels and the inside edge of the rails. It was positively hurtful to be knocked against the sides of the iron truck. Add to that the sand coal dust and smoke from the engine, and it will be realized that travelling was not 1st class.

Arabs with watermelons

Nothing for it but to stand all night. It soon became very cold and damp, almost quite wet, with the very heavy dew, big drops of water were hanging to all parts of the truck, and ones sleeves were soon wet through if rails leaned upon (almost an impossible task).

I do not wonder now that it is possible to grow water-melons in the very middle of the desert, for we saw many large patches of the same in different parts. To make up for this I was privileged to see two of the largest stars I have ever seen. One was bigger than the other, but they attracted attention of all. There is something peculiar and fascinating about star light skies of the East (small hand drawing of stars). Hour after hour went by, every now and then passing through some small railway siding where everything looked quiet and deserted.

25th Thursday

In the very early hours we came to Rafa. Should have liked some more Rafa water-melons, 1½ hours more travel brought us to El-Arish. We had a better view of the wells and date palms this time. The sea looked absolutely glorious, for it was still grey morning. Some Tommies were enjoying a swim. Cocoa was brought from the Canteen and bought at a low price. Standing and balancing one's self all the time, like a man standing in a spring dray going over rough roads, soon got sick. However, having 120 miles still to go, we had to chew it. The distances are marked in Kilometres, and eagerly watched the numbers getting lower down. Now it started to get hot, and as the sand dried, so it began to blow all over the place, and the old engine did not improve matters in the least. I was doctor in charge of our truck, and removed coal and dust and sand from eyes a good many times. With ears full, eyes full and nostrils blocked, we were quite comfortable and happy. We were now passing through country we came through at night before. The 2ft-6in pipe which carries water from fresh water supply at Kantara could be plainly seen near the line these parts. Water pumped as far as Ludd. Wonderful scheme of course, is all filtered first. During this morning just at dawn, we noticed small trains of Camels, pack and mounted by Bedouins, waiting at the line for the train to pass. Here too we noticed a stray now and again picking his way amongst the dunes. Great desert wanderers these people.

Travelling in cattle trucks

Wailing Wall Jerusalem

Garden of Gethsemane - Russian temple

Church of St Anne Jerusalem - Well icy water

Absolom's tomb - old burial ground

Site of King Solomon's temple

Way to Wailing Place

Railway station at Jerusalem

Outside old Wall Jerusalem

Travelling in cattle trucks

Church of Nativity Bethlehem

End of journey Sgt Biggs

Front of station at Jerusalem

Donkey venison - Rabbi on left - Butcher on right

When about 10-12 miles from Kantara, I had the misfortune to lose my hat, the one that Sgt. Northey gave me at Mitcham the day I left. It was a good hat, too hot to have chin strap down, so a strong gust of wind blew it overboard. There were many other soldiers belongings on the side of the line, as well as many bales of compressed hay which had at various times fallen off the trucks. The traffic never held up betweens stations, so all these belongings will stay there for a generation at least. Worst luck, I had kept that little ditty, an old paper-seller had put into my hand at Manchester, in the band inside. Expect wire repairers of telegraph will someday pick it up. On one side of the line runs the tel-wires of the railway, and the other those connected with Jerusalem and the firing line proper, and are solely used as these communications. The sun seemed to get hotter now just to please me. Luckily had two handkerchiefs, rolled one up and placed it over my head, and enclosed it by making a capelin of the other.

Reached Kantara East at last, noticed the sea of canvas, different training camps, marquees, prison camps, stores and goodness knows what not. Took photos of Turkish prisoners not long arrived. A motley looking crowd poorly dressed and half starved looking, but chaps of big physique taking them all round. It is about 1½ miles to Canal from Station, and I thought for sure that I would have had a stroke. The heat was exceptional and we all had parcels to carry. Talk about perspiration, we were wet through and through. The atmosphere was very muggy. Shouldn't care to be in camp at Kantara with drifting sand and heat like that.

Came to pontoon bridge across the canal, and when ½ way across the sentry who noticed me without a hat kindly handed me a Tommy Topee, he seemed to have plenty, having raked them in as they float down. Made enquiries re our train for Suez. Had time for a snack of a description at the Aust. Camp Canteen near the Station. Most of the chaps were for going back to the boat and putting in an afternoons sleep and rest, but finding I could catch another train from Cairo to Suez at about 9 o'clock, I stayed behind to put the afternoon in at Ismailia.

Haye came with me, and Rundle went onto Moaska to see his friend Robinson attached to No. 2 a Stationary Hospital whom he had missed on way up. Hayes and I made for lake on the canal, went for an hours sail in a very nice yacht for 1/- each, boatman went about 5/- to start with. There were three other Australians there also, and we bought a few melons. Old boatman tried to prevent the lad from putting them on board. He reckoned we would make a mess, but we had our way in the end. Sailed right out into the lake, a fine stretch of water, and up to the English cruiser and mine layer laying at anchor, there were other large vessels there also waiting their turn to either proceed up or down the canal. All were painted camouflage. Next had a walk to the gardens, which are very beautiful indeed to take photos, 1st having a look through some shops in main business centre. Ismailia is a very pretty place, big high trees of all descriptions are planted along the avenues and in the gardens, and in the avenues up many, long clustering creepers are growing.

After walking for miles and ready to take photos, poor old Hayes found he had left his camera in the boat. That meant a walk all the way back again. In these gardens are many old relics from Cairo and other places. When we get back to the Signal Station pier, we found the boat out again, so meantime went for a swim in the baths no charge, only 2½ pt. for bathers and towel. A mixed bathing place for bathing done in the lake. We entered the gents dressing rooms, diving board etc. rigged up in gents enclosure. Along the beach are a good number of bathing and dressing houses, some rented by Officers, but mostly owned by French people who are much in evidence along places near the Canal. French run the show, altho' England has great interests in it. More than the French really. Plenty of them in bathing, as we found when we swam from gents dressing apartments. The water is fairly salty and buoyant. Enjoyed the swim very much and got rid of our Sinai dirt. We now noticed the N.Z. Hospital Ship which had just come in and took up moorings, a nice looking ship and well fitted up by all accounts. Too late for photos now. Hayes got his camera, we bought a fine big melon and ate it at Y.M.C.A. put in the rest of the evening, by looking round the native markets at the other end of the town. Bought melons (sweet etc). A very interesting hour and a half.

Caught our 9pm train and met Rundle and his friend at Moaska. Had a short nap in the train and arrived at Pt. Trewfik at 12.10am. There were also with us chaps from Alexandria and Cairo. We walked to the wharf near the Indian Hospital to our ships boat. Waited a long time for fellows that were missing, so had to leave them. Three Sisters on board who all this time howled about those left. Cpl. Hadison in charge of the boat, and he amused us by asking who shook the Matron's beer. It seems she had left a couple of bottles in her ice chest, and they had disappointed her by walking. Hear the 'KANOWNA' departed, and that we are likely to be staying here for some time yet. The Sisters think I am an Officer, not knowing me in the Topee. Had to take an oar and a pretty stiff long pull to the ship. Find that the Col. has gone to Jerusalem on finding we were able to get there soon after receipt of our telegram. He was not on board when it came, otherwise may have had our extension. Orderly Officer could not grant it, Capt. Southwood wished to go but was not given permission by authorities. Thus ends our trip to the Holy Land, it is pleasant to know that we were the first troops to get to Jerusalem on leave. Cost us roughly (just bare expenses the big sum of 8/-) for at R.P.O.'s office at Jerusalem we got a through ticket right to Pt. Tewfik. Different chaps state that they wished now they had tried to get through (of course). Slept soundly till Reveille.

26th Friday

Local leave only granted, and all leave goers to pull the boat ashore. Mitch and I intend visiting the fresh water canal, and having a look around there. First bought a big watermelon at Suez, and ate it between us on an old punt tied to the wharf on northern side of Suez.

Walked to the old Roman wall (on an old rubble hill) recently discovered, a very thick wall and in parts remnants of old rooms. By the way it is built I should say that at one time it was an old Castle. Then to the lock. Here Baffra were being washed and having a wallow. Cows were likewise having a dip. Walked along further to place where there are two huge tanks on a very high elevation. This is where this water from Cairo is filtered for use in the town. Entered a fruit garden and were given some good grapes, altho' not one half as delicious as those of S.A. Donohue from Mt. Barker has gone from Austr. Camp there, as camp is entirely deserted. Tracked back to Suez and put in remainder of evening buying small things and watching native markets.

Should have mentioned that at daybreak the party left on shore last night, J. Rundle amongst them, turned up in a launch. Put the night in on wheat bags on the wharf. Gave Rundle a melon bought at Ismailia. The party appreciated it during their experience. Had to catch 9pm. boat for ship so caught 8.31pm. train from Suez. Mitch nearly came to blows with an Egyptian re change he had given me over a small purchase I had made.

27th Saturday

Still no orders. On boat party for day, boat leaves ship at 11am, 2pm, and 6pm. Returns 12 noon, 3pm, and 9pm. At times especially in the morning we found it a good stiff long old pull for these life-boats are a dead weight. After getting rid of our passengers on leave, we invariably tied up to breakwater and had a swim except at 6pm. boat when we either walked round Tewfik, or had a swim inside the basin. Not a bad stunt this, and notice all of unit looking better, brown and fit i.e., those who had stayed on board during our absence, and had continued to do this work.

28th Sunday

Sunday. No service. Biggs the shark hunter caught a big female shark 11-6ins in length. There were three round the vessel. On post mortem, 22 young ones were discovered, and by appearances would soon have been living an independent life and away from such close confinement in different surroundings altogether. She strained the rope severely, and put up a lot of playing before finally passing in her cheque. Noticed the pilot fish swimming about. It had led the shark to a wrong sort of feed this time. Lugged it over promenade, and tumbled down companionway to aft of well deck. One of the Sisters present at P.M. said it was like a ---------- (*nothing written*).

29th Monday

In the evening the boatswain took some of us for a sail. A fair wind at times but occasionally dropped. Succeeded in bumping the cruiser 'TOPAZ' ? knots at a pinch, gave a chap in his bunk a scare, but pushed off easily. Tide very strong and finally had to pull ashore. Three of us walked about the esplanade in Tewfik until return trip.

30th Tuesday

Hear we may sail Sunday next. Native fisherman tied his boat at stern of ours, catches two 'gummies' (sharks). These are sold for meat, quite a small line used, and several hard smacks on head with heavy stick settles the shark. Our lost reinforcements taking exception to Capt. Southwood's remarks to them on previous day. He classed them as dirty, slovenly, and inefficient and consequently failure. These remarks unfair to some, as good honest workers amongst them. Most threaten to apply for transfer when next in Australia.

31st Wednesday

As boat party arranged for shell hunting expeditions a couple of days ago turned out a success, another arranged today to visit quarries at foot of ranges 5 or 6 miles away. I was one. S.Sgt. Gray in charge of boat. Started off with two of ships crew, baker and night steward, and reached there alright. Party divided, some walking along beach shell hunting, and others, myself included to the Quarries. Tremendous reefs of stone. French bosses and Egyptian labour. Stone loaded into trucks, of wooden structure and wooden buffers. The whole scheme is very antiquated. One pocket of stone resembles mixed cement and stone allowed to dry. On closer inspection found the pebbles to be fossils of shell- fish of some sort. Obtained a good sample of, and found embedded in the mass a tooth of a fish, (small drawing of tooth). This dislodged from the very top, we got there just after the blasting. The mountain a solid rock. Of what age must this fossil be? The big stone is taken in these trucks to crushes further down. Crushes of same pattern as those at Humm?cks Hill, but not so large. There loaded in very small trucks drawn by the tiniest engine I have ever seen, a proper toy. Runs on the narrowest gage railway I have known. A steep incline. Trucks parted ? on latter. Part gave poor old Arab as he (sitting on last truck of other), a good old bump. Nearly dislodged him for he was seated on top of the stone.

Walked to end of the pier and found the others waiting in the boat. The sea had come up very rough and as we could see besides the wind, the tide would be strongly against us. Somebody rung up Suez for a tug to assist us, not liking the look of the job ahead. Saw a small steamer approaching after a long wait, and hopes ran high. However, she tied to wharf, knowing nothing of us and intended going back next morning. Only a tiny village at the place with one or two houses tenanted by French bosses. So no hope of a sail. Several of us agitated for a move on, seeing no use in waiting. Eight oars were put out, and party arranged into two sections, to take rowing in relays of ¼ hour each. Talk about stiff, we were lifted all over the place, and if ever an absolute dead weight existed that boat was a sample. At the end of the first ½ hour we were not more than a chain away from where we started, (and had 6 miles to go). We struggled and wrestled with these adverse elements like madmen, and before long we found the job ahead was a call on all our combined strength and perseverance. We dare not lose a stroke between shifts, for we found the boat soon drifted back, so each man when his turn came sat near his man to be relieved, to take the oar immediately and without lose of a moment. This went on for 5 solid hours. L/Sgt. Chidgey lay in bottom of boat trampled on by everybody, seasick and done up. We kept a constant watch for any boat, tug or one sent from the ship as we were well over leave time. Being pitch dark, we had to simply guess our way by lights away in the harbour. Any other time, the ship has her lights on and is easily distinguishable from any other, but this time of course, they were not on. Going out we noticed the beacons on, either side of a rock reef just above water line then. We watched for these and this, and just as we thought we were quite safe, rose up and fairly bumped right on them. No damage and backed out, another mile to go to get round them, this at 11pm. Donawa now acted as 'look out', and it was laughable even then to see him leaning over nose as far as he could, gazing into water for more signs of rocks ahead, and trying to pick up the ship. Resembled a figurehead somewhat. Rowing a bit easier now. Deemed to be less wind and tide, sighted the ship, which all reckoned was 'good' now.

Came to gangway and everybody on board seemed to be ? The 'wind was up' amongst some of the heads. Now 12.10am. We find that a relief boat had been sent for us, had actually gone right to the pier we had left and had carried a light. The boat was sailed by Jimmie, the ships carpenter. They had arrived back at 11pm. However, the chaps were very good having prepared supper with coffee. Nothing was said to us about being late, too glad I think to see us back safe and sound. Hearing the reveille was to blow at 5.30am, in order to prepare the wards for patients now soon to arrive, we lost no time in turning in, meant about 2 ½ hrs sleep altogether. The two ships crew were excused also so everything ended happily, but if it ever came to choosing a consistent crew with grit, some good specimens could be picked from the chaps out in the boat this night.

AUGUST, 1918

1st Thursday
Reveille at 5am. Could really have done with a longer rest. Embarked 60 patients from 5.30pm from Egypt and Palestine, after preparing wards and proceeding into the basin. Patients coming in dribs and drabs from various hospitals.

2nd Friday
Completed embarkation with men from France. Came from Southampton in 'WANDILLA' to Havre in France, then overland by rail to Marseilles, thence by P. & O. Hospital Ship 'ASSAYE' to Alexandria, from there to us by rail. The Hospital train a white one, painted with the crescent on each carriage. Not nearly such a good train as the camouflage one we saw several times in Palestine, which was a gift by public subscription in England, a handsome affair. It seems that our delay was caused by the sinking by enemy submarine, one of the Castle Line of Hospital ships. She was to bring our patients who were ready for her in England. We had ample, ample time to have gone over there and get them ourselves. Patients state that they passed the 'WARILDA', Adelaide Steamships Coy. old boat, when on the 'ASSAYE'. The 'KANOWNA' took her patients. ('Warilda' *Hospital Ship was torpedoed and sank in English Channel with loss of 123 lives*).

3rd Saturday
Les Delgaris came on board previous evening with patients and slept here. Saw him next morning, and had a yarn re Egypt and our chance of transfer here. Hear that Max Dumas my old Mt. Barker friend is on board. Left at 10am. Mitch in hospital with bronchitis.

4th Sunday

In Red Sea. Phew!, the hot winds from the desert blow some. In the afternoon after a long time catching up, we pass a British Standard Hospital Ship. She looked odd, no masts, these being lowered and lying across her hatches. Only a low thin mast showing for use of wireless. Her funnel was no higher than about 4-5 ft, and at first we wondered where the smoke was coming from. A good bow and travelled at a good speed. Looked anything but a slapped together job.

5th Monday

A Royal Mail Packet Coy. Steamer, two funnels passed us at 8am. First time on record left behind. Chief Engineer grumbled a bit about it.
 Saw Mr. Scott, Lient. (BE) and belonging to Engineers. Volunteers to teach me Chemistry. Started tonight with Capt. Southwood in the laboratory.

6th Tuesday

Travelling slowly, heat too much for firemen. Mitch allowed up and out of hospital. Started Chemistry.

7th Wednesday

Passed Abu-ail 4pm, just after passing the two funneller 'ROYAL GEORGE', a fine big ship painted grey. Reached the straits, and find a remarkable change in temperature of water to Red Sea.

8th Thursday

Much cooler now and sea smooth. Thunder and rain. Three patients confined to cells for refusing light duties ordered by their M.O's.

9th Friday

Sth. Wester springing up and something like a bit of a toss on. Canvas taken down from Monkey Deck.

10th Saturday

Nothing doing, early hours in morning and late at night.

12th Monday

Staff Grey caught phosphorus in bath, examined it under microscope, found fish with head and feelers like a lobster and tail like the ordinary – very tiny.

13th Tuesday

Concert in the evening. Pens is appreciated with his 'Doreen' from the 'Sentimental Bloke'.

14th Wednesday

Bert Cuthbertson feeling unwell and struggling against it for days, at last faints away and put to hospital. Patients on look out for land.

15th Thursday

Arrive Colombo 11am. Leave for troops 2-7 pm. Mitch on piquet duty in the town not far from spot where we last did this work. Staff leave split 2-4.30 and 4.30 – 7pm. I was detailed to the gangway and assisted patients into the boats. Some were taken away in a steam launch. It was the fun of cork listening to the yabber and chitter and yelling of these boatmen to each other, the Water Police cuffing one occasionally. All were striving and straining themselves to be 1st at the bottom of the gangway.

On leave at 4.30pm. Chap whose boat we jumped in, refused to take the three of us, so promptly jumped in another boat at which he kicked up a fuss, and made off to reach the Water Police before we arrived. He tried to make out that our boatman induced us to jump from his boat into theirs. No such thing, and we had to give evidence. Very strict regarding these matters in Colombo.

Jumped in a Rick-sha a went out to Borella, a pretty little suburb about 3 ½ mile out. I prepared to go by tram, but Indian begged of me to let him take me while I was waiting for the car. Had beautiful drive through cinnamon gardens and Victoria Park. Was shown the Cinnamon tree, rubber and a plant that shrivels right up when just slightly touched. I will never forget that sunset, and the glorious shades that it cast over the road and amongst the trees. I have never seen tints like them. It seemed to be like a fairy- land. Bought two jars out there for 5d, so that I could make pickles and store them in these.

All on second leave supposed to report at G.O.H. at 7 o'clock. For the rest of the evening had to parade the streets picking up 'strays'. None found however, and I think most of us did all the shopping we desired. Bought cigars, crockery and handkerchief box. Met Mr. Saul on a boat starting out for the ship to take some flowers aboard. Gave them to me to take for him. No patients worse for liquor this time.

16th Friday

Embarked wireless patients from India and Mesopotamia at 10am, and sailed at midday. Saw lighthouse on southern point of Ceylon 8pm. One English sovereign worth 28/- each in Colombo, and had many offers at this price.
Big swell on, and as the huge waves dashed up against the harbour breakwater, it made a fine sight.

17th Saturday

Mitch had molar removed and sent off duty. Ptve. Sheehan a 'silenced' R.C. priest died in the early hours of the morning. Post mortem at 9am. I had to attend. My first, but, took it well. Carcinoma of small size found in oesophagus near epiglottis. Buried at sea and had to form one of funeral parade. R.C. priest Capt. Bossence performed ceremony.

19th Monday

Mitch starts op. theatre today in case Westy at any time falls sick.
Travelling at a very slow speed, lowest mileage on our record, bad coal.

21st Wednesday

Lumbar puncture for Cerebro Spinal fluid from Arnott E6. Patient suffering from T.B. Meningitis.

22nd Thursday

Passed very close to Cocos Island at 4pm. Cocos, one of the Keeling Group, a fair sized island. A good sea on today and with naked eye could plainly see the reef running almost parallel with the beach and just a little way out from it. The waves smashing into foam against it. Plenty of vegetation on the island, trees growing almost to water's edge. As we proceeded further, we saw a large bay or basin between Cocos and another island. This wholly protected by a coral reef up against which the sea was breaking at a distance of not more than 5 or 6 miles from us. With Nank's glasses very plain. Behind the reef, the water was as calm and still as could be and quite green in colour. Must be like those transparent pools we read of in Sth. Sea Island stories. More islands round about as we proceed further along. Just fancy that reef on a very rough day. Would be a sight to look upon. Beaches white and sandy. No sight of the 'EMDEN' this side of the islands. Could see no inhabitants or poles of the Wireless Station. Beautiful moonlight night.

23rd Friday

Sea calm, and weather getting quite cool. Chemistry going strong, with Lt. Scott til 10.30 every evening.

24th Saturday

Anxious to reach Fremantle so as to get news from home.

25th Sunday

Hear we are to reach Fremantle Wednesday the 28th. Ralphie's birthday. Many happy returns dear kid. (*younger brother*).

28th Wednesday

All on the lookout for land, and sighted Rottnest at 1pm. Got in at about 3.30 or 4pm, taken in by Pilot. Mail comes aboard. Say goodbye to Mjr. Nicholas, a fine fellow and very anxious to get his discharge, is a sheep grazier down Bunbury way, runs ? sheep per acre down there, keen on getting back to his place, has given me many tips worthy of note re starting on land first i.e., sheep grazing.
Four letters from Mother, one from Mrs. Mc Kinnon who rejects my offer re land. One from Crofty, now a Corporal in his old transport section, left Austr. on 26th last month, and another from young Giles. Fancy some home letters are missing. Wrote two to Mother and asked her permission to go on to Sydney this trip. All well at home.

29th Thursday

Still in port. Nobody granted leave. Jap war boat lying in stream near us. Everything quiet, left at 2pm, rain having delayed coaling operations. On going to laboratory discovered cigars and handkerchief box purchased at Colombo for father and Vere, stolen. This is most vexing, and feel deeply disappointed at not being able to send them home, where I know they would give pleasure for those they were intended for. Reported to Adjutant, he and Chief Officer making enquiries. Interviewed boatswain and he on look out. A few of crew working next the lab. early this morning. Ship leaves port at a good rate, seems like an express train when going like this near the wharf. Passed Leeuwin light at 11pm.

30th Friday

Regret not being able to get Mother's birthday present home in time. Sea very choppy and blowing hard, but fortunately right behind us. Should put up a record, 'KANOWNA' left Fremantle only last Sunday morning, stand a fair chance of giving her a go to Sydney.

31st Saturday
Many happy returns of the day dear Mother. May happiness be yours all the rest of your life. Still running with sea and strong wind behind us. Passed vessel going in opposite direction, she was plunging her nose deep in water. Arnott, Tasmanian guy passed away 5.10pm. tonight. Pay for staff cancelled.

SEPTEMBER, 1918

1st Sunday
Had a very busy day at ? this morning, and cleaning up test tubes this evening. Sea much calmer, wind practically dropped. Hear we are to arrive Melbourne early Wednesday. Arnott committed to the deep 1 pm.

2nd Monday
An iceberg certainly very close to ship judging by cold wind.
Capt. Southwood fixes me up for Sydney trip.

3rd Tuesday
Mitch consents to take present for Mother home for me. Rough boisterous and cold wind, these sudden changes in climatic conditions in various parts of the globe which we experience, give us nearly all colds. No luck in exhaustive enquiries re stolen articles. Afraid will have to give up all hope of ever tracing same now. To get same leave as Sydney men. Capt. expects a heavy blow during night and preparations made.

4th Wednesday
Arrived Melbourne daylight and went straight in when tide had turned. Missed Mr. Scott, cot cases having been disembarked early, left at 3pm. The S.A. boys all gone, feel properly lonely tonight. Vic, S.A, and Tasmanian patients all disembarked, only Queensland and N.S.W. remain. Pretty choppy outside Heads.

5th Thursday
Witness to the noise between Charley Smith and Clarke. Clarke cause of the worse, which I think served him rightly enough.

6th Friday
Sea pretty rough. Sterilizing most of time. Arrived off Heads at 2pm, and met by Pilot boat. Tossing about some, even after going through. A very windy day and huge breakers on the rocks, and on Manly Beach. Went to Woolloomooloo and discharged patients. Immediately afterwards were to go straight into dock, but having a mishap with one of tugs, knocking her propeller off and damaging our port propeller blades. Had to wait until morning now, troops on leave go off at 7.30pm. I am posted to gangway.

Note from Official Record AWM
The Pathological Laboratory was another department which did excellent work, and for the long voyage it is absolutely essential on a Hospital Ship. The occurrence of cases of cerebro-spinal meningitis, malignant tertian malaria, diphtheria etc., where the early diagnosis and the early segregation of patients is so important in itself, justifies this department. The scepticism from certain quarters as to the necessity of this department on a Hospital Ship is hard to explain, as on a long voyage where

the patients are cut off from all contact with land for weeks at a time, and serious operations and serious medical problems have to be faced, every aid that the Medical man in charge can have is only what is due to men being returned to their home after being on service for their country.

Note from diary Cpl. C.R. Mortimer

Right on the top was a sort of cubby house, part of which was used as a workshop for dental mechanics and the rest as a laboratory for the pathologist to wage war on various germs and microbes. The remainder of the space was occupied by a steam sterilizer, as a good pressure of steam was available, this sterilizer was the most efficient seen on active service to that date.

7th Saturday

Went into Mort's dock at Woolwich at 7am. Everything being ready from previous evening when prepared for us, lost no time. Different gate to docks in England. Scrapers washed growth off the sides and water receded. All were curious to have a look at our propeller, but bar a few gaps in it, not much repair was necessary. Simply filed off the edge, rounded it and sharpened. She is a perfect model. A long dock prettily situated, right in a hill and trees all round. Very long, built so for Austr. warships. Noticed the fish left in dock after pumping out. Pumps capable of lifting 460 tons per minute. Viewed the ship from all points. Made enquiries during day regarding places to visit, and how to see them etc. Were quickly pointed and let out at 5pm. A most interesting sight to see, flooding of docks. Proceeded past Cockatoo Is, where the destroyer 'ADELAIDE' was lying, having been recently launched, to Mc Ilwraith's splendid wharf at Millers Point. All had to leave the ship at 7pm owing to fumigation. Went with Sgt. Biggs to the city. He stayed at the 1st Hotel, I went to pictures for the evening.

8th Sunday

Back to ship to meet Prideaux, who was to be on guard duty today. Had promised him that I would stay at his place for a day or so. Missed him however. Had done his guard, and obtained leave to go home. Went over to Manly for the afternoon and strolled round the beach and parade. Visited the old spots and enquired for our friends there, but they had removed. A pleasant little trip in the ferry.

9th Monday

First thing paid a visit to Tourist Bureau for information re proposed trips, handed numerous bills, leaflets etc. Received my registered letter from Mother at P.O, and walked through Domain and past Cathedral to Art Gallery. Spent a very profitable time there and chose my favourites.

Came back to Anzac Buffet in Domain for lunch, and caught 2pm. boat at Circular Quay for the Lane Cove river trip. Passed Woolwich Dock again and various stopping places, all the way up to the 'Fig Tree'. Noted all the private swimming baths behind the sea wall at foot of the houses. It is really beautiful scenery up here. Houses seem to be built in all sorts of impossible places to get a view, and be in close proximity to harbour front. This land very dear, altho' quite rocky and good for nothing in places.

At 'Fig Tree' we change to motor-boat and proceed as far as 'Fairyland', a popular picnic ground in the summer, fare 1/3 return to Fig Tree. Sea tide reaches right up here, and owing to low water had to zig-zag a good deal. Walked with a couple of Tasmanian lads to look out at top of hill, and noted the wonderful expanse of country up a long and broad valley about N. West. Walked to Chatswood and caught train for Gordon, and visited the Swanson family. Expected, and were pleased to see me.

Went to Staff Gray's home at Roseville later on, but he had returned to ship to do piquet duty. Walk during afternoon was great and really pretty hills covered with gums, peppermint, and stringy. Returned to ship myself for the night.

10th Tuesday

Had intended doing the Hawkesbury trip today, but seeing young Price on my way back last night, and being asked to take Cpl. Griffith's place should he not come, on a trip by motor to French's Forest, Newport and other places round about as well as Church Point on the river, I accepted it. Caught 9am. boat to Manly with Hills and Ph? (Griffiths not going), and met Price and his Father on wharf there with their very fine motor-car.

Were at once driven to their house, a grand little place and overlooking the entire beach of Manly. There were introduced to the family, who kindly packed a very large hamper and placed in car. Started off, and made for French's Forest. Inspected houses built by voluntary workers out there. A splendid idea, they look well and substantially built. Came back to main road, pulled up and went into scrub hunting wild flowers, Waratahs etc. After travelling thro' very pretty country, roads stiff in some places, caught a glimpse of the ocean and found ourselves at Pittwater, proceeded to Newport pulled up at the lawn and had lunch from our hamper, which we found was filled with good things. Ham, turkey, apple pie etc. Inspected Mr. Price's summer house there, strolled along the beach, and afterwards went for a swim in the surf, which is excellent, only drawback being a strong back current, and a dangerous looking channel. Hosts would let us pay for nothing.

Then get ready and went to Church Point on the Hawkesbury. I liked this spot as well as any. A motor-boat filled with youngsters on their way back from school, called at the jetty. They are put off at different places where their homes happen to be. Could plainly see Lion Island from here. Many motor launches and fishing boats about. Land here for building sites a big price too. Being so close to Barenjoey, should liked to have seen it. Came back home via Pittwater, and followed the car-line all the way back along the sea-coast to Manly. Had a freshen up and a good tea. Price a very fine family. Caught steamer and reported to ship for duty, being my second guard stunt at 7.30pm.

11th Wednesday

Wrote letters all the morning and went on top to have a view of Darling Harbour. Although I got lost several times trying to find my way to the ship at night, it looks all very simple now. The well lit ferry-boats look fine at night as they ply to and fro' to every part of the harbour. Ship left at 1pm. Had a little trouble with a drunken sailor before leaving. Prideaux came on board this morning. I got his address. Sent telegram to Mitchell and walked to 'Lady Macquarie's Chair' near Woolloomooloo to watch 'KAROOLA' steam out. However, she had gone just before I got there. Later went to Roseville to pay promised visit to Staff Gray again. Had tea. Mrs. Gray a lady. Had a pleasant evening, thinking I was to stay all night, they had made preparations for me. However, later caught train to Chatswood and jumped in a tram for Willoughby, and arrived at Dad Prideaux where a goodly company had collected for the evening. Soon found I could make myself thoroughly at home and slept well.

12th Thursday

Old Dad, a girl staying at his place (his niece) and self, took all day harbour trip on 60 miles of beautiful harbour scenery for 2/6d. A guide on board to point out places of interest. Visited most of bays and coves, and have a permanent mental picture of all spots visited. Parramatta and Middle Harbour particularly good. Viewed at close range the 'BRISBANE', and Jap war ship. 'KANOWNA' which arrived in Sydney two days before us, still in port.

13th Friday

Caught 9.25am. train from Sydney to Mt. Victoria (6/- return). Mountains look fine from distance. At Mount find no motor to Jenola until 10am. tomorrow (day practically wasted)! Looked round at local sights, beautiful valleys, walked to Blackheath and out to Gavottes ? and Bridal Veil Falls, and Great Canyon. Met Mc Arthur family there, walked back with them to Blackheath and had tea with them. Stayed at Mrs. Phillips Boarding House, after enquiring from all motor people in Blackheath and Katoomba re probability of trip for full day to Jenolan, thereby allowing me to see Wentworth Falls tomorrow and Jenolan on Sunday, thereby saving a day. Nothing doing. A most up to-date and splendid boarding house.

14th Saturday

Walked part of way back to Mt. Victoria and a lift by Govt. Tourist Bureau cars for the rest. Saw my old friend the swaggy from the previous day, and threw him some cakes and buns. Paid my fare at Imperial 30/- return. A good car. Met party, who met with accident at Junction of Jenolan and Lithgow roads. Party were Shaw S.M. from Broken Hill. He had broken 'ulna', wife, shock and bruises, daughter broken leg, and another lady severe shaking and abrasions. Dr. in tourist cars just ahead in attendance, I assisted him with splints etc, and fixed as well as possible. Used my car to take to Lithgow hospital, and I followed in a Scripps-Booth owned and driven by the young postmistress nearby. Was glad to get to Lithgow, 9 miles out of our track, but made up for lost time. Ride itself to Jenolan worth the 30/-, simply wonderful. The great valley nearly all way in sight, a fascination. 36 miles from ? Vic. Put up at Caves ? Saw a significant Cave 2pm, inspection. Gen. Pan of French Commission arrived in afternoon. Walked in evening 1800 ft rise in 2 mile of road.

15th Sunday

First thing climbed right to Lucas Rocks. Trout feeding at 9am. Con-Arch, Devils Coach-house and Grand Arch once again, and before breakfast. Left Imperial Cave at 10am, at 1.15pm. left for Katoomba. Simply impossible to relate impressions re caves and other things, a huge task as I wasted no time in looking round. Spent hour or two at drivers house in Katoomba and slept at a boarding house, but before dark, walking out to Three Sisters and Echo Point.

16th Monday

Up at 6am, and walked to Leura. Heavy fog, could see nothing. Now set out for Wentworth. Rained heavily nearly all way. Sole of boot came off at Leura Baths, and caused great inconvenience and discomfort all way to Wentworth. Jamieson Valley completely obscured. Get to Wentworth in due time, but see no falls altho' right against them. 10.30am. train to Sydney, 3½ hrs wet in train. Glad of change into dry clothes for rest of afternoon at Prideaux. Caught 8pm. train for Melbourne. Report ship 1pm (beautiful country en route) took particular note at various places.
Evening leave granted. To sail tomorrow.

Diary 2.
Arrivals and Departures. 1918.

Arrived Fremantle	4th January 1918
Left " "	
Arrived Melbourne	10th January
Left " "	
Arrived Sydney	13th January
Left "	16th "
Arrived Melbourne	18th January
Left "	23rd "
Arrived Fremantle	28th January
Left "	29th "
Arrived Cape Town	13th February
Left "	16th "
Arrived Fremantle	3rd March
Left " "	
Arrived Melbourne	10th March
Ship gone to Sydney	
Left Melbourne	23rd "
Arrived Fremantle	29th March
Left "	30th "
Arrived Colombo	8th April
Left "	10th "
Arrived Pt. Tewfik	20th April
Left "	27th "
Arrived Colombo	8th May
Left "	9th "
Arrived Fremantle	20th May
Left " "	
Arrived Melbourne	26th May
Ship 1 ½ days in Sydney	
Left Melbourne	12th June
Arrived Fremantle	19th June (1 ½ days overdue)
Left "	20th "
Arrived Bombay	3rd July
Left "	7th "
Arrived Suez	18th July
Left "	3rd August
Arrived Colombo	15th August
Left "	16th "
Arrived Fremantle	28th August
Left "	29th "
Arrived Melbourne	4th September
Left " "	
Arrived Sydney	6th September

Diary Three

Dear Mother,

This is more like a letter-book than a diary, but I have written it so, that you may be the better able to get an idea of the surroundings and happenings of each of our days as they come round.

Not always being able to get the news through to you owing to censor etc., and not always having the time to tell everything even when I see you, I here record them that you may read at your leisure for I know they would interest you above all people, and this accounts for the detail of it all.

Your loving Son,
Rex

SEPTEMBER, 1918

17th Tuesday
Further leave from 4pm. till midnight. Smithy, Jim and self go along to Y.M.C.A. for tea. Having received a letter from Mr. Scott, Lt, telling me of his retention at No. 5 A.G.H. at St. Kilda Road, I afterwards go along to see him. Find him doing splendidly, and having new treatment for his leg. Seems comfortable, and is fortunate to have his S.A. friend Lt. Col. Catchlove in charge of the hospital. Delivered his French 75 shell cases to him. Remainder of evening put in with Jim and Smithy. Given my box of goodies from home by Jim, but no time to look inside yet, turned in about 12pm. having written to Mother.

18th Wednesday
Reveille 5.30am. (everybody yawning). Send telegram to Westlake in W.A. re ships departure, leave at 11.30am, but wait in offing for firemen who had not turned up at sailing time. Some were intoxicated and had difficulty in clamouring up the gangway, and getting from the motor-boat which brought them to foot landing, as a good sea on. Whilst waiting, take my box to No. 4 hold, and have a good ½ hours thorough enjoyment fossicking into things from my loved ones. Cake, chocolate, toffee, fruit of best quality, pyjamas and socks. Dear Mother has had a good hand in all this I can see. The cake an excellent one, and a present from Bobs for my birthday of last July 8th.
A nice fresh breeze and buoyant sea on reaching Heads.

19th Thursday
Somehow seems good to be at sea again. Understand the restless, roving spirit of seamen better nowadays. A good swell on. Troops allowed to occupy E5 and 6 as sleeping quarters again. Good-O. The 6 S.A.'s occupy same beds as last trip on portside E5. Began flag-wagging once again.

20th Friday

I love to hear the seemingly distant moaning of waves breaking of surf which is caused by ships bows churning the water. Great to stand on promenade and look over the white foam. Not a movement or vibration can be felt from the engines, but just a gentle dip and a pleasant roll largely from side to side, but only slight. The sea is azure blue, and to get a vision overhead of the life boats, and underneath the wall of steel, all rising up and coming down together, everything white-like, a phantom ship, and as far as the eye can reach on all sides, nothing but water, and yet here we are but a tiny white speck in comparison, heading to a point on the compass across this vast expanse of blue water. Coming aft, the ship certainly feels like some moving living thing, and the throb of the engines like a heartbeat, pulsating all over this portion distinctly felt. In evening held a little gathering to commemorate 8th July. Ham from the stewards, and all dainties from my loved ones, make a tidy and creditable spread. All S.A. boys of the 'clique' present.

21st Saturday

Half holiday for troops. Cricket and hockey on boat deck. Cool winds.

22nd Sunday

No duties today. Church parade 10.45am, evening service by Nankivel. Tells me he wishes a transfer from ship, having had nearly enough of this work at sea.

23rd Monday

Saw land early this morning and this evening, expect to arrive Fremantle early tomorrow. Whilst flag-wagging saw a very large shark make several grabs at brass instrument at end of log-line. On previous trip one swallowed this, but took it away with it, to show those at home. Resembles a fish as it rotates in the water. Pay to date.

24th Tuesday

On waking see Rottnest. Arrived Fremantle 7am, and tied to our usual berth. Plenty of dirty water coming into the stream from the Swan and a good flow. Must have had rains higher up. Same old Jap tub cruiser in port. Noticed the big coal hulk with masts just above water. Sunk near wharf by large coastal steamer backing away from wharf. Letter from home. Leave 11.30am – midnight. Went to yard, saw Uncles Charley and Alf. Hear of Aunt Graces illness. Rode Chas' bike and visited Bill Toms and presented with nice bag of choice apples and oranges. Saw Uncle Dave and spent evening with him at home. Aunt unwell from influenza, so could not take little trip to Pt. Walter etc. Went for ride on left side of breakwater near baths etc. 'WILTSHIRE' with returning troops on board, a monster. Hear of poor old Mr. Anderson Y.M.C.A. Sec's sudden death. Took up evening by relating few Egyptian and Palestine stories and events to Aunt and Uncle. They were keenly interested.

25th Wednesday

Left 8am. "WILTSHIRE' just ahead of us going east. Our course eagerly watched until rounding Rottnest, and we decide on Colombo.

26th Thursday

Water unbroken but a big side swell on. Rolling considerably as we are painting and cleaning up the Op. theatre, find it difficult to keep balance on the platform erected for the purpose, which sometimes all but topples over. Higher up on the ship, bigger the lurch from side to side. Passed a 5 masted schooner, a Yank trader. Warming up already. Capt. Southwood gives me pictorial of Blue Mountains.

Note from Official History of 'Karoola' by Lt .Col. T.G. Wilson

The performance of surgical operations on board ship offers very little difficulty, and during the 22 months I was O.C. I only remember about three days on which it would have been impossible to do an ordinary emergency operation, and I have operated in all sorts of weather. We averaged 60 to 70 operations between England to Australia each trip. The ordinary acute abdominal, and head operations, fractures, and amputations etc., but the bulk of the operations were for removal of foreign bodies.

Note from diary Cpl. C.R. Mortimer AWM

One of the original smoke rooms was equipped as an operating theatre, being roomy, well lit, and ventilated, and conveniently situated to minimize the effects of the ship's movements. As a result only on very few occasions weather conditions prevented surgeons from carrying out their duties. In convenient proximity to the operating theatre there was an X/Ray room, well equipped. The dentists surgery was close to the theatre, dental work for patients and staff well in view.

27th Friday

Euchre party hold their tournament on well deck. Flying fish numerous. Busy darning socks and mending torn clothing.

28th Saturday

Half holiday. Helped in E3 ward a bit. Party there decorating and arranging the ward for concert in the evening. The get up looks fine on completion. Concert met with unparallel success. Pens and Fredo took the floor. Port lights a novelty. Moving pictures during interval, Bill Holdup "Shellshock" the operator. Many amusing and humorous incidents. See Souvenir programme. Finishing Sis. Ronaynes book 'Quiz of nursing'.

29th Sunday

Church parade. Nank held service in evening. Now to begin renovating laboratory. Want to get down to Chemistry again as Capt. Southwood brought a good book by Remsen on board for me to work on.

30th Monday

Nothing especially doing. Said to have passed Cocos at 4am. Nearly finished the op. theatre job. O.C. pleased with same.

OCTOBER, 1918

1st Tuesday

Saw Capt. Southwood re getting hair cropped for treatment of scalp for dandruff. Mitch shaved my head. By no means adds to my appearance. Fully recompensed however by the curiosity of other members of the unit. Many uncomplimentary remarks passed, some are really funny. It does indeed make one look like a savage. Flock down in twos and threes to see the '9 days wonder'. Glad to give some amusement.

2nd Wednesday

'Wonder' still on. At breakfast parade and every other place by those whose curiosity not yet fully satisfied. Very muggy inside.

3rd Thursday
Having finished the theatre, now on the laboratory. Wish to get the painting done and dried before coaling operations at Colombo.

4th Friday
Passed a vessel at 9pm. going same direction as ourselves. Only the Port Starboard lights showing. Took some time to catch and pass her.

5th Saturday
Arrived Colombo 5am, rattling of the winches woke us. Hear that the steamer we passed was the 'PORT DARWIN', and that Sgt. Duncan and L/C. Freeman on board, two members recently transferred from the unit. She came in about 10am. Leave (after battling by O.C. with shore authorities) granted from 10am – 11pm. Went off in Military boat with a Capt. from the 'PT. DARWIN'. A decent chap. Told us that he thought a lot of the ability of our two ex members. Said that owing to Fever and Influenza in the town, none of his troops were to be allowed leave, so we were particularly fortunate. We had to take two measles cases from his ship, so he said he would send Duncan and Freeman over with them, so they may see their mates.

Mitch and I went to dealer for our promised motor-car trip to Kandy and his country residence. Made arrangements for two o'clock, so meantime posted letters at Y.M., hired a Rickshaw and had a ride to Galle Face, had a look through and back to town via Malay-town. Made several purchases. At shop no cars turned up, and the excuse was difficulty in obtaining tyres, as one new one was needed. Waited till 3, so made up our minds to go to Nogomba if any train. None till 5.15pm. however. Nothing left but to walk about. Went along breakwater. Mitch taken in over a ring properly. Splendid view of the harbour and ships, caught a rowing boat back and called on 'PT. DARWIN', but Freeman away somewhere and Duncan down below. After coming back went through Pettah library and gardens near Govt. House.

Remainder of evening after having tea, spent around the streets and shops. Mitch buys a tea set during afternoon. Arranged to have my breakages in set purchased last trip, made good. Sovs. bringing 30/- in silver now. Told by dealers that we could purchase as many opals as we wished in Austr, and a ready market would await them in Colombo. Met a good many troops on shore from the 'PT. DARWIN'. Some had swum ashore, others stowed in coal barges and water hulks, and got ashore. Their dress was very mixed and certainly untidy. One boy with a shirt over bathing trunks reaching no further than half way to his knees, another with old white shoes, shorts, no socks and leggings and so on. A guard sent out from the ship to hunt them up. Been on water 3 weeks and no leave since leaving Sydney. Pretty hard on them.

The O.C. & W.O. greatly worried over non appearance of Keys and Moss on board at 11.30, preparations are being made to leave at midnight. Not on board at 12.30am, but hear something wrong with engines, so we have to wait till morning. Walked on Galle Ocean parade, watched the breakers, saw the lights, and had a quiet sit down on seat to watch the waves before joining the ship.

6th Sunday
Nice sunny day. Yesterday it rained during morning, and last night simply poured in torrents. Heaviest shower I have seen. Good enough to keep away all day. Started off at 8am. Passed close to stern off the Port boat, and were loudly cheered by the boys. Freeman was standing amongst them. Would seem strange to him I daresay, seeing the lights of his old ship at sea and meeting us in Colombo. A coincidence. Their bugler

'bugled' to us and received a worthy reply. Keys and Moss to foot the carpet. Hear they would have had to come on to Suez by the other boat, had they been left behind. Lucky for them engines needed attention. Another patient isolated in E2 and meningitis suspected (from other ship also). Sunday services. A good many Catamarans at sea, as we come out. Value of rupee 1/6 at Colombo.

7th Monday
In the old trade route again, and passed several vessels today. Saw one resembling an oil tank towing another of the same kind. Water very smooth and unbroken. Wonderful to watch waves from bow roll out and curl round almost without a break. Can see our propellers distinctly. At night we leave a thick track of phosphorous. As waves roll over also, has an illuminating effect on water round about. Stars reflection on water as distinct as beacons. Signalling at 6pm, and passed Ninikoi. More than one island near it. A big lighthouse, with soft yellow light. Palms. No mountains. Large stacks of coal kept for traders requiring it.

8th Tuesday
Only found out last night that we have patients on board besides the measles cases from 'PT. DARWIN'. Housed in E1 ward with Messner, whose tonsils were removed. One is from the Naval Fort, and another from old 'SAPHIRE' an old British Cruiser in Colombo. There are 4 Tommy chaps all told, but have not had the chance to talk with them yet.

9th Wednesday
Lad suspected of CSM in E2, lumbar puncture today. A positive test at laboratory. Isolated, and orderly attendants ordered germicide for their throats etc. Poor lad, very stiff luck for him. Suffers a great deal of pain after anaesthetic. Passed very closely large Str. last night. Could plainly see her during lightning flashes.

10th Thursday
A splendid day again today, and a beautiful sea. Said by a fireman to be the best trip he had taken on the ship since coming this way. Agglutination of blood serum tests finished at the lab.

11th Friday
Passed Socotra today, about 100 miles long, and in sight for 8 hrs. Through glasses saw a sailing vessel evidently a Dhow trading there. Now in Gulf of Aden. Notice many sea birds fluttering over top of water and pursuing flying fish. A strange little bird absolutely unafraid alighted very near me on the ship. Resembles a shore bird and not unlike our ground larks in Austr.

12th Saturday
Saw land again towards evening. 36 hrs Socotra – Aden. Completed microscopic tests of serum during afternoon with Capt. Southwood.

13th Sunday
Passed Aden this morning, and further on came to two steamers bound there. One was a standard ship and only hull could be seen. At 5pm came up to Pirim and stopped by 'TOPAZE' (same as we saw in Suez last trip). Signalled to us and we went to her. A small

tug boat was with her, and evidently had something to do with her patrol work. When quite close, a message was signalled from the bridge in Sema 4. 'Please report yourself arrival at Suez. Sorry to have misled you!' A fine little packet sister to 'SAPPHIRE' age 14yrs and now 22 knots. Signal Station and lighthouse on our left. All round here on both sides, nothing but God-forsaken looking country.

14th Monday
Passed the 12 Apostles today. Hundreds of dolphins playing near the ship. Splendid wireless war news still continues. Huns still retreating in disorder and confusion, and a few weeks ago they were close to Paris and boasting of their achievements and making all sorts of threats. Palestine front going strong, 7,500 Turks captured, and our troops right up past Damascus now. Kaiser said to have abdicated. American and German peace notes being considered. Warmer today by a good deal. Expect to arrive sometime on Thursday. Staff Gray and I intend going to Aswan in Egypt if leave permits. Had some interesting chats with naval patient re his experiences on 'SAPHIRE' in the East Indian Fleet.

16th Wednesday
Still having beautiful weather. Trial by mock court of Alf Moore in the evening for breach of contract, in that he bet his hair being cropped if he ever appeared before the foot lights in concert. Tried and found guilty, and ordered to have it cut immediately (which was not done of course), as it is 6in. long in front. Would look an awful guy. War news still good. England and France insist that Germany hands over Kiel Canal, Heliogland and Rhine fortifications. All belligerents mistrust sincerity of G—s peace proposals.

17th Thursday
O.C. promises to do his best re leave, and railway passes to Aswan. Says he would like to go himself and asks if a week would suffice. Reading book by Stevens 'With Kitchener to Khartoum' in order to learn a little of the country we may visit. Off Sinai Peninsula during afternoon, and later can see both sides of Gulf of Suez. Passed a ship (a three mast sailer) on our left. Right in shore and with a big list. Looks like a wreck. Arrived Suez at 9pm, and anchored. 'Wires' (rumours) already afloat that we are to go through.

18th Friday
Our Tommy – Austr. patients taken off in tug this morning. No work today. Our Welsh officer friend, particularly of Sister Cooks, of Embarkation Office soon comes on board again. Rumours getting stronger. O.C. goes ashore. Later ordered to hand in brassards, looks like Mediterranean at least. All rumours substantiated when at last a tug and punt come alongside with our Canal lamp. Same is fixed and all ready to start at 5pm, now waiting orders from Signal Station. Mitch and I read messages. Everybody seems satisfied at the prospects now. One in hand equals 5 out of it. Lot of apparatus in connection with the search-light. This morning a large P. & O. Hospital Ship the 'EGYPT', (2 funnels) and later a French trooper carrying French troops from possessions, making about 20 in port.

At 6.30pm we follow the latter for the canal. Pt. Tewfik viewed from the top of dental surgery looks great at night. How in day time? Get many Coo-ees from people walking or sitting along the Parade. Drop down to low speed, only supposed to travel 4 knots p.h. Even then the wash along the banks is tremendous in places. Good moonlight night and see the banks distinctly. Our search-light, lights up very brilliantly both sides for a distance of 2-300 yards ahead. Notice stations en route and British camps close to canal. Lights on our starboard and red buoys on our port, leaving room for 1 ship comfortably.

See the trenches occupied by our troops during attack by Turks on Canal. Informed by Capt. Southwood of probability of proceeding to England. Arrange to go to Cornwall together in such case. Just before leaving Tewfik, the 'PORT DARWIN' arrives. Sorry not to have seen Freeman, as I wished to hand him one or two little things belonging to him left in the lab.

Where sand dunes are highest notice that edge of banks lined with stone, idea evident. Come to one of the lakes where canal is broader. Passed the French trooper here, but had to wait until she caught us again. Before going to bed, went up to forecastle head and had a look at the light. Shows up brilliantly both sides, box so large that a Egyptian is able to stand inside and tend it, generator driven by steam from our forward winch and current sent to another box of accumulators, thence by cable to light. 4 Egyptians accompany us on this job, and we carry their rowing boat on board. Supper with Harry the night steward.

19th Saturday

Travelling more like 10 miles per hour early this morning. Said to have passed Kantara between 4 and 4.30am. Hard cheese I missed it. The 'Froggy' still ahead. To break the wash, which is enormous at times, seeming to lift the water clean away from the bank as if by suction, and followed up by a surging torrent, is a bed of stone built much after the natural formation of the Basalt at Giants Causeway at Port Rush, N.Ireland (small Drawing). See one of the branches of the Nile, similar at Kantara last trip. Later see Pt. Said ahead and pass the Armenian Refugee Camp on right bank.

Came to ships basin and near us are 18 big ships and many more further up, all camouflaged. Standardized (2) all watering and coaling and some waiting to get through to Mediterranean. One torpedoed and undergoing repairs. Garden on our left, adds refreshing after otherwise dirty, coaly outlook. Dates look good. We find that at midday the 'KATOOMBA's Officers are on board, and there she lies, our sister ship, camouflaged and waiting amongst the rest of the troopers. What a strange meeting place in this corner of the globe. She was converted to a trooper only a short time ago, has been conveying American troops to France and we hear now that she is bound for Salonika. Recognize the old Chief Engineer who was on this vessel when I a passenger went to the west as a youngster. Have taken water and are to leave at 1am.

A lad from No.14 A.G.H. showed me the hospital buildings. Says the unit at 14 are doing O.K. Put the motorboat on board, and a French pilot starts us off. Pass the seaplane base on our right and the No. 14 comes more plainly into view, a large one storey building and covering a large area. Now come into full view of the 'KATOOMBA'. She looks grand, old Fred the boatswain at work I guess. They raise Mc. Mcs. House Flag to us and 'shake hands', and what a shouting from one vessel to the other. How the voices ring in this big basin. There are all the crew on forecastle and old Alf amongst, bawling out as loudly as the rest. A rough diamond old Alf. The other troopers must think we are mad, but do not know probably that these are old employees of the same Coy. way out in Austr, and that we are sister ships.

I have never seen so many vessels in such a small space. Over 40 large tramps alone, and talk about naval craft, Suez canal craft and the rest, there must be 80-100 large ships. Danes, Japs, Italian, French, Swedes, and best of all mostly British. B.I. boats carrying Indians and French, their colonial troops. Torpedo destroyers, light cruisers, mine layers, patrols, mine sweepers, belonging to England, France and Japan, and all mixed up. Makes one wonder how all can be accounted for and controlled. Many tramps are waiting on water and coal, and flying the flags for same. Note the prop gun on the 'KATOOMBA', and extra wireless installation. As far as ships are concerned you are left with the impression of old boats, new boats, tramps, and war craft, 2 funnels and twin screws, single funnel and single screwed, and all differently painted all nationalities and different owners.

The 'KATOOMBA' blows us no. 'Home Sweet Home' as she did on a previous occasion, when a neat looking passenger ship. Notice the buildings and streets and vast improvement on Suez. Note the British camp right in centre of town. See the Admiralty Buildings and many naval motor boats tied to the landing. Pass the Signal Station, a lofty tower with Semaphore signalling apparatus on top, also the Suez Canal Coys. buildings which are good-o. Come to another Hospital Ship on our right and find it the old 'DUNLUCE CASTLE', another surprise. By sight of her am reminded of the chap, one of our patients, who came off her at Cape Town when we went to meet her there. (All brassards signed by O.C. and ordered to be worn, and identification discs to be hung round neck). Guess the chaps on her do not forget the stir he caused on board over the starvation food!

As recorded in previous diary, had patients from her the second time, when she put them off at Alexandria. She followed us out of the harbour, through the breakwater and for some miles to sea, then sheared off and as some say for Lemnos to hospital there. We preceded by small craft through mine field and keeping in constant touch with her. Now in the old Mediterranean, an experience often longed for. One of the rules of the game in the Mediterranean is that we must carry a Spanish Officer (a Neutral). No safety of Hospital Ships guaranteed without. Came on board at Pt. Said at noon, cannot speak English, and elderly gentleman, so Pte. Toby who speaks several lingos, detailed to be his batman. (no good to me). Boats swing out at Pt. Said, and ready for emergency. Tonight reminds us of old times as Promenade lit up with kerosene lamps also a rule, and used in case explosion stops ship's generator. A beautiful night and expect to reach Alex. after 12 hours sail from Pt. Said.

Note from diary Cpl C.R.Mortimer AWM

When near a danger zone, the life boats would be swung out ready for instant lowering, hurricane lamps would be lit at dusk, and hung at various places in case the ship was mined or torpedoed, and the electric lights failed. We were given 'boat stations' generally about 4pm. The signal was 2 blasts of the ship's siren. First thing to be done was to get into a life belt, the next thing to fasten down all the port holes, then fasten up all water tight bulk heads, then get the life belt from under the cot patients pillow, and fasten it round him, then get him into a stretcher, and rush him on to the part of the promenade deck in front of the boat set aside for that ward. The O.C. would then go around and see if all instructions carried out. The Officer in charge of each boat would report to him as he passed by, the bugler would blow the dismissal and then we proceeded to take the patients back to their cots and get the poor nerve wrecked bits of humanity quietened down to normal again. Every time something happened the mental cases became very agitated and had be settled down.

Boat stations were at frequent intervals helping efficiency to the extent that wards could be emptied and occupants in their positions on deck in 7 minutes. There were times when most of the patients thought it was the real thing. If the boat kept up for 10 minutes after being mined or torpedoed, the boats would have been loaded and be clear of the ship.

20th Sunday

Woke up to find no trace of land. Here we are forming letter S's, circling round in our own length, and otherwise doing all sorts of fantastic manoeuvres. All the time preceded by a tug boat, and the one that came with us from Suez acting as a moving buoy and setting our course. Four patrol boats come to meet us and they seem to have something to do with us. One drops a buoy with a flag on it and we turn right round and pass it. Now see land in the distance and a few spires of Alexandria. This submarine problem baffled the Italian and French fleets in earlier part of war in the Mediterranean until

British took over laying of mine fields and protection of ports. A wonderful system this must be. By aid of glasses, can see a big war ship and Hospital Ship in port. Only 100 miles from Pt. Said, and at most 8 hrs run from there in normal times, now midday.

On morning parade, strict injunctions given re censorship of letters and Kings Regs read regarding mention, description or facts re any place left, or any destination bound for. Also told to treat our Spanish Officer with every respect, not to say anything detrimental to him or about his countrymen etc., to be careful in anything we said or did. He to leave us here, but same to apply to his successor when he comes on board.

Now come to another Hospital Ship at anchor and waiting to go out after we come in. The 'ASSAYE', the ship that brought our last patients from Marseilles. Used to carry Indian troops from India to England and vice-versa in peace times. A fine ship and about our own size. She lay inside the horseshoe of mines. We had but a very narrow passage to pass through. Notice a buoy (green) with words 'wreck' on it, just near our port, and salvage operations were being carried on, we could see lengths of shafting in bottom of punt, and further over again another wreck with decks awash. Pass breakwater and through its channel into harbour. Many vessels in and a good variety, naval etc. Mine layers 34 and 35 remind us of these craft at Liverpool. Pass by Sea-plane sheds on beach on our right. A battleship, destroyer, and P.& O. Hospital Ship the 'VALDIVA' a larger vessel 9800 tons.

On our left and towards sea shores is the 'Ras-el-Tin', Sultans old palace, and now used as Australian Hospital. Tie to 2 red buoys and towed by an old paddle tug. We stir up mud considerably and cause a stench. Just behind us is a large 2 funnel steamer, just lately raised from the bottom, having been under water for eight months. Sunk thro' an explosion in coal bunkers. Never think to look at her now, that she had been so, resembles a new ship. Very clean, with transport no. up, and wireless installed. Will soon be ready and completed for sea.

Leave to those not on duty from 6-10pm. Go ashore with a boat load in these fine sailing boats and have a look round. Mitch and I leave No. 6 gate and do the outskirts of the town, through it, and then back via esplanade to No. 6 gate. Post letter to Mother. See one or two Egyptian concert shows given in under canvas places. See native fish market. Town as bad as Manchester at night though. All lights shaded for fear of air raids.

21st Monday

Watering and coaling. Leave 10am-10pm. Smithy being off guard, he, Mitch and myself take a run on shore. First send a cable, and postages and a run in the tram from the terminus to the Nouzha Gardens. On the way out, very up to date and large buildings, some flats, but majority residences of wealthy Egyptians. A little further on, our car collides with a bag of flour on back of donkey. This knocks another off and catches in dog catcher of tram, and also knocks the chap down leading the donkey. The other bag is nearly hidden by dirt for it falls into a hole of dust. The donkey is quite unconcerned and begins to eat bamboo close by. The owner however, tries to make out his foot is crushed, and with much gesture, hand wagging and yabbering 'tells off' the car driver.

See banana plantation and many date palms, with their huge bunches of dates tied up and covered in bags. Arrive at the gardens and take a walk right through. A grand spot, and well laid out. Many tropical varieties of plants and all sorts in Egypt. Help ourselves to mandarins which are good. A small zoo there and Aust. bird and marsupial life represented.

On a trip back we overtake a Gharry, when suddenly the driver jumps out from his seat, leaps at the head of our tram car and tries to strangle the driver. Car stops and wrestle proceeds, ticket collector gets hold of assailants legs and coat and tries to drag him off.

With that he turns on the collector and a hand to hand combat takes place. Both receive pretty hard cracks till we stop them. But the collector had just received the last crack unfortunately, so not being content, he watched his opportunity and flew for the other fellow. It turned out tit for tat and both bled at the mouth a little. Anyhow the car started and both were obliged to give up, at least collector was. Fancy such a thing happening in King William Street. But such is eastern life. There had evidently been an old score of some sort.

In afternoon hired a Gharry and went for inspection of catacombs, 1st to Pompey's Pillar. A magnificent granite column of 5 pieces. Granite said to have come from the Soudan. Went under the earth and saw the Roman Wells and burial places, about 400 BC. On top and in another part, fresh Roman Baths and pillars are being excavated. The Sphinx, male and female are fine pieces of work in granite. The other is about 5 minutes drive from here and overlooking the sea. This is a wonderful place and takes time for inspection. Light by electric light underground. A great well with windows in the wall, admits of fresh air and ventilation. Note the rooms with tombs in walls like so many tiers, the sealing up of them with stone, the bones, skulls etc, of ancient Egyptians. Have a sample. Only small men, but large thick bones. Lower burial places inundated by rise of Nile. Note also the royal tombs, worth a good 1/- to see. Must buy books re history of these places. Remainder of evening spent at Casino (a good place with a peculiar name), and an Egyptian circus. The performers were really clever especially one little girl. 'Boss' a Jap.

Note from diary Cpl C.R. Mortimer AWM

The Hospital ship was along-side the dock, the coal being tipped into the bunkers through the side of the ship - a much cleaner way of doing it compared to handling the coal on deck. Coal trucks were shunted onto the dock close to the side of the ship, one side of the truck being let down to make the shovelling easier. Some natives shovelled the coal into baskets, and others carried it to the side of the boat, and tipped it into the shute leading into the bunkers. If a few coppers were thrown onto the wharf, the natives would cease work, and tumble over each other in eagerness to get the pennies. Occasionally, one would get away down to the end of the boat further from the coaling, and entertain with a song and dance in return for the threepenny bit thrown to him from time to time by those on board.

22nd Tuesday

Were entertained for awhile this morning by flight of sea-plane from its base. A very large machine. I am wondering when we will get away from here. We have finished watering and coaling. What is the delay? Seem to have plenty of time to spare anyhow. Ships Capt. gave instructions to Egyptian contractor this morning to put a rail on deck and enclose the matrons cabin, now to be used by a fresh Spanish Officer to come on board. This is a state cabin, with sitting room and bathroom. Not nearly good enough for this foreign gentleman, so same are to be redecorated etc., we hear. An absolute waste of money. This ship costs the Commonwealth Govt. a fine fortune I guess. 'But the taxpayer pays'. Being held up from time to time, the delay causes many expenses in one way and another, and does not make burden any lighter to a ship carrying no cargo or passengers. Mitch on guard-duty.

Smith and I walk to Museum, both it and the War Trophy Museum closed. Catch a car for Victoria. A very enjoyable ride along sea-coast. Note the many bathing houses at sand, and hear that it is a favourite bathing place. A fashionable line altogether for streets of large mansions passed all the way. Note the large and fashionable looking burial ground at Chatby. Many fine edifices erected there.

At Victoria we had a look through No. 17 British Gen. Hospital, formerly a College for English and Egyptians. A very large place and capable of holding 2,000 patients. Very few Austr. patients at present there, but otherwise crammed full of Tommies. Scores of tents erected outside in the sand and all full, over 1,000 patients, more expected and 500 arrived from the line while we were there. (hand drawing of layout). A.M.C. quarter being shifted, orderly room and all the rest of it for more marquees. V.A.D. nurses and Sisters here, great many V.D. in hospital. Egyptian orderlies do all the stretcher work, but Tommy A.M.C. a poor looking lot.

Have an enjoyable ride back to city, and all this a distance of 7 miles out for 1p.t. return. Smith went off to play Govt. officials (Egyptian) football at rear of Ras-el-Tin, and I had a look through the War Trophy Exhibition. Found it very interesting indeed, especially German propaganda, aeroplanes and old curiosities from Mosque at Gaza. Very interesting to note the most up to date weapons from Germans, Turks to the most obsolete, and antiquated by the Bedouins and Arabs. Noted the old finger post which I saw myself at Jerusalem. Believe more trophies to follow in about 3 wks, since successes past Damascus. At 6.30pm, went to Union Club and attended Masonic 2nd passing of Scottish Constitution. My first since leaving home. Much enjoyed myself. Made very welcome and met interesting folk. Had my leave extended to midnight for this purpose in company with three others from the ship. Our concert party pays a visit to 'H.S. VALDIVIA' to arrange to give a concert on board her.

23rd Wednesday

The old three together again. This time take a run out to Alex. from the tram junction, a distance of 7 miles (return p.t. 1). An English Veterinary Camp out there. Walked past Signal Station near the beach and old forts (evidently Turkish) to the Salt Works. A light railway runs out over the lake (Lake Mariut) and a train just having returned with a bagged load of salt and about to return for another, jumped on and took a run out. Well worth while and having the salt gathering explained to us, found it very interesting indeed, especially how the salt forms round the myriads of sticks, placed in the pools. Simply beautiful formations, similar to the white-pinkish formations of Jenolan caves. Came back and had a look through works. Salt is only crushed here, and exported in this state as much as 10,000 tons per month at seasons of the year. Had the whole system explained to us by son of the manager. Engines burn a sort of copra-coke. Makes good fuel.

Walked back, noticed a convoy of about 7 ships coming into the harbour. Also notice the 'DUNLUCE CASTLE' in again. Find she has taken a short trip to Jaffa. Came in previous evening. Go back to Museum and War Trophy Exhibition as others have not seen them, not forgetting the most distasteful and unpleasant 'perfume' ever experienced from the tanneries on way back. Skins laid out on footpath to dry. Abattoirs fine buildings not far distant.

In the city, hire a vehicle and take a pleasant drive down promenade way to swimming beaches, this at 6pm, when aristocracy usually come out from their houses and either parade or drive about the main and best streets. This place a most cosmopolitan one indeed. Egyptians, Greeks, Italians, French, Spanish, Maltese and Assyrians. Between 5-6pm. is the time to see them at their best. Have something to eat of a kind at Soldiers and Sailors Institute, and put in remainder of evening at Casino where the Xylophones take the attention of all. Very cleverly played – gent a genius.

Give Smithy a short ride by pick-a-back through town. The Tommies wonder what is the matter. Meet a naval chap on one of the trawlers, and get interesting facts re sunken ships and sweeping for mines from him. Seems to be a shortage of flour everywhere. Have seen a few fights and struggles for supply by natives at various bakeries, but none to surpass this morning. Two women had disagreed upon some flour handed over the picket fence in a basket. The way those women screeched, howled and yabbered to each other and to those nearby for support I shall never forget. From old men and women, down to the young girl with a baby on her shoulders, each and every one had a say, and after a struggle amongst them all for 1st serve over the fence. Empty baskets were thrown from time to time back amongst the crowd belonging to those who had thought to get quicker supply. Even the old women crushed, made ugly faces as they were squeezed, gowns over their heads and lace over their faces, were pulled off, and all the time everybody yabbering, yelling and shoving like mad. Will not forget it, altho' only one little incident from the eastern life.

Another large Hospital Ship came in but went out again before we could get its name. They seem to be busy and in a hurry, why not us? Met Cliff Taylor from H.Q. in Cairo. Came up for Col. Dawson to invite volunteers from the M.O's to go to Egypt and Palestine owing to shortage of doctors.

24th Thursday

Orders. No further leave will be granted to N.C.O's and men while ship is in port. So nothing doing all day. Were supposed to have sailed today. Having Red Crosses painted on Port and Starboard side of funnel. Whole ship has been washed and looks a bit whiter now. Welsh and Newcastle coal mixed 1-3, very dusty and makes a mess. Work in wards preparing. I to get X/ray room and Lab. up to ? An Egyptian diver is doing well by getting up coal dropped over the side while coaling. Fills his old boat, which must hold between 2 and 3 tons, everyday. Coal only about 8 pounds p.t., so does not matter much. He stays down as long as 2 hours at a stretch.

Owing to a fresh Admiralty order today, leave is granted the troops 6-10pm. Do not go ashore as I anticipate a sail round the harbour if moon comes up, as it did last. A good wind too. How rumours are flying again. The other Hospital Ship yesterday was the 'ASSAYE' again. We learn that she and the 'DUNLUCE CASTLE' have been busy bringing sick and starving refugees from Beirut, Assyrian Coast just north of Damascus. Naval order says we are to do likewise and sail at noon tomorrow. No bread here, one would have thought it better to have taken food to them. Many died on the other ships, some 20-25 each, deaths take place even while they lie in harbour. Must be more on account sickness they are bought down. Malaria and dysentery is playing havoc also with troops up there. One Austr. squadron out of 500 strong have only 50 left. Just as well 'Jacko' has the 'wind up' for us. Terrible news from Cape Town today. 500 dying daily from this new fever, called Spanish Fever and 1/5 of these Europeans. Seems to be traversing the whole Southern Empire.

25th Friday

A battalion of 80 men came on board this morning and got straight to work on painting everything white on the boat deck, including funnel and masts. A real phantom ship now. During the last three days the engines have been undergoing a touch-up in order to guarantee a speed of 16 knots if called on in submarine area. Got away at 12.30pm with Egyptian Pilot and led by the same boat as brought us in. Read of the terrible state of affairs regarding inhabitants in Beirut and refugees there. My word the old 'KAROOLA' has come to life again doing our 16.4 knots at 5pm. At 2pm, all wards stocked with medicine and mattresses, but owing to short voyage no covers on them or pillows. C3 prepared to date as these latter are shifted from there.

Working till 8pm, and expect to do long duty on way back. At 11pm, we are travelling even faster, and lab. shakes like a spring. Spanish Officers quarters completed and same old chap on board. Smithy and I spent remainder of evening studying a chapter from Staff Gray's book on Beirut. A splendid little treatise and fortunate to have it.

26th Saturday

At 11am, a storm threatening. Running into an inky black mass. Bridge awnings put up, and air vents turned round. Rain falls heavily and sea looks choppy. If this continues, our arrangements for putting patients on deck will be spoiled, as anticipating a big load, the decks are to be used, and mattresses and blankets etc., have been put out accordingly.

COPY OF CORP ORDER TODAY WHICH IS INTERESTING

Corps order no - No. 1 AHS 'KAROOLA, 1. DUTIES.
Orderly Officer, Lt. Crouch, Orderly Sister, Str. Richardson.
Orderly Sgt, S/Sgt. Gray.
Embarkation. Immediately on arrival of patients in the wards, or at 'Deck Sections' the N.C.O. in charge will obtain the following particulars:-

Regimental No. Rank. Name. Unit. Disability

If patients should be too ill to furnish these particulars, they should (with exception of disability) be obtained from identification discs. The disability should be obtained in all cases if at all possible. A foolscap sheet should be ruled ready for the purpose, so that there will no delay. These lists should be furnished to the Orderly Room immediately embarkation is complete. Should any cards be attached to the clothing of any patients on embarkation, these are not to be removed on any account, but are to be made secure so as to facilitate disembarkation at Alexandria.

Deaths

In the event a death occurring during the voyage, the ward N.C.O., or 'Deck Section' N.C.O. will at once remove the identification disc from the deceased soldier and send same (together with his pay book, will, monies, or any article of sentimental value) to the orderly room. All other belongings are to be clearly labelled with the man's Reg. No., Rank, Name and Unit, and handed over to Quarter-master for custody until return of the ship to Alexandria. At Sea.

A.R. Southwood.
Capt. And Adjutant.

At midday land is showing up clearly. Surprisingly high to any we saw on our trip to Jerusalem. Book says they are snow capped certain times of the year. We suddenly take a sudden turn in towards shore, and in about an hour or so come up close to trawlers and one or two middle sized steamers. Can now see houses on the hills, and a little later find the mountain sides scattered with villages. Without the glasses they resemble large rocks. The town is built on an Isthmus, facing due north. Can see electric cars about the streets, and all are surprised at the large and up to date buildings with red tiled roofs. Pvte. Toby's old home only 2 hours ride by train from here. The dark green olive trees, and mulberry and lighter bush, all in plenty, so I confess blending help to make this one of the prettiest places visited by the ship since I have been on her. At rear of town are the 'Mountains of Lebanon' and are very high. St. Georges Bay, named after the Patriarch is on the left.

A good substantial breakwater, and a good mooring place for ships, guarded by a chain of mines, thro' which we pass, and drop our big pick at 4.45pm. Several French Navel craft here. Sunset considered by some to be the loveliest they had witnessed. Certainly remarkable. Beautiful sight as sun sank over corner of Isthmus, leaving a peacock reflection on the bay and hills behind. Some fine houses and date palms in gardens. We are only a short distance away. Detailed to C1 pantry for return voyage. News come that we embark 750 patients at 7am, including 100 Indians. Reveille at 5.30am. Feel very glad now that I know something of ancient history of the town. 1912 census, 150,000 inhabitants. Old School of Faculty of Medicine and Law, studied by ancient Greeks and Romans 300B.C.

Proceeded to wharf through breakwater. Began embarking at 7.30am. All cot cases brought down by Ford Ambulances, and walking patient by lorries. Some of the chaps look really terribly ill. Am one of the stretcher party. A temporary companionway erected to working ally-way from wharf. Note the dray loads of bones on wharf, and odour not too good. Evidently food from ships cook houses thrown to hungry inhabitants. The French transport which proceeded us thro' Canal from Suez here, and discharged 1,000 troops (French). Hear that British and French and relief ships brought provisions and eased starving populace somewhat. Nevertheless women and children came off to the ship in boats, and begged for food, which when thrown to them, was fought for, and devoured as if by wolves. Even old scraps of bread falling into the sea water was dived and swam for, and greedily eaten by the boys. Most of the Syrian women and girls very good looking.

Toby went ashore with O.C. and given a short time to see some of his friends. All our patients from the Damascus front. They have had a hard time of it, living on bully beef and biscuits for weeks, and being utterly run down have become easy prey to Malaria and dysentery. Thousands still waiting transport. Patients include representatives of various English Regiments, Scotch, Austr., 1 N.Zealander, and Indians among them, a few Gurkhas, who are the nearest approach to Japs I have seen. A Turkish gunboat sunk in the harbour. Hear many stories told re the stunts in these parts, but generally considered by all to be the worst sight seen is the Damascus Turkish Hospital after its capture. Filth beyond description, and dead in wards and passages number scores. Turks have been in bad way and unable to bury their dead, so cremated by British. Damascus 94 miles from here. See Turk prisoners under French Gangers, shifting and tipping bones referred to into the sea.

British occupation only last Oct 1st. Hospitals numbering 3, in frightful state as yet, no medical attention and no medicines or drugs. Some clothing sent for sterilization in shocking, filthy state – infested with parasites of most disgusting and annoying kind. Left at 2pm. How pleased are patients with our white bread. Assist with bedding on decks, and boat promenade decks lined with them, no spare room. Duty till 10pm. At 9pm, one of funeral part of deceased 'Black Watch' soldier. A fine big fellow, 6ft 3" in height. Very ill when brought on board. Sad incidents these. Note the flashes to the north as last night, thought by patients to be a battery at work.

28th Monday

Patient on boat deck turned mental this morning. Am sent for to assist remove him to lower ward. Through the poor fellows wandering, learn something of his bitter experiences and terrible, crushing and unbearable living at the front. Only allowed to give all patients soft food. Such as milk diet etc. Passed a convoy of 9 ships today bound for Pt. Said. Hear we may disembark patients at Alexandria tonight. Suddenly we turn nearly right about at 4pm. Away in the distance are two torpedo craft, and anchored near them a very large kite balloon. Evidently on look out for subs. Engines stop and we hang about for 2 hours. A Hospital Ship the 'DUNLUCE' passed by us. A great sight. Red cross and green lights. Evidently waiting for her, for we start again. E1 patient died. Too late now to disembark, so to start early tomorrow. Different berth, about No. 20 gate.

29th Tuesday

All patients breakfast at 7am. Only a few ambulances available, so looks like a slow job. Tommy A.M.C. assist. On stretcher work again. Pretty difficult getting loaded stretchers from C1. to wharf. Lots of delay and fooling about, finish at 2pm, afterwards had to remove bedding from boat to promenade deck. Cleaned up wards and disposed of linen. 'ASSAYE' goes out at 3pm, bound below Beirut. Leave again at 4.30. Many fresh ships in port. A few of these trips and we will have had a strenuous time. Hear we may go to Tripoli. News says our troops have captured Aleppo, and have joined hands with the

Mesopotamian forces. Wilson's note and Western Front seem satisfactory. As soon as all duty finished and beds prepared, 30 of our own staff and crew go to bed with the old fever, Mitchell and Nankivell among them. All feeling quite ill, extended pains and looking very sick.

Note from diary Cpl. C.R.Mortimer AWM

Bandages were washed in laundry each trip when last lot of patients had disembarked. When dry they were placed in pillow slips and given a few minutes in the steam steriliser, and then stored until opportunity to have them rolled up, and put away according to width.

Some in twos with a bandage roller to each couple. The roller consisted of a small wooden frame with a piece of iron bent for a spindle, and handle. The roller would be fastened to a form and one orderly sit one side of the roller and turn the handle, and the other sat at the other end of the stool to let the bandage run between his fingers as it wound up on its spindle, this keeping the bandage spread out its full width and free from creases.

Sometimes they had races to see who could finish first, or which team could do most before lunch or before tea break etc.

30th Wednesday

To proceed only at 7 knots to give time for trawler to proceed to Tripoli and take soundings, as we the 1st big ship to enter close. Meantime to strike for Beirut for instructions. Just crawled along all day. Sea choppy. Started letter to Mother giving her account of the last trip. Red crosses on funnel enlarged at Alex. More ships staff and crew to hospital. O.C. not too good.

Capt. Southwood in bed and several Sisters. Arrived off Beirut at 7am, this morning. Met by Naval Officer in a trawler and received the megaphone message to proceed at once to Tripoli, lat. and longtde, at 6 ½ knots, his boat to proceed. Several large new ships in Beirut harbour. A French destroyer went in just after our arrival. A bonzer looking craft. A thick fog over St. Georges Bay. Passed Hospital Ship at 12.30am. this morning, probably the 'DUNLUCE'.

31st Thursday

While on parade, sea plane comes from Base, sails round the harbour and finally soars aloft. A good exhibition. Arrived at 3.30pm, and proceeded very cautiously. The old 'KAROOLA' picks her way and seems shy of new ground. Anchored. One or two other trawlers here. One comes alongside and gives our Skipper instructions. Her Skipper says only military folk here, the N.T.O. (Naval Transport Officer) away as Lient. on a trawler.

One or two N.C.O.'s go ashore in motor boat. The town looks O.K., but learn that real town of Tripoli further up a river which runs out here. A sailor took lead soundings each yard or two we proceeded. Anchored again in 5 ½ fathoms. Note the peculiar hills, and one in particular is the result of a volcanic disturbance. Note also the groves of trees lining the shore, the better houses on hill higher up, one demolished building on sea front, punctured with shell holes evidently result of naval bombardment. On hills are trees which are mulberry or figs, planted out as in an orchard, and many villages as at Beirut. Beautiful sunset and a perfect night. Another trawler Skipper says his drinking water supply is finished, and his crew drinking the boiler stuff. Request a replenished supply which will be acceded in the morning.

Wireless operator - Top of ship

Sports on ship

Sports on ship

Meal time on board ship

Group of ten on ship

As we gaze on this country so recently held by the Turks, wireless news comes thro' that Turkey has come to an Armistice and hostilities are to cease against allies. His day here is finished. First of staff to get the news, came direct from operator to O.C. then to me as I was working on Monkey Deck. News that Smyrna also captured by British, only 200 miles from Constantinople. As well for Turkey she is giving up sponge at 12.30pm. today. Tripoli is 40 miles from Beirut. The famous forests of cedars are only a few miles from here, between Tripoli and Baalbek. Would love to see them.

NOVEMBER, 1918

1st Friday

Up at first streak of grey, and everything got ready for embarkation at 7am. At 7.30 patients began to come off from shore, cot cases on an old barge 30-40 at a time, and walking cases in large rowing boats, sharp at both ends and both out of water. Staff down to half strength, so all stretcher work done by Egyptian Labour Corp. Heard earlier in the day that a German and Turkish Officer to come on board and Turkish sick prisoners. Patients comprise English and Scottish, many Indians, (including a few Ghurkhas) and Serbians. Some are from the furthest advanced Infantry in Palestine i.e. 7 miles north of Tripoli.

Could see the point at which the camp was, very near the coast. In due course the German and Turkish Officers arrive, and both are in a very low condition indeed. Embarkation finished 2pm, but Skipper judging his time to arrive Alexandria in daylight and early so as to disembark, decides to stay for the night.

At 5pm. at low tide find ourselves on the mud, but tugs assist us off. OC. sees to the change of dressings of German Officer in C2 ward. Amputation above right elbow, and ugly deep long wound at base of right scapula, and many abrasions and deep lacerations left hand, and wounds partially healed over abdomen. The two former were very bad and septic. He is a Flight Lieutenant and the story he tells the O.C. who speaks German, runs like this. 'He was reconnoitring over Aleppo on 19th Oct, when two British planes sighting him, set off and engaged him. Brought him to earth, machine badly damaged, himself shot thro' arm, (medical history sheet says tibia and fibula fractures). He lay in a helpless condition for some time, when a band of roving Bedouins attacked him, and one at four yards distance shot him, the bullet lodging in his right side beneath the shoulder, others assailed him with knives etc., the result being the lacerated wounds above mentioned. His right hand, altho' arm broken, was subjected to the awful, barbarous cruelty of the thumbs screw. Altho' only a lad of 23 and of big statue, and intelligent features, he certainly seems to have suffered much. Further states he lay for dead from 10am. to 5pm, when a band of Arabs more friendly, and seeing the gunshot wound in his side, removed the bullet with an ordinary dagger knife, making the terrible ghastly, yawning wound as it is now, and this without any anaesthetic. Of course turned septic for it was 8 days before he came under treatment of English Dr. Howls and pleads piteously to the Sister and O.C. as dressing is done, and small wonder poor wretch. Altho' his country our bitterest enemy, doers of deeds the world will never forget, one cannot help but be kind and humane to him in his unfortunate position. As for the Turk, he has Malaria and very sick indeed. Thinks he is going to die and mentions Allah several times. Both are very thankful for any consideration shown.

All patients are from the 74 C.C.S. late American School in Tripoli, and on the whole are very much better (condition) and not nearly so starved looking as our last lot. Hear myriads of oranges in orangies ashore, and just ripening. Am told they are as good as the Raffa of world fame.

Group of three on ship - Rex Sargent in middle

Group of one on ship

Group of five on ship

Group of six on ship - Rex Sargent second on left

Sports on ship

Sports on ship

2nd Saturday

Looking after the Officer prisoners today, and get on tip top with both. Find that with a little tact easy enough. The German however, has the Turk under his thumb, and Jacko gets very afraid at times. Leave punctually at 6am. The sweeper leaves too, but we leave her miles behind, and are travelling at a good rate. Have several yarns with the German, for altho' he speaks only a little English, make ourselves understood pretty well. Says war will last only 3 weeks longer. He has a sister, no parents, shows me his birthplace on map, and points the route he took from Berlin to Constantinople to Aleppo 3 weeks (all by rail), also said he went to Baiffa by rail, and from there to Constanza by ship. This on business in Black Sea. During the night Jacko woke him up by getting out of bed, as being hot he wished to get on promenade for a cooling. Night staff put him to bed again, and in doing so turned on the lights at which the German went for him. Told that he looked horribly fierce and cruel and requested that the lad strike him (Turk). I noticed this morning his irony towards the Turk. Only 23 and a real young blood and iron alright, he can frown, but is nice to me.

3rd Sunday

A large percentage of V.D. cases on board. Four Indian Officer patients (one an M.O.) not bad fellows, have seen a good deal of service, also have one English M.O. (Septic sores). Arrive Alexandria at midday, which is jolly good going. Disembarked and soon finished. Many fresh vessels in port. The old 'EMPIRE' is now a Hospital Ship. Painted white and green lines. Ptve. Roberts came from Hong Kong in this ship years ago, but good enough yet to do work. German thanked us as he went off. Leave to be granted us this evening, but after tea, all ordered to roll blankets etc., and store up ready to be exchanged from on shore. Evidently finished Syrian runs. Noticed a sea plane returning to base before tea. Went to Offing and anchored close to 'VALDIVIA'. O.C. and Spaniard obtain particulars from two prisoner Officers, so as to advise Germany and nearest relatives respectively.

4th Monday

Still messing about with mattresses and blankets. Leave from 5.30 – 10pm. Smith, Robbo and I went along to Casino. A change of programme, but same performers as last. Rumours re Austria's Armistice substantiated by latest bill in Y.M.C.A. Lloyd George in Paris and telegraphed news to Downing Street as definite. Coaling and watering up. Have no idea where bound for yet, but hear we are to sail Wednesday or Thursday.

5th Tuesday

Finished coaling, and native diver soon out with his boat and gear recovering the coal fallen overboard. Barges alongside to take bedding off and a gang of 20 Egyptians. Funnel being scraped and paint hammered off. The old 'KANOWNA' comes in, having been up Smyrna way, a little later the 'ASSAYE' comes in also, and both loaded with patients. The 'VALDIVIA' goes out, and is to follow the fleet sent to the Black Sea and act as their Hospital. Several Russian war vessels there, taken over by Germans, two are battleships and their capture will not long be delayed now that Dardanelles are open to British.

6th Wednesday

Mitch not having yet paid a visit to Victoria, we set out, first ringing up Mr. Mitchell at Mah-moudie Canal. Could not go out there as he was ill with Spanish flu. Coming back from Victoria got out at San Stefano, and walk along beach past bathing houses and swimming sheds to Ramleh Casino. A reef of rock runs along parallel with the beach, and against this the waves dash up and break. Only a very small piece beach, looks anything like inviting. From San Stefano came back on a different line via Schulz and Bulkeley. This is well worth the ride, passing by mansions and good gardens, some splendid. At Y.M.C.A. for latest war news. All oil trains through Austria from Romania held up and communication all seized, 20,000 tons food stuffs stopped. Germanys main route of supply. Witnessed a handsome hearse, 6 horses draped and grooms of Italians – funeral during afternoon.

7th Thursday

Arrangements having been made to play football against the Royal Welsh Fusiliers on their camp ground at Abekieh, Mortimer and I take a run out that way. Just as well it is mid-winter here, for it is a long way from Sidi Bishr tram station to the camp. Hear they are the best soccer team in Alexandria. Noticed 6 aeroplanes returning from a cruise and alighting out there. Welsh in good form and in training, our chaps unused to the sand, untrained and off ship lose by 3 pts only. Scores 8-5 points. This camp composed of 4/5 divisions and very large. Large Turkish prisoners camp at rear. Walked to beach and followed it back, past old Mosque. Tea Y.M. and pictures at Majestic. Afterwards had a look in a small Casino run by an American, but a very rough house indeed, so left and walked back to ship.

8th Friday

Still wondering when we are to get out of this, but nothing known yet. 'ASSAYE' comes in. She and 'DUNLUCE' busy and we doing nothing. 5 of us went for a sail round the harbour, 1½ hours for 2/6d. Visited old 'KANOWNA' and were shown over her. Several things exceeds us, but in main our ship much better fitted up and more roomy. Their cricket team on board us and playing on boat deck, as no arrangements could be made to secure ground shore. The Aust. ship 'WANDILLA' a British Hospital Ship near her. Looks fine, just came from Marseilles empty. Went ashore and just strolled about.

9th Saturday

Dear Father's birthday. Many, many happy returns of this day, and may this be the last under such conditions. Went out to Nouzah again, with Mortimer this time with the intention of taking photos, and afterwards walking along Mahmoudieh Canal to see Mr. Mitchell. Much enjoyed the stroll round the gardens again. A good band (Military) played during afternoon. Rather a long walk to Travers Asphalt Co. on canal, Mr. Mitchell's address, but very interesting. Found Mr. M up 1st time since sickness but still feeling groggy. Thunder and lightning most wonderful I have ever heard or seen. Bright as day nearly all the time. Pleased to see us. Caught tram back, Mort went picture card hunting and I went to Rosette Skating Rink to watch on.

German Peace delegates on their way to French lines by road, directed to interview Gen. Foch and others, looks hopeful. Fearful riots in German Navy, carrying red flag and movement spreading to dockyards in many places, also to Army for both join hands when army ordered to restore order.

10th Sunday

Old 'ASSAYE' in again yesterday. Went to St. Andrews Scotch Church with Mitch in the morning. Several other of our chaps there. Came back to ship for dinner, and the trio go for a sail. Went into all the docks and round the sailing ships this time. Had a look at the Naval ships, and a cargo boat recently torpedoed now undergoing repair. Got a surprise to see the Aust. ship 'CANBERRA' here, also the 'INDARRA' just coming in. Went round the 'mystery' ship, certainly looks an innocent harmless looking thing until one gets close up and then entirely different. Get a close view of the Standardised ship 'WAR ----' loading raw cotton for all she is worth. Go ashore again and have a look at Cairo Railway Station.

Not a patch on Cairo Station at Cairo. Hoped to go for a ride into the country for a little way, but no trains until 6pm. Hear from two A.M.C. from 'ASSAYE' that she has been running to Haifa 60 miles from Jaffa, and bringing troops from Damascus. Had many Austr. deaths, some dying whilst on their stretchers being brought on board. Before this work here, brought Chinese from Marseilles to Alexandra, to China. 'DUNLUCE' been going to Jaffa. 'ASSAYE' to go no up near Smyrna probably 'KANOWNA' trip at 'Fushi and ----where exchange of Turkish and British prisoners been taking place. Church to Methodist Military Church. Chaplain Roberts a splendid preachers text, 'out of darkness shall come light'. Singing an inspiration, fine music, good sermon, and church filled tightly. All much enjoyed.

11th Monday
Old 'DUNLUCE' comes to light again. Death from double pneumonia following 'Spanish fever' occurs amongst one of the stewards in hospital. Leave our berth between B.I. boat and Russian ship under British Admiralty at 4pm. for the wharf.

12th Tuesday
Have never felt so 'fed up' with things in general in all my life before. This infernal delay and waste of precious time makes one feel 'nervy', let us hope we get a wriggle on as soon as embarked. Started patients at 9am, and all sorts come on. Many English Officers, French ditto, and an Algerian Officer, belonging to French Army, Tommies and B.W. (British West Indiamen), and French private with their personnel of A.M.C. B.W.I. chaps speak English fluently. They tell me no other language is taught in their country, and are taught English from the cradle. Fine looking chaps, well built and intelligent. Only one Australian and he turns out to be old Peter Hamilton, of whom Cliff Taylor in H.Q. Cairo gave us a full account. Being a Scotchman and wishing to have his sick leave for 6 months in U.K. Taylor works the business for him, fortunately for him, as this a most unusual and unprecedented favour. We know him well, and of clearing hospital fame at Mitcham. A different fellow now altogether. Has had wonderful experiences in Palestine.

Get the latest re other chaps of our ken up there. Many Officers and men exchanged prisoners who came down by 'KANOWNA'. All complain bitterly of harsh and cruel treatment of Turks towards them. Funeral of deceased steward goes off after all patients on board. Hear now after many rumours all this time that we are to go to Marseilles and unload there. 'DUNLUCE' and 'EMPIRE' leave the port. Raining in torrents.

Omitted yesterday.
Last night Mitch and I went into the town to see if news confirmed re Armistice with Germany. (Brought by Pilot yesterday). All true, no demonstrations, but great rejoicing on board and a bit of jolarity.

13th Wednesday
News re Armistice seems too good to be true. One can scarcely realise it. Day of all days, a day prayed and yearned for. Note the terms which have been accepted by the Huns. Terribly drastic. With Kaiser and Crown Prince, and many other responsible heads abdicated, what a marvellous sudden humiliation for that great tyrannical power, which only a few months ago had planned what she would do with us after the war, and had decided our destiny. Riots in Germany seem to be spreading to revolution, nearly whole fleet affected. Now a fresh Naval Order comes to light. We are to go to England, but Naval and Military people here have to re-cable England stating Frenchmen on board, and already booked them for Marseilles. More delay, have to wait further instructions. Still nothing doing. The expenses of this ship must amount to a very great amount by time wasted. Could have gone to Marseilles and back, and been ready for another load by now. Fireman who died also of pneumonia last night, buried on shore this morning.

14th Thursday

Pompey's Pillar distinctly seen from the ship, 88ft high, 10ft radius at bottom, and 8ft on top (small drawing) of 5 pcs. granite and largest column blocks in the world. Got the oil now that we are to take the Frenchmen to Malta, disembark the West Indiamen here and more patients to fill the ship (as only 400 or so came on yesterday) to take their places. The French places to be taken at Malta by fresh Tommies. Patients come from No. 21 and 19 British at about lunch time. 'WARILDA' came in and took 'DUNLUCE' berth near us, from up Beirut way. All think we are going to get away at last when we move off at 4pm. When near many other ships near breakwater however, stop and drop anchor. The Chief Engineer and Purser on shore, looking up firemen. 6 of ours sick, so will have to wait until tomorrow. Just in nice time to get out of mine area before dark too. Sorry to lose our B.W.I. Discover more Algerian troops on board. French and they occupy nearly whole of E2. A Brig. Gen. Anderson among the new patients. A big 2 funnel, 4 mast ship lying close to us, came in today. Four of Aust. Coast largest ships in or near Alexandria now. 'KAROOLA', 'INDARRA', 'CANBERRA', 'WANDILLA', 'KATOOMBA', not forgetting the old 'EMPIRE' of E. & A. line.

15th Friday

Our motor brings back 2 firemen. We start off at 2pm, and by jove a different feeling in everybody. However, just outside the breakwater we touch bottom. Not much difficulty in getting off. People on bridge seem to be paying a good deal of attention. Stop again, and notice a motor boat racing from the harbour to us. Lower our gangway again and a Naval Officer comes on board, his business being to take away a patient with him. It appears owing to a clerical error, an Aust. was booked to go to England with us. At the last minute the mistake was discovered. They found him, but came aboard dressed in Scotty clothes. Daresay he was delighted at prospects of going to Blighty, otherwise he would have said something about it.

Poor beggar, if we had not been delayed yesterday for need of firemen, would have been safely away by now from motor boats or aeroplanes perhaps. Through wireless most likely put off at Malta. Sweepers working outside, but proceeded by, no tug now for the first time, so presume mine field opened a bit. Lookout rigged up to watch for floating mines. To receive orders at Gibraltar re destination in England. Spanish Officer an elderly, portly man with his wife on board. He in civil clothes. Both seem a happy couple.

16th Saturday

Nice quiet day. Patients on English rations. Food over from C1 pantry being saloon fare, is eagerly accepted by the men. Many Officers and men have stated that they have had no such meals for the past four years. Work looking up in the lab. French and Algerian fully satisfied. Thinking out a scheme for a little stay in England.

17th Sunday

Ship going good. 318 miles. Expect to reach Malta tomorrow morning. Make a suggestion to W.O. re sounding of ¼ and 5 min. bugle warnings. Westlake takes a photo of French and Algerians. In one of parcels which just reached the ship before departure for Officer patients, being sent to them while prisoners of war in Turkey, but sent back to Alexandria again since their repatriation, was a bottle of pepper. This given to me, and I keep this and bag in which enclosed as a memento.

18th Monday

At daybreak could see land ahead. At about 7 arrived with a large tramp steamer, off the Island and waited escort to the harbour. Followed immediately behind the sweeper. For several miles proceeded along the coast. Very showery, but nevertheless we able to see the land very clearly. Remember learning at school that this the most fertile country in the world. Looks doubtful at this time of the year at any rate. Draw in much nearer to the shore and pass the forts close against the entrance. Cliffs to the sea front, and sea has worn large tunnels in parts. Forts on both sides simply bristling with big guns and look formidable enough. On right hand side is a fine breakwater, joined to the mainland by steel bridge. We were all simply amazed at the picture after passing through a bit. Had been longing for a long time to see this place and having heard much about its terraces, were soon fully convinced. Noted the painting of a horse and hotler on both sides of cliffs.

See a Hospital Ship in front at anchor and as far as I could make out the name was 'KANARARA'. Turned into the naval base, and I believe every variety of naval boat under the sun was there. A submarine moved away from the berth we were to take, and having just been under repair, went out for a trial run. Interesting to watch. Berthed at Hamilton's Gun-mounting wharf. Our French and Armenian patients taken off by ambulance at 2pm, and Tommies take their places. Mostly men from Salonika, who have been waiting a long time for a boat home. Just ahead of us large guns were being taken out of a decoy ship, a small sailing vessel, by a huge crane and placed in a truck.

Supposed to sail at 4pm, but now find we are to sail at 7am. tomorrow. Col. ascertains from on shore that we may have leave from 7.30 – 11pm. Leave divided and I strike 9 -11p. Go ashore with Little, Rundle, take ferry for old 'Valetta'. Walk along street after inspecting one or two shops for lace, under Victoria Gate, and ascend those wonderful steps from terrace to terrace. The whole town one mass of stone seemingly. Passed St. Jeans Church and as far as Royal Opera House, a grand building and back to the Guard. Visited several shops and purchased various little mementos. Should love a roam round this charming place in daylight. As we descend the steps again, the lights of and around harbour present a grand spectacle. Go back a little early with intention of having a run round the docks, but somehow time goes all too quickly, and only have time to get on board.

Near us just on opposite side of our wharf is a large dry dock, and in it a big steamer recently torpedoed and undergoing repair, further down is another where a mine sweeper is having a cleanup, and on right of that a big destroyer in another dry dock. Submarines are down there, and I wished now I had gone down there as I first requested, for some of our boys take a stroll down and are shown all over a submarine of E Class. Near here is lying the M1, the largest English subs yet built, about 350ft long and carrying 12 – 15in guns. Seems hardly creditable, but same is a fact. Built especially for purpose of bombarding Constantinople, and only arrived just prior to Turkey giving in. Another large one nearby of same class. No leave to look over these of course. Sunset simply beautiful. Rained in torrents prior to 9pm.

19th Tuesday

Sunrise. Good-oh. Many shrill whistles blown from naval craft at about reveille. The Jap boats also in harbour seem brisk enough. Ahead and on our right side looking towards the dry docks, right up high are long regular buildings resembling Naval or Military barracks. The roofs against sky line. Leave at 7am and towed by paddle boats, one howls like a dog in pain and gives us a long drawn out farewell as she 'leaves go'. Did not take long to find out that the sea was choppy outside. Passed an oil tank-steamer coming in. Later wind comes up and a heavy head sea. Pitching a bit and takes some time to pass Gozo Island, one of the Malta Group. This island particularly known for its lace manufacture.

Hear for the 1st time that the gent in civvy clothes (a Spaniard) is not the Naval Officer, but a Spanish Ambassador from Salonika. He and his wife were travelling by English ship when torpedoed. Rescued and given permission to travel on any hospital ship bound for Spain. We drop him at Gibraltar, so that he may reach home. A little podgy chap with squinting sore eyes. Neither of the couple speak English. The dinkum Spanish Officer rarely shows his face but is a lively, sporty sort nevertheless. Sea nearly as rough as the Aust. Bight last trip.

20th Wednesday

Sea going down a bit. Fair amount of laboratory work. Have discussed a little trip thro' South of England with Capt. Southwood. Staff Gray also going to go down that way, and has been making enquiries from Tommy patients. Most of R.A.M.C. staff attached for the voyage, tending mental patients in E6.

21st Thursday

Algerian coast in sight most part of the day. Between 4 and 5 pm passed Algiers, but could not see the town, altho' only 15 miles off. Hills very high in background with a low long ridge running along the shore line. Through glasses could see 2 lighthouses and dwelling houses on the ridge. Most northerly part of Africa. Find amongst the patients a young Ceylonie, father an English planter in Ceylon. Came down from Smyrna by 'KNOWNA' 2½ yrs a prisoner in Turkey. His battalion gives option of going to England or returning home. He chose former, so as to see his father's relations in England. Promises to send me anything I require from Ceylon, when he gets back home.

22nd Friday

A perfect day. About noon sighted the coast of Spain and kept in view all the afternoon. Going a bit slow in order to reach Gibraltar at daybreak, 10 knots. Arrange with night staff to call us early, as anticipating our arrival during early hours while dark, wish to see the wonderful searchlights at Gib, we hear so much about. Had a yarn with another patient, a Burma boy from Rangoon. Very intelligent and well schooled in English. Recites some of his experience as prisoner in Turkey after surrender of British troops at Kut-al-amara's 5 month siege. Troops from Rangoon and various parts of India sent out as same Brigade to Basra and to Mesopotamia. He and Ceylonie are the two given permission to go to England. A few of our boys have applied to transfer in England on arrival. The lookout gave the alarm of wreckage on our port bow. Altered our course accordingly and went towards it. Passed it quite closely and found it to be an old timber, copper bottomed sailing vessel. All we could see was the keel and part of stern, and the shape of the bottom (small drawing). Altho' sea quite calm swell was breaking over submerged bow. Had evidently upset after torpedoing. Resumed our previous course again.

23rd Saturday

Only lights seen at reveille were a stationary one right ahead of us and a good way aft, and that of a ship which had been following all night. At daybreak found land on both sides, the coast of Morocco on our port. Very high, cragged and steep mountains lined the shore. Some room for mountaineering here. Caught up to and passed several vessels all bound for the one point. At 7am the old Rock came into view and a big massive, grey object it seemed. Remember well what taught at school re this immense fort, key to the Mediterranean. Could see other vessels approaching it from opposite direction, thro' Straits of Gibraltar, and four or five from our side. Heading a little to the east side of it, we turned and steamed pass the Signal Station, a place standing over top of many other large buildings below it.

A beautifully built breakwater runs across the harbour in two sections. Outside, this near where we were, two British light cruisers 'LUCE' and 'ADVENTURE'. A Yankee destroyer, also an old timer apparently. Dropped anchor and were soon met by a naval boat. Having a chance to come up on Monkey deck and use glasses, saw a grand sight. Naval craft of all sorts and sizes were here, inside and outside the breakwater. Myriads of masts and funnels, some going out and some in. Two submarines tied to another naval ship. Two other Yanks came in and went straight behind the breaker.

Skipper goes ashore at 8.45, and Spanish folk shortly after. Looking up at the rocks we are amazed at its immensity and height. One of our patients who has been thro' the forts points out different spots. Camouflaged guns can be seen on the very top and foot of Signal Station, and high above it again. Of course batteries cannot be seen, altho' if seen mountain would be found brisling with them. Sides all covered with a dark green brush growth. Note what appears to be an Ariel railway running to the top. Wireless Station, and terraces of stone, to the highest point. At the very foot is a well built, and clean looking town. Some very fine buildings in red brick and white stone work there. Looking north and much further the country looks O.K. Undulating and green. An isolated little township is there quite white and with a large tower in the middle. On our west is the town of Tang---- where the agreement was signed between England and Germany about 15 yrs ago, over the Agadir affair which nearly caused war. Also quite white, and a large tower. A three funnelled cruiser in harbour there. Note the green crops and well ploughed land about this part. The timbered hills behind make a good background. Notice one or two big gullies yawning towards us. A typical S.A. scene. Behind and south is Morocco, the straits are only a few miles wide. On 6 of the ridges, (their peaks really) are built square looking arrangements, which presumably have something to do with the fortification of Gib (small drawing). One mountain over that way particularly 1 of same colour as Table Mountain (a bluish manganese) goes straight up from the foot of it on ocean side, and sharply peaked.

A naval chap tells us that the 'KANOWNA' departed from here two days ago, so evidently her arrangement re Marseilles had been upset. Her chief steward and one of the Sisters put in hospital here with Spanish Influenza. Stiff luck for them. Pity we were not here yesterday, for since conditions of Armistice being effected, no less than 83 German subs gave themselves up under white flag. All these under escort, departed for England yesterday. Only hope we catch them up, or run across them somehow. Left at 12.30 and passed big 2 funnel steamer, port of registration Geneva. Had many alien passengers on board of men, women and children.

Many handkerchiefs were waved as we went by. Got into the Straits, passed one or two other vessels going out and left the town of Algiers on our left. Several big naval vessels in harbour. Country very steep and craggy near the shore, but looked more arable inland a bit, and clothed with timber. A few miles further and we came to the very North West point of Africa. Right on the very tip is a large lighthouse. Coast running from there south, does not appear so steep, in this vicinity at any rate. On our right we see another little town and above it on the side of the range, a regular, white wall in the form of a ring. Said to be a bull ring. Had heard of this previously.

Dark at a little after five, but do not forget that we are sailing over the water, in which the great battle of Trafalgar was fought and led by Nelson in the old 'Victory'. Received orders at Gib that we are to proceed to Southampton. Strange, for this is where the historic old 'Victory' now lies. At 9pm on going to bed just catch the rays of a lighthouse, so cannot be far from the Spanish coast yet.

24th Sunday
Passed a floating mine about 11am. 2–300 yards from the ship. Must have put wind up the Skipper, for a boat station was held at 4pm. Things a bit topsy-turvy and many things not arranged for, which causes the Skipper to become angry with those concerned in the negligence. Skipper informs W.O. late last night that we are now in very dangerous zone, many drifting mines about. In case of emergency, night staff to close water-tight doors in forward E wards in all haste, first thing. Arm amputation operation today.
A good following sea.

25th Monday
Real Blighty weather today and brings back memories of our last trip this way. Misty and drizzly. A good sea, but following us, and the old ship dips her nose and rushes forward on top of the big waves. Doing a good speed by these means. Very much puzzled to know whether I should apply now that I am in England, to transfer to a land unit, which may probably relieve some man who wishes to get back home. Gets me thinking properly. Only wished I could confer with loved ones at home re the matter. Entered Bay of Biscay this morning.

26th Tuesday
Still doing a jolly good speed. Run into a real Scotch fog and after a while ship slows down, and later stops to allow of mine sweepers being lowered overboard. Strange that they should have been left until so late. Cold enough towards evening. Ships whistle blows loudly at frequent intervals as warning to other ships of our proximity.

27th Wednesday
Arrived at Portland Bill at 4.30am this morning. Awake in time, but could only see a few lights through the mist. The bill is a sort of promontory ending sharp and steep. Has a prison there. The harbour has a large breakwater built entirely across it. On the left is Portland and on the right Weymouth Is, marvellous to think this is piece of the little country that owns so much. Mistress of the Seas and wealthy. Pilot comes aboard and we start off about 7. Country all along the coast looks good and much under crop. This is Dorset here, but shortly afterwards find ourselves opposite the Three Needles on corner of Isle of Wight.

This country beautiful and passing very close to the shore have a good chance to view it. Notice several pretty little villages, two of which are Peel and Ventnor on Sth Est. corner. A war ship with two assistants of a class I have never seen before went by and looked majestic enough. Turned the Isle and headed for Portsmouth. Noted the two funnel wreck. Pass thro' the camouflaged forts and submarine boom. See the old 'Victory' at Portsmouth. Going up the gulf leave Cowes on our left on the Isle. Any number of naval boats notably.

Went on up the gulf (Spithead). The scenery on either side was beautiful. Aeroplanes and seaplanes like as many flies were flying on top and closely round the ship. Many others were anchored, and we notice that the body is really a boat. One float (on left wing) reaches the water and thus balances it. For such glorious scenery in winter, what must it be like in summer. A large Naval Hospital (Netley) on the right. Passage only about ½ mile wide. Could see 4 funnel ship ahead and on arrival Southampton find it is the 'OLYMPIC'. A ship I have often longed to see. 'KANOWNA' lying just ahead of her. A great number of ships of all sizes here. Berth 4.30 and do not anticipate disembarkation, but all have a hurried tea, and train which has been waiting all day for us, backs into station and disembark at 5.30. Soon finish.

Prisoners from Turkey go by different train to London, and others to Liverpool where there is a special hospital for treatment of tropical diseases. See in paper of 100 odd German Subs in Scotland (Harwich) just lately surrendered, open to public exhibition. Hear cinema are showing same in town. Must try and see it.

29th Thursday
Finish cleaning the ship up and waiting reply from O.C. in London re leave, transfers etc. Night leave granted. Mitch and Smithy on guard. Westlake and I have a look round the town. Notice many lights now uncovered and exposed. Seems more cheerful than when last in England. Go over the 'OLYMPIC' together and have a thorough good look all over, even getting so far as right through the engine room, swimming baths, pantries, gallies, smokerooms, saloons, and state rooms. All over the decks, and noticed her large guns. Recently this ship for which two German subs were waiting – sank both of them in about 5 minutes, hitting one with a 6in shell and ramming the other. Went to Southampton West Stn and enquired trains for London. To have 2 days leave, 1 guard, and 7 days leave again – do me.

29th Friday
Ration books issued. At morning parade, told of O.C.'s efforts, and his success in obtaining free warrants for us in any part of U.K. To get a free trip to London, report at H.Q. and obtain leave passes and the warrant. All highly delighted at the prospects. To catch 11am train, except those on duty for the day.

Arrange with Staff Gray re trip to south with Capt. Southwood previously. All muster and proceed on L. & S.W. Railway, through Winchester. Pretty scenery all the way and see several pheasants strutting about in the fields. At Waterloo Stn met by a Sgt. from H.Q. who conducts us in marching order to Horseferry Rd. This seems as funny as a circus to us. Go down, up and through many strange streets until we come to the old familiar Westminster Bridge. Crossed over and pass the Houses of Parliament and then to H.Q. by back entrance. Here we were given a cup of coffee, sausage, roll and scone. Very acceptable. Handed in our pay books for leave passes to be made out.

Assembled by Capt. Southwood out in yard and told we had come abdominals as far as warrants were concerned. No free ones to be issued, but tickets at ½ pre-war rates. Not so bad anyhow. Change Aust. money etc. Mitch and Jimmy go off to see a pal in H.Q., and I to Anzac Buffet in Victoria Street. Had a snack and given tickets to Drury Lane. Go round to Shakespeare Hut our old camping place, but find all beds taken, try American Y.M.C.A., Aldwych ditto, Holborn and all same result. No beds to be had anywhere. Hotels alike are full up. Told never such a rush on accommodation.

30th Saturday
Walking about until 2am and pull into Aldwych again. Wait till 2.30a, and ascertaining that a bed booked up earlier is untaken, am given it. Got out at 7.30 or so and find a party is on foot to inspect Houses of Parliament (open Saturdays only). In due time go along with a fine gentlemanly guide. Proceed via Thames Embankment as far as Westminster Bridge by Big Ben, 22ft dial, noted for its wonderful accuracy (Greenwich set by it). Enter by door leading to reception chamber of the House of Lords the 'Guilded Hall'. Note the entrance door to this for the King, also the many beautiful paintings on the walls. Through passage into House of Commons, shown different members seats. Wonderful to think this is the room where such momentous questions have been and being discussed, during this national crisis. Many Americans about.

Walked back with the guide via Trafalgar Square and Fleet Street, and saw many fresh objects of interest. Guide encouraged questions and gladly answered everything to his utmost ability. A man who has taken a great interest in English history since a youngster, and his chief hobby. Names given to places, buildings etc., a by-word with us, but at import really as he knew their meanings and reason for so called. Back to Aldwych. Pay a visit to Somerset House, and start out for Chiswick to see Mother's cousin. On way to Temple Station, meet Capt. Southwood and make further arrangements re trip.

Arrive at Mrs Oswald-Jones house, but could make nobody hear. Two ladies call also, and I hear that she is ill and in bed. About to go, when one of the woman, who is her sister, advises me to stay until she gains admittance. Taken in at last. Mrs. Jones very pleased to see me and wanted all news of Mother, whom she adores by those beautiful letters she writes, and which I so well know. She and younger boy laid up, and find they have had rather a bad time. Her sister Mrs. White brought out some goodies and was preparing them. Had a long chat with Mrs. Jones and find her an intellectual and interesting woman. Mrs. White when asking how I managed re housing accommodation in London, and learning what I had experienced, asked me to go home with her as she kept a Hotel in London. Started off after hearing about Lt. Jones's doings in Egypt.

Arrive at the 'Lonsdale Residential Hotel, just near the British Museum . A bonny place. Am introduced to her house-mistress and son, who spread a ding-dong tea before us. Yarn far into the night beside a good warm fire and turn into a bed in a room all to myself. Quite a change these days. Rather a select Hotel I find, and patronized by the 'upper'.

DECEMBER, 1918

1st Sunday
Having slept like a brick, son of the mistress woke me early to catch train for Southampton. Had a good breakfast and found mistress up busying herself for me. Drizzling rain, caught 8.25am train at Waterloo. Sent wire to ship as train arrives at noon, and supposed to be on duty at 11.30am. Would very much liked to have been in London today as Gen. Foch, leader of Allied Armies and French President arrives from Paris and are to be given a public reception. A very quiet days guard and a windy one. Most chaps have a stroll round. Got a letter from Staff Gray re their movements. Get things together a bit in readiness for the trip.

A new experience for me today. Most of crew being on leave, and taking advantage of free warrants in England issued to them, the Chief Officer asked for volunteers among the staff to assist in moving the ship to new berth. I went to the bow and found it good fun, taking rope from winch, dragging lines etc. Some sailing. Berthed at Dolphins at entrance to Harland and Wolff's dry dock and next to a well known old Orient line Austr. trader.

2nd Monday
Finish guard at 11.30am, got ready and waited for a letter from Gray. Meantime, went ashore and had a yarn with Yankee soldiers on their way to France from leave in Blighty. Good chaps. Saw dozens of big guns captured from the Germans piled up on the wharf and in the sheds. Many were marked 'captured by the A.I.F.' All camouflaged. Came back to ship. Got the letter requesting me to meet Gray and Southwood at Salisbury noon tomorrow. Catch 2.30 train to Salisbury, buying a through ticket to Launceston. Country en route to Salisbury tip-top, would love to see it all in the summer. At Salisbury booked a cubicle at Y.M.C.A. After tea met another Aussie and had a stroll round, and I made enquiries of places to see prior arrival of train in the morning. A bit drizzly during the evening. Dark at 4pm. Walked out to Laverstock village for a stretcher.

3rd Tuesday

Slept like a brick and rose early. Went first to King George Hotel a place of quaint design, and historical because of the fact that past monarchs used to visit there. Old oak panelling, and same of gables. Down same street enter by old gate through wall of Close into the Sarum. Notice boards still to the effect that gates close at 8.30 or 10.30pm each evening. A very old custom. Soon notice the famous old Cathedral on large open ground, quite flat and with beautiful lawns all round. Spire does inspire one. Said to be the highest in England i.e. 400ft. Seems as sharp as a needle on top. The west side is adorned with statues and figures of Saints and Monarchs, but wind and rain has had a marked effect on some of them. Note the huge, massive oaken doors. When inside the visitor is awe stricken with that beautiful building. The massive columns are composed of several smaller and thinner ones to make a whole and each meets its beautiful arches at the roof. The cloister inside second widest in England. The Chancel lavishly decorated with marvellous carvings in oak and choir seats the same, the floor and walls decorated with old tablets to the memory of those gone before. Shown through the outside cloisters. Wonderful stonework, where old processional services held by clergy etc. In centre is an ancient burial ground with holes, small square one in the turf, exhibiting the tablets of those in whose memory they are placed. Shown into the Chapter House. This is most wonderful, every design on the walls is of different pattern. The roof resembles an umbrella, and arches its stays. The whole supported by a single column in the middle. The plaster marked in black makes it look like tiles, so very white and regular are they. The same is noticeable in various parts of the interior of the Cathedral. At the back of this in spacious gardens stands the Bishop's House, a fine old mansion. In one of the Chapels inside the Cathedral are the Australian colours and flags of various Aust. Battalions, also other of ancient regiments which have seen battle. The place warmed by heat conducted from large round, phalanged fire places in various parts of the building. Note the worshipping seats of distinguished persons, one resembling a bird cage. Made from parts of a tomb from an ancestor of the present owner from the other part of the building. Many costly and gorgeous tombs of ancient notorieties.

Getting ready for a service, so left and went for a walk into the country a couple of miles. Aeroplane flying about overhead. The old lanes are great. Make straight for the market place, for it is market day and sale begins at 10am. This is quite in the open and well bricked floor. Sheep, pigs, a few horses, vegetables, fish seemed to be the main centre of attraction. Plenty of old 'Farmer Giles' type about, and the good healthy complexions of men and women alike speaks well for the atmosphere of Wiltshire. Got my baggage at the Y.M.C.A. and strolled along to have a look at the Poultry Cross, a structure of the 16th century, where nothing but poultry was once sold. Many quaint, half timbered houses in Salisbury. (Cathedral 1220) so no wonder we can get a fair idea of an old English town.

Met the others at the Station. If time had permitted would like to have gone out to Salisbury Plains via Wilton, Denton and seen some of our Austr. camps. However, we boarded for Exeter @ 12.40pm. Southwood done up like a jolly roger. Travelled 3rd class, no Sam-Brown belt or stars on his tunic. Has books and information galore on places he intends to visit. Have a jolly little ride together and am tempted to go along with them. Find much room for admiration both for surrounding country and places passed through. One of which is Okehampton, built completed in a hollow and long way below the railway line, where I change trains for Launceston and leave the others. Arrive in the darkness 5.30pm, and find my way to the town first ascending a very steep hill. Look around shops till I find my way about, make a purchase of an ashtray and enquire of Trewarlet at Lezant, from a Mr. Geoke who offers all assistance possible and recommends old identities, students of Launceston history and all the rest of it. Learn that a Mr. A. Wise, councillor lives at Trewarlet 3½ miles out. Ascertain a Miss Sargent lives in Launceston. Put up at a family hotel, where the good old landlady promises me some Cornish pasties, two in the morning.

4th Wednesday

Well on the war path. Leave gear behind and after a look through the church of St. Mary Magdalene, set off for a walk to Lezant. Launceston by daylight is a very pretty place, some buildings are old and antiquated, but others such as banks etc., are quite modern. The church is a wonderful piece of architecture and as a guide book says, has few more excellent exterior decorations and designs in stone in England and none in Cornwall. Built of Devon Granite, it appears that a very wealthy man once living at Trecarrel Hill had this stone prepared in order to build a mansion for his son, but the youngster died, and the stone being given to the townspeople, this magnificent building was erected. Gained admittance after the service. All wood work of oak, pews etc. Has a large pipe organ. In room at back which is evidently used for meetings etc., is a large board hanging from the wall and in gilded type, expresses the eulogy of an old Noble and his wife, who so admire the Cornish people for giving men, material and money for the war waging at the time. In old English, spelling peculiar to us, and some of words now almost erased. In grave yard read some familiar names from head stones. On a path leading through I notice the very old head stones used as flags for a pavement, one of these dated 1678. See names of L?agman etc.

Soon put in direction of Lezant and altho' foggy and damp underfoot, enjoyed the walk very much. Met several people who all speak distinctly Cornish. A dialect of their own almost and reminds me of the Cornish people of Pirie and Moonta. On the outskirts of Lauceston some fine residences, but majority are quite modern. My book says Launceston (pronounced, Larnston here) is the most oriental looking place in Cornwall. Went over the old Norman Castle ruins, from tower a panoramic view of Launceston is obtained. Portions of wall still standing, once entirely round it. Supposed to be the 'Castle Terrible' mentioned in 'Morte-d'Arthur'. Church and tower of St. Stephens plainly seen from here looking about East. The country to Trewarlet Crossing where an old smithy shop stands and cottage in which farm labourer of Trewarlet now lives, is beautiful indeed. Have never seen so many hedges and woods are plentiful. What a place in Spring or Summer this must be! An old fashioned pump over a very old wall yields good sparkling water. Had a good drink and I know father would have enjoyed the same.

Now walked down the main road to Lezant and either side are planted oaks, ash, beech and chestnut trees, the same forming a beautiful avenue. Came to a prosperous looking farm house on the right, with a large courtyard, and many thatched roofed sheds on each side. See a farmer coming from the back door, jump into a gig which is waiting and come towards the gate leading to the road. Open gate for him. Asks me where I am going. Ask him if this is Trewarlet. Replies in the affirmative and says he is going via Lezant to a mill to get flour. Tell him I am going that way, and asks me to jump up, first asking me if I should like to stay the night at his place and asks his wife in turn and makes the arrangement. Right in my hands. Tells me his father owned Trewarlet, his grandfather before that and a gent by the name of Sargent before him again. Cannot think of anybody who would know them now living. Tells me of what he knows of the Doctors Sargent, and that one of them still comes to this parish fishing and shooting every season.

Leaving him at the Church to wait his return, intend enquiring for two old ladies of whom I was told in Launceston and who have lived here all their lives, and keep a little shop. However, see the old head stones in graveyard first and find Sargent and Pearses names there, some going back as far as 1713. Have a look through the church which is a splendid and well kept place. The old clock rings out the ¼, ½, ¾, and hour and sound really very quaint. Seek out this little shop and ask the young woman serving about any old folk who may have lived here many years. Says 'Yes'. One in the very next room would be very pleased to see you! Invites me in and find the dear old lady Miss Uren? by name, ailing a little. After a little whimpering asks who I am. Tell her as much history as I know and she is delighted. Says that her sister could have told me all about them had she been alive, seems she died 12 months ago, and poor old soul whimpers again at recollection of deceased. Says I look like a Sargent, but should have more curly hair, as all of them were noted for that. Have heard Aunts say same re grandfather Amos. Does not yet know I am from Austr., but says there was one boy she recollected who went to the Colonies. The best of them all she said. Surprised to hear that I am his grandson. Then tells me of John, Grandfathers nephew, the finest and most handsome man of the parish, and like his father John in that respect. Must have been gay days at Trewarlet, for she tells me of the hunts, red coats etc., but adds that the brewery which Great Grandfather John started spelt the ruin of the family. Of course have heard Aunts mention the brewery and grandfather Amos, eldest son seems to be only one who escaped and did good for himself. Johns father's cousin went abroad, visited Australia and has not been seen since I believe. An unhappy page in this branch of the family which I believe was wealthy and affluent in those days. Feel a bit at sea, as she mentions so many names unknown to me.

Wish her goodnight and promise to return before I leave the district. Mr. Wise, my Trewarlet friend comes along and I accompany him home. Road hilly, but having a good horse, soon reach the farm, unharness and introduced to his family, Mrs. and a daughter of 12, also the maid. Make a hearty meal, and sit over a good fire, trusting to see round in the morning. Chat away, but being early birds, turn in and shown to a room upstairs. Struck at once by the huge, massive cedar bed, a double one, with drapings. Too jolly soft for me, not used to it these days, almost buried in a hole, mattress, springs etc., being so soft, but after while fall into a jolly good sleep, after ensuring myself that they wake me first thing to see the cows being brought in and milked. Am anxious to get an idea of farm life in England, and how farmers go about the jobs.

5th Thursday

Mr. W did not wake me thinking I was tired and should appreciate a good 'rest'. Thanks for their thoughtfulness, but preferred to be up all the same. However, early enough to get breakfast between 7.30-8, and afterwards went along over the fields with Mr. W to collect rabbits in the traps set for them, gins as called them. Didn't take long to get damp feet. Great fun climbing over the fences, which are made of a mound of earth with hedge on top. Inspect his potatoes and turnip crop. Come to the field where his gins are set. The dog shies clear, and goes off with his tail between his legs, having been caught in them before. Marvellous Mr. Wise knows their whereabouts, so completely and cunningly hidden from poor bunny. As for myself, I keep constantly putting my foot in one and setting it off. Caught 5 bunnies and a big rat in another. Search the fields for fresh places to set other traps, go through gates, the hinges of which are marked S.S., being initials of Sargent. Sargent of old days, the gate posts are blocks of granite. Tells me the extent of Trewarlet is 190 acres, a fair size farm in England, and keeps 3 or 4 men employed all the year round. Mr. Wise says he will take the day off with me, and have a shoot for the rest of the morning.

Come back to the house, find more hinges marked S.S. on doors of pigsty's, and am shown the old oak, beech and ash tree in front of the house which one of the Sargents had planted. The old road to village used to be between these and the house, still see the old track, the back of the house faces the present road. With two double barrelled guns go down to a river, and work along hedges through woods and furze. See two pheasants, male and female, the latter is fairly close, but missed bringing it down, the other too far off, a fine bird tho'. I knock down a rabbit which our water spaniel hunts out. An excellent dog this and kept especially for hunting. Lays the game at ones feet etc., and works like mad.

Come back to owner, after this novel piece of enjoyment. Inspect his Devonshire cows, which are housed at this time of the year and fed on mangles and many mixtures. Also see the old Brewery. Has been repaired in places, but the old boiler place not so, but walls still standing, basement of stone and ? made from chipped slate, lime etc. Most of old building and sheds on the farm built of this. Hear that old copper gear etc., from brewery sold at a sale from here by Mr. W's father not so very long ago. At the rear of the house is an old fashioned pump, find the water very good indeed. The front of the house is tiled with slate, after weatherboard fashion. Very interesting to watch Mr. Wise grinding corn for the cows, for whose milk he gets 2/3d per gallon, which he reckons is a great price, pre-war only 8d. The corn grinding is done in a round shed, where horses used to work after the style of our old chaff cutter in Austr. Done by petrol engine now in this place.

Being advised to go and see Miss Eliza Husband of Trecarrel Mill who would be more likely to know anything re the Sargents, we set off, and start on the main road by way of the Trewarlet Cross, down to a valley and up a hill again. At the bottom of the valley is a creek and near it a little cottage. Mr. Wise says that tho' now empty, people lived there but a few years ago. Told it is labourers of Bottonet, this name had no significance just then. Went into a wood and hunted for Chestnuts, but found that wood-pigeons, partridges and pheasants had got most. However, found a few which had begun to sprout. Came to the little village of Trebullet. Mr. Wise says that some of the Sargents being devout Wesleyans and connected with the chapel here, were buried in the graveyard round it. Had a look round, and the name of Sargent and Pearse conspicuous enough. Hear from an old lady who greets Mr. Wise that Miss Husband may have gone to a wedding, anyhow in case she should be home.

Walk past the old Smithy shop and down a very steep incline to Dobbin's Cott. Looking straight across and in the distance, the Dartmoor can be seen. Walked up to this very snug, pretty little two storied cottage and found nobody home. In the garden in front is a large variegated holy tree, an old rustic garden seat under shrubs and 2 large Cyprus trees. The fence on the side of the garden is decorated on top by odd, but perfectly modelled pieces of granite, evidently part of an ancient arch or door. Afterwards hear that these found under the earth and are supposed to be part of a very old Priory, which at one time stood near this spot. From the front door one looks over the river Hinney, which later joins the Tamar, the boundary between Devon and Cornwall. Dobbins' Cott is right in a hollow, a sort of basin, where 5 valleys meet. On most of the surrounding hills are thick woods, the autumn leaves look good-oh. The ivy, which is so abundant in these parts, has not overlooked many of the trees up which it has climbed and growing luxuriantly gives the tree a tinge of summer or late spring.

Go through a gate and notice an old mill-stone once used for grinding corn to flour, also an old stone apparatus for the manufacture of cider. Go to the river, which we find running very fast. Over it is a good old stone bridge and this road leads to Tavistock etc., I understand. Learn that this a good trout fishing stream, and one the Drs. Sargent make good use of. Go back the same way home, to while away the time tell Mr. Wise of some back country experiences, and the little that I know of bush life in Australia. Very much taken up with the yarns, so very different from any experience ever likely to be had in this country. Tea and a good warm fire afterwards with Mrs. Wise mending alongside, beguiles the time till 9.30pm, our bed time. Make an attempt to dry my boots and socks over the fire in a fire place large enough to live in, in the kitchen. The warm flags and stones do the trick.

6th Friday

About time I sent a wire to the ship, if I want an extension of leave, so tell Mr. Wise I must walk into Launceston today sometime, and afterwards go to Dobbins' Cott again and see if I can find Miss Husband at home. He presumes I can ride evidently, for he says he will lend me a horse. So getting ready, walk into the stable and find black Dobbin ready saddled and waiting. Rode into Launceston by the road I came out. Rather embarrassing to notice people stopping to look and gaze at an 'Australian Light

Horseman' riding through their town. However, leave the nag at the stables, send the telegram and ask for a reply at Plymouth, for being told by Capt. Southwood that we could be pretty sure of 4 days being granted, I intend coming back this way and spending the extra days in London. Go down to the L.& S.W. and Gt. Western railway stations to enquire departure of the trains on the morrow.

Meet a gentleman there who kindly consents to take me over the ruins of the old Priory. This was discovered whilst digging a cutting for the railway. Built in the fifteens, only portions of the wall now stand, but on the ground are many beautiful cut pieces of granite, similar to those at Dobbins Cott representing the crowning pieces of pillars and other pieces of archways. Several tombs of old Priors can be seen. Evidently some history on record of the place has been located, for references are made of various things on a board enclosed in glass on the door leading to it. On the same printed form is a plan of the building as it was in olden days. It is supposed that a secret passage-way led to the Castle on the hill under the earth from this place.

Back to the town, through the castle grounds and pass the prison of Fox the martyr, a strongly built, cold uncharitable looking place. Shown the Free Library, and a glance through book dealing with the history of Launceston by a local resident, whose hobby the study of this is. Have a pleasant ride home and arrive in time for dinner. Take stroll over to Dobbin's Cott again. On the same little private roadway leading to the cottage are two more houses and an old mill. This place goes by the name of Trecarrel Mill and is a separate place altogether from Trecarrel, a village further over, and behind a hill from here.

Noticed a lady standing at one of these, but went on to Dobbins. Arrived there and found no one home again. Just coming away in despair, when this lady came along. Asked her if she knew whether Miss Husband would be likely to return soon. Said she was Miss Husband, and lived here. Told her she would never guess whom I was, she replied; No, but I think you are a relation! This afterwards proved to be somewhere near the truth. Told her at any rate, and she was more than delighted. Asked me inside, made a fire, expressed her pleasure of my coming and asked after Grandfather Amos, his descendants and all about them. Had a most interesting yarn re old ancestors of whom she seemed to know not a little. So many names were mentioned, their children etc., that I soon found myself in deep water. However, later and by the time I had seen their likenesses etc., a little history of each came to be bit better off. Her house is packed with old china, and some very valuable. A lot of this belonged to some of the Sargents and Pearse group. Had a cosy little tea over an old fashioned round table, I was asked to stay for the night, but scarcely cared to do that as I did not tell the Wise folk that I would not be back, in fact told them I would only be a couple of hours at Dobbin's Cott and then intended calling on Miss Uren, to keep my promise, on the way back. Making this fact known to Miss H, she promptly said that she would come with me to Miss Urens, as she wished to see her since she had been ailing, and as far as the Wises were concerned she was sure they would know where I was and would understand that she was sure to have asked me to stay. Anyhow I did not feel so sure of that, but she busied herself by preparing a bed and bless my senses, warming it! Never such luxury these days, nor would I care to think I always should. At any rate I did not like to refuse her, so my mind was made up for me.

Grandfather Amos had an Uncle named George. From his descendants have sprung many doctors. All the boys in one instance were medical men. One of these named William, now lives at Padstow, a Cornish town near the North Coast noted for its fishing industry. He moved here from Wales where he had a large practice. He had a son named Shone (Welsh for John), who an only child was Fleet Surgeon on H.M.S. 'TOPAZ', the ship I have mentioned on previous dates. This poor lad had been on duty in the Persian Gulf, and received a sun stroke. He died at Bombay somewhere about June of this year, probably just before we arrived there. Saw her (the ship) in Suez that trip, and remember bumping her when Bob the boatswain sailed us ashore in one of the ship's boats.

His mother was expected at Dobbin's Cott any day now. The three of that family come here regularly for holidays, but father and son have shooting rites over several estates this way. See a photo of Shone in his naval uniform. A splendid looking fellow and appears to be the essence of kindness. Have a very enjoyable walk to Lezant and hear many more stories, mostly concerning Richard Geddies Pearse who died at Dobbin's Cott in 1913. Owned Larrick, and was commonly known in the parish as 'farmer Dirk'. Another farm owned by the Pearses called Larrick, but this in South Petherwin in another parish.

Another story concerns old George Sargent, who told it to her. We were passing beneath a big oak tree over the road and I suppose it reminded her of it. It seems that while going to school two girls had a quarrel, one was George's sister and the other smacked her pretty hard and made her cry. George could not stand that so beat this girl for so doing, but she afterwards became his wife. This happened beneath this old tree, (beating I mean).

Arrived at the church and found it lighted up. A service was being held. Went in and sat down. It soon finished, and I was made known to the clergyman and his rather gushing little wife. Did not tell them I had seen inside before, but was shown round the church, alter etc. On hearing my name, he says that in their old books of records, the name of Sargent's very conspicuous in that they are frequent. Were leading members and evidently had offices of some sort. Invited to visit them whilst in the parish, but of course time would not permit. Oil lamps used. Outside Miss Husband points out a tombstone of one of her relations which had been moved in order to extend building. I think she rather resented its removal. It certainly should have been placed in the wall as others are owing to extensions of other walls.

Step into Miss Urens. Her neice staying with her this time. Have another little chat, and succeed in getting a smile and a laugh or two from the poor old soul. Must say I like old ladies providing they are not too talkative. Promise to write her a letter later on, which I shall certainly do. Leave about 8.30pm, and stroll back to Dobbin's Cott. Hear of the Pearses in New Zealand whom father has mentioned to me before. One of the daughters came over here, stayed at Dobbins and later married a London doctor by name of Shaw, I think she said. A good cup of coffee and that old bed was very nice indeed.

7th Saturday

Up pretty early. Miss Husband milks her cows, which she keeps for a hobby, have breakfast and set off for Bottonet, which she is very desirous to show me. She is a remarkable lady and although must be between fifty and sixty walks round these steep hills with heavy boots, like one thing. Well loved and respected in the parish for her charity and care of the sick. Call at Trebullet Chapel and shown the headstones, some of which I had not seen previously. There are two vaults belonging to the Sargents, one of the family of George Sargent, and the other of Johns father's Grandfather. The former has a headstone and the latter not. Miss H, says that it is a puzzle why this should be so, evidently for some reason, for the matter could not have been overlooked. Both are of granite, and being low are hidden by earth and grass.

Shown inside the chapel. A very cosy little place indeed. Shown the seats which the Sargents used to occupy. Has a large reed organ with imitation pipes. A kero lamp burning behind to keep it dry from dampness of mist and fog. See several things, such as tables, wash stand and basin, and a room for meetings donated by various members of the Sargent group. Next, inspect the hall where tea meetings and harvest festivals etc., are held, also the stables, which are quite good enough for anybody's horse. One or two small residences and P.O. on corner of grounds, and this owned by the Church. Introduced to one or two people who mistake me for Dr. Shone. Am told there is a likeness.

Could see the village of Trecarrel walking over, and noticed the Hall there at one time owned by the Husbands and considered to be some place in the old days. Walked over to Bottonet. Could see the effects of last year's winter upon the corn which lay about the field in heaps. This farm said to be absolutely the best in the Parish. Could see Landue in the distance, a lovely looking bit of country with a mansion built amongst a clump of trees. Squire Tregouning lives here now. Old grandfather Sargent (George), farmed this place originally and tried hard for years to buy it. Efforts all in vain, so purchased Bottonet instead. In those times money only used in coin proper, and it is said that he carried a small bag made from an old farm bag, full of gold, on his horse, resting it upon his saddle and riding to the owners house. Hid the cash in the horse's manger and made the deal. Afterwards handed over the cash directly after walking from house where the bargain was settled.

Went up to the homestead, a two storied place and rather modern. Learn that the old homestead was burnt down, and in words of Miss Husband, was a grand aristocratic looking old house. One can see now where portion of it stood, for altho' this house is built on original site, does not nearly cover it. The old house had a glass casement veranda running along its entire width. In the trap shed lies an old piece of granite of historical interest. A long drive with avenues of big trees leads out to the road on to the place I mentioned as the old cottage yesterday. She showed me several fields in which Dr. Will and Dick Pearse went shooting and hunting together, their picnic grounds etc. Her life seemed to be wrapped up in Pearse whom it seems she nursed through a long and eventually fatal illness. She came as far as the Cross with me and I was loath to say goodbye to her. I know she would have liked very much for me to have stayed longer. Anyhow, I left her and I felt that during this very short space of time, I had been privileged to meet a perfect lady of genteel manners, and striking personality because of its gentleness and kindness and courtesy.

Went along to Wises very sorry at having to allow Miss Husband walk back home alone. Found the Wises in good mood, but wondering what had become of me last night. Had stayed up till 11pm, an unearthly hour. So my presentiments were correct. Anyhow after due explanation soon got jolly. Mr. Wise going into Launceston this afternoon to attend weekly market at Launceston (Saturday), so arrange to go in with him. Have dinner, put a calf into the gig, and after goodbyes and thanks to Mrs. Wise, and a little present to little girl (now sick in bed) drive off and soon leave the land of my forefathers well behind.

Go the longest route in order that he may call on an aunt. Cross several main roads to various towns. Leave him in the town and go to have a look at the museum. This is the upper room of over the old South Gate of the town. South entrance and exit through the old wall, which surrounded the town in olden days. In these rooms too, French prisoners were kept during Napoleonic wars as also at Dartmoor. Many old types of coin etc., but two most interesting things, an ancient man trap (a horrible thing) and French carvings in oak. Another very interesting thing was an old hard-stone frying pan picked out beneath diggings on the moor. Visited the market place, a broad street. Poultry, rabbits, game and vegetables seemed to be the main items. Made one or two purchases, cards etc., said goodbye to Mr. Geake, asking me to let him know if I should get another opportunity of coming again and gave me a card accordingly.

Collected my gear from the Hotel and met Mr. Wise. Walked with me to the Station and caught Gt. Western Railway train for Plymouth. Sorry to part with my good friends, it seemed all too short altogether. Another Aust. boarded too, so had company. A little over an hour's ride to Plymouth, but being dark could see nothing. Loved to have seen the Saltash Bridge, but only heard ourselves going over. Plymouth a big enough city, judging by shops and people in streets etc. Enquire way to P.O. and receive my telegram. Advised that I may have two days extra, to report back on 10th. Now this does not allow time enough to go back to London, so if I had not placed quite so much confidence in statement of Capt. Southwood, may have had a ? replied back to Launceston and stayed there for two days, and been thus enabled to visit the Dr. at Padstow which Miss Husband had already suggested. There being no trains from Launceton on Sunday, thought it advisable to leave on Saturday and be on the safe side should the worst happen, and should have had to report on the Sunday 8th, could easily have reached Southampton from Plymouth on that day. Never mind, better luck next time. Had to look for a bed for the night, but found every Y.M.C.A., Soldiers and Sailors Institutes etc. crammed full. This being a week-end, and rush on these places from men in Barracks here.

Walked to Devonport and found the same at every place there. Tried a political meeting to pass half an hour, but no good. Walked back to Plymouth and was obliged to book a bed at an Indian Herbal Doctor's place. Did not go much at sleeping at Indian houses, looked too sand baggy etc. for me but risked it. Bedroom small, containing two beds, one double and one single. I took the single and noticed sheets not too white. Three Jews occupied the double and learn from them that they are from America and enlisted in English Army to be sent to Jerusalem and various parts of Palestine, to rebuild and clean up the country. They asked me a good many questions re Jerusalem. Told them all I could and wished them bon luck. Hope they like the country better than our boys do at any rate.

Heard some time ago of Gt. Britain's intention of settling the Jews in their own country. Think of our lads lives, their suffering from disease and death in this hell. Wonderful Britain and yet she gives it away to people who have done practically nothing for it, and pays Jewish soldiers to rebuild it for their own use. Well the country is no good to us I suppose, and if the Jews succeed and make good use of this land of milk and honey, good luck to them. Soon forgot my troubles and my money in this strange place and slept the sleep of the just.

8th Sunday

Cleaned up a bit and went out into the street to see what was doing. Walked over to Davenport. To get over here from Plymouth one must cross over a toll-bridge. The lord of the Manor gets a fine thing out of this, the Tramway Coy. has to pay a very large sum. A ridiculous idea to say the least. I wished to see the mystery ship, which had come to Plymouth and had been thrown open for inspection. Asked a Jack Tar the way and he said she was lying down the other end of Plymouth. He happened to be going that way so walked back along with him. Found him a very interesting chap. Belonged to H.M.S. 'RESOLUTION', Admiral Beatty's flag ship and was present at the taking over of the German fleet at the surrender, and taking them over to Firth of Forth.

Left him at P.O. and went along to the wharves. Found no vessel there bar a fleet of sailing fishing luggers. Picked up with another chap, a civilian and he promised to take me to the mystery ship. Came to the old emigration wharf and jetty where the Mayflower left for America with Pilgrim Fathers in 1620. There is a granite slab placed in the roadway to this effect. Tells me this is the same wharf where emigrants to the Colonies departed from years ago. So probably my poor old grandfather and mother Barber left this same place. They sailed from Plymouth as we know for certain. Father's cousin John left from this port, so evidently grandfather Amos did also.

The sun came out by way of a change, just to see if the earth was still in the same place in which he left if (some time ago evidently), it was grand walking along by the water's edge. We at length came to the Hoe. This is of historical interest, in that this is the place where Drake was playing bowls, when the arrival of the Spanish Armada was announced. This is a fine open space at the top of the cliff with greensward growing over it. Further back is a park and around it big houses, where, as my companion stated, 'the torfs live'. A big stone lighthouse stands to the front of it. This was brought from rocks at sea, where it was originally built and re-erected here. Tower open to visitors but not on Sundays of course my luck, while looking over the water towards the Channel, saw a very long, large submarine pass out. I wonder what Drake would say if he could see now what was going on in his old port. A large warship lying out there too. At the bottom of the cliff is a gents bathing reserve and on the right the Plymouth or Grand pier. A jolly fine one. Military band plays here every Sunday evening. On the green is a large statue of Sir Francis Drake. Walking along the promenade come to a large salt water bath built of concrete and filled and freshened by the tide flowing in and out of it. Come to the dock, which belongs to Sth. West Railway Coy, where the mystery ship is lying. Find however that hours for inspection not till later in the afternoon. Stiff luck.

Pass one or two factories and come to the Millbay Station (where I arrived last night) made enquiries re trains for Exeter, crossed over the main street again, and had a lemonade at this chaps house. He however, had beer and I noticed he seemed rather fond of it. A decent fellow all the same and described himself as good old Britisher and accordingly made me welcome. Only has two rooms on second floor. Has a niece there who is amusing herself cooking cakes and things. Both are fond of music and give me a few tunes with their harmonium and banjo. Open hearted folk these English. Set off for a jaunt round the town, frequently asks me to have what he terms a 'wet'. Find that hotels, during the war are open on Sundays from midday – 2.30p and for a similar number of hours in the evening. However, he had wets galore and I had one lemonade. Told him it was no good to me, and pubs and their motley company gave me no pleasure or pastime, seemed perplexed to know what to do, for I plainly saw he wished to stop for awhile. Told him I would go for a walk whilst waiting for him.

Besides the women in next partition of bar, were gabbling and screeching to one another, like so many at a Christening and it was anything but pleasant. When the house closed @ 2.30 saw these 'ladies' come out only 6 in all, and were carrying their bottle or bottles of stout away home with them. Nothing in England to see women in bars drinking like, and sometimes with me. Awfully demoralizing and am glad that such things are not done in Australia. Had a look at the Reservoir, a pretty spot with water spouts and fountains playing in it. Big catchment area and basin further inland and this kept full from there.

Went home to his dinner by way of the markets. This is where a good many people from Launceston and surrounding districts come on Saturdays, but by the Callington or Kellybrae line. He went to dinner, I declined his invitation and went to the Y.M.C.A. Met again afterwards and boarded a tram at the Clock Tower for a ride round Plymouth and Devonport. It is possible to do this for a single penny, but we changed trams on several occasions. First of all went past the Reservoir again, the other Railway Stn. and over the hill. Soon found ourselves in the open country and actually passed a farm house or two. Through Davenport, past the Naval Engineers college and docks. Saw the gun mounting wharf and huge crane used for this purpose.

Kept in the tram till we came to where all the Dockies houses are built, all of the same pattern and thousands of them. Got out here (tram goes no further). This is the top end of Davenport. Walked to the river Tamar with the intention of seeing the Saltash Bridge. Of all the structures, both huge and delicate together, or any engineering feat to equal it. I have never seen anything to equal it. It consists of two spans only, is of the suspension type and capable of withstanding the fastest and heaviest of trains. Saltash is on the other side of the river, in Cornwall I suppose that would be. An Australian camp and hospital there, where men held prior to embarkation in troop ships for Aust.

A chain ferry runs across the river to this place. The bridge is worth walking miles to see, will try and get a photo of it. Returned to Plymouth my very communicative and really excellent companion to a hotel, and I to the Guildhall where a service to be held. This situated in the square amongst other public buildings and a very old church. New Plymouth is noted for its music and world famous bands and choristers. In the latter I was not disappointed for a lady and gent sang beautifully. The organ one of the world's largest, and best, was justified by its organist. A good ? which I was very pleased to see. The interior of this building exquisite indeed. On the walls are allusions to Drake, other famous 'Stout hearts of Devon', Walter Raleigh and the rest. The steel grey granite pillars give wonderful effect to that richly decorated ceiling. The sermon and lesson were good. Some people outside were still fiddling about the guns placed there for public inspection. These are German, captured and drawn up on the tar paved square. All beds still occupied at soldiers houses and institutions, so obliged to go back to Fords the Indian Herbalist. Quieter than last night, no Jews. Tommy soldiers 'hopping out' American sailors from their beds and rowing outside. Asked to be wakened at 6am. Bedroom a refined attic, but did not mind that. Read a paper until I felt sleepy, and with overcoat as an extra blanket (badly needed) dreamed sweet dreams.

Monday 9th

Caught 8.30am train at Millbay Stn. and started off. A very long train, and took quite a lot of grunting to get up the long incline not many miles from Plymouth. Country here in Devon simply beautiful. At length arrived at Teignmouth, a water-side town. I reckon this was perfectly lovely, and should like to have had a look round. A very small place, with a small comfortable little harbour. For some distance now the line runs absolutely right along the very coast, trundling through the projecting cliffs and along the sea wall against which the waves were splashing, and over the line itself. This is a rare treat and well worth a journey to see. The soil, and even on the beach is of iron stone coloured clay, and comes from the hills through which the cuttings have been made. Lovely views out to sea all the time with an occasional glimpse at the green-sloped hills and forms on the other side of the train. By and by round a gulf and on the other side of it, see a fairly large town, which I believe is Exmouth.

Arrive at Exeter 10.30 at St. Davis Stn. On the platform were several German prisoners, hospital patients. Two on stretchers. Were in charge of men of the St. Johns Ambulance. All were put into the train I had arrived by. Made my way up the town. Saw the very fine statue of General Buller of S. Africa, and the fine clock with tower and drinking fountain underneath it. Made straight over High Street to the Cathedral of which Exeter people so proudly boast. Situated in fine grounds, and amid wide lawns, the west exterior present one block, weather beaten and venerable with age. Like Salisbury, figures in carved stone, presents the Ancient Warrior king etc. Three entrances, each door of heavy looking solid and massive oak. One enters by the side door and is immediately struck with those wonderful arches, naves etc. The pillars here are single, not of several smaller ones as at Salisbury. Ones notice is soon attracted by the huge organ which is mounted high over the front carvings of the Chancel and from the back, inside the Chancel this is made the more beautiful by the exhibition altogether of all the carvings in oak of the chair seats etc. The floor is of tiles and the pulpit of exquisite alabaster carved too wonderfully to describe. The richness in decoration of the vaults also are worthy of note. One of a Bishop of the place has the deceased figure in stone lying prone on the top of it. This is of pure white stone. Others (two deckers) show up well with their gildings and coats of arms painted on them. On the walls proper of the church are tablets to memory of past leading lights and attendants, also bronze, and brass plates in memory and honour of soldiers killed in famous Devonshire regiments in various battles. I am fully satisfied that Exeter's boast of its Cathedral is fully warranted.

Now pay a visit to an old shop, of a very old design. On top is an oak panelled room where meetings of Drake and the rest used to take place. Postcards and stationary are sold at the shop and visitors are conducted to this room free of charge. The whole is in a wonderful state of repair. This is just outside the Cathedral grounds. Noted the seats placed round near a fence for use of wounded soldiers and sailors only, and on the back printed 'Don't cut a friend', in Austr. we have, 'Don't ill use a friend'. Do not know which appeals to 'would be's' the more. Heard of the old Guildhall, so had a look through. This is a very old and interesting building dating back centuries. Drake and other bold Devon sailors have met here. The hall is entirely lined with oak, fine paintings on the walls, one of Monks particularly attracts ones notice. The building is till of importance and periodical assizes are held here. Several flags of England regiments are hanging on the walls, also one was very proud to see that of Australia given to the citizens by an Austr. Commander as a token of appreciation for kindness and hospitality shown his troops while quartered near the town.

Caught the 12.40 train at Queen Street Stn. (L. & S.W.Rly) for Templecombe, where I changed trains again. Having plenty of warrants in my pocket, wrote out one for myself to Shepton Mallet, and after a wait caught the Somerset and Dorset railway train. A good deal of flat country to Wincanton where there is a race course. Passed through Evercreech Junction. In same compartment were chaps bound for Bath and the far towns of the North West. Train met by coaches from various hotels, but walked to village, and altho' raining found it a pleasant little walk.

Once in the town and in main street, recognised precisely where their house would be owing to the Market Cross which the Butlers had shown me a picture of. Went straight to the shop and entered. Caught them all by surprise. Shop open till 8pm each night. Introduced and gave my reason for calling. One boy George in Palestine. Mr. Butler a real Butler judging by those in Aust. Mrs. B., a buxom rosy cheeked lady of exceedingly charming manners. The younger a boy of about 14, a very nice gentlemanly youngster. Soon felt quite at home and over a big fire had a comfortable and homely chat. Told them all I knew of Edgar's family. Find that two of the boys from W.A. late of Alberton, have already been there. Had no intention of staying there the night, had already schemed on putting up at a hotel, but invitation to lodge for the night was pressing. Having heard the tramp of marching feet earlier in the evening, was told that German prisoners were bought to and from the Union every night and morning to the village, where farmers employed them as farm labourers.

Tuesday 10th

Woke early and heard the prisoners coming through the street. Jumped out of bed and could see them on road below. Noticed they turned down a side street, so made up my mind to go there when I got up. Most hospitable and homely folk, and received kindly morning greetings. Had breakfast, and a promise from Mrs. Butler that she would come for a walk if afternoon fine. Cleaned up a bit and made out for the Workhouse where prisoners kept, at the same time having a chance of looking round the town. Entered by the front gate. Part of the house still used by original inmates. Old chap at gate gave me many blessings for filling his pipe with good tobacco. Went round the back, but could not gain admittance owing to armed sentries being posted on guard. However, learnt all I wanted from them and walked back to the street up which I saw them go.

This led to stables which had been taken over by the Govt. and used for Military horses kept for farming purposes. Labour in England being short these days, Govt. undertakes to plough the fields of farmers, either by motor traction or by horses. For this purpose men have been enlisted under a force called the National Service. A fee is paid to the Govt. by farmers (who compulsorily have to work so many acres of their land), for so much per acre ploughed. The labourers are in many cases girls (two of whom I saw at Launceston), and these German prisoners who are given 6d per day by the Govt., and Govt. being paid for their labour by the farmer. Somerset farmers report satisfactorily regarding their work and behaviour. Very good treatment they receive, for farmer here does not know shortage of food yet. Very different to see poor lads, the prisoners in Germany and who tell a very different tale indeed. Saw some of horses used by the Service Corp, mostly above Military age and x service men. The horses in the main also are army horses from

France, recovered from wounds etc. Good stables and well cared for. Saw two prisoners here grinding corn for them. Seemed civil and obedient sort of chaps, and not forced to work hard, for they stopped when the Sgt. went away and restarted when he came back. Still wore their caps, legging boots and clothing of their military equipment. Horse a dear item in England 70 pounds 80 shillings for a decent draught, and Mr. Wise tells me he gave 100 pounds for cow and calf day before I came.

Had dinner and rain began to fall heavily, and thought no chance of a walk now. However, cleared up a little later, so while Mrs. Butler getting ready, went with the boy to have a look at the Church. It is a jolly fine building and no exception to the rule of English Churches in England. The ceiling is panelled in plaster with three hundred entirely different patterns, and on the other side of the arch running lengthways along it, are twelve angels. The bullet holes are to be plainly seen to this day, made by bullets from the rifles from Cromwell's soldiers. Plenty of oak in evidence also. A fine old tower, with a large slate-faced gilt handed clock. The bells are charming and ring out the quarter hour. Has always struck me as quaint and beautiful in these little old fashioned towns. The bell was ringing at the time on a/c of the funeral of a babe. Climbed the tower, and by permission of the bell ringer went into the bell room. A set of 8, one of which was ringing now. Went higher and above the clock out on to a balcony all round the tower. From here a splendid view of the surrounding country obtained. Made good use of the glasses. After the burial, bell stopped for ringer can watch proceedings from his height. Just felt I should like to have stayed here for a month. Such a pretty picture and already learnt enough of the little town below for imagination. Just the sort of thing one sees in paintings of villages, and country round, in England.

Had a look at the old Market Cross, built in 1500. Inscription in old English to effect that a noted villager and his wife died, and buried somewhere near, and a few words of respect to their memories. The old shambles round the market place still standing. This is one of only two or three still left in England. Goods were exhibited and sold from these old benches. The roofs are of red tiles, and benches and supports of rough hewn oak. At present it is a matter of consideration whether these are to remain or not. Not used now, some wish to retain them, others not. Do not present a very tidy spectacle, just about the reverse.

Went back to the house and found Mrs. Butler ready. Started off by one of the smaller roads leading from the town for the railway line, passed under a very long and massively built stone bridge over which it runs across a valley, soon found ourselves climbing a hill. On top of this a road branches off to the City of Bath. Turning to the right, climb gradually higher and from here a beautiful sight meets the gaze. Away in the distance looking towards the sea-coast is the town of Glastonbury. Right in the town can be distinctly seen a lofty, isolated sharp, peaked hill (supposed to own its existence to a sub-earthen disturbance) with its old lookout tower right at the very top. At the bottom of this a Holy bush grows, flowering once a year, at Xmas time. Legend has it that a priest when travelling country at this part, unknowingly carried a seed of this bush on the bottom end of his staff from its native place. Looked upon as a remarkable object even today. The sun shone out from a gap in the clouds for our benefit. And I must say one of the most lovely effects I have seen in England.

Turned to the right again and back towards the town over an old Roman Road, one the main track to Bath. Old stone walls on either side in places are to be seen yet. Passed by an old Brewery. Quite a tiny hamlet on its own. Employees from Heads downward live here. The manager and the boss of the show both have good, substantial old houses, the whole typically English. Ivy, oaks and poplars much in evidence. Next went through the gardens and park given to the townspeople by a successful local tradesman. Very fine grounds, but only in its infancy yet. Fish ponds, swings for children, and band stand, also seats are evidence that movement is on its way. An oak tree planted there by present King when Prince of Wales, at opening of the place. Arrived home just before dark so while Mrs. B. preparing tea, went to stables again and found two prisoners just returned from a farm after their days work. One a young chap, speaks English fluently. According to report Australians their pet enemies, for from captured documents, it is learnt they fear the Aust. more than any other ally. However, decent enough to me. A sentry took them off the Union and I went with them a little way. Same as the others, their habit or Battalion distinguishing badges worn over the right should-blade. A round hole about 4" in diameter cut from the coat, and of a patch of different colour, red or blue or as the case may be inserted. Had a cheery tea, and after thanks due to them for their hospitality, and requests to come again if possible and a desire that I should see their daughter a nurse at Bournemouth if time permitted, I left them.

Caught 6.10pm. train for Templecombe. Had to wait a little over an hour for Salisbury train, so went for a walk up the street. No lights about, so could not see much. Seems a very old fashioned place for there were many thatch roofed houses about. Passed through Dinton on Salisbury Plain. A large Austr. camp here. Had time to walk down Salisbury main street again. Had Flying Corp. chaps as far as here. This train bound for London so changed. Left for S'ampton at 9.22 and arrived at Dock station 10.30. Found the ship had moved to new berth, but did not take long to find her.

Whilst on this job noticed fresh American lake steamers in. These camouflaged and now used for carrying troops to France. Resemble house boats more than anything else. Also saw hundreds of motor - vehicles on the wharf of all kinds, pieces and parts, some whole, but all stacked on top of the other like as many bales of stuff. All for repair. Some beauties amongst them from a General's car to an A.M.C. Ambulance lorry. Hear that 10,000 of these on the way. First thing on board ask for the Austr. mail, been looking forward to this for days, but find to my great disappointment that only one or two received letters from home. Found Jimmy and Mitch in bed, but woke (voluntarily or involuntarily) on my arrival. Got all the latest news from them before finally turning in.

Wednesday 11th

In orders I find I am posted for guard today, but those of yesterday not coming off until 11.30am, take the morning to myself and with Jimmy Smith go round the wharves looking for the German Sub which we hear has been brought in. Find her lying not far from our own vessel. Its number is U67, one of the smaller type. Large enough however, and considerably longer than a very large tug lying alongside her. Saw the gun mounted on her deck, and the shaft hole at the nose and into which is fixed the net cutting gear. Several Jack Tars on board fixing things up and setting things straight. Went round the docks as far as Harland and Wolffs. Noted the large Castle boats already released from War Service, being painted in fresh greyish white over their war camouflaged paint. Funnel, Black and Red similar to Mc.Ilwraiths. Several of the Castle line Hospital ships have also been released. Fared badly, during the War this line. In evening had the night out with Smithy and Mitch. Saw a variety show and afterwards went round a back street to have a look at the old 'Tudor House'.

Thursday 12th

First parade not until 9.30am. Worked in the wards, but myself exempt owing to having done night guard. Wrote a promised letter to Miss Husband. Evening leave granted. Mitch stayed on board, but Smithy and I went on shore. Hearing that the 'MAURITANIA' had just arrived from America, we went along to have a look over her. Having only just arrived, and a large consignment of mails on board, were not allowed on. She is another leviathan, 32,000 tons, smaller than the 'OLYMPIC' by 1,300, (difference near twice our size). Went to a show in the city, and afterwards had a stroll through one of the parks. Had not forgotten my promise to father to buy a thermos flask. Went to several shops, but unable to procure one. Learnt that these articles not now manufactured owing to the war. Other kinds in stocks, but besides being a tremendous price, were not recommended by the sellers, as only an imitation, so did not buy. Bought other things to try and make up. Fully expect this will be my last time on shore so, said goodbye to Southampton for awhile. The worst of it is, no letters have arrived for us, and we know several Australian mails have come in.

Friday 13th

Cleaning up in the morning, the ship has been painted inside and out and looks very smart and clean. Embarked early in the afternoon and finished by about 4pm. Patients are a pretty bad lot and plenty of stretcher cases. Mostly a surgical crowd and worst of all are the poor fellows suffering from spinal injuries, 14 in all. To see these good chaps, makes one feel sad, but they are usually a cheerful lot, brave boys. All staff a little concerned about Pvte. De Meyers and Hayes. To sail at 7.30p. But O.C. sees a chance of staying awhile longer in order that should these chaps come by a later train they would be in time for the ship. De Meyers eventually strolls along, but gets a great surprise when he hears of his close shave. They had applied for extended leave and granted passes till midnight tonight. All thought we would be sailing at daylight tomorrow. However pulled off between 9 and 10, and made for the open water.

All feel sorry for poor old George. Personally I know he was anxious to get home, as when we left, his father was dying. Thanks to our thoughtful O.C., he had written a note to H.Q. requesting that Hayes be transferred to the 'KANOWNA' for duty. The old tub now at Portsmouth undergoing repairs for her propeller. As one of the N.C.O's and their O.C. made this ship his home for a few days, our O.C. must be pretty well in with them, so Hayes chance of getting on their staff is likely. Has the advantage of seeing a little more of Blighty. Most of our chaps expressed the wish that they should like to be just behind Hayes when he heard and saw that the ship had gone. Has a great reputation for airing his g.... in most admirable and feeling language regardless of any hearers, when annoyed or disgusted with anything or anybody. Guess he was properly disgusted tonight when he came along. Fancy I could see how he would screw his neck and head from side to side and let forth.

Saturday 14th

Find that the mine sweeping apparatus in use. The Otters drawn in during the afternoon. Sea fairly choppy and patients not used to this tumbling aboard, and consequently many are experiencing sea-sickness. Even old Smithy has a go. Too much land for him lately, so has to start over again in getting sea equilibrium.
Foggy and dark about 4pm.

Sunday 15th

The old Bay of Biscay anything but friendly. A bit rough and none too pleasant attempting work anything like that of a tender nature in the laboratory.

Monday 16th

Same Padre attached to strength as going over. A padre patient named Mr. Lynch (RC) on board, (might be pious at Church services or on Sundays). Have not met too many Padre I could respect since in the army. Except our own non-conformist.
Passed small sailing ships. Cannot be far off land.

Tuesday 17th

More sails today. One no bigger than an ordinary Dhow with a single mast close by. In sight of land most of the afternoon. At night passed plenty of ships and knew we must be somewhere near Gibraltar. Shortly entered the Straights and were opposite the Rock @ 8pm. Did not have to call there this time as no Spanish Officers needed now.

A glorious starlight night. Smithy and I went on Monkey deck to look round. The night was cool, still and calm. Could plainly see the twinkling lights of the town and higher about 2 yds distance up a larger light, which looked at you like an eye, from a hole in the rock. Opposite on the Moroccan side, by aid of the glasses, saw the shore lined with lights. Take it this is Ceuta. A lovely picture, here were we, sailing between these two continents, air balmy, everything pleasant, and stealing past the greatest fortress in the world, like a ship which passes in the night. Sat for some time, drinking in and admiring it all. Have good prospects of a good day tomorrow.

Wednesday 18th

As predicted, a perfect day. One feels glad to be alive, and yearns for a limb stretcher or a run about. Reminds me of a perfect early spring morning at Mt. Barker. Everybody who possibly could, left the wards at short intervals on some pretext or another, to get a sun bath. Suit we Australians better than weather we have been experiencing in England. Land of Spain early on the port bow. Sailing ships, resembling miniature 3 masted barques passed today.

Thursday 19th

A following sea, and a good wind behind. Do our 345 miles up to mid-day, averaging close on 15 knots. Ship does not forget to roll a bit. Now find some of our patients are from 3rd G.H. of Dartford. Wordsworth and others from Southall.

Friday 20th

Did 347 miles today, jolly near a record for us. Tail wind and sea still holds good. Had to steer clear of an island. Passed it very closely and had a good view from Monkey deck with aid of glasses. Nearly the whole of the sides of the hills are terraced. Fields are green, plenty of trees, hedges etc., these aided by the pretty little white houses dotted everywhere about, made a pretty picture. Just such one of those places that one feels a weeks roam round in a small boat amongst its many bays and landscape would be a novelty long to be remembered, and a rare treat. (Good size drawing of shape of Island, and position of terraces, house, lighthouses etc.,) Said to have once been a convict settlement for French breakers of the law. The Island goes by the name of Pantelleria.

Saturday 21st

Nothing special doing today. Another very good run – 345 miles. Passed the large two funnelled mail steamer, which we think is same as one we met coming through Abu-Ail last trip.

Sunday 22nd

Patients seem very much quieter than our usual Australian chaps going home. A very contented lot nevertheless. Discover Capt. Lewis on board, one of our Medicos from Gawler at Mitcham Camp in our time. Always a jolly good fellow and same now.

Monday 23rd

Another good run yesterday, and same today. Expect to reach Port Said tonight. Arrive off the Port @ 7pm, but not allowed to enter. Had to hang out and steam slowly round and round in big circles all night as no anchorage outside here.

Tuesday 24th

Came somewhere near @ 8am. this morning, and make in. The masts of sunken vessels above the water in different places surprise us. Victims of U. Boats I suppose. Past the old breakwater again and find de Lessep's monument still there of course. Not nearly so many vessels here this time. Take up our berth near the old obsolete French Battleship. Very anxious for my mail, most important thing at present. We have the purser from the 'Katoomba' on board, he was on this ship for our first voyage. Joined the 'Katoomba' in Australia, went to England and left behind on the sick list. Brought him here to rejoin his ship. Heard him tell the Skipper today just after he had been ashore, that his ship just returning from Terante (South Italy) and expected in two or three days.

Alas, no mail, but O.C. wires Cairo and requests if any mails in Egypt, to have them sent to Suez, where we can pick them up on our way through. Expect to be here only a few hours meanwhile to load coal. After finishing in the ward came as usual to monkey deck to sterilize. Had a good chance then of looking over the immediate vicinity. Plenty of small craft jogging about such as tugs, motors and rowing boats, but the most interesting of all was the 'Shooter', a vessel of the type lately used by the British Govt. in their anti-submarine campaign. Resembled our Hydroplanes on Lake Alexandria very much. Manned by Blue Jackets and Officers. Very little noise, but possessed the speed of an express train.

Left great waves behind on the water as it passed over it and tossed the water up from the stern, like a huge water spout. (Hand drawing of vessel and water spout as described). The object of these vessels is to chase towards the enemy vessel at great speed and drop a weapon (latest and unexplained) over the stern. This now chases after the motor, but later in the night time she turns suddenly off, and the missile proceeding on its own accord towards its object. A thrill ran though me as I watched. Ran into a flock of gulls swimming about in great numbers together. The birds literally had no time at all to get out of the way. No sooner had the boat come from behind a breakwater, than it was in amongst and on top of them. During the afternoon Mitch tells me that a chap below wishes to see me, turns out to be a lad named Uren? from Ballarat Vict. A jolly good chap and after awhile took a great liking to him. Says that his cousin Palamountain would be on board @ 5pm to see us. This is good news, not having seen old Pal since he left us at Keswick, altho' been near him a few times.

At five he came and my word didn't we have a good old conflab. Brought him up to the lab and all our S.A. lads trooped along to have a chat. A very interesting noisy sort of chap, but sees the right side of life. Had to go and do shopping in the town for Xmas day, but came back afterwards. Hearing that 6 Sisters have just arrived as patients @ No.14, Smithy is anxious to know whether his sister may be one. They go on shore back to the hospital to find out. No luck for Smithy, but brought back a young pathologist by the name of Stevens. This lad knew nothing of this work until rostered for No. 14 lab. Has a good all round knowledge now and has the opportunity of learning well under Mjr. Fairlie of Melbourne, (an authority in this business) and splendid scope through numerous tropical diseases. Rather a slow Xmas eve for many, but we had a pleasant little supper together. Posted letter and parcel of sultanas to Mrs. Wise of Trewarlet as promised.

Xmas Day
Wednesday 25th

Greetings knocking about. Later we find 7 more barges of coal alongside. Rumour goes round that we are to call at Aden and then straight for Freemantle, hence taking so much coal. This turns out later to be unfounded. Supposed to sail @ 4pm. Stevens promised me last night a number of malaria slides. Brings them on board. Introduce him to Capt. Shield. He interviews the O.C. re my going ashore to No. 14 Laboratory and obtaining a stain for our own use. Same is granted, catch a boat for the shore @ 11am.

Pulled up through the Canal Company's Docks and Basin and walked over to the laboratory. The whole hospital is to be moved to Cairo within a few days, the Canal Coy. having obtained permission from British Govt. to take over their premises again. Everything up to date in the lab and was able to pick up a few ideas. Mjr. Fairlie a young chap, two Sgts. also at work. One came over to Egypt by the ship on her 1st voyage as a hospital. She brought whole of No. 14 Original Unit. Had a look over these beautiful buildings, told they were built by a German firm and installed with machinery by the French. The whole of these are electrical and driven from a power-house near the Canal. In some wards machinery still stands. Patients having Xmas cheer today. The Officers ward, a lofty, airy building and beautifully decorated for today. Porcelain wash-basins run right down centre of ward. From end to end floor is tiled. Went along to another (men's wards) similarly decorated. Tables nicely set. Shown the theatre. Near the door of the wards noticed dozens of Xmas puddings being brought in. The poor lads were eager and enthusiastic over the meal. Great credit due to the Sister in charge of decoration.

Preparations throughout for removal of hospital to Cairo in a few days. Have a flower garden running about whole length and parallel with the hospital. Egyptian flowers from here, and chains of beautiful variegated leaves from shrubs. Steven tells me that people for treatment from Armenian camp, further along the bank of the Canal, come to the hospital. Consequently, many interesting tests in the lab. Left him as desirous of getting along to the ship by dinner time. The mess deck had been decorated with flags, and behold! the benches with tablecloths, fruit arranged etc, before I left, so would like to show appreciation. Had a look at docks first though. No big ships there at present, except an Italian destroyer undergoing repair in dry dock, and a few of the Corp's own Canal boats. Passed out through sentry-gate and immediately rushed by rowers of boats, offering to convey me to the ship. Many told me of each other that they were macuoons, and not to take his boat etc., but I chose the most unlikely looking' macuoon' and started out. The old ship looked good from here, and compared favourably in size to most others in port. The old 'ALDIRIA' our friend of Alexandria is astern of us, but all her nice new white paint, green lines, red crosses etc., being painted over with a coat of jet black. Evidently now being converted to a trooper.

On way to the ship had to pass two submarine chasers, the (M. L's). Could not resist pulling over there. Found a New Zealander on board, now in British Navy. Made me very welcome and offered to show me over. One is 5ft shorter than the other, and one of the original of which England bought 500 from an American yacht builder at a cost of 10,000 pounds each. The bridge is like that of a miniature steam ship, being fitted up with set and cabinet of International code flags, telegraphs (sending and reply) for port and starboard, speaking tubes etc. Small mast and wireless telegraphy installed. Carries a lifeboat above engine room and a crew of eight, all of who sleep in forecastle. In charge of Naval Lient. whose quarters are aft. Decks of timber and hull ditto 1 1/8 in thick. Engines are a marvel, 200hp. each, not want of copper and brass, charge their own batteries and supply own electric light. Petrol driven, capable of driving 18 knots. The 'Shooter' seen yesterday built in England. These M.L's carry depth charges, and a 3 in. Hotchkins gun on bow. This pair lately used for patrol duty only.

Found things agreeable on the boat. All staff received their Xmas parcel from British Red Cross. Not myself however. They contained a packet of American cigarettes, chocolate, packet of dried fruit and tobacco. Pantryman of C3 extra sociable today, and Mitch now being on this deck, make a very enjoyable 'tuck in' together.

During the afternoon other old S.A. boys from Mitcham and Keswick attached to the 14th or in Rest Camp came aboard to see us, Godley from Bordertown, (the Densley's acquaintance), Presgrove. Mitchell when standing near the gangway, noticed old Bill Gillan being rowed about, my predecessor N.C.O. at Keswick. Called out to him and he came alongside. Had a word or two. Have often wondered about old Bill. Looks well, is in Rest Camp and attached to the Band. Caught him on his way to No. 14 to participate in a band concert to the patients. Having had the search light and motor apparatus attached to the bow and all else being quite ready, we get a move on. Now hear the reason no leave granted is because previous Aust. troops have played up so, many hand to hand, and street brawls having taken place. Foreigners having fell foul of our chaps. The English Embarkation Officer has the 'wind up' regarding Aussies.

The passage past other ships in port and further along the Canal will remain in my memory. The night altho' not hot was perfectly still. From a ship here and there in the darkness comes the calls of 'Coo-ee'. Some were made by Egyptian along the banks but we could well distinguish the difference. Jimmy Smith and I came up here on the monkey deck to see and hear. On the promenade below us a concert by our chaps and patients was in progress. A good pianist at the piano. A stray Egyptian walking along the bank would call out 'Merry Xmas Australia', and as we passed the Armenian Camp, a whole squad of youngsters of the Camp, sang very lustily and at top of their voices without a break, and in real good English 'God save our gracious King'. Should loved to have been on shore and seen the ship. All lights up. Here we were with our returning heroes from the great war, conquering heroes, a boat load on a white ship with a big peering eye at her very nose, stalking her way cautiously through a narrow waterway in pitch darkness, the music of instrument and voices echoing out into the night, songs common to we Australians, bound from one part of the world to another and under this Eastern Sky.

Cannot help thinking of that statue in bronze at the Port Said breakwater, representing the person who made this thing possible. Guess he did not dream that hundreds and thousands of Australians would travel to and from this terrible conflict by way of this track. There are the boys below, nerve wracked, shell shattered, maimed and suffering, unable to leave their beds. Men as soldiers, having earned an undying name for Australia. Australia has been brought before the eyes of the world and Australians are popular everywhere, and all Allies admire them. As soldiers they are said to have no equal. Their happy-go-lucky, yet manly ways have caught on. People in England knowing scarcely anything of Aust. before the war, and now making every enquiry about the country. There is scarcely a village in England which an Aust. soldier has not at some time or another, visited, and they are as popular now in England as they were on arrival. This is very noticeable in England and judging by careful notice taken of the English people in ourselves, and in anything Australian, I foresee big emigration from England as soon as things are settled a bit.

Well here we have a boat load of them and as music always stirs one, I have no wonder, that English camps along the banks of the Canal, whose soldiers are either sitting or walking along the edges or get up from their bunks and lean against the tent door or against the tent pole, and cheer our lads and give three Hip-Hip, hoorays! We are wished good luck, the voices are very audible and our boys return the kindly sentiment.

All the time the old engines go plug, plug and we move slowly along. To my mind this is an experience, there is something grand, novel, and weird about it, gives you a feeling you can hardly explain. How many other lads of different nationalities have passed this way, through this gaping old desert engaged in different ways on the same business as ourselves. British to India and Mesopotamia, Indians to Palestine and France, French from the Colonies, in some instances Chinese, men from the West Indies, American, Italian, men from and to East Africa and Australians, both to Egypt and England via different routes, some through Italy, others France, and others Gibraltar. It is wonderful, and before that, the tourist on his way to other parts of the globe on some of the best ships in the world which come this way. Have read books re these experiences and mention has often been made of the time passed, coming through this waterway. Can well imagine it now.

By and by came to Kantara, the new steel bridge: the bridge was open and waiting for us, everything seems so automatic and silent, save for a train which rattles along the line close to the Canal. Came to the old pontoon bridge where I was supplied with a topee hat on way back from Jerusalem last trip. One feels in a real muse as the imagination lingers, but the bugle for 'lights out' extended till 9.30 tonight, breaks the reverie. We all wonder, especially the staff if this will be the last trip of the good old ship as a hospital through the Canal.

Thursday 26th

Have passed by Ismalia during the night, but expect to reach Suez at 11am. Much slower than our last trip through. Pass several Canal-Stations, fitted up much like a port or sea-shore signal station and used much to the same purpose. Come to one of the big lakes and stopped. Waiting on a vessel coming the other way. A fine ship beautifully camouflaged. English soldiers on board evidently from India. After she had passed, noticed the idea of the stripes and colours over and about the stern. Now looked like a steamer approaching us, the wash from the propellers, appeared like foam at the bow. Indeed from this position, stern looked like a bow itself. Able to steam faster through these lakes. Could see the familiar old mountain ranges and Suez in the distance. When we came to Port Tewfik, everything quite familiar of course. A couple of English officers came out of the clubhouse to watch on. A few French damsels wave to the boys and of course as may be expected not everybody ignored them.

On our left a vessel flying the Aust. Flag and with a swan painted on funnel denotes that she is a W.A. Govnt. vessel the "KANGAROO" by name. On war work for she is camouflaged. All wonder where Sister Cook's friend is, seeing that he was not along the parade, a common saying on board here now, 'Goodbye Cookie' for in the darkness when leaving here for England he stood on the Bank and called out several times these words, at the top of his voice. All guessed whom it was, but presently we see him chasing after us in a steam tug. Several call out these words to him, but he comes on board when we are anchored in the anchorage, all the same. A little Welsh Officer, but has been good to us. Used to tow us ashore etc. when on the boat, parade stunts everyday when we were here before. Learn from him, no mail for the ship. What stinking luck! Punt soon comes up to take lighting gear off. Not many vessels in port, but a fine big 5 mastered Shire liner lying at our old embarkation wharf in the harbour. Tip this is the vessel which is booked to take of load of Aust. light horsemen back. About the same size as the 'WILTSHIRE', well known to Aust. soldiers now and of Anzac fame. Only stayed a few hours and made off. Keep up a deadly slow pace and hear from Firemen that coal is old and over exposed, owing to old stock. They cannot get a sufficient pressure of steam up. Now we have to wait for Colombo in the hope our mail if not already sent to England by Aust. P.O., may have been sent here for us. What a nark if we have passed it on the way so far.

Friday 27th

We really thought that speed slow on account of ashes un-dumped being in the way, the consequence being that fires cannot be properly raked. All ashes have to be kept whilst in Pt. Said or anywhere in the canal. This speed is rotten, only 200 miles for the 24 hours. Now we hear we are burning Indian coal, which if true would probably account for it.

Saturday 28th

Commemoration Day in S.A. today. Guess a great day at Glenelg. Don't anticipate getting any letters at Colombo, so by jive I will be glad when we pull alongside that old wharf at Fremantle. Good job it is not hot in the Red Sea for us, travelling at this rate. Sleeping on deck of course.

Monday 30th

Very warm but nice. Passed within a very short distance, a large 4 mastered American barque in full sail. Unusual to find sailing ships in the Red Sea. Could see the men at the wheel distinctly and others in forecastle head. Dipped her flag to us and ours responded. This is one of the prettiest practices at sea that I have seen yet. Knocks our old red tape. Military salute into a cocked hat. Pass Abu-ail during evening.

Tuesday 31st

5 operations today. A good many lately. Death occurs in D1 ward, from aemia? following nephritis. A P.M. held at night, and I had to attend. Capt. O'Brien performed and I assisted in things not hitherto my lot. A nice New Years Eve for me. Up pretty late on the job. When finished went below and found others making merry in Red Hills cabin. A contrast to my experience. Trust next will be with my loved ones at home.

JANUARY, 1919

Wednesday 1st

Through Perim and Hells Gates 9am. Our longest trip yet through Red Sea. One of funeral party. Deceased buried at 1pm. An impressive service by Staff Padre. Very quiet New Year's day. Only did 248 miles today.

Thursday 2nd

Beautiful days and nights. Saw Southern Cross for first time tonight. In sight Socatra all day.

Friday 3rd

Three operations today. Mitch kept busy at his new job, which he is learning to like O.K. Much better for him than down below. Is able to get fresh air sometimes and already looks better for the change.

Saturday 4th

Patients to be paid before Colombo. Officers 10 pounds, men 2 pounds. Plenty of work in the lab. Captain S. often comes up for a yarn. Going to make a study of malaria slides, from No. 14 lab.

Monday 6th

Sky looks stormy ahead and big black clouds. Later come into torrents of tropical rain, which however only lasts for a couple of hours.

Tuesday 7th

Passed Minikoi 7.30-8am. Much closer than usual. Three small sailing vessels close to shore plainly seen. Also light house, quite white, itself standing amongst the palm trees and undergrowth. Just the sort of place I should like to go ashore in. Drop a dingy over the side and have a roam round, and along others who express the same wish. Hear from Wireless chap that 'WILTSHIRE' in Tewfik the day we were there, is already at Colombo. Heard her wireless working and reports, two Coolie Stowaways in bunkers, also says to take 18 Australians as passengers, having been lent to British Govt. for work in India. Hottest day so far.

Wednesday 8th

Intend spending all spare cash in Colombo this time. Have prepared a list of things I wish to purchase for those at home. Puzzled as to what to get Ralphie (*younger brother*) though. Patient died of Miliary tuberculosis this afternoon. A post-mortem ordered. To be buried ashore tomorrow. Kept me at it till near midnight. Had a most enjoyable evening I don't think.

Thursday 9th

Arrived during the very early hours of the morning. Wake just in time to see water barges coming alongside, altho' could see the light-houses of Colombo when I went to bed at about 12.30am. Being full of hope for leave ashore and mail from home, imagine disappointment when this notice read on parade:-

Special Corps Order 9/1/19
By O.C. troops

Port arrangements.

Orders have been received on board that, owing to restrictions, no troops are allowed to land in Colombo.

Spanish Influenza is very prevalent in this port, and cases have occurred of troops breaking leave having become infected.

This disease exists only in a mild form in Australia and the Commonwealth. Authorities are determined to prevent the possibility of an epidemic being introduced. Patients are strongly impressed, that the precautions taken are for the protection of their dependants and relatives as well as their own.

If above order not obeyed, a rigorous period of quarantine will be necessary on arrival in Australia.

Patients should also avoid coming into contact with coaling gangs.

M. Mc Intosh. O.C. troops
No. 1 Austr. Hospital S. 'Karoola'. Colombo

This has been worrying a good many of us, when thinking how the disease has travelled, and just wonder if to Australia yet. Seems to be a world epidemic. Anyhow get the washerman (Dhobie) to take letter ashore to old customary trader and try arrange for purchases this way. Arrange with an Officer and Rundle to divide a role of about 20 yds Assam Silk between us. The 'WILTSHIRE' here (only!) 28 hours before our arrival. Mr. Saul, Y.M.C.A. Secr, kept busy making purchases for Officers and men. Another man died last night, a Special case in D1. Both deceased taken ashore in coffins @ 2pm. Sad this, brave lads so near home, where mortal remains are to be buried in a foreign country. Waiting round anxiously till late for arrival of parcels, for contrived to get another message ashore, as well as for the silk we three bargained for. No luck however. Mr. Saul brought all his parcels for patients who had ordered through him on board late. No luck this time and usual pleasure of giving things on arrival home, and the pleasure to them will be missed for nothing has come by anybody addressed to me.

Friday 10th

Woke to find ourselves well out to sea. It gives us some pleasure at any rate to know that we are just about on our last lap for home. Steaming slowly as really started before steam properly up. Kept in sight of land (for our first time) till well after dinner time. Hear we got away between 1-2am. Patients on awakening today, were pleased with contents of their parcels. Met young Day 1st night, one of our E6 patients. T.B. Cystitis. Spoke to me at gangway and after a bit recognised him and remember him well. Used to be boy in Verification Dept. in Adelaide Office, when I came down temporarily from Pirie and attached to the Verification Dept. myself.

Saturday 11th

Pretty warm. The Chestnuts I obtained at Bottonet Wood are growing splendidly in dirt from Southampton Wharf. Altho' entirely out of season, the hot weather seems to have no effect. Notice smoke on the horizon at the rear of us and we are told it is the 'WILTSHIRE'. Supposed to be only a 12 knot boat, but she is gaining on us for we can see the funnel later in the afternoon. Going rotten speed ourselves again, 250 at 12 o'clock today. Sleep on deck, but a storm comes up suddenly. The wind is almost strong enough to blow self and bed away. Heavy rain falls, and forced to find new position. Washed out of this and tried another. Alright for an hour or two until water from boat deck not being able to get away quickly enough in scuppers, teems over on to the promenade. Soaked out again and getting up, find the old 'WILTSHIRE' right opposite at a very short distance. Seems a monster and has very many large lights alight. Passes us. Had to sleep below in the rat hole this @ 1.30am. Lay awake perspiring freely for a long time and awoke at reveille in a dead sweat.

Sunday 12th

There is the 'WILTSHIRE' just ahead of us. Has 600 men on board from Egypt and Palestine. Are in hopes of catching her up when fresh watch comes on. Hear that Officer patients offer 20 pounds to firemen to give the other ship a go to Fremantle. A neck to neck race would be most exciting and certainly vary the monotony a bit. One of our spinal cases walking now. Thank God for this blessing. Able to get up and visit his friends on other side of ward for 1st time. Put a pretty straight notice on board re thefts from my lab. This causes comments from some which is amusing to hear.

Monday 13th

Pretty warm. Many large sea birds flying about. Expect to pass Cocos tomorrow. Capt. Lewis very low and to use his own words, is properly 'fed up'. 4 operations. One last night for appendicitis. Quite an emergency, so Mitch kept busy. No hope of catching 'WILTSHIRE' now, all other firemen watches except 12-4 willing to get a move on. Lists for all patients prior to reaching Fremantle to be carried out. Made a start on E1 and F1 today, so expect to be kept busy.

Friday 17th

A queer experience befell me today. Happened over an incident of yesterday. Our 3rd Wireless operator is a boy who is always saying things he does not mean. On the monkey deck here yesterday he casually mentioned that this ship was to be quarantined in Aust. Well this wire always goes about when we are nearing home. Of course Rollason and I paid little heed to it, and laughed at the idea, as we have had infectious cases on board before and escaped isolation. Operator did not ask us to treat it as official news or keep it secret on account of it being a wireless message. When I went down to lunch, by way of sport and trying to get the 'wind up' I told the other chaps in the pantry. Of course it met with much derision here also. Anyhow the pantry man told it to somebody else, and so on until it reached the O.C. Had dismissed from my mind all thought of the affair and had quite forgotten it, until the W.O. came up here today and informed me the O.C. wished to see me. Paraded to him and asked me point blank if 3rd Operator had told me about the ship going into Quarantine. Not knowing what he knew or how he came by it, of course had to admit that he did. Told me this rumour true, as all ships advised on a/c of Spanish Flu' restrictions, but added that he hoped we may be exempted. Also said he would not drag me into any trouble re this matter, but stated his reason for going thus far. It seems the Ship's Captain has been complaining that information entrusted to the Military Heads on board, has been leaking out and has spoken to the O.C. about it. O.C. of course does not approve of accusation, altho' unable to prove the Mid-officers innocence.

Seeing his chance here to justify his denials, he brings the poor wireless operator to book. Tells me always had idea the leakage in the Naval Quarters and that this lad previously cautioned for big indiscretion. Anyhow I am exceedingly sorry for the boy and could not have had this happen for pounds, but to make matter worse O.C. comes up to the Monkey deck for Rollason and to act as witnesses to his charge made of the operator before the skipper. Put tunics and caps on and went along to the cabin. Poor kid was there, his chief of department, our O.C. and Skipper. Youngster looked very white and skipper nervous and agitated. Surprised at this, but hear this is customary for him on such occasions. Answered his questions straightly and to the point. O.C. seemed nervous also, an unusual proceeding for him I suppose, and certainly for me as I hate this sort of business. Only feel I would like to know the 'pimp' who informed O.C. in the 1st place. O.C. came up here again afterwards and says that message true enough and reason he takes such drastic action is because if this story spreads amongst the patients, they may not take it quietly and so cause trouble of all sorts, and asked us to squash any talk we may hear regarding it and so stamp the rumour out of existence.

Lad goes on duty @ 4pm, so go to him and ask him to look me up @ 8pm which he does. Talk things over with him here in the lab, and glad to say he seems satisfied quite liberally taking the onus upon himself. Says that Skipper unremitting in his decision to report matter to Naval Office, as he has signed declaration contracting to keep all secrets entrusted to him, has to declare that he has broken his pledge. I do not like this and worries me, but I hear from other quarters that this only intended to impress him and teach him a lesson. I trust this is true, for altho' an utterly indiscreet, irresponsible lad, is quite harmless. Intend to see O.C. at 1st opportunity with view of asking him to use his influence on lads behalf.

Saturday 18th
Just under 1,000 miles to go at midday today. Beginning to realize that nearing Fremantle a fact now. Every twist of these old propellers puts us a little nearer to our mail.

Sunday 19th
Traced the report to O.C. as having come from Taulty W.O. of Orderly Room, of course cannot do anything, but feel satisfied now that I know. Had an idea it was he somehow, because nobody who did not know actually the truth of the story would have bothered about it. Told the operator for his own sake. Good old swell on today.

Monday 20th
Today's orders state that patients and staff may send wireless messages @ 6d a word. Handy, but no good to us just now. A wire at Fremantle would reach home about as good. Should we have to come away again this would be useful.

Tuesday 21st

Expect to reach Fremantle in the early hours of the morning. A strong cool breeze blowing, but from the wrong quarter to get a whiff of the old gum leaves. Turned in pretty late, but could see Rottnest light before going to bed. Old Southern Cross shows up well. Awoke to find ourselves anchored in the harbour. Other vessels in, and some in quarantine. At about 11, moved off in. See the old barrier has been removed on the wharf, and a new one erected further along. Overway Bridge to Railway Stn. now opened. Do not know if we are to have leave yet, but hopes of leaving intentions re the ship and receiving my mail will make up for that if none granted.

Disembarked patients and sorry to lose Mr. Leak and Everett from C1. Both jolly good chaps. A good muster of people outside barrier. Patients to leave from 12noon to 8pm. Staff in two sections 4 hours each. Mine 4-8pm. Got Jimmy Smith (on former) to go round to Uncle Charley and make arrangements with Uncle Dave re going to Pt. Walter with Aunt Emily. Sent wire to Mother. Bitterly disappointed with my mail. Letters only since middle December having reached me. Mother states written regularly every week, so all letters since Sept. missing.

Went along to yard, met Uncle Dave and went with him to his new home at East Fremantle. Saw Uncle Rex and learn Aunt Grace now better after her holiday. Find Aunt Emily well, but have no time to go to Point Walter, so after tea, have a stroll down to the Swan, a 10 min. walk. They are very keen on having Mother over for a holiday, and I feel I must see what can be done before very long, as Mother should have a change of some sort, and this an ideal spot. Reported back to the ship, but found Uncle Charlie waiting there for me to have a yarn, so had to get a few minutes extension from the W.O. Coming on board again, the Officer on shore in charge of Guard picked on me to try and coerce a drunk (one of our patients) to come on board which I had to do, having failed themselves. Found him well on the way, but after taking him in hand, kicked and shouted a good deal. Had to carry him up that wretched swinging gangway pick-a-back, and he was no lightweight. Several of the patients intoxicated in spite of all Hotels being closed. The fellow I bought on board shifted to the cells for rowdiness, and abusive language to the 'heads', later in the evening. Supposed to pull away from Wharf @ 9pm. but plenty of water to be taken in yet. 'BOONAH' loaded with troops comes in just after our arrival.

Wednesday 22nd

Early this morning (about 3am) as sleeping on well deck, wakened by commotion on wharf. Here were 7 or 8 intoxicated chaps from the troopship 'BOONAH' (which had gone out again last night) on the wharf arguing with the guard and amongst themselves. Another managed to get on board by the stern, and for abusing our O.C. had been pushed and run off down the gangway by W.O. and N.C.O.'s. He of course tried to retrace and bring his 'mob' on board for revenge, but it would not work. Officer on shore had rather a lively time of it. Still, one known to be on board somewhere and presumed he stowed away by stoke hold. After row had subsided went to bed again. Left @ 7am. Fremantle not yet awake.

At breakfast learn that our star passenger had given himself up and put down in the 'Clink'. Let out at dinner time. Seems a decent sort of fellow, but says that drink bettering him, remembers nothing of last night except that he was aware he had missed other boat and knowing we were bound for Melbourne, got aboard. Found himself lying in No.14 lifeboat on waking this morning. Does not remember going with his mates at all last night, but expects they will fall in pretty heavily for having missed their ship. Says he got a surprise on finding himself well out to sea. Would have looked foolish if we had been going away instead of home. Hear from Mother of Ralph's illness and poorly health again of Aunt. Old 'SARDINIA' over which so much trouble by troops returning lodging complaints, came in yesterday too.

Thursday 23rd
Passed land very closely at 8am. today. Note the blow holes in rocks. Passed Albany 12 noon quite close to entrance. Many bush fires along shore. Very cool in afternoon. Our old friends the albatross joined us again this afternoon.

Saturday 25th
Learn from O.C. that 3rd Wireless Operator will most probably be let off, measures already taken were to teach him his lesson. I am very glad. Ship has a terrible list on, most uncomfortable and risky for patients with artificial legs. The old Bight seems quite friendly this time. Water unbroken and smooth as glass, but for a side swell.

Sunday 26th
Put in for various items of new clothing today. Q.M. does not see way clear to make certain issues, so see adjutant about it. Orders at morning parade to the effect that old Unit Colour patches to be changed from chocolate and gold to chocolate and green. Issues of green made. This in accordance with A.I.F. H.Q. London. A mad idea now original are so well known, and this business nearly finished.

Monday 27th
Pass good old Adelaide sometime today. Still a big list on.

Tuesday 28th
Cape Nelson passed @ 7.30 this morning. A beautiful sea, day misty and a little rain. Close to Cape Otway and land for latter part of afternoon. Melbourne Heads lights come into view about 8pm. and not long after passed through. Had a good view of all proceedings as I got along on fo'castle head. Do not remember having seen water more phosphorescent. A very pretty and interesting sight was afforded by a dolphin. Could see it making for the bow of the ship by the silvery line caused by the phosphorous. It then swam just in front of the bow, not a yard from the very nose, for quite a long time. Resembled a mass of moving silver. Anchored behind Heads opposite Queenscliff, but nearer the other shore. Many lights about. Have had another medical examination for quarantine purposes.

Wednesday 29th
On wakening, find ourselves at Portsea Quarantine, with about 5 other ships. One the 'BURMA' just arrived before us. The 'SAXON' also in with returned troops. Wait for some time until quarantine motor boat comes off with Officers to inspect. Detailed for duty on gangway. These Officials wear anti-infection masks. Look peculiar and meet with remarks from 'diggers' re gas-masks etc. Orders come that 'BURMAs' Queensland patients to come on board ours for Vic, S.A., and Tas. to go on to her, she to go into Melbourne with them, the ship afterwards to be quarantined. We to go to Sydney and Brisbane. All states except S.A. and Queensland, declared 'black' (on a/c influenza) two days before our arrival, so no leave for S.A. staff. For above purpose, a tug sent alongside and disembarkation begun. Patients to be transferred to other ship in this way. Mitchell and I detailed to assist in this job. No easy matter at times, for tug being on windward side, rocked to and fro and put the 'wind up' some patients, especially the shell shocks to whom this business did a great deal of harm, especially to one poor fellow who utterly collapsed and fell from gangway into Mitchell's arms. The old dancing tug and distance from gangway at times enough to disturb any one armed, or one leg patient. Now come the thing, which disgusted and caused vexation to us all. When disembarkation had all but finished, the O.C. came down to us and informed that all had to be brought back on board again, as we ourselves were to go into Melbourne.

This was the limit. The tug itself of course could not proceed to Melbourne with us, take the patients already on and so save all this extra trouble. Anyhow we did it, much to the detriment of the shell shocks whom I believe lost all the good in this short space of time, they may have gained on the whole voyage out. Such is the Military. Goodness knows what will happen when brains begin to work.

One H. Ship in 6 months and a cable from Colombo for instructions and no reply. Right on top of them in a heap and a muddle. In England thousands of troops arrive every day and everything goes without a hitch. Started off for Melbourne and reached the Quay in 3 hours. Found the band waiting for us, which rendered brightening arias. A crowd at the barrier, 'BURMA' followed just behind and berthed opposite. Discharged patients who were ready before. Said goodbye to Capt. Lewis and received an invitation to his home at Gawler when he is better. After things straightened a bit, took on 100 Queenslanders from the 'BURMA'. The chap who voluntarily joined us from the ship in W.A. sent off. Got wire and letter off to Mother. Am afraid I would frighten Mother with contents of letter, as I wrote as I felt at the time, (pretty awful). Having been told last night to pack up and be ready to disembark when called on, and Brisbane now being certain, I confess I feel disgustingly disappointed. Crowd were now allowed on wharf. Started off @ 6pm. 'BURMA' to Melbourne. Anchor for the night at Portsea.

Thursday 30th

At reveille found ourselves outside the Heads and close to land. Passed Wilson's promontory later in the day, not so very far from Cape Schanck. Went quite close to Skull Rock, and also to the lighthouse. Note the burnt or probably ring barked trees as of last trip. Pass another lighthouse at a point a little later on. Kept in sight of land most of day. Doing good speed with winds and sea behind us.

Friday 31st

Pass Gabo Island @ 2.30 this morning. 18 hrs usual run from here to Sydney should reach there tonight at latest if enter straight away. Caught up and passed a sailing ship going jolly near as fast as ourselves, but with only a few sails set. Having started the making of a kit-bag yesterday, almost completed it today. Pass 40 mile beach this afternoon, but slow down considerably so as to reach Sydney daylight tomorrow.

FEBRUARY, 1919

Saturday 1st

Saw land on dressing, waited for pilot boat 'THOS COOK'. Skipped the pilot and passed through Heads. Note 4 or 5 steamers in quarantine at North Head near Manly. Ferryboat comes alongside between 8.30-9am and disembarkation commences after the 80 fresh Queenslanders are brought off ferry. Things went smoothly. Water boats and coal lighters alongside. N.S.W. members of Unit bitterly disappointed at not being able to get home so no leave will be granted. However some of them being able to get messages off to their people, some come off from shore in rowing boats.

The water police kept them at a reasonable distance from the ship. Later, some come in motorboats, and to see the expressions and hear the exclamations from some were really funny to one indeed. One or two of the motors kept running round and round the ship afraid to stop, because of the police, and each time they passed their 'loved one' I had my ½ penneth of fun in watching. Pte. Martin late of the Unit, having a motorboat for hiring, bring out the Commanders and O.C's wife. They are fortunate for the boat is allowed alongside and these two gentlemen were able to go down, talk to their wives and nurse their kiddies for ½ hr or so.

During the afternoon had the pleasure of watching a 16ft champion yacht race. All passed very near to the ship and turned round a point not far from us. Could see all the people and able to speak to many as they passed by. Many people wearing masks. This to be a compulsory measure on Monday next. Women look queer objects. All wards except C. and F. deck closed and cleared up now, patients to occupy only these. 'S.S. SAXON' lying at Quarantine Melbourne with us, anchors near us in Watson's Bay. In England I travelled with Australians from Plymouth to Exeter, on their way to Liverpool to join the 'SAXON' and here she is. The chaps were from camp at Saltash. Ferryboats look good-o, as they at night, making splendid reflections on water with numerous lights.

Sunday 2nd

Left Watson's Bay @ 8am, Brisbane a 38hr trip, but do not intend reaching there until Tuesday morning. Proceed out to sea for several miles before turning northwards. Coast in sight all day. Lovely day. Some of patients sing hymns on their own account on promenade during evening. Have no Padre to take evening service.

Monday 3rd

In sight of land all day. Perfect warm day. Many bush fires along the coast. Pass entrance to Clarence River at 1pm, and a township (which lights we can see) and the lighthouse of Point Danger at 9am. Have quite a mixed crowd on board. Those we brought right from England, those from 'BURMA', with some brought from Egypt on way out (Aust. Light Horse) and those from Sydney and the "Pt ------" from Plymouth. Anniversary day of my going to Pirie. Poor old Nank in hospital suffering from kidney trouble. Told by one of sailors that 3 ships wrecked up near entrance to River Clarence. A town 60 miles upstream supplies driving piles for export, but only small sailing vessels can get up the river. Scenery en route is beautiful am told.

Tuesday 4th

Very close to land early this morning @ about 7am, steered straight for a point of land with a high white lighthouse on top and signalling station installed. This is Point Moreton. The peninsula is cliffy and of rock. Land about grows large trees, but bush fires had ravaged these. The beaches appeared good, with long stretches of white sand. Behind the Point found a Pilot waiting for us. We were now in Moreton Bay. Pilot not coming on board, (treating us as infection) followed his boat closely. Could plainly see breakers over coral reef here and there, so guess we are in dangerous passages. Pass close to mainland on ones left (going westward). Covered with large trees. Also two lighthouses on shore edge. On opposite side of bay, a remarkable view is to be had of hill and mountain formations. Two hills are so situated and shaped that they remind us all of Gaza Pyramids. Near them are three more very abrupt sharp peaked hills, the 3rd absolutely the sharpest peak I have ever seen, far and away beyond any of those at Cape town. (small hand drawing of peak shapes) Go as far as the Pile Light, the light is itself built on a steel framework, and on top of this, much resembling a balcony, is a house where the keeper lives. A signalling apparatus in use. Threw out our anchor here. This is as far as any ship can proceed without examination and serves as a temporary isolation.

Another large ship in all her war paint, here also, the 'SOMERSETSHIRE' with a cruiser stern (small drawing of stern). Hear that this ship torpedoed three years ago, taken to Devonport, where the original stern, which was blown off nearly, replaced by the one of present pattern. Has telescopic masts. Troops had dinner on board – notice came out that disembarkation to commence @ 2.30pm. Troops assemble and no doubt they are a fine body of men these Queenslanders, fine big stalwart chaps. Look O.K in their uniforms. Many of them, (all from the 'Pt......", embarked at Sydney) 1914 men on leave. They have their red stripe and 4 blues on forearm and colour patches (small drawing of patch design) in red, white and blue on tunics near shoulder sleeve. The Light Horse men from Egypt besides this, have their feather cockades in hats. Looks O.K.

A barge comes alongside with tug to take them off, the former succeeds in taking away our notice board re 'This vessel has twin screws etc', with her steel rope guys. The rope catches between the boards and looks as steady as if placed there on the barge. This raises a laugh for she looks very much the opposite to possessing twin screws. Next the same ropes catch against top of our aft gangway. Expect it to go, but instead as each guy comes into contact, they are snapped in two like twigs. This raises more roars of course. The 220 men with 4 or 5 cot cases are duly put on board the old barge. The tug tow them to quarantine. Seems an awful pity for these poor chaps, for it seems an almost un-glorious homecoming and welcome back.

Would have given anything to have gone into Brisbane. Our present position 15 and 20 miles from there and Brisbane –47miles from Cape Moreton. Am told that scenery en route along the river exquisite. The 'KAROOLA' at Brisbane on her first return trip as a Hospital, but assured if only we could get into Brisbane again, would meet with a great reception. Boats of nearly all Australian Interstate Steamship Companies anchored not far from us (mainly on Queensland coastal trade). Arrange with the Chief Steward that if he gets stores for the ship, to remember and get a few doz. pineapples and bananas as this the very time of year here for this tropical fruit. However, we were destined to come a thud over this as too far away from Port.

The harbour here has several small islands in it. Seems strange to have no patients on board after all this time and quite deserted. Waited for a while and started off about 6pm. Met the Pilot boat again further out and followed her. Took a slightly different course this time and kept well out from the point. 'Oil' now floats round that we are to go straight to Melbourne and pick up S.A. men and others for Tasmania from quarantine and in camp in Victoria and take them to their respective states. Trust this is so as I am anxious to get my kit bags home at any rate.

Wednesday 5th

A meeting of the sports committee having previously been held to arrange as to how the 18 pounds, 10 shillings donated by English Officers on our way over, to the club, should be spent, a sports tournament was arranged to be held on voyage to Melbourne. Money to be distributed to successful competitors. Obtaining O.C's permission to hold games during afternoon accordingly started today. Games held. Old Buffens winner, Argate potato race winner. Throwing at wicket winner Pens, sack race winner S/Sgt. Coldwell, and quoits tournament also begun. Results were most amusing and a pleasant afternoon spent. Land in sight most of the day and passed a point closely.

Thursday 6th

Games continued. Obstacle race winner J. Rundle, a difficult proposition this, as competitors has to crawl thro' the long wind shutes used for the tropics, then take an apple from a bucket of water by the mouth. This intensely amusing, especially when some of the wags of the unit competed. Pillow fighting on rail, winner Hall.

Friday 7th

On party to clean well deck aft. See by notice to crew that they invited to stay on ship for further voyage to Adelaide or Hobart, place not yet decided. All who claim to be paid off in Melbourne to furnish names, and these to be sent by wireless to the firm. Later in day hear it is to Adelaide we proceed. Good luck.

Saturday 8th

Of course do not expect to meet Mother when in S.A., but write and let her know I am coming. Reach Melbourne Heads 6.30am. pass through, but thick fog and smoke from bush fires impede our progress. Take soundings, ring bell and blow siren at intervals, and steam slowly and cautiously.

'S.S. MILTIADES' proceeds immediately ahead of us. Has few English wives on board for Aust. soldiers (more immigrants). Both of us berth just off Williamstown. Go in after awhile. Coal barge comes alongside, but coalies after consultation agree not to board the ship tonight, as having waited all day whilst wasting time in the anchorage. However say they will work tomorrow at double rates i.e., 6/- per hour. (Have been drawing ½ pay all day though for waiting.) Leave granted troops 2pm. today until 11pm. tomorrow. All applicants for transfer on previous parade informed that Head Quarters had written a letter to O.C. He read it himself and it's gist was that no man could transfer or obtain his discharge (i.e., being an A Class man), unless for urgent family reasons, or to go back to business or industry of welfare to the States. If granted for consideration even under those headings, the application would have to further go before the State Commandant and his decision final. A good many were disappointed at this.

Those folk to do all present guard, but somehow unfortunate am put on list in error and have to report back @ 2pm. tomorrow. Mitch, Jim and self go along to the favourite old spot, the Y.M.C.A. on St. Kilda Road for tea. Given a good warm reception. Hard to get used to breeches and woollen tunic on a hot sultry day like this, after shorts so long. Young ladies served, insisted upon us having plenty of iced lemon and drinks, which were much appreciated. The influenza epidemic has killed Melbourne. No indoor public amusement of any kind is allowed, so took a run down to St. Kilda, and spent the evening lying on the lawns and within reach of a sea breeze. Good crowd, but no bands etc.

Sunday 9th

We three after breakfast walked over to Yarra and followed the road into Melbourne. Often wanted to see the old Yarra properly, having heard so much boasting by Melbournites against Sydneyites re their 'arbor', so wish at last gratified. Previously walked along beach where it seemed most horses in Melbourne were having a dip, and being washed, thence across golf links to Yarra bank. Had lunch at Y.M.C.A. and caught tram for Pt. Melbourne. Reported ship 2pm. Unit informed that all had to report daily for medical inspection re flue stunt, and forms stating place to attend whilst in Melbourne filled in. Dr. came to ship @ 2.30pm, and inspected all those on guard who had desired to present themselves at this place. Sudden change towards evening strong winds, cold, and rain.

Monday 10th

And now we come to the end of a perfect day so to speak, for this is the biggest muck-up, and disorganised scheme I have ever witnessed. Previous daily papers inform that we are to take 510 men to Adelaide, but today contains an advertisement that the 'transport' 'Karoola' (this a perfect end) will take any man to Adelaide (being a S.A. man of course). Must report at the Pt. Melbourne pier not later than 2.30pm. Only start coaling this morning. Now we have heard a few yarns about the S. Aust. men being in Quarantine and isolation camps, breaking leave, running wild in Melbourne, getting into trouble of all sorts, quite strays and running loose and this confirms it. Some have been here days and others weeks and represent men from many various ships. At 2pm. they started to roll up, some rolling drunk and others without a bean in pocket. Some consisted of men from S.A. on lease and caught here by Quarantine regulations, some from bases, hospitals and camps, being in due form and order of course, their papers etc. would be sent to the ship for later use at their destination, but the others, goodness only knows what a tumble up they have caused, for no papers accompany them or record of any kind, how this mess will eventually be cleared up, I cannot think. But all this while something else was afoot on board.

Orders came last night that the men applying for transfer were to be taken off and sent to Moore Park Convalescent Hospital which is now used as an Influenza Hospital, for duty there. All these chaps about 30 in number from N.S.W., Vic., and S.A., getting their gear ready and packed. They leave us at about 3 o'clock and thus I lose my old friends Mitch and Smithy. Best of friends, must part, but I guess I will feel lonely for awhile without them. Altho' not definitely promised transfer for good, still they are hopeful, as this seems a step nearer. Nankivell also goes with them. Now a big crowd have mustered on the wharf and all of all the drunks I have ever seen, this debauchery was awful. S. Austs. have always had the name for being the most sober, diligent and orderly men of all the states, but here I feel ashamed of them. Fully 2/3rds of the whole, if not wholly intoxicated, were in all the worse for liquor. The Head Quarters staff officers who had come down to see the embarkation were powerless, and bottles were smashed and liquor drunk beneath their very noses.

The noise and commotion at foot of gangway, by some who did not at the last wish to come on, their mates insisting and struggling to drag them on, some stopping on gangway to raise bottle to their lips, thereby holding others following, these in their turn arguing and scarce a pocket that did not indicate a flask of spirits, or bottle or bottles of beer. Never have I seen such a bosh-up, lack of discipline, and disorganisation and there were the Officers, begging, humouring, and trying to coerce them to come or go on board. Well every vessel has only a certain holding capacity, so not knowing whether 500 or 1,000 men wished to come on board, so H.Q. Officers kept tally, but this was futile and useless for some of the men whom only half way up the gangway jumped over the rail and on to wharf, so at last took all we could see, and who 'wanted' to come for a ride. Coaling being finished put to sea, and a crowd were allowed on pier to see us off.

Proceeded slowly, this at 5.30pm. When we reached Portsea, stopped there for the night. Firemen were drunk, and some came on board so. Most of it was obtained from 'diggers'. Drink seems to be Australia's besetting sin. Have noticed it on a big scale on other occasions. Not sufficient steam, so cannot go until morning. This will probably upset Mother's arrangements for I have wired her to the effect we reach Adelaide about Wednesday morn. Amongst our troops are Sisters from Egypt and England. Three are from Keswick in my time, Sisters Johnson, Whitfield and Kitson. Have heard often of Whitfield in Egypt from Taylor and others, also many A.M.C. boys of Mitcham and Keswick. Goft, Conway, Redding, Twelvetree. Some of our original patients from England this trip here again too, also my chemistry friend Lt. Scott, have a good yarn with him and with Capt. Lewis. Who should be here also, but young Hopkin's brother of Hopkins in our Bank. A Tommy Officer now. Enlisted in England when war broke out, having gone there to study medicine. About 8 of our Sisters only left now. Others gone to do duty in Victoria also.

Still not knowing how many on board, find difficulty in finding beds for them all. Mattresses and blankets spread on decks for surplus sleepers. Reminds us of Tripoli and Beirut. Have every reason to believe there are N.S.W. and Victorian men on board as well as our own state, having listlessly walked down to ship and jumped on. Every corner of ship, Officers quarters, smoking room, wards etc., full of lounging fellows, an unheard of thing heretofore on this ship, being regular, orderly and a place for everything, and everything in its place as far as hospital itself concerned. Alas, Mother, we are no longer a hospital ship, now we are a rough and ready trooper, altho' still painted white with red crosses, but they will soon disappear when ship gets back to Melbourne.

Tuesday 11th

A few sore heads and sorry hearts this morning, I can see one Officer still in a trance. Started away between 7 and 8am. Have a yarn with Lt. Hopkins, whose father is now stationed at Mt. Barker I hear, in place of Mr. Dunk at National Bank. Tells me poor old Reg, who has so long been insane from shell shock at Gallipoli now recovering his mental balance. Good news as he is a favourite at the Bank. Steam slowly at first but more steam, more speed later on. Pass Cape Otway 65 miles from Heads during afternoon. We have now quite a family gathering on ship.

Wednesday 12th

Another thing to delay us. A thick heavy fog this morning. Ships siren sounded frequently, and steaming slowly. At 7pm. pass between Kangaroo Island and Cape Jervis, close to mainland. To show what a mess the records of patients are and their whereabouts, following is an extract from Corp Orders:-

Troops are to arrange themselves in two ranks in the following order

S.S. THEMISTOCLES, ORONTES, BURMA, AENEAS, MAMARI, SAXON, ARGYLLSHIRE. Other 'details' to report to orderly room. (Goodness knows what other details may be). Passed Brighton and Glenelg (lights of town) and dropped anchor at Semaphore anchorage at 11.30pm. Slept on deck.

Thursday 13th

Medical Officer came off from shore and carefully took temperatures of all on board. Went into Outer Harbour and began disembarkation immediately. Big and enthusiastic crowd on wharf. Saw Reg Hopkins now quite well and Hopkins family, and Jack Treloar. All the time kept a look out for Mother or the girls. Band playing. Said by all on board to be the heartiest reception ever witnessed. Saw Mother and Renie looking for me after crowd had dispersed a bit. Glad to see Mother looking so well. Had a good chat. Donned my tunic and jumped on to wharf. I felt very pleased that she should at length be able to see the good old ship. Both of us extremely disappointed at not being able to go home, for it is definitely settled for the present anyhow.

Interviewed O.C. and Adjt. last night to this effect, but find Melbourne have issued instructions no staff to be granted leave. To see my dear Mother for an hour is something to go on with at any rate. Ship moved off at 1pm. I stood on Monkey deck and waved to them till lost to view. Jack Treloar took kit bags to Woodville Stn. for me. Good old pal. A good run to Cape Jervis and by 6pm. passed very close to Island this time and saw 'KARATTA' on her way back to Pt. Adelaide. Fresh rumours afloat of our going to West now after docking. Still seems strange why these troops of ours get leave immediately, having only done 2½ days quarantine on ship and right from 'black' Melbourne. See Premier made a fuss when mentioned, but 7 days isolation not carried out all the same.

Friday 14th

Passed not many miles from Cape Northumberland and Nelson today. Plenty of porpoise about. A perfect day, sea with a lovely old rolling side swell on. Busy clearing ship and cleaning up, as hear now that ship going into dock. Passed Otway midnight, expect reach Melbourne early hours, 6 hrs from here. Now question arises as to what will be done with us. Are we to follow the others into epidemic camps or not, or be granted leave. I intend going to Gippsland, if not allowed to cross Border into S.A. Voluntary inoculation today, anti-pneumonia influenza. Assailed myself of opportunity in case this should be handy in getting home

Saturday 15th

More fog in the bay, slowed down very much, taking soundings the while. Siren sounded often. Heat intense due to bush fires. Proceeded straight up the Yarra (our first time) and berthed at No. 9. Gave a coal hulk a squeeze on the way up. More papers to sign re attendance at Quarantine Office for 4 days. Leave granted until 10am. Monday, so S.A.'s and Vic's asked to do all guard duty. Am anxious to see Mitch and Jim, I hear they are on duty at the Exhibition building, connected to a civilian 'epidemic' hospital. Go ashore with B. Allen and book a room at Victoria Coffee palace. Find the woollen rig-out most uncomfortable and clammy this weather after used to our shorts so long. And now everything is a mass of uncertainty. Half staff attached to P.M.O? Victoria, and half on board, so nobody able to get home and goodness knows what will be the outcome of this split.

Thus endeth, altho' in Melbourne on two occasions this is the end of our voyage – Melbourne to Melbourne originally, but one of the most uncertain, spasmodic voyage I think possible.

Arrivals and Departures. 1918–1919

Arrived Fremantle	24/9/18
Left "	25/9/18
Arrived Colombo	5/10/18
Left "	6/10/18
Arrived Suez	17/10/18
Left "	18/10/18
Arrived Pt. Said	19/10/18
Left "	19/10/18
Arrived Alexandria	20/10/18
Left "	25/10/18
Arrived Beirut (Syria)	26/10/18
Left "	27/10/18
Arrived Alexandria	28/10/18
Left "	29/10/18
Arrived off Beirut	31/10/18
Left "	31/10/18
Arrived Tripoli (40 miles)	31/10/18
Left "	2/11/18
Arrived Alexandria	3/11/18
Left "	15/11/18
Arrived Malta	18/11/18
Left "	19/11/18
Arrived Gibraltar	23/11/18
Left "	23/11/18
Arrived Southampton	27/11/18
Left "	13/12/18
Arrived Pt. Said	24/12/18
Left "	25/12/18
Arrived Colombo	9/1/19
Left "	10/1/19
Arrived Fremantle	21/1/19
Left "	22/1/19
Arrived Melbourne	28/1/19
Left "	29/1/19
Arrived Sydney	1/2/19
Left "	2/2/19

Arrived Brisbane	4/2/19
Left "	4/2/19
Arrived Melbourne	8/2/19
Left "	10/2/19
Arrived Adelaide	13/2/19
Left '	13/2/19
Arrived Melbourne	15/2/19

PAPER CLIPPING ON LAST PAGE DATED 29/1/19

TWO CONTINGENTS ARRIVE
NUMBER GO INTO CAMP

Difficulties in connection with troops who are bound for 'clean States' had to be met today by the military authorities, when the hospital ship Karoola and the transport Burma arrived late this afternoon. The two contingents numbered in all 1,120 men, and it was necessary to provide accommodation for many of them in Melbourne. Disembarkation had to be postponed from the time originally fixed owing to the vessels being delayed at Portsea.

Patients from the Karoola for Victoria were taken to the Caulfield Military Hospital, where their relatives met them, and the invalids for South Australia and Tasmania, who numbered 51, were also taken there, and will await a change in present restrictions before proceeding to their homes. The men for New South Wales and Queensland went on by the vessel, as did the Queenslanders from the Burma. The New South Wales Soldiers from the transport left by special train later in the afternoon and the men for Tasmania and South Australia were taken to the Broadmeadows camp which had been hurriedly arranged to accommodate them. Invalids from the Burma were, however, also taken to the hospital. The Victorians from the same ship were brought by train to the Flinders Street Station and marched to the Sturt Street drill hall, where their cases were dealt with and where their relatives were met.

Diary Four

My dear Mother,

I seem to have naturally dropped into the habit of keeping my diary in a letter – book fashion. However I think you yourself would prefer it, for should I be prevented from coming home again at some future time, this would not only be handy to me, thereby saving me the task of writing letters giving you an a/c of the voyage, but getting them home in time as well. Dear old Auntie's son too I should think, would like to read it. Of course you will see that this is merely an account of the pleasurable and better side of this life. I have omitted the pathetic, the sordid, and worst side incidental to the daily grind of duty which this duty entails.

Yours loving son,
Rex

FEBRUARY, 1919

Saturday 15th
Went on shore with B. Allen from Orderly Room. Met Chunder Morris and hear from him that Mitch and Smithy on duty at Melb. Exhibition Influenza hospital. Would have paid them a visit, but says they are on night duty and evidently sleeping now, so put it off. Allen and I booked room at Victoria Coffee Palace.

Sunday 16th
Take a stroll to the Exhibition and find both in bed, but owing to the heat of the day and closeness of the building, Mitch is awake and perspiring. Sees me immediately, gives poor old Jimmy a dig and both come along to another passage where away from all slumberers, we exchange news. The Exhibition is similar to a big barn so far. Everything is upside down and topsy turvy with mismanagement and unpreparedness.

In the hospital are some 300 patients, two wards, male and female, with children in cots in each. Staff Gray is in charge, and Cpl. Mc Queen over night staff. They tell me that the Matron is a splendid woman and thinks the world of them for coming at a time when she and her staff nearly distracted with overwork and fatigue. Many had already contracted the disease themselves and were now laid up. Many deaths were occurring day after day (all turning quite black giving the belief to a good many that it was the old black plague on another visit to Melbourne) and many more admissions to hospital. Our poor boys for being only here two or three days had had a pretty rough time of it.

No food in pantries for their patients, this being scoffed off by the many hangers-on supposing to be working and assisting there. This proved to be great source of inconvenience and worry to our chaps for simply not knowing who was who, finding these civilian male nurses giving hunks of meat at any old time to any patient for the asking (when they were supposed to be milk diet) and when a patient with a temp. of 106, was ordered a sponging, these people simply washed the face and hands. No soda water could be found in the middle of the night when wanted, and some patients unwashed for 6 days, floor like a stable, beds just dragged and bunched up together in any old order, dirty sheets and covers, beds absolutely unchanged and filthy, no diet sheets, kiddies howling and in pain and mixed up with adults, dirt everywhere and always people dying and more coming in.

However Gray soon saw to these hangers-on and with the help of V.A.D's and Sisters got a list of those properly connected with the institution. Beds were put in line and numbered, floor sodered and mopped, diet sheets made up and many other little things incidental to the proper management and easy running of a hospital. Anyhow, Melbourne is ringing with their praises now, for many lives have been saved through their extra attention and care. Mitch says he feels now, the use of his time put in at Keswick, for here, his chance had come to put into practice his nursing experience. We often have spoken of this, and wondered if Keswick had not been a waste of time. Smithy says the Matron wishes to do all in her power for them and already pay besides their Military allowance, has been spoken of. Their quarters were being improved and their mess, where the V.A.D's were in attendance, were also gradually coming up to scratch. Anyhow, they seem properly done up these two, both had said that they had never had such strenuous times in their lives, so lively and constant the attention required.

Went out onto the balcony and saw our boys amongst the ward patients. The female nursing staff wore masks, but the medico in charge, said our fellows may smoke as much as they desired, and it seemed queer to see them all 'puffing' away at their work. Even Mitch and Smithy bought some cigarettes. Arrange to meet them at the Y.M.C.A. during the evening, and which we accordingly do. Have a nice quiet tea and they seem relieved to think they are away from the hospital for awhile and are able to forget about it.

Monday 17th

S.A. and Victorians asked to do the guard, and all have to present themselves at Quarantine office for three days successive medical examinations. Forms had to be filled in, to comply with this order as soon as we had come from Adelaide. My guard 1-6am. this morning. Ship fumigated during yesterday and goes across stream to Victoria dry dock. In another dock just next, ties the Dutch Mail Steamer 'HOUTMAN', the one once suspected of laying mines about Gabo and New Zealand waters. Spent evening at St. Kilda beach. As soon as dock dry, tail shaft removed and propellers taken off. All staff reported back 10am. to see what further development in hand.

Tuesday 18th

Raining all over Victoria today and squashes Allen's and my own proposal to go for a little trip to Ballarat. However, decide to wait until tomorrow in case weather should improve. Intend to try to work Bacchus Marsh in as well. Later owing to Taulty's good chance of getting off the ship, Allen has to stay on board and do orderly room work. Go to see Smithy again and it being his night off, spend the evening with him and get him to come back to the ship with me, to sleep, which he does, reminding me of old times once more. Make arrangements with him to go to Bacchus Marsh on the morrow, for the day only. Hear from him that Dr. Mannix, R.C. Archbishop is to take over management of the Exhibition hospital very shortly and place his Mother Superior and nuns as staff there. Hear that there is likely to be criticism and resignation of present Matron and staff immediately if this scheme entertained.

All hotels, billiard saloons, picture shows, all houses of amusement in fact being now closed in Melbourne, schools have followed likewise. Funds previously coming from R.C.

Colleges for upkeep of convents etc., consequently ceasing, this is 'Mannix' idea of getting fresh income for his various institutions. The most disloyal man in Aust. during the war, and literally hated by Protestants in Melbourne for his disloyal utterances, and public attempts to hinder recruiting.

Wednesday 19th

We caught the 7.40 train for the 'Marsh" at Spencer St, and arrived about 10.00 o'clock. Went for a stroll up the street, and after making a few enquiries, found the place we were looking for, the Federal Milk Coy., this firm has joined hands with the Co-operative Milk Coy., (the producers own factory, 1st in Bacchus Marsh) and having extended their premises, do a very large business. Had to obtain permission from the manager, a real hard-headed business man to go through the factory. At first not willing to let us through, citing a case where two chaps whom he let through previously, really belonging to an opposition firm, there for the purpose of finding out the latest ideas and methods. However, after stating that we were disinterested parties, he said, 'Well it's against our rules, but go through, I don't see you'.

We had an interesting couple of hours, but the whole scheme seems simple enough. Girls are employed on the lighter jobs. Saw the milk fats being tested by the Sulphate test, which was interesting. Some 15,000 tins manufactured every day when season in full swing. Then went for a walk round the district. Bacchus is a goodly flat in a hollow cut into many sections and all growing lucerne, being irrigated from a weir further up the river. Methods appear rather primitive, but seem to answer very well.

Made a contour of the river, walked along it for two or three miles and finally crossed over a footbridge. Smithy had certainly shown 'nervy' signs in, but today he is in high spirits and his old self again. Feel quite satisfied that this is doing him good. The lucerne (everywhere) gave a delicious and invigorating smell. Came out on the main road to Ballarat and walked back again to the town. Had a look at the trees (oak etc) planted to memory of lads enlisted from the Marsh. This is a good idea, each tree bearing an inscription, and will make a fine avenue some day.

Caught the 4.30 goods train and after signing our risk notes, were invited to take a seat in the guards van. He was a good old sort and seemed to think it encumbered upon him to make our little journey as pleasant as possible. Travelling very slow though and many delays. Jumped out at North Melbourne Station yard and caught a suburban for Flinders St. Arrived about 8.20pm. making it too late to have tea together as intended as Smithy had to go on duty at 9pm. However, went to Y.M.C.A., had tea by myself, Jimmy getting supper at usual hour at Hospital. Went up afterwards to see Mitch, and these two induced me to stay the night, so occupied Mitch's bed. Guess Mother would not have liked this, but I learnt ship was out of dock and present in Victoria Basin, a jolly long way off, and no other means of getting there except by ('Shanks').

Thursday 20th

Intended going back to the ship this morning, but as walking down from the Exhibition, meet the bugler and he tells me the 'HYGEIA' leaves Pt. Melbourne for Queenscliff and Seranto at 10.30. Catch the 10 train and for 4/- buy a ticket for the trip. Had a very enjoyable time, meeting on board an elderly gentleman, whom making himself known to me, tells me of his boys at the front. At present a member of the Com. Trav. Assoc., and the 'Fathers League', doing all in his power for the welcoming back and treatment of returned soldiers. Starting in the Riverina and still holding sheep country up there, but now retired. I was much interested in his knowledge of sheep raising etc. Went to the forts at Queenscliff, alighting here for a look round, (for I hear nothing doing at Seranto) until the steamer returns. Walk along beaches etc. and watch kiddies bathing. Some very fine summer residences and hotels here and numerous boarding houses, at the same, there is a distinct countryfied air about the place. There are many farms round-about and farmers coming and going about the town. Hear that the belt of country running along slopes of ranges, some of Victoria's best wheat producing areas. Had a good run back and met old gent again. Went to Y.M. and caught Smithy. Walked to hospital with him and make arrangements to go through Dunlop's at Montague tomorrow morning.

Friday 21st

Had to do a day's guard today. Cargo now on the wharf, lead for St. Helen's Smelting Coy. of Liverpool, wool and preserved fruits and jams for London. Lead into No. 4 hold and the other into Nos. 1 and 2. No. 3 still reserved for mental patients. We are a transport lot now in reality. We have been stripped of our green promenade lights and the huge red lights next to the funnel. Surprised at the size of these crosses when taken down. The ship has been painted all over, a French Grey, the funnel bears the colour of the owners, red with black top. Now lying in Victoria basin, on other of side of Yarra altogether, and just ahead of the 'AENEAS' the ship, some of whose troops we took to Adelaide.

Met Alf our old Bosun who is in charge of shore gangs for the company. Tells me of some of his experiences while on the 'KATOOMBA' making use of her name with very great emphasis and pride. Just by the way he told me that as soon as the ship was fitted up as a transport in Sydney, they proceeded through the Panama to New York. Were engaged in carrying American troops to England under escort of American Navy, which ships he thinks much inferior to our own. Latterly the British Navy took this job over, and it was while an escort of 8 or 9 vessels were somewhere close to the Irish coast, that one of their number was torpedoed. Instantly the order was given 'take stations' and they all proceeded on their way. Alf's chest filled when he related the wonderful smartness of the Navy in his decidedly emphatic and true seaman's language. After we left them at Pt. Said going through last time, they went to Salonika again under escort. Two of their number were blown up, and the guilty subs sunk by depth charges, which he said, being exploded not so very far from their own vessel, caused her to shiver from stem to stern, and lifting her bodily higher out of the water. A while later the S.O.S. signal, also that unfortunate vessel was sinking fast and immediate help was desired. The distance was 40 miles, and it took them only two hours to reach scene of disaster and pick up survivors. Alf is 'decidedly' engrossed with the speed of his vessel with the aid of the best Welsh coal. At Salonika they took English troops on board, but when embarkation was complete they were ordered to disembark again. Fresh troops came, some from Bulgaria and comprised those who had originally landed on Gallipoli with our Anzacs. They met the portion of the British fleet commissioned to proceed to Dardanelle's, land troops at Constantinople and capture German war vessels in the Black Sea. They followed the fleet, the old hospital ship 'VALDIVIA' immediately behind them. This was at the time when this vessel left her berth next to us at Alexandria to join up, as we then heard. Going through the straits, various points of history now, were pointed out by the troops as 'Lone Pine', and many others, places which cost our brave Australians so dearly. The 'KATOOMBA' landed her 2,000 troops, taken off by barges sent alongside. Not allowed ashore himself. When coming back through a mine area, one of the Otters on being hoisted, suddenly dropped from its suspended position, swung and with all its weight jammed him against the ships bulwark. This gave abdomen trouble, and he was sent home by transport and now awaits an operation. His old ship is expected back shortly.

Saturday 22nd

Off guard at noon. Take my Xmas cake down to the Y.M.C.A. so that when Mitch and Smithy go along to have tea, they may partake of the same with the three ladies there on duty each Saturday. Caught the 4pm. Adelaide Express for Ballarat. Train pretty well crowded and only going as far as Serviceton. There owing to influenza regulations, the mail and goods are transferred to the Adelaide train (two specials, taking stranded S.A. people in Victoria to Adelaide are run each a week now, the passengers going into Quarantine for 6 days in S.A. prior to going to their homes).

Opened the locked apartment leading to 1st class and with other soldiers took a seat. The carriage we left was crammed. This is a ridiculous state of affairs, seeing that no shop or saloon in Melbourne at the present time is allowed to contain more than 20 persons. Became friendly with a young returned soldier whose ship called at Adelaide. Being there for 4 days he says he had absolutely the best and most enjoyable time, of any since being away from home. Promised to show me around Ballarat on Monday morning. Many fine crops of potatoes to be seen along the line, nearing Ballarat. Arrived there just before 8 o'clock and straightway booked up a room at Reid's Coffee Palace. Beguiled the evening with a young discharged soldier by walking round to the Returned Soldiers Club, and up and down Sturt Street, at the same time making enquiries re anything doing tomorrow.

Sunday 23rd

Take an early walk through the streets to see how they look by daylight. At once struck by their width, trees and splendid clean looking buildings. Walk to Lake Wendouree and have a stroll by the shore. Note the yacht and rowing clubs, ferries etc. to Botanic gardens and Fairyland on the opposite side.

In afternoon took electric tram for gardens (about worst service in the world, only one entrance and that by the motorman who collects all fares, by watching you drop your coins into a box behind him, dispensing with the services of a conductor). At once struck with the beauty and careful laying out of these. The finest bloom of flowers I have ever beheld are in the glasshouses there, and as for statuary, it stands alone to anything I have seen, especially those of 'Susannah', 'Ruth', 'Modesty', 'Rachel' and the 'Flight from Pompeii'. The former is a wonderful piece of sculpture, quite a favourite, by Summers, an Australian in Rome. These are housed in a fine glass house. 'Susannah' has had the offer of 20,000 pounds, (cost 1,800) but being a legacy cannot be sold.

Spent a very enjoyable hour or two here, and walked along banks of lake on way back. Then went to Motor garage and booked up seats for Gong-gong etc. tomorrow. See there is no chance of going down any mine, for all in immediate vicinity closed down. Meet acquaintance of train at P.O. according to appointment. Engage a cab and pay a visit to the Woollen Mills, but find epidemic causes 'no admission allowed'. Then went to the old 'Stockade' where only battle fought in Aust. took place. A pillar erected over sight of stockade, of the fifties sometime. Miners claiming their rights and meaning to have them, here collected and made a stand against Imperial soldiers sent to capture them. Caught napping and a good many shot. A monument to their leader now stands in gardens in Sturt St. This leader lost an arm in the fray, but rose high in public life years afterwards. Tried to get through tile works but same scare prevailed.

Went to 'Orphanage', but met with same result, altho' had the satisfaction of having a yarn with the Superintendent, a grand old chap, who explained their system and showed us his book of accounts etc. in his office. (Interesting to me). (Similar to Boys Home at Mt. Barker). Had a look through Coliscum where competitions of music and singing are held each year, also the Travellers Club etc. The public library (and excellent one I hear) 'flue' up. The motor trip being put off on a/c of no other passengers turning up, we had dinner at the Coffee Palace. Caught the 3pm. train for Geelong. Had to wait here for an hour and a half, so took a jaunt down to the wharf to see the wheat ships, and wheat stacks. Met an old miner there, who knew the old digging at Ballarat well. Had an interesting chat with him.

Rain has destroyed a good deal of wheat, when stacks opened up for loading. To make matters worse, weevils have played havoc with the grain, it is necessary to clean it before shipment. Several seasons grain stocked up, but now a brighter opening for shipment to England offers itself, for according to news, about 50 large vessels already on water on their way to take it. Mice plaque, damp, rotting of bags etc. have all been serious discomfits to the wheat lying here so long. Walked back along main street and caught the 5.40 train for Melbourne, the remainder a fairly fast journey.

Tuesday 25th

Reported for guard duty as all Red Cross goods coming on board. Six more men leave the ship and we hear our new O.C. has been unsuccessful in bringing his new men on board with him to replace us all. Greatly disappointed at having not received a single letter from home since Adelaide. Can blame mail arrangements 'flued up' for this. Walk up to Exhibition to say farewell to Mitch and Smithy during night, as we expect to sail at mid-day tomorrow.

Wednesday 26th

Will not get away before 4 now, so our new O.C. being sporty gives us 2hrs leave to enable us to do any little thing we may wish to finalise on shore. This is especially handy to me, as, having by some wonderful means or other, received a stray letter from Mother, telling me she had forwarded my kit-bag with contents to Spencer St. Stn. (Glad, though unexpectedly) find my parcel there, the contents being from her dear, thoughtful love, a big packet of almonds, chocolate and other sweets. Go into Melbourne and there meet Col. McIntosh, who came and shook hands, wished me good luck and a bon voyage. We are all sorry to lose this most excellent man for who we have every respect. Leave at 4.30pm, a few of the boys being off duty for awhile from the Exhibition, come down to see us off. Some of ours on board, entice old Duncan McDonald, (a favourite sailor) into bringing his bag-pipes along. He plays plenty of Scottish Airs on this which proves rather a novelty even Hon. Admiral Mc. Ilwraith not objecting to it, altho' very close to his ear, before casting off. Once outside 'Heads' met with a good old sea. Slept on deck but soaked out about 2 in the morning by waves dashing over well deck. Hanging mattress up to dry, somebody made off with it, for it had disappeared when I returned for it at day-break.

Thursday 27th

A good sea still on, but having good ballast now, the old ship sticks and steadies to it. We have with us a patient Sister (a cot case with flu) her sister is with her to nurse her, altho' one of our own staff Sister's detailed for duty. Our poor patient is a thin, wasted form and not long for this world I should say, but is remarkably content and cheerful withal. In fact it is a pleasure to talk with her. Contacted the disease, by being placed on duty, after serious illness of her own, in a 'chest' ward, before she nearly ready and fit to resume. Also there are 4 staff Sergeants, returned dispensers from India. They know our old dispenser friend from Keswick well. (Staff Rowe). Occupy Sergeants cabins, some now occupied. Jolly fine fellows and associate with our fellows well. Came from Bombay to Sydney direct, by 'THERMISTOCLES', and having found their way back as far as Melb, are indebted to this ship for their final lift home. One of them knows the Uncles at Fremantle well, have a good many chats of interest re various places in India, he having put into my head to take a run to Nasik if I get a chance while in Bombay this time. Good for brass work he reckons.

Note from diary of Cpl. C.R. Mortimer AWM

Under Geneva Convention we were only allowed to have water as ballast. (A British Hospital Ship was sunk by Germany for having Pig Iron as ballast), so ship riding light and tossed around.

When at Pt Melbourne, all tanks were filled with fresh water, and as went along ships journey, these tanks would be filled with sea water after the fresh water was used. At one stage the tanks were not properly emptied out of their salt water at Fremantle, so that from there to Cape Town there was brackish water for cooking and drinking.

Friday 28th

Have not seen much of O.C. to date, but came along this afternoon and takes an interest in the cricket on boat deck, and in evening certainly seems sociable as he listens to the music, leans on the piano and tells funny stories between times. This is the man of whom the W.O. and Lt. Luton would have us believe, he was a very strict and severe officer. Nothing of the kind. This said for their own benefit. Promotions are out. Swift Ord. Room Sgt, Tomroy Cpl, McElhone Cpl. A few aspirants disappointed, but cheered by fact that Luton stating on parade, that further promotions to be made from this staff, when staff reinforced in England. No ambitions myself in this matter, in fact would refuse stripes now altogether, so no hoping for same.

MARCH, 1919

Saturday 1st

Nothing doing, but a quiet pleasant sea.

Sunday 2nd

Passed Leeuwin and kept in sight of land all day. Arrived in the Roads about 2am. and anchored for daybreak. All on board medically inspected, and temperatures taken. Allowed to go to our usual anchorage and began coaling. Flying yellow flag. 'DIMBOOLA' arrives with mail from East.

Tuesday 5th

Considered to be in quarantine until 5pm. today, and our patients not allowed off. O.C. tried to get off at about 3pm, but Dr. says owing to clock going back 2 hours, must be taken into consideration, i.e. for 7 full days isolation complete. Much amusement this morning, when apples (300 odd cases) sent on board, to be stowed on bridge. The 1st sling sent up from barge loosely tied, so when raised in air above our deck, cases fell out and smashed 2 or 3. Imagine what followed. Everybody dived and ducked for the strays, even the W.O. and chief Purser, Mc. Ilwraiths sub-manager in Melb, (on a trip for his health) condescended to partake of the spoils. These apples, as on other are a gift from the firms Managing Director for troops returning. However we never get any, and they are allowed to rot and decay, baked by the tropical sun and all thrown overboard, cases unopened, as has actually happened, without a single one being issued.

Made good use of our opportunity this time anyhow. Coaling 600 tons, but slow on a/c of being placed by chutes into bunkers from vessels sides, no one being allowed on board for 'flue up' reasons. Got off at 6pm. by tug sent alongside. Officers sent and patient Sister by another, have leave till midnight. Saw Uncle Chas. and with him went to Pt. Walter by tram. Evening warm, found this an enjoyable spot. Dancing, and boat-loads of pleasure seekers from Perth, who bring a band with them, make a lively scene on the big open lawns, by playing 2 and 3's, and other homely games. The river looks fine from here, so strolled down to the jetty for awhile. Took tram to Uncle Dave's. They were retiring to bed, and having written a P.C, stating not much chance of my getting leave (an early prediction) were surprised and pleased to see me. Getting more and more comfortably settled in their new home, which I like too, very much indeed. All abed when I reached the ship again.

Thursday 6th

Left punctually at 7am. and headed for the old Briny again. Pretty rocky too, rolls so much tonight, that it is impossible to sleep on deck. One cannot keep still, spread arms and legs as you will.

Friday 7th

An 'Influenza' suspect today, a donkey-man. Jolly detailed for special duty and both sent to isolation ward. Patient kept his condition secret at Fremantle.

Sunday 9th

One of our new sailors, quite a young fellow, one of the party of three who set out from Medlin Is. in a 20ft. life-boat for Fanning Island (a thirteen day's sail) after their ship the old 'JOHN MURRAY' had been wrecked (Melb. training ship commissioned to take wheat over to San Francisco and return with a general cargo). Were taken to Honolulu by Cable Coy's 200 ton schooner, others at Medlin, by an Austr.-America ship later. Had a very rough and trying trip in their small craft.

Monday 10th

Cold storage apparatus in engine room broken down. 5,000 pounds worth of meat in the balance. All engineers working hard last night and all day today. Chief very doubtful as to their being able to mend the very big break in pipe. Late tonight its fixed, but he a bit pessimistic as to its remaining so.

Thursday 13th

We have with us two discharged soldiers, both Englishmen. One enlisted in Aust. Army and now returning to old country. Arranged their passages through Repat. and Defence Dept. The other of the English Army, was wounded and gassed in France. Advised by his Medics to take a trip for his health to Aust. When his ship the 'MONGOLIA' 40 miles out from Bombay, she struck a mine and sank in 15 mins. Survivors picked up by Dutch Steamer. This chap went on to Dutch East Indies in her, North Territory and New Guinea, and finally found his way to Brisbane, Syd, Melb, Adel, and the West where we picked him up, so has had a trip right round Aust. Lives at Windsor and wishes to show me round London a bit on our arrival there.

Saturday 15th

Crossed the line today, getting warmer but a good cool breeze at evenings.

Monday 17th

At 8 o'clock this morning passed land on our right. Supposed to be the Malabar Coast of Sth. India. Low lying foreshore, but very high mountains not far inland. Notice 1 or 2 small sailing craft, and a large 'neutral' steamer lying off a small port with a lofty white lighthouse at its entrance. Tall palm trees line the shore and plenty of small growth. Sunsets these days are beautiful. As from the 15th, all wireless news officially cut out, as per intimation from Colombo Radio. Trust no fresh trouble has broken out on the other side. O.C's final inspection today. Expressed himself at 2pm. parade, as being very pleased, and quality of work, 'very, very nice' and as a sign of his appreciation would give us the afternoon off and free use of the boat deck. Also said we had a high reputation to keep up, and as this probably last trip of the ship, to keep up high standard nevertheless. Said he would now insist on all future promotions i.e. 2 Sgts, and 4 Cpls, being made from present members of unit when staff reinforced in England.

Passed an old Dhow heavily laden towards sunset. If Admiral Jellicoe's programme on his visit to Aust, kept to time, we should see something of him or his party at Bombay. Supposed to arrive there on the 15th.

Tuesday 18th

Passed Pigeon Island this morning (a high brown coloured mound). (small drawing of same). 4th Officer says small port passed yesterday was just north of. During afternoon many more 2 masted sailing ships pass – land in sight all the time. 350 miles to go from midday today. Southern Cross about 40 degrees.

Wednesday 19th

Passed the Bombay floating light at midday, followed by a large steamer we had prev. overtaken. Had to turn to a right angle here, and a little over 20 miles from Bombay. Reached the light ship, the other also has a bell which rings with every roll and movement of the boat, and stopped at the pilot boat to pick up the pilot. Could see the 'NEW ZEALAND' distinctly from here. Her hull had been scraped and an 'army' of sailors were repainting the sides. Pass the 'OSTERLY' the Aust. Liner of Orient Coy, going on her way out. Went straight up to the "Mawl" i.e. the entrance to Alex. Docks, where steamers lie in wait for the tides. A large new building has just been erected here, where Indian Mails are received and sorted. Many English and Anglo-Indian girls work here and our chaps try hard to attract their attention. Notice a fair sprinkling of British-India boats in. Very pleased to get to the wharf so soon – for last occasion, nearly 2 days wasted in anchorage.

Leave is granted from 5-midnight, but Rundle and I having previously arranged with W.O. to do first guard, these duties are assigned us. A bit disconcerted though at the news that Lt. Luton insists on 14 men on guard. Since only ½ staff now, there is double number of guards than usual. A bit hot. Would readily complain to O.C. for altho' 'tis said that thieving has taken place in Red Cross holds, these precautions are grossly overdone, fancy 3 men alone posted to bridge to guard a few apples, and I guarantee there are more apples disappearing tonight than all the voyage hitherto, three to patrol the decks and two to Red Cross etc. Never heard of such a preposterous over-estimation. The thief of course could not be watched for during the trip when things were said to be disappearing from time-to-time, but precautions must be awaited until in port and everybody goes ashore. Mc. Elhone, striving hard to get Sgts. stripes, arms himself with hammer, talks quietly, condescendingly, explains the magnitude of the task of running down the burglar, the 'importance' of it as he terms it and hosts of other disgustingly babyish things about the O.C. and Major saying they would gladly mend broken bones and other rot if we came into conflict with this terrible nightmare of an impostor. The whole tone and manner is so appallingly crawling, and red tapey, I am sick of the business. This fellow complained very bitterly when he discovered his own name in the extra list for duty and 'was going' so far as to see the O.C. about it, however coming into contact with Luton first, of course to such a crawler, all these ideas are at once knocked in the head, and now he tries to impress us. Finally resolve to see the O.C. in the morning and explain, for I am certain he knows nothing about these arrangements. At this rate we will be doing guard every other day and Luton has always been a hindrance to the troops in the matter of leave, the whole trouble being, that the men of this unit have always been too good and soft, never failing in their duties or work or discipline required of them, this 'Pomey' finds it an easy matter to impose on them. The apples for instance are in charge of chief steward, brought on by him for use as other ships stores as meat etc, and why have we to have 3 men on the job. The steward who thinks of his own staff – has a mutual friendship in the way of money making with this chap, of course talks him over. Things instead of improving are going from bad to worse and after all 'the war is over'. Being a new Adjutant he is termed a 'nark'.

Thursday 20th

Rumoured that English Officer's wives, and children will return with us. May be a novelty if true. The rumour appears to be true for natives are bringing quantities of timber, mostly teak, for the purpose of making cots for children and beds for the women. Hear that the 'TOPAZE' in naval dock. This must have been the 3 funnelled cruiser I noticed there coming in. Roberts and I go off at midday to the dock yard, leaving poor little Rundle on board, ill with fresh boils, poor kid. Get permission from an officer to visit ship. Being refitted, so no Officers on board, but find a Petty Officer and others who knew Shone Sargent (*English relative*) well, and how they speak of him, 'top hole' a gentleman and sport. The P.O. takes me round to the 'MAJESTIC' to see his P.M.O, a Staff Surgeon Egan. Met his comrade Naval Officer first, who asked me to sit in lounge while he went to dining hall to tell him of my desired interview. At length Egan came, greeted me pleasantly and shook hands, and in a perfectly frank and open manner, told me all he could of Shone. Expressed his sorrow of losing what he termed his fast friend. Appears he took ill in Red Sea and not Persian Gulf as told me by Miss Husband. Came overland thro' Italy just after Egan to join ship, and had been on board some 6 weeks or 2 months. Always complained of his head, and one day (after always warning his crew against such a practice) lay in the sand at Aden without his topee (a very dangerous thing to do). It was first supposed he had received a sun-stroke when he took ill, so Sgt. Egan, having no decent accommodation on board, had him sent to the hospital at Aden, where reasonable care might be taken of him. After a time came to Bombay in a hospital ship, and died at Bombay on 25th June, 1918, (just before we got there). Egan stated that his father wired his intentions of coming out from England to see him, but Shone's death shortly afterwards prevented this. He himself received the news while still in the Red Sea, and all on board were saddened by the news, having learned to love and respect him for his quiet unassuming manner, and untiring attention to wants, and in cases of sickness, to the crew.

Sgt. Egan a tall, rather thin man, with short moustache and beard. A splendid looking fellow and I shall not forget him. Stated further, re the enquiries his mother had made re the missing belongings sent safely enough from on board to her. It appears she had complained to the Admiralty re various losses, and other damage sustained by the remainder. Admiralty had written to the East India Stn. for an explanation. Said he was perfectly satisfied in his own mind that the Italians would pilfer the luggage on its way through Italy. He landed the gear in Egypt and it being customary to send all Sailors and Soldiers gear overland by this route, via Taranto, this is what most likely happened, further proved by the fact that two suits of clothes, when received at Padstow, were torn, dusty and had the appearance of having been dragged or thrown about on the ground, evidently by railway men in search of loot (a not unusual thing this, and their dishonesty well known to travellers). Said he had sent binoculars and medical books, but the former missing on arrival of package at his home. He had written and told his mother all, and asked me to convey his kindliest regards to her and inform her of his intention of coming to see her when his ship sailed to England, probably in the near future.

Very sorry to part company myself, but met Robby by appointment, after finding out from Sick Bay Steward at 'Sailors' home, where the grave of Shone was to be found. (Had written Miss Husband stating I would visit it if possible should I ever come this way again). Buried at Sewri Cemetery, so will go out tomorrow. Robby goes to Crawford Markets and I to Roosevelt House in Appollo Bunder to see Miss Cowdrey, having learned from Y.M.C.A. just previously that I should find the Sisters at the flats. Both were having an afternoon nap, Indian 'Wallah' did not seem at all anxious to wake them, but on considering that our uncertain occupation, the opportunity may not again present itself, I had one called up. Was not at all put out at being awakened. Just the reverse for was delighted to see me again, not only did she say, but I came to this conclusion by manners and words.

Not long afterwards my real friend came, and we had a good friendly, homely chat of events since our last visit. Spent a very pleasurable couple of hours indeed and arranged an appointment for 9 o'clock same evening to go for a motor drive with a couple of American Y.M.C.A. secretaries, friends of hers. Met also at the flat a young Y.M.C.A. Lady sec, just arrived last week from Sydney by the 'OSTERLEY'. Seems very glad to meet another Aust. for she has signed on for India for 5 or 6 yrs. Having arranged with Keys to meet him at Lodge Emulation near Railway at 6.30pm, set out to attend the Lodge. Same is a fine building where things are done in style right enough. Lodge Em – run entirely by Parsees and jolly fine, conscientious, and painstaking chaps they are. Much enjoyed myself. At festive board, candidate just through his first, made a very interesting reference to his captivity in Turkey. Appears he came down from Mytilene by 'KANOWNA' when we were in Syria. Disembarked at Alex, and repatriated very soon after to India. Gave a detailed a/c of his impressions of Austs, our coo-ee call from the staff as the ship approached them, and recited their experiences with submarines on the way back. We took her English compliment to England with us. This I regard as a novelty. Met the party at the flat, went to Malabar Hill and round-about, then to Calabar. A perfect night. Aust. lady in front with driver (male sec. Y.M.) and Miss Cowdrey another Y.M.C.A. Sec for Bastra and Mesopotamia and Caspian Sea, (where British troops are fighting Bolsheviks in South Russia) and self at back. A real hard case and kept us well entertained. Both these gents have been to London and the latter and Miss Cowdrey wish to visit Aust. on way back to America when their terms finish.

The Cowdrey's are unpaid Secs, and can go back anytime. Their father is a doctor in America. Had to tell her all I saw of American soldiers in England of whom she is very proud. Stood below the Parsi Towers of Silence and overlooked the city beneath. Many lights of those 4-6 story eastern buildings shining through numerous oblong windows. Could distinctly hear natives singing their weird songs with the accompaniment of their still more weird finger drums. As we looked and listened in that still, quiet starry night, Miss Cowdrey made the remark, 'How small one's efforts seem and how little accomplished against the sin and degradation of an eastern city like this!' I daresay the something in the atmosphere prompted this remark, for my own mind was in a similar strain and I agree. From Calabar drove to the flats, but secs. insisted on driving me to the docks. The famous Taj Mahal Hotel big and towering even at night. Roosevelt House is just at rear of this and Greens Hotel. From the driver I learnt that they are going up country a little way tomorrow to take photos cremating of deceased natives. Could go but have too much else on hand. Saw the place where hundreds of tons of wood was stacked when bodies were cremated at time of Influenza outbreak. By way of a change, walk round the docks from gates to ship at No. 12 berth, having gone in during the afternoon. Notice a large ship painted in what is known as the Zebra Camouflage.

Friday 21st

Leave today, fresh detail of 7 going on. Saved the trouble of seeing the O.C. re the extra men for guard, the W.O. having seen about and righted this matter himself. The W.O. lets me off soon after parade in order to go to Sewri Cemetery, by me sending a cablegram for him first of all. From Railway Stn. Master, learn that best train to catch would be one for Dadar, then Gharry to cem.

Caught the 10.10am. Only a few stations up, but on arrival found no vehicles. Would have been better to have gone to Parel, but set out to walk it. Being a warm day, and sore feet with blisters on heel on a/c tight boots, being obliged to wear them, because a native who had taken others to sole not having returned them at time arranged, found this a bit tedious. To make matters worse missed the turning at meeting of 4 roads at Parel Village and walked long past. Noticed cotton mills etc. on the way, and had another chance of seeing native life through little places on the way. It was amusing to see a boy and girl in one of the yards behind some buildings dressed up like some heathen gods, saying things which seemed to amuse and fascinate the crowd who gave money. Seemed a little disturbed by my looking on, but proceeded after awhile. Came at length to a road which seemed to lead to nowhere. However, there was a large bungalow here, and I espied an English lady who gave me fresh directions. Had to retrace steps to Parcel Village. I could see the sea from this point, but had not gone far, before a native boy caught up to me and gave me to understand that the lady wanted me.

Went back and found another lady, and a gent on the verandah. Offered me lemonade and a sit down. Gent is a Scotch engineer on a big scheme whereby monsoonal waters drive machinery for generation of electricity I understand. Another big plant to be started, but American firm secured contract, owing to England's inability to supply machinery during the war. Offered to show me around anytime I felt so disposed. Learn from the lady, that all Englishwoman out here medically examined and classified accordingly, and to be given the opportunity of returning to England in their order of classification. Sent their servant with me to show the way, a short cut, thus missing Parel Village, and inviting me to come back if I so desired. Passed many large cotton and other mills on the way and hosts of natives seem to be employed.

Arrived at the cemetery and interviewed the clerk, an old Indian pensioned soldier of many 'brushes' who spoke excellent English. Find the directions given me at Sailors Home incorrect, for instead of grave being Plot 23, Line C. No.4, should be (P-) N11-(L)1, (No) 16. Found this after turning up good many books of record. Even while I waited a notice to the clerk came, giving instructions for a grave to be dug for a deceased Lt. Col. whom I learnt afterwards quite accidentally was an old and respected veteran, having fought many battles for the Empire in these outlandish eastern countries and won distinction for doing it. Proceeded to the grave and found it, with aid of a lot of natives working in the place, ever ready to oblige when they think baksheesh may be forthcoming. The spot marked simply with a white wooden peg, rounded at the top with this inscription in black E.J. SARGENT 25.6.18. (small drawing of same). Piece of ground quite flat. Believe this peg only temporary until Admiralty office puts something better over it. Miss Husband told me that a stone would be probably sent from home later, which is so much the better still. Arranged with clerk to have a couple of decent pot plants I saw nearby placed there, which he did. Gave a native a little money to look after them through the clerk. Took two photographs which I thought would be nice for his far-away mother to have when I get to England.

The cemetery is a long narrow one, between two low hills with cliffy looking sides, a general burial ground and not for soldiers only, altho' the latter are in plots according as to Protestant or Roman Catholic. Could not help feeling the strange experience for me to be standing over the grave of one whom I should have loved to meet, but who now beneath the earth in these foreign parts, at a spot never probably thought possible. My mind then flew back to his old haunts of 'Dobbins Cott', his guns and fishing lines there. How I wished it were possible to have arrived at Bombay a little earlier last trip and known of him then. I should have known of him and his whereabouts most probably if I had paid a visit to Cornwall when in England the first time there, as I intended if the ship had stayed at Avonmouth, instead of going further north to Liverpool. Was shown the entry in register later and under proper headings read thus.

'Edwin J. Sargent, Age 25 yrs, Naval Surgeon H.M.S. 'TOPAZE' buried 25/6/18 by Chaplin W.R. Garrad'. Had to ignore the gravediggers on leaving. All full of 'Salaams Sahib' for baksheesh of course. My poor old guide directed me to the train line, having decided not to go back to the house. When at Governor's old residence, dismissed him and made for Bombay. Jumped out of train on one occasion on seeing a brass maker at work, but the stuff I wanted proved to be too expensive. Arrived at the Victoria Gardens and having an hour or so to spare had a look through. Met other of our chaps there. The gardens take the form of sort of zoo as well. Lions, tigers, bears, elephant, birds etc. all on view. Rides are given on jumbo and a camel. For the garden itself, have seen plenty better. The remainder of journey was slow, owing to arguments and other things on board the train. While some native quarrels with the conductor over his fare, both yelling like maniacs at each other and others joining in, for or against, the train pulls up and stops.

Met Miss Cowdrey at 4.30 as arranged, had tea, and set out to buy. Hired a Gharry (all sorts of ways of spelling this word). She seemed delighted to do this, and said she felt it an honour to have the freehand to buy what she thought good quality for me. Went to a brass shop first in Hornsby St, and bought Cashmere beads, making intentions to buy brass offered if nothing else better in market. Went to Silk market and bought Assam silk for Mother and other cream for blouses. A fair price but best quality. Next to Crawford Market and purchased a bit of brass. Had a look through the fruit stalls, there as last time arranged fit for a show. Spices smell very strongly, all sorts of different aromas from these, some very nice. This was a most pleasant three hours. Drove back to flats at 7.30, Miss Cowdrey having a meeting to which she had to attend. Retained the Gharry, went to the Walker's house near Crawford Market. Met them all at home. Were just as sociable and nice as ever.

Had supper and the young chap whom Mitch and I met here before being present, were provided with plenty of amusement. The girls provided singing and music. All knew me on first sight, thought they would have forgotten me. Made enquiries after Mitch. The young chap above referred to is now stationed not far from Nasik, and now down for weekend. Is in motor transport and offered to drive me up on Monday when he returned. No hope I am afraid, expected to sail that day. (Side note on this page). The Zebra camouflaged ship is the 'ZEALANDIA' a popular Aust. Coaster taken over by British Govt. some time ago.

Saturday 22nd

Hear no more leave to be granted. Begun to prepare the wards and get things ready. All buck in and make good headway. Being on the safe side for embarkation tomorrow, leave is granted from 12 o'clock. Go on shore with Rundle, his first time poor kid. He has a friend, a S.A. nurse at Freeman Thomas Hospital, who having sent for him, go along, first changing some of our Aust. money at Currency Exchange in Hornsby Street.

Stay at hospital till 4 o'clock and have afternoon tea there. Nurse shows us over the building, erected for the purpose of School of Sciences. On the road in front are placed pontoons used by Turks on their attempted attack on the Suez Canal, and Turkish field guns from Mesopotamia captured by Indians. Believing that no leave would be granted, earlier in the day, I had written to Miss Cowdrey asking her to purchase some coffee trays we had seen yesterday. Now able to relieve her of that trouble, so go round to see her and I am glad I did so, for she had received a call to go and see a sick friend at Poonah, and was determined to get the trays etc., before she left, so consequently found her in great haste. My coming relieved her considerably. Said goodbye for the last time, and I confess I was sorry indeed to do so. She has been so good to me. Arranged to come back to the hospital to get a parcel from the Sister for her brother at Horseferry Road in London. We then went to Crawford market to purchase cigars, which we accordingly did. But the number of beggars who followed us into the shop and waited outside was most distressing. An old fellow crawling along the ground, some deformed and young mothers with tiny babies in their arms, muttering and gabling, pointing to their own mouths, then to their stomachs, doing the same performance to the youngsters at their breasts. If you give to one of course the others will stop and clamour still more. They made such a din it was impossible to hear what one was saying to the shopkeeper. Went round to Walker's, but they were away at the cinematograph. The old 'COOLYANNA' which I remember so well when owned by the Ilwraiths on the Singapore trade, but now purchased by the B.I. Coy. lying just ahead of us. Our Chief Engineer on her for 9 years.

Sunday 23rd

The new berths have been finished, E4 is to be used by the wives of soldiers in India such as W.O's and non-commissioned Officers. These constitute the 2nd class passengers, using Canary Cottage for a mess room. Tables similar to those on our mess deck have been provided for this purpose, but tablecloths laid of course. D1 to be used by wives of Officers. This is a much better place, and curtained off by use of the railings rings put up on ceiling when this ship carried Sisters to staff No. 14 in Egypt in old days. All there to use Saloon for meals, 2nd class children to use Canary Cottage for 1st sitting. 1st class ditto same place at 2nd sitting for meals. Have to work until 4pm. today and do further jobs in the wards. All mattresses and blankets carried to beds, and staff on C deck had to prepare C3 ward after these had been taken from here, where they are always stowed. Took some going to be finished by 4. On guard but Keys stating his intention of not going on shore, get him to take my place till 10pm.

During morning have shifted from No. 12 to No. 1 berth. The large shed here is decorated handsomely with flags and cloth of many various colours. It is here that Indian troops are given a welcome back and entertained. We will embark at this place. Robby and I go ashore to try and have a trip out to the H.M.S. 'NEW ZEALAND'. Go to pier near Taj Mahal. Meet an English lady who wonders if the ship is open for inspection. Papers state Mon, Tues and Wed, but three of us with her, her little boy, sail out to try our luck. Made very welcome on board, and a cadet detailed off to show us round. Several fine inscriptions in brass are to be seen such as 'Fear God, honour the King' etc., on the turrets and other places. Were shown the guns, taken to conning tower, searchlights and other places. A fine ship, presented to the Royal Navy by the New Zealand Govt. some years ago. Sister ship to 'AUSTRALIA' battle cruiser, still in the Nth Sea.

Saw the great piece of armour knocked by a German shell from off the base of one of the midship 12in. guns, of which these are 8 altogether. Shown the silver teapots and utensils presented by N.Z. Govt., also the silver cups and shields won by the crew against other competitors in the fleet in gun practice. On the decks plates of brass showed the various engagements participated in, such as Heligoland, Dogger Bank etc. Much amusement was given to us by an excitable Englishman who had joined our party, asking such ridiculous questions of our young inexperienced guide, for we learn that the whole crew was provided fresh from Devonport, many are new cadets in training. We are shown into Lord and Lady Jellico's apartments, but they are at Delhi. On the dining saloon table is a beautiful model of the H.M.S. 'IRON DUKE' in solid silver, presented by the crew to Lady J, when the Admiral used this vessel as his flagship in the North Sea with the grand fleet. The boatswain was a typical Jolly rolling sea-dog of Devon breed. He was very good to us. A Capt. Mac Kenzie son of High Com. Snr. of New Zealand is a passenger bound for home by this vessel. He, poor fellow, is quite blind having lost his sight in France.

Met another A.I.F. man, his friend, who is accompanying him home and looking after him. Mac Kenzie went ashore. This chap told us to keep an eye open for him when ashore during the evening, hoping to spend the evening together, as he was going to see his charge later. Our lady friend a Mrs. Clark, (whose husband is in the Civil Service in India) is returning to England early next month. Rather reserved at first, but thought it a huge joke having to climb up and down so many bar ladders. A pleasure steamer came alongside, provided by sort of 'cheer up' Society ashore for entertainment by them of Officers and men of 'NEW ZEALAND', and here a real difficulty came from her, (having made up our minds to go on shore in this boat) by having to climb through two lots of close iron railing, but she managed the task admirably. Reserve had all disappeared, as she asked us to dine with her at the Hotel Majestic or lunch tomorrow. She was staying here prior to embarkation. Neither invitation could be accepted, as tomorrow sailing and tonight we were to go round to Cooperidge Hut.

Now the Misses Cowdrey had more than once mentioned that they should have like me to meet Capt. Woods. R.N. of the 'TOPAZE'. So happened he was in charge of evening service at this hut. It is a Y.M.C.A. mission to soldiers and sailors in which the Cowdreys are interested. Could hear the sermon and hear the preacher. Waited until it was over and interviewed him. A Miss Withers, another American Y.M.C.A. worker was there, and was helping with the supper always provided after these meetings. A Jack-tar from same ship made arrangements for me to see the Capt. I found him an earnest quiet, and very gentlemanly young chap. Told me that Surgeon Egan had mentioned to him that I had looked him (Egan) up. Told me practically the same story, and seemed concerned about the missing luggage, mentioning how carefully it had been packed and forwarded. Invited me down to the ship in the morning, but had already seen over her yesterday. Went back to the ship at 10pm, and straight on guard with the two others on duty over the apples till morning. Simply beautiful up there and delightfully cool.

(Omitted this yesterday) Rundle and I had long spoken of trying to take a run up to Poonah or Nasik, before our arrival here. Made enquiries at Station yesterday, but found no trains to suit. This a great disappointment. Having promised myself a good look over the "TOPAZE' when chance offered, did so yesterday afternoon with Rundle. Next to her in the naval dock is the 'OUFFERIN' a beautiful ship, always until recently used for bringing troops to and from India i.e., before the war as well. Being now converted into a mail steamer. The 'TOPAZE' altho' a smart looking little cruiser, is a hell on earth inside for the Officers and crew alike. I have never seen such terrible conditions under which her 300 odd men are expected to live. No baths, sleeping where they eat, and so terribly cramped. I wonder how the men exist in the tropics. I am told that for 6 weeks the crew lived on bread and dripping. While on patrol work in the Red Sea, firemen lived also on this, and worked in holds like rat traps, and right up and crammed in against the fires. Some went right out, others had often to be bought up exhausted. Saw Shone Sargent's cabin. After his death his friend Surgn. Riley expired. Hot, stuffy, and little cabins they are too. Shone often said he detested the ship and no wonder. The crew get 6d per day extra in summer, but what a difference their conditions and environment to those on the beautiful 'NEW ZEALAND'. The former deserve the Victoria Cross each I reckon.

Some poor beggars have had to 'stick it' for over 18 mths. No freezers on board, and Capt. Woods has often had to beg fresh meat from passing ships. Have never seen anything so awful for Englishmen of the present day to have to put up with. The men idolize their Captain. One had told me that many fine, rosy cheeked country men have come out to serve in this Station, but nearly all end up sick and poorly in health. These looked pale and thin, goodness knows. Ship being fitted out for England, when it is supposed that with many other older vessels, she will be 'scrapped'. The engine room was also a horribly cramped place. In our trip back from the 'NEW ZEALAND' tonight (23rd) we pulled up in the Naval dockyard and landed just by the stern of the old 'TOPAZE'. Capt. Woods also stays at the 'Majestic' when on shore. How these Officers must appreciate the comfort there after being at sea for any length of time. Asked him why he made us go right over to his ship while proceeding through Red Sea last July. Remembered the incident well, but says he did not ask our skipper to do so. Said it suited him alright all the same, for he obtained a good photo of the 'KAROOLA' at close range. Said he only wanted to know what time the 'old man' expected to reach Suez, so that he could report it. Nevertheless, customary to hold up all vessels going this way.

Monday 24th
Soon after breakfast a troopship loaded with Indians came in. Twenty five R.A.M.C. men as re-enforcements to the staff arrived on board. Not a bad looking lot of chaps, and quite a departure from the usual run of this Corps. Fifty five women and 47 children are to come on board and we expect to see some fun. Embarkation began at 9 0'clock with patients and troops coming on board, the latter (mostly Gordon Highlanders) with full

pack up rifles. Shortly the luggage began to roll along and what a stack. All this carried by Indians. Knowing what an excess of gear English Officers always carry, we could see a lively time ahead, for they are most fussy and lardy-dar about their belongings, and do not at all like being interfered with re their belongings. But here a fine fuss was caused by the P.M.O. on shore sending the women and children on board in the midst of loading troops. Their arguments with their lackeys, stacking and fussing about their luggage on the landing, soon began to interfere with the correct running of things. Our O.C. stopped them and ordered troops first. This caused the P.M.O. to go off pop and 'telling everybody off'. Made a great song about it, but to no purpose. Women had to wait, and rightly so in this instance. Amongst other things I was detailed to gangway to stop all luggage over and above the usual amount being brought on board and taken to the wards.

Well I saw a few scenes. One woman accompanied by her husband, a Captain, screamed, stamped her feet and tugged at her luggage and went on in a terrible manner tugging all the time, and said she was determined to take it on board with her. I however was equally if not more so, that she should not. Her husband was pushing behind, but Sgt. Biggs who was helping me, told the Capt. he should be ashamed of himself, acting as he was, in a way against our orders. This brought him to his senses. He ordered his wife to stop her noise, and we explained that in order to prevent cramming of our limited accommodation, only luggage absolutely immediately required could be taken with them, the remainder to stay on the wharf and loaded into places set apart for it in the ships holds, where it was available twice weekly or when specially required. We won, but being a tall, broad, fierce looking man, he did look fierce. The old P.M.O. then explained to the 'lady' that (in a very pathetic way), 'I cannot help it lady, this is an Aust ship, and you know what they are', with the emphasis on 'they'. I guess some of them will find out what we Australians are before the trip is over, same as many before them, not like the poor Indians whom they boss so, or the Tommy soldier who is looked upon as so much dirt.

This is not a passenger ship anyhow. If old Col. Wilson had been on board now, he would have refused to take them as he did on a previous occasion. Others told me their night attire was in such and such a box, and children's clothes in another, said they were already dirty as monkeys and must have change for tomorrow. To see some of the artful tricks played to get some of that stuff on board was an experience for me, but how strange and entirely new life this seemed. I confess it was not half bad. English people are thoroughly spoiled out here in the East, have so much waiting upon, used to giving orders and having them obeyed and almost too useless now to help themselves, this does not wash with we Australians. However there are always some good ones to be found everywhere, and this case no exception. Little incidents of today will long live in my memory, being as they are, so entirely new and out of the ordinary for us, but it is impossible to tell them all here. An Indian Military band had assembled just after we had finished embarking, to play into the shed the Indians who had returned in the ship this morning. While waiting for them the band struck up 'Auld Lang Syne' for our benefit and other airs. Presently the troops came along, and jolly well they looked as they fell into step, and marched decently to their places in the shed. A fine spectacle, must have been over a thousand troops. Ladies had assembled to meet and greet them. Glad to see this sight. Backed away from wharf meanwhile and sailed at 2pm.

Tuesday 25th

Ptve. Price having brought a monkey on board which he had purchased from a native, and the W.O. finding out, he is requested to dispose of it. Instead he let it off its chain, hoping to capture it again before reaching England. Hides itself in potato lockers, and finally Sgt. Biggs workshop. Is taken prisoner and one of the N.C.O's administers an anaesthetic (4 doses) while animal enclosed in a box. Buried at sea in Lat —and Long --. Price had an in-growing toe nail removed today by local anaesthetic only. Caused him considerable pain and he was chaffed about this. The lads reckon the monkey received more humane and expensive treatment. Seems so queer to see women sitting about, and children romping and playing on the decks, the noisy young scamps darting through the ward landings, rushing and tearing about the place and playing hide and seek in every conceivable corner. Some good rewards are offered by the 1st class folk to any of the unit, patients or troops, who will look after and mind them while parents are away at lunch etc., but it is not likely any Australians would take the job on. A Sgt. of the reinforcements detailed to assist Cpl. Cox in keeping these young bounders within boundaries. It is better to see them thus than crying all the same. Babes in arms of course, usually squawk at night, but that does not annoy us, being well away from the arena.

Officers in G. are O.K. and very nice, in C3 is an old retired Col. 83 yrs of age. Retired from the Indian service years ago, but returned on a visit to his 4 sons in India, with wife and daughter. While there took sick with Cholera. Poor old lady sleeps on a form outside his window on promenade. Promotions came out today. To be permanent L/Sgt. Mc Elkone, and Sgt. Grove to be acting Cpls, Mullinger, Pens, Mortimer, and Shaw, ditto L/Cpls. Gilchrist, O'Sullivan and King (a 4 ½ service man!). Can easily be seen now who are to be the permanent N.C.O's for return voyage. Nobody is picked or will be chosen said Luton some time ago, before the authority is given from London. This looks like it. Apples on issue every day now, just as well for some are already rotting, in fact there will be an abundant supply I can see to get rid of before they become inedible.

Wednesday 26th
Pvte. King voluntarily reverts to the ranks. Kohn made another temporary corporal. We have several medical men of the Indian Medical Service with us. One, a Mjr. Mackworth, a very fine fellow and we have interesting chats.
Has cured 7 leprosy cases during the last 6 months with new discovery of another Indian Medical Service man. A R.A.M.C. Major has been attached to the staff, for attendance on the women. Also an Army school teacher with his wife on board, from one of the Indian Stations. Have a French lady too – a Mrs. Dart. Rather interesting and out of the way to notice the evening dress of the ladies at dinner time 6 and 6.30pm. Some dress and others decidedly 'undress'.

Thursday 27th
Have read books often, of travellers here in the East, of their coming through the Canal on some big liner or other, their sports and pastimes and life on board generally. My mind has gone back to these stories, especially when at Suez Canal, of travellers to other parts of the Empire through this narrow but wonderful waterway. Feel glad in a way of this opportunity of witnessing a bit now for myself. Took blood film from lady, a suspected Malaria.

Friday 28th
Nice and warm. Invited by one of additional staff to his home in Warwick. Four English nursing Sisters to attend women. Only one lady has an Indian nurse girl. Red Cross issue. Chocolate for children. Still see Southern Cross at night. Water bright with huge lumps of phosphorous.

Saturday 29th
Concert held by 1st class passengers on boat deck during the evening and dance following. Deck ornamented with flags. Lady violinist good, her husband a Mjr., a clever pianist.

Sunday 30th

Passed Aden @ 8am. Knew land to be about, by numerous sea-birds, flying about @ 5.30 reveille. Life in the East certainly spoils women, (i.e., if these may be regarded as a sample), for besides being unable to do much for themselves, having always been waited upon hand and foot, smoke and drink spirits, and in public without any show of modesty. I think this is appalling, and although have seen quite a lot of smoking amongst women and other masculine habits, am afraid I can never reconcile myself to this lowering of a woman's standards, tending as it does to damage ones respect for the better sex and more refined when noticed (i.e., to individual concerned). Through Gates of Babel Mandel, @ 5pm. A large steamer berthed at Pirim and another came out and passed us going opposite.

Monday 31st

Boat Stations @ 4pm. for all. Very funny to see women unused to their life-belt attire wearing them probably a bit lower than their waists, just flippity flop style, and without tying them correctly. Seemed as if youngsters seemed weighed down with their loads.

APRIL, 1919

Wednesday 2nd

Children's concert held this evg. in aid of Shipwrecked Mariners. All tickets sold and good funds realized. Wireless news re Bedouin trouble in Egypt and Syria. Much damage done and railways destroyed. Scheme in hand to move Europeans from troubled districts. Mail closed today, wrote home folk.

Thursday 3rd

Pretty blowy today and the coolest ever I experienced in the Red Sea. Notice where sailing ship aground ashore last trip, that she has now gone. Off Gulf of Sinai this morning, land both sides. Further wireless news of riotous Egypt. Rupture likened unto 1882. Pretty windy and choppy for the Red Sea. Arrived Suez at 9pm and anchored.

Friday 4th

Not many ships here this time. Moved off into the Canal later in the afternoon. Notice more camps in Tewfik and in and around Suez. Officers watching us before their club house, I notice are armed with revolvers, at their belts. ((Received X/Mas card from Miss Husband of 'Dobbins Cot' and letter from Mrs. Mc Kinnon Cumberland re land). Reached Ismalia at about 8pm and anchored in lake until 11 o'clock amongst other vessels waiting there. Had to wait for another steamer coming down canal. Her search light very brilliant and notice her miles before she reaches us. Nights rather chilly now, but good for sleep.

Saturday 5th

At Pt. Said 5.30am. Dozens of large vessels here, the 'CALEDONIAN' (a beautiful old ship) "MALWA' and 'PT. DARWIN' amongst them. Anchored opposite Signal Station and began to take in water and coal. A beautiful large passenger ship, port of regis – Trieste, came in and passed us. This is a Hungarian steamer captured by the Italians during the war. Some few Italian troops on-board. Officers and 1st class ladies granted shore leave until 3pm. from 10 am. Officers compelled to take revolvers. Rowing boats loaded with Jaffa oranges alongside. Vendors do a lively trade 10 for 1/-, others 8 for 1/-, but larger. Oval shaped – good-o, world famed. Very cheap in Palestine. Only wished they had been in season whilst we were at Jerusalem that hot weather. Completed coaling by

4pm, but watering not finished at 8pm. Took on 8 cot cases, and 40 odd other patients to fill E1 and E6. Some from Kantara I believe. No life or activity about late No. 14. A.G.H. and no visitors of old acquaintance, so presume they have all shifted to Abassia. Left at 9pm. for Southampton direct, cabled to arrive evening of the 16th instant.

Note from diary Cpl. C.R. Mortimer AWM

Coaling was a dirty process and leaves ship in dirty state. Cots were swung back on their staunchions, and washed down with hot water, soap and soda. Ceiling and walls were also washed. Officers inspecting the boat at various ports before and after embarkation always unstinted in praise regarding cleanliness of the ship.

Sunday 6th

Children's service 3pm. Passing other ships. New passenger a Lt. Col. says that Australians would deal most effectively with miscreants in Egypt if given the chance. Says that enough troops massed to quell trouble.

Tuesday 8th

Chilly, and a pretty choppy sea. A very large British warship passed closely, and we saluted by dipping the Mercantile flag. Could plainly see her tremendous fore-guns. Ascertain later she is the 'CENTURIAN' proceeding at a slow rate, a recent super dreadnought. Concert to be held tonight, put off owing to weather.

Wednesday 9th

Many passengers sea-sick. A jolly big swell on. Youngsters very noisy and well. Some wish the thing would reverse, put them in their parents places, and have quietness. At noon passed within 10 miles of South Sicily. A not very high ridge runs not far from shore, but parallel with it. A lofty lighthouse on beach and could plainly see large breakers dashing along shore. The range and foreshore studded with houses a good distance either side of lighthouse. Have not come so far north on two previous occasions. Fairly cold and wintry. Wind very strong from port, causing slight list of ship. New patients from Egypt delighted with food on board. One a S/Sgt. of Vet Corps came from Mesopotamia through Palestine when forces joined hands about the time we were at Syria. Tells of the hundreds of beautiful horses shot up the line, to save expense of bringing them down or sending to England. Turkish ponies, Arabs, and donkeys bring enormous prices by conducted sales at Gaza and other places to desert Bedouins. Arabs selling for 100-120? Donks which cost Army 4 pounds selling for 20, while English and Australian horse 5 pounds only offered.

Thursday 10th

A big swell on this morning and heavy rain. Many seas coming over bows. Caught up and passed a two funnel cruiser, but soon lost sight of her in the misty rain. Supposed to be one of the Eastern Station boats going home for 'scrapping'. Many of the boats are being weeded out, and already booked to be sent home, as 'SAPPHIRE', 'DORIS' and 'TOPAZE'.

Friday 11th

Old cruiser of yesterday must have caught up and passed us last night, for we pass her again today, but at some distance off. See the coast line of Algeria from 11am. Sea quite smooth again and day sunny. Concert previously postponed held. A great success. A Major and his wife leading artists. Lady a wonderful violinist. Coast of Spain in sight at 7pm. and lighthouse passed @ 8 o'clock. 310 miles from mid-day yesterday – noon today. Blowing off overload of steam at frequent intervals today. Sunset over Spanish coast glorious.

Saturday 12th

At 5.30 reveille land close on both sides. An hour afterwards the Rock of Gibraltar shows up quite white in the morning light. Sea as calm as a pond and air as fresh and invigorating as could be. Reached Gibraltar at 9 o'clock having proceeded thence by wireless instruction of yesterday. The old Rock looks magnificent and majestic. Anchored near breakwater. Dozens of vessels in harbour behind. Shortly, a smallish steamer comes out with about 8 fresh patients for us, and several of those are cot-cases being Jack-tars of the Navy. They lay in their hammocks (stiff), and brought on in them. Also a German prisoner of war, but O.C. refuses to take him without a guard over him. Consequently he is sent back.

The steamer comes out again with 4 Sisters of the Queen Alex Reserve, who have been doing duty in Garrison hospital here, to be taken to England. Now ready to go, but authorities seem anxious to get rid of German, for a guard is found and he with them come back, and we have to wait. Guard consists of 12 men (all told), with a few N.C.O's, but it appears they have been waiting for a ship to England so this a good excuse and a good chance to send by us. Hear they received only 5 minutes notice in which to pack up and get ready. Many smaller naval craft in and notice a large two funnelled French liner in the anchorage, also a steamer recently raised from the bottom, all rusty and top decks smashed through gun fire. Vendors of oranges, lemons, tobacco and cigars, come alongside in small rowing and motor boats. Spanish folk, but oranges being no good, were pelted by their own fruit by buyers of it, at which treatment showed no delight.

On the Moroccan side as well as the Spanish, beautiful parcels of arable land in patches on the hills and slopes, some just cultivated and some under crops of some sort, in places hedged off reminding one of England. Remarkable though to notice the high buttresses and peaks of rock, reaching to great altitudes amongst it. Left at 1pm, followed by the French liner, which taking shorter course, close in to land, soon is out of sight. Can see Tangiers by daylight this time and not dusk as on our last voyage. A large cruiser lying off, and a really nice looking town. About the best time of year for these parts. We are now a full ship and no room to spare. Extreme point of Africa extends further West than same of Spain. A fine lighthouse on turning point for south, i.e., West Coast of Africa. Pass a tramp steamer going in and she Semaphores to us. Many ships all told going in and coming out of this channel, the Straits of Gibraltar, causing me to realize the huge trade of English shipping to the East. Atmosphere perfect, with a good moon, a clear sky and stars showing out vividly. Unfortunately missed the big gun practice from top of Gibraltar forts, a short time before our arrival. Just as we were opposite the beach on mainland behind Gibraltar, a large flare was used which starting small at first, leapt up into the air many feet in height attaining a bright salmon coloured glow. After a minute or two gradually died down. Caused much curiosity.

Sunday 13th

Meeting held by Adjt. of members of unit, to receive and discuss any suggestions re arrangement of duty roster and leave in England. Cpl. Keys idea to be submitted to O.C. Adjt. wishes to retain the 10 men on guard as in former days. Meets with much opposition and rightly so, our suggestion is 6 at the very most. Will hear tomorrow opinion of O.C. Passed Cape Vincent early this morning. A lighthouse on point. Still doing good speed, as firemen receive no pay if out during Easter, so by their effort, to get into Southampton by Wed.

Monday 14th

Entered the Bay today, and towards afternoon, a good wind and sea came up. Fairly rocky, wind howling thro' the rigging. Spray coming over boat deck from waves smashing against the ship. Rain falls. Huge white horses as far as eye can reach. At 8pm. passed a steamer with a sailing ship in tow, no easy job in this sea, I guess. Later passed a steamer going in opposite direction, only funnel visible as she got into the trough of the sea, when she very quickly bobs up again and disappears. The wind partly behind us, if other way, would be bad going. Naval Commander a Sea Captain say this one of the best sea boats they have ever seen, or travelled in.

Tuesday 15th
Wind heightened into a gale and very big sea on. Scarcely any women about. Passed a tramp, but shortly after she 'hove to', the sea being too strong for her. Came up to a small sailing boat, but going dead with the sea and only a storm jib up. Seems to ride well in this direction, but is no larger than an ordinary ketch, in fact is similarly rigged. Many things smashed by extreme rolling of the ship. The fine electric incubator in laboratory damaged through falling to the floor. In fact this place presented a terrible spectacle when I came up here this morning. To meet easterly winds in Channel tomorrow. Difficult thing to hold on here in the lab. Floor is awash and the ship shakes and trembles like a leaf in this spot. Heavy rain and driving hail today. Would like a photo of some of these waves, which at times are much higher than the ship. To me there is a certain amount of glory in this, for it is a mighty deep right enough.

Wednesday 16th
Much calmer this morning. Water greener looking. Sight land @ 4pm, which turns out to be the Isle of Wight. Came right up to Ventmore and ran along the coast. Met by pilot in sailing vessel and proceeded past Spithead through the forts and anchored opposite St. Helens. Patients and passengers, in spite of severe cold wind, are on deck and looking out, with pleased expressions. Sunset glorious, a deep red sun, caught it just as sinking behind the hills, through tall trees along the horizon. A good many craft steaming and sailing about. Another wreck, with just mastheads showing above water near shore of Isle of Wight. Clock goes forward one hour, in order of the daylight saving scheme. One hours shorter rest tonight. (Bob's birthday). *(Nickname for sister Vere.)*

Thursday 17th
Went into port @ 7am. Early breakfast throughout the ship. Had a splendid view of Netley Hospital as we passed by. Two tugs took hold as soon as inside docks, very soon swing us around and put alongside in a berth as if dealing with a naughty child, so powerful are the tugs of Southampton. Very many ships in port and in our dock the old 'WEST AUSTRALIA', two American lake steamers and several others. While at the anchorage this morning an American lake ship loaded with Tommies came in, and another British vessel, with Australians from France on board. Coo-eed us and waved. Guess a good many of them know the old 'KAROOLA'.

Now the fussing over luggage and baggage begins. Cox, Gunlay, and other big shipping agents appear to make arrangements for its delivery. Hear terrible rumours about trouble in Bombay and other parts of India. If true are pretty fortunate in having got away when we did. No crowd at wharf to meet us. Officers in ward desire to show appreciation of my services by making a gift, which I decline, but later a Ltn. Fusby gets to work and practically forces it upon me. Troops go off and taken by train before the passengers. Find it necessary to assist some of the Officers with their terrible amount of gear, otherwise I do not know how they would have managed. Seems too much even for some even to look after themselves. Hear that owing to dockies refusal to discharge their cargo over the Easter holidays, we are to proceed to Devonport at 4pm, and have it discharged there. Posted letters to Miss Husband and Mrs Oswald-Jones.

All off by 1pm. Did all the sterilizing and left punctually @ 4pm. A great many ships waiting in anchorage to go into wharves, and amongst them about a dozen of the small steamers which follow up battle ships with coal etc., similar to those we saw on our way from Portland last trip. Wonderfully camouflaged. Hills and slopes, on either side of Southampton waters look simply beautiful, for the fields are green hedged and heavily timbered in parts. Vessels right up till bedtime, all round us, coming or going, big and small, in an endless stream as it were. Ship seems good again after getting rid of the crowd. A few Sisters off and O.C., and Adjutant gone to London Headquarters. All bedding etc, stowed away and wards cleared this afternoon. A glorious day today and different to our last day of arrival in Southampton.

Friday 18th

At Plymouth very early. Anchored behind the breakwater. Another lovely day and see plenty of people coming down to the Hoe. Spent morning on board reading messages from the Port, and cleaning out the laboratory of the mess made during the rough weather at sea. Leave granted, but no launch available under seven pounds.

At 3pm went to Mill-bay wharf by motor boat, which owner wanted to charge 6/- return (15 minutes rowing), but eventually got him down to 4/-. Rundle and I walk along and about the Hoe. Go to top of old Eddystone lighthouse and have an excellent view of harbour, city and surroundings. To Saltash (or Royal Albert or Brunel) Bridge. Again struck with the beauty of this bridge. Hear steamers now going up Tamar to Caldstock (20 miles). Will try to work this in with Callington railway, for trip to Launceston. By punt to Saltash, a very historical and quaint little town and then walked along banks to Defiance Stn. Dozens of war boats in and around the river Lynher and Tamar, and further up the former, destroyers were either moored to or anchored close to the banks. At Defiance, so named on account of an old training ship there of that name, lie two other vessels with her just off the land, and connected by a foot-bridge and the three being connected also by the bridges. One is of the old 'Victory' type is roofed in, resembling a huge houseboat, same is a torpedo school, and has turned out best class of men in this regard, in the Navy. The other is dismantled, and was once a recruiter, in fact bears that name used to gather new recruits from Southern parts of Devon and Cornwall in the old days, for the Navy. Stood on Stn. Bridge and I think the tints and hues, and river later when a good moon came up, would take some beating, (in Cornwall now). Returned by rail, having gone by car to Morice Sq, and another St. Budeaux. Hear 'RESOLUTION' in dock, must see her if at all possible. Collected at pier and found that a Dutch American liner had just arrived with mails from New York, and tug had just brought them in. Luton arrives from London with leave. Hear 9 days only granted, today being included. Stiff luck and throws plans out.

Saturday 19th

Went into Millbay Docks @ 8am to discharge cargo. (this on side of diary).
Those starting leave today to catch 12.40 for London. However, Luton fools about as usual and states his intention of coming as far as station with us. When on wharf tho' fools about for more than ½ hour, looking for Transport Office, to go through some red-tape proceeding or other. Takes us to Millbay. GW, and does not know which way to go, fools about again and we find ourselves at train terminus. Then gives up, he goes his own way to get warrants for us somehow, and we pay for taxi to shake him up a bit. We ourselves tram to North Road Stn and wait for him, so have to act on our own initiative after all. Catch 12.40 train. Goes over same line as my first experience here.

The country as well as the sea coast is simply beautiful. Many fields ploughed, and plenty of sheep and cattle about. This more noticeable in Devon than Somerset, although the latter magnificent, flatter if anything. Travelled with a most interesting, educated and pleasant lady, and reached London (Paddington) 6.20pm. Went to H.Q. and with a certain amount of despatch this time, received passes and railway warrants. Found Base medical stores closed for Easter, so could not see Westlake. Thinking it too late to go Chiswick, went round to Lonsdale Hotel. Found Mrs. White and Mrs. Hearn in good spirits, and not so surprised as I had expected, for Mrs. Osw-Jones had told them of my coming. Found the Wertheimers there, from America, supposedly multimillionaires, and a Mr. Philps, another wealthy influential American. All were engaged in cards and seemed decent enough. One of the lodges took Mrs. Hearn and self to pictures in Holborn. Stayed the night at 'Lovedale', and very comfortable indeed, Mrs. White insists.

Sunday 20th

Up early and met Roberts and Rundle at Westminster. Caught tube for Commercial Rd, formerly known as Petticoat Lane, and paid a visit to the market places. Made a few small purchases, and no doubt things are sold much cheaper here than in shops elsewhere. Jews are the prevailing element and are sharp, shrewd, salesmen. The place was simply crowded and one had to go along with the crowd. Both in shops and stalls in the streets, everything from a needle to an anchor can be bought. Went back to 'Lonsdale' and collected traps. Took underground to Hammersmith, changing for Chiswick. Found Mrs. Oswald-Jones, in good spirits and certainly stronger than when I saw her last. Gave me an extraordinarily homely welcome, having made arrangements for my coming long before I arrived.

Had a good old chat, mostly concerning my dear Mother, in whom she is greatly interested. The boys are well. In afternoon went to Kew Gardens just across River Thames. Strand-on-the-Green is on river bank and have to pass thro' here to reach Kew Bridge, a fine structure. Gardens are lovely, clean and spacious. The fern and other tropical house are superb. Daffodils grow in profusion among the trees, which in a few weeks hence, will be out in full leaf. Coming back notice white swans on the Thames, also many old barges, tied and huddled together, which remind me of 'Dickian' days. Mrs. Osw-Jones gives me a splendid watercolour painting of 'Strand on Green' by her husband. My room most comfortable and nice, makes me feel I should like much longer here.

Monday 21st

Up early and on Basil's bicycle went for a ride through Kew to Richmond. A splendid road. Came to the river again and rode along the bank and back again. Noticed the Locks along the way and pass many very fine open fields. Opposite Kew Gardens are many workshops and small docks for river tugs, punts etc. Rather cold at this hour. Made a good breakfast and caught train for Westminster and proceeded straight to Horseferry Rd, to try and arrange the transfer to duty in England, which I had already interviewed our own O.C. about, but found nobody at office owing to Easter holidays. Came back and had a glance through Westminster Cathedral as of old. A good many visitors there.

Walked along Thames Embankment, had an interesting chat with a couple of Policemen re night life in Fleet St and Embankment, - Blackfriars Bridge, then to Lonsdale Hotel. Arriving there, hear from house-maid that Mrs. White, Mrs. Hearne, her house-keeper, and Mr. Philps, an American, a Film Coy's manager living there, had just left by motor car for Chiswick, for the express purpose of taking me out for the afternoon to Hampton Court and a run round, afterwards to go to some of the favourite haunts in London with Mr. Philps. My disappointment was great, but no means of catching them now. Went straight to Chiswick, and caught bus from Hammersmith in hope of catching them returning along main road. During evening went along to see a Lizzie Martin, one of Mothers' cousins, who, hearing that I stayed at Chiswick had called in afternoon to see me. Thought this being the case, had better go and see her. Mrs. Jones enjoyed the walk, for having been very ill and laid up in bed a good deal since I saw her last, has not been able to do much. Still pretty weak however.

Tuesday 22nd

By tram went to Hampton Court with Basil. Several cities en-route which takes an hour. As we neared the Thames again, noticed large house-boat, tied to the banks. Just before Hampton Court is a river resort called the Casino. Here were boats to be had on hire, dancing halls etc. The Royal buildings present a noble appearance on approach. Two main wings are connected with narrower buildings, and one walks through arches under them to each court in turn e.g. (small hand drawing of same). Over top of middle court, is a clock, the only one of its kind. Has a huge dial and gives many particulars as do our latest 7day watches of nowadays. At the end came out on a glorious park, beautifully patched, and with many waterways and huge trees thickly, but regularly growing. Water lilies and white swans graced the water surface, which was for all the world like a mirror.

Came back to buildings again, and for a small sum were allowed to look through the upper rooms. This is an old palace originally belonging to Cardinal Wolsey, but taken by force from him by Henry 8th and thence occupied by Royalty. The original paintings (mostly), beds, tapestries are still there. As one walks from room to room a notice shows this to be Queen Anne's bedroom, another her sitting – room, parlour, library etc, etc, and other Kings and Queens as well. An abundance of oak everywhere. Beautiful stuff, but now nearly black with age. This scarce timber was used extravagantly those days. The buildings are now occupied by wife's and families of deceased Naval and Military Officers, high in command, i.e., for those unable through misfortune to keep pace with society and 'high jinks', so are given a sort of retiring 'snuggery' here.

Coming back to entrance again, notice a large field, where yesterdays crowds had gathered. Dray loads of paper and other rubbish strewn about. Gypsies striking camp and 'scavengers' searching amongst rubbish for valuables. Mrs. Jones tells me a little of her mother's family history, which should be interesting to Mother. Sorry to part company with her, for I have been made very much at home, but having made arrangements by telephone at Hampton Court to spend afternoon and evening with Mrs. White. Mrs. Jones makes me a present of a water colour painting by her husband, of Strand-on-Green, near Kew bridge. Leave her with regret.

Train to Westminster again. Find Col. Millard in H.Q. Put matter re transfer to him, but says he cannot owing to strictly definite instructions, grant any fresh transfers in England. Unfortunate for I had a lad from Base Medical Stores, anxious to get home, to take my place on ship, and all my work on board arranged for this. Tea at Lonsdale. Taxi with Mrs. White to 'The Bay' where we spent a most enjoyable evening indeed. Supper and tube for Paddington (midnight train). (Tubes are more than wonderful). Train for Plymouth crowded with Aust. and English soldiers, but most of former change at Warminster for Sutton Veney Camp. Manage to get a wink or two.

Wednesday 23rd

Arrived Millboy Station, Plymouth a little after 7 o'clock, and having an hour or so to spare prior to reporting for guard duty, go for a stroll round by the Hoe, and to see if any ships in the Sound. All quiet on board and still discharging the cargo, a slow process owing to limited room up through hatches. The ship is now being painted black with yellow line, quite her old original colour. Mrs. White having asked me to look up her son in Plymouth, do so today. Found him a decent fellow. Managing a large cordial and mineral waters Coy. Wished to have dinner with me at a further date, but I could not arrange it. As an Officer, has seen service in Mesopotamia. Went via the Cape-Bombay. Walked to Lond. and S.W. Railway, Friary Station to make enquiries re trains for Launceston or Callington for tomorrow. Visited 'Mayflower' wharf and Fish pier as I did last time in England. Large smack just arrived with fish. Sting-ray by dozens, considered a delicacy in England. Dozens of fishing schooners etc, part of Plymouth fishing fleet, anchored or tied to their base. Walk back to docks via the Citadel and over the Hoe.

Thursday 24th

Roberts and I caught 11.40 train for Launceston, accompanied by Lumsdame who changed at Yelverton for Princetown (Dartmoor). Undecided at first whether to go by motor from Saltash to Callington and walk the 7 miles to Lezant, or go with the others by train. However as rain began to fall, I thought motoring and walking would be but a spoilt pleasure, so soon then made up my mind. Lodged Robby at Temperance Hotel at which I stayed when in Lauceston last time, had a cup of coffee and set out to walk.

Took a road in a slightly different direction this time. A mile further, but just felt like a walk. No doubt the country looks magnificent. The sun shone for awhile, altogether improved things a bit. These fields and woods are simply beautiful, with their many tints and shades defy my powers of description. Fir trees are just coming into leaf and Hawthorne sprouting nicely, and furze is yellow. Come to Little Comfort, a tiny village boasting a few houses, a Chapel and P.O., then across a bridge and following a road which leads past Landue and directly to Trewarlet Crossing. Called in at Trewarlet. Mrs. Wise did not dream of seeing me again, and for quite a minute looked at me wonderingly, thinking I had left ship in Australia. Mr. Wise busy with his cows came in, and we had a most pleasant tea, cream being a delicacy. Hear they received my parcel O.K. from Pt. Said. Asked to stay of course, but after making arrangements for Roberts to stay out here, continued my walk to Dobbin's Cott. By jove, I do not doubt when told now, that this about pick of country in all Cornwall and Devon. These fields simply superb. Many times lean over gates in the hedges and gaze over the panorama from the hills. Thrushes and larks rise up everywhere, while it being nesting season, the rooks make a great noise from their lofty perches. Miss Husband having received my letter, I find waiting for me. Am made very welcome indeed.

We look through a house on her property recently vacated and undergoing repairs for new tenants, also an ochre factory, also under repair, being let @ 100 pounds per annum. Ochre is very plentiful in these hills. There is a lovely spot near here. The old mill of Trecarrel with its old wooden water wheel, moss-covered and split, the canal from the weir higher up the river, one time used for the Mill and huge iron wheel of Ochre factory, the many fine trees, the rushing, gurgling river below, and the high thickly wooded hills opposite the valley belonging to the Duke of Cornwall (Prince of Wales), and Trecarrel Bridge lower down, all as neatly and snugly placed. The old mill is the original of a beautiful picture now in the Royal Academy. Hearing we are to go for a drive tomorrow, clean up the ponies harness till about midnight and after chat by a good fire retire to bed, first of all going outside to listen to the river and watch the stars, which tonight are very brilliant and air is crisp. How I should love to see this place in summer time.

Friday 25th

Walk over to Trewarlet with intention of going to Launceston and bringing Robby back. A boy named Rundle at the farm however, lends me his three speed geared bike, so I ride in. Roberts not at hotel, but hear he has gone out for a walk to Chain Bridge. Ride out there in hope of meeting him. Cross over River Tamar into Devon, and a couple of miles further on, put bike inside fence and walk across fields to it. This chain suspension bridge has been carried away by debris brought down by floods, (this a small river, and not Tamar). He not to be found, so come back again.

As he was expected for 12.30 dinner, spent the time in looking over the Castle and St. Mary Magdalene Church. When at last he did arrive, we walked it by way of Little Comfit. Met two lady school teachers walking their bikes up hill and of course Robby must have a word with them. One is a red-cross worker, but both come to this part for their Easter holidays and live at a farm near Trewarlet. Wises make him very welcome. I go back to Dobbin's Cott. Catch the pony in what is known as the 'Island', a paddock between the mill canal and the river. Miss Husband's turn-out is called a carriage, a little low four-wheeled affair, with bent shafts and 'steel' wicker work seat and back and very conveniently low steps, a real invalids chair. Drive over to Lezant, with intention of paying a visit to Vicar's wife and Miss Uren. Call on the latter and found the dear old soul still in a whimpering mood every now and again cheers up though, especially when Miss. Husband is absent in the shop, and tells me a little more about the Sargents of Trewarlet. John re father's cousin, who once came to Aust. and never heard of again, seems to be her favourite. Said she was proud of the letter I had written her.

Not enough time now to visit Vicar, having got a late start, but go into graveyard and see the grave of George Sargent of Bottonet, late of Landue. Died Nov 1st, 1801, and next to him, his father before. Forgot to mention that we called at Trewarlet on our way out, and passed St. Lawrence, a smaller farm owned by the Sargents and farmed with Trewarlet. Father's grandfather John, after selling Trewarlet, lived here. Saw the very gate at which he was found dead, lying over his horse's neck, whilst the animal waited for admittance. He died of a stroke. A good old house being two storied. Richard Geddie Pearse subsequently farmed this property prior to living at Dobbins' Cott in care of Miss Husband. Slept the sleep of the just in a bed, the deep soft mattress of which nearly buried me. Having sent a wire for extension of leave while in Launceston yesterday, asked for a reply to Trebullet P.O. Received same on coming back from Larnson this afternoon. Had to go to Sth. Petherwin parish first (nearest telephone) and then delivered to Trebullet. Same was brought right down to Dobbin's Cott here, by 2pm. Pretty quick work. Extension granted till 1/5/19. Very handy. Evidently ship delayed for some reason.

Saturday 26th

Lot of timber felling about here. Two discharged soldiers with a two big splendid army horses on the job. Not needed for France now, but being taken just the same. A shame, but I believe afforestation has already begun on a large scale. We arrange to go to Padstow for the day, to catch 11.30 train from Launceston. Caught the pony from the 'close' after his playing round a bit and trying to kick me (old Granny's horses are tricky sometimes), put him in the carriage and made ready to start. Had to lead him up steep hill at back of house, but little beggar played up as soon as I touched him. Behaved in a most unseemly manner, backing, screwing and turning round and back, the turn-out nearly over into a hedge. If ever I wished a woman further, I did then, for I believe I would have skinned him. As it was Miss. Husband, making pets of all her animals, began petting and coaxing this little brute, in a very frightened manner, and he was aware of her scare I think. However, knowing too well how offence may be caused by doing anything to pets that the owner may not like, I did nothing. Got over his sulk in time, but poor Miss Husband would push behind as we went uphill as I led the pony, although she had a very bad foot. I at length prevailed upon her to get up and then I had my way, for I guess I pulled the brute faster than he could have comfortably walked. As we had little or no time to spare, how I wished I could have had charge of him. It was likewise torture going downhill, for it thought it had full responsibility, in spite of a good brake, of preventing the vehicle getting out of control, and seemed afraid that it would push him over, for he would at once begin the zig-zag tactic, and oh, slow slowly. Had then to lead him down-hill and this sort of thing does not improve one's patience. Somehow felt we were running very late and good soul Miss Husband, although saying she would make 'Tommy' make up for lost time, lifted the little flick of a whip high into the air, but I noticed it came down very sparingly indeed and only tickled his rump of which he took no notice.

Anyhow arrived too late for the train and I'm sure I could have done it by walking, taking us more than an hour to travel about four miles. This was most disappointing, and really had upset all my arrangements. However as it was market day, and meeting Roberts and Mr Wise, spent an hour or so with them while Miss Husband shopped. Rob was to report to the ship tonight and after doing guard, to proceed to Liverpool for rest of his leave. Drove a little way out of town with Miss Husband, for it was arranged that I would go to Padstow by 7.12 train and return as soon as possible. While driving passed Miss Anne Sargent's house and noticed her looking out of window at us, pulled up and went inside. Miss Sargent, having heard about me, was glad that I came. Appears she was on look-out last time of my visit to Launceston, when hearing that an Australian was enquiring re Sargents of Lezant. Present owner of Bottonet, and very nice, apple cheeked, middle aged lady. Saw picture of old homestead of Bottonet. A grand old house, surrounded by glass houses against the walls and fine gardens. Tells me the pride of the Sargents, but being burned down, the present large and up to date house, built in its place. House called 'Tor View' and commands an excellent view of hills for miles.

Caught train and travelled with farmer who had come to the market. The country further north this way, does not look half so good as at Launceston. Appears patchy and poor in places. Even the hedges seem stunted in growth. At junction for Padstow and Bodmin, the train comes close to an inlet from the sea, and keeps this in sight until Padstow is reached, first crossing a fair sized bridge beneath a high monument on a hill, before reaching Padstow. Leaving the station, one comes right upon the Hotel Metropole, a favourite hotel for tourists and visitors, and easily the largest building in Padstow. Intend riding back tomorrow if weather fine, being only 40 miles by road. No bicycles to be hired in the town however. Make these enquiries first. Little houses and streets could not possibly be more quaint than these of this old fishing industry town I think. Have no trouble in finding the Doctor's house. Knock at the door and meet Mrs Sargent, who welcomes me. Explain Miss Husbands absence, and take a seat in the surgery. The Doctor is a bright, witty grey haired little chap, and made me very welcome. His cheeriness is wonderful after his recent sad bereavement, which I hear he took to heart very much, and is really just recovering from a recent serious operation. Go into the sitting room and over a nice large fire, have a long, interesting talk on many matters until bed-time, Mrs Sargent first making sure I had had a good supper. I fancy their Cornish cake, which is plain, but very good. Shown to my bedroom on top floor (3 storey) and hear I am to accompany him tomorrow on his round near the coast. Bathroom close handy. Soon find myself in a soft bed again, and nearly buried alive through its depth of mattress and softness of it. Seems a favourite idea here in England.

Sunday 27th

Had instructions to lie in this morning and have a 'laze' as they call it. No time to waste these days however, so got up early and had a good warm bath. Found my way through a field to the wall facing the inlet from the sea, with the hope of walking along the water's edge to the 'Heads' or Point. After a short distance found this impossible for I came to cliffs, where the water was against them. Besides it came on to rain heavily, and my boots leak like sieves, so turned back and went for a jaunt round the wharves, and fish market, also to the little one where the fishing luggers are berthed. All have brown canvas and hulls painted black. Hear from one of the fishermen of the terrible losses of lives and ships off the coast and sinking by shell-fire of numerous fishing craft by Huns during submarine warfare. Huns used often to scuttle all fish on board, sink the craft and submerge themselves. Notice steam life-boat lying in the stream, quite as large as the average tug boat. The fishermen's houses, and 'Taverns' or 'Inns' are small, and exquisitely quaint little arrangements.

One old place facing the wharf, but standing back from it a little way, looks very odd. It is quite round, low, slate roofed and much resembling an old town market. Is now composed of dwellings and shops. Tide at Spring comes right up over pavement and 3 or 4 ft up walls of this place at times. Hear from this chap, that Navy now requiring more mine-sweepers in North Sea and other places, for sweeping up our own fields. To receive 7/6d day and 2 pounds put on one side each week for them, not to be drawn until discharged from Navy. At the house by 9am and in time for breakfast. Mrs Sargent is without a maid, (a real problem in England), but the Chauffeur who by the way is a survivor from a British man-of-war, which was wrecked some years ago on Lundy Island, is a handy chap, and cooks and waits on table and does housework as well as any woman. He prepared a jolly good breakfast anyhow. The motor was brought from the garage and we made off towards the point. The day was extremely cold, boisterous and rough. Came to fields, and had several gates to open, and at length reached a little clump of neat looking cottages and bungalow, into one of which the Doctor went. Opposite is an ancient French burial ground, recently unearthed in a sand hill.

Mrs Sargent and myself meantime had a look at this. Many skeletons are to be seen under glass covers. Walked to the water on our right, and viewed the Point (entrance) from the cliffs. Course sand which blew from the beach off the little cove below was blinding, and smarted and stung one's face with all the force of a pepper-corn blown from a blower, so fierce was the wind. Gathered a few wild flowers. Started off again, and the motor ploughed her way up hill through very pretty country lanes, to a little village called St. Mervyn. Doctor pulled up here again, so we went for another stroll. Now on north shore proper. A little cove nearby with steep, raggy, cliffy sides. How these huge breakers dashed against them. One great fragment of rock off mainland, high out of water, was completely hidden at times. On the beach we saw, spars, timber and various other objects washed in from wreckage. Mrs Sargent says that often explosions could be heard, as some unfortunate ship was torpedoed. On one occasion survivors brought ashore at Padstow, and a relief committee started by Mrs Sargent. Money, food and clothing, as well as housing soon collected and arranged by willing hearts of the townspeople. On the left side of this cove, is a funny looking little house, sort of bungalow, built by a Captain of the P. & O. Coy, where he lives during certain season of the year, or when on holiday from his voyage. The old sea-dog spirit again. Coming back to the road, find lovely wall-flowers growing in abundance.

After this we motor home again, with all cob-webs flown, after such a severe blow. Put car in garage again, meanwhile Mrs Sargent went to an old lady's house to arrange a look through the Squires mansion after dinner. That over we called for this lady. The sun came out for a little while for our express benefit evidently. Walked through a splendidly wooded park, with daffodils growing everywhere, then reached an open field in which the Squires deer were feeding. Came to the mansion, a huge place, with a high wall (with its strong gates of iron and oak) all round it. The whole is built of Cornish granite and steel grey in colour. The place is 'Prideaux' place and family the Prideaux-Brunes. The old squire is a Colonel and all his sons have joined up during the war. One killed first night in France, and the other rendered a cripple for life. Entered by the front door and being an old-timer is studded with iron bolts. This house is one of the typical old English-houses, handed down for centuries from father to son. The family at present away in a city home. A description of every part of this great house and all its details would be a task on its own. What interested me most was the library. There were books and manuals there entirely of parchment, some in Latin and others in Old English. Scores of rows and shelves of them, and mostly leather bound. Made a fine show. This large spacious room is in the tower which is joined to and forms part and parcel of one wing of the building (small hand drawing of same). From the window a fine view is to be had of lawns and shrubbery and over surrounding country. On the walls and staircases are paintings of ancestors French and English, the record of which are kept in a book for the purpose. Dozens of rooms, some lined with tapestries of the first order. Cedar and oak used lavishly. Schoolroom and nursery all in the same house, interesting. Billiard room a picture, for ceiling and walls decorations original and exquisite indeed.

Visited the kitchen and servants quarters which are excellent. Then went to the diary and this is a revelation. Special coppers and heating arrangements made for heating milk and skimming the cream. There were dozens of pans and buckets simply full of rich golden and white cream. This is from a Jersey and Devon herd. Patent churns used for conversion of cream to butter. The plate and old china in the house, worth anybody's while to see. Left with regret although really saw nearly everything. Followed a gravel path and when nearing a wall on the eastern side, and suddenly descending, came out through, under the wall, a gate in an opening made in the solid rock, and see hewn in the stone on old inscription re 'industry and labour', probably put there when opening made. This lodges us right on the roadway.

At the house found visitors with Doctor. They are the wife and daughter of his brother Doctor of the town. These two families get on well together, in fact I think Dr. Sargent could be popular with anybody. A genial, easy going style and not in the slightest proud, but a real gentleman all the same. It now came up cloudy and cold. For the first time in my life I saw snow falling. Slowly the tiny flakes came at first, but quicker and thicker after a bit. After visitors had gone, went for a walk for about 2 miles to the monument above the railway bridge, I mentioned yesterday. From here a wonderful view can be had. Farms all round. Bridge spans a branch of the inlet from the sea known as River Canal. The Obelisk is of Cornish granite and commemorates the Victorian Jubilee of 1887. This is on the peak of the hill and easily the highest point about here. In front and at intervals down the side of the hill, seats are placed, but used on better days than this I guess, for I have never been in stronger wind. One leaned over to the wind at 30 deg coming down, placing ones weight against it and then balanced comfortably.

Walked along the line and hopped the station fence, and back to the house. Spent remainder of evening looking over the silver plate etc., for which indeed is grand. Have boxes full, for which they have no use. Doctor told me same was insured for 300 pounds. Much of it given them by miners of Wales who appreciated his willing and untiring services to them, as a sign of their goodwill on his leaving Wales for Padstow (see newspaper cutting). Also presented him with an address the best I have seen. After the Doctor went to bed, Mrs Sargent and I talked till late about Shone. Poor soul, her heart was full. Showed me his clothes and luggage sent from 'TOPAZE' which I mentioned. He was in HMS 'CARMELIA' sweeping off Irish coast before going to the East. Says she will not speak about her son before the Doctor, owing to the upset it causes him.

I saw photo pattern of stone she intends sending to Bombay. In his pocket was found an application for Special Service in another Station. Glad to hear all I had to tell her. Had a photo of grave sent her by Padre Garrard. Not a very good one, but I explained exactly the position and the surroundings of the place. Glad to talk to someone who had actually seen and been there, and I think it was comforting. Told me of the awful experience of them both, when the tragic news came through. Feel they have lost their all through loss of this boy. She does not appear to be very strong. Chauffeur to call me for breakfast for 1st train in the morning.

Arrivals and Departures. 1919.

Left Melbourne	26/2/19
Arrived Fremantle	2/3/19
Left "	6/3/19
Arrived Bombay	19/3/19
Left "	24/3/19
Arrived Suez	3/4/19
Left "	4/4/19
Arrived Pt Said	5/4/19
Left "	5/4/19
Arrived Gibraltar	12/4/19
Left "	12/4/19
Arrived Southampton	17/4/19
Left "	17/4/19
Arrived Plymouth	18/4/19

Left Devonport	5/5/19
Arrived Southampton	6/5/19
Left "	6/5/19
Arrived Sierra-Leone	14/5/19
Left "	16/5/19
Arrived Capetown	27/5/19
Left "	30/5/19
Arrived Fremantle	15/6/19
Left "	16/6/19

Copied newspaper cuttings etc.

Extracts from paper-cuttings re our lads on duty at Exhibition Hospital Melbourne.

Sydney Sun NSW.
    Lost Platoon
    Flu's duty by the Yarra
    Exhibition Hospital Control
    By Pvte. W.B. Hardy A.M.C.

I am one of a merry company, a round score of 'Noo South' Army Medical men 'dumped' in Melbourne to await events. This pleasant afternoon I am 'free' to sit on Port Melbourne beach, watching the blue haze of boiling-down works drifting and eddying in spirals over 'the tanks' from overseas. For a few hours I am going to linger in these sylvan surroundings for I love quietness. The rattle of Melbourne's streets disturbs me and lorries laden with stone ginger-beer bottles anger me, for be it remembered that to indulge in a 'legitimate' gargle, means many locking and boltings, much whispering through key holes and strange passwords. We members of the lost platoon, humble servants of the A.I.F., duly recommended for discharge, find ourselves a very 'mobile' body, being neither fish, flesh, fowl, nor good red herring.

The Brass Hats. We were told to report at Military head-quarters to go before a board. We promptly forgathered in the square of execution, but a certain 'Brass Hat' quite as promptly disowned us and in the Military custom, referred us to another 'Brass Hat', who in turn posted us for guard duty in Hades.

That is some eight days ago, but on the second day we were detailed for duty at the No. 5 Australian Garrison Hospital.

There was nothing to do in the establishment, for with 95 patients and 190 staff, it requires no arithmetician to work out the detail concerning a fair division of labour. It is certainly not an ? problem.

Another 'Brass Hat', however, made the important discovery that our appearance in the hospital was more decorative than useful, and, strange to say, we were given immediate orders to depart, not to the Harbour City, but to the Exhibition Building for 'duty'.

With boots, belt and pack, we have made our ? to the officer in charge, and so far as we can gather, the matter of our discharge 'hangs gracefully from some file in the office of the P.M.O, the S.O.P, or the D.P. X Y.Z.

Philosophic Soldiers.

Consequently we are in the peculiar position of being governed by a civilian administration body, with Dr. Marnise? on the horizon as the 'High Panjandrum'.

We have however, taken the matter philosophically and without in any way being desirous of blowing hard blasts on a bugle, the lost platoon has, since its appearance at the 'Big Barn', occurred some measure of order and uniformity from chaos – that is to say, patients are grateful, which is the Alpha and Omega of any army medical man's existence.

The Matron – God bless her – has expressed the opinion that with the present staff she can cope with any emergency. The nursing staff is not fully qualified, but it is ? with a few who have gone through the mille from probation to full matronship and that is something.

Some there be who do not know the difference between the simple Haut Tussi and Mist Alba' mixtures - but they are learning.

Nursed by Foreigners.

Altogether, the 300 victims of 'pneu-influenza' are now getting a 'fair go', and possibly it may be that we stranded soldiers, knowing our business are doing some good. But our hopes of seeing Sunny New South Wales are somewhat remote, and it would appear that Victoria, panic-stricken, masked, and 'eucalypted' to its boots, has left its liege subjects to be nursed by strangers- 'foreigners' from over the border. In our spare moments we wash our shirts and socks, take what nourishment is thrown at us, and read 'Bolshevikism'. Melbourne itself is a ghost city, and St. Kilda has gone right out of business.

A "Diggers Verse".

A 'Digger' has produced some dogerd verse extolling the army medical man in this manner:-

The A.M.C., they have a good time
   Parley Voo;

The A.M.C., they have a good time
   Parley Voo;

The A.M.C., they have a good time
   Painting the 'diggers' with iodine
   Inky, pinky, parley voo.

We are making no growl, but as our claims for discharge are legitimate (medical and urgent domestic reasons), we wish to shake the dust of Melbourne from our regulation boots as soon as possible.

We are 'temporarily lent' by the military authorities to the Health Department.

The question as to whether military regulations or law can so dispose of us whilst waiting the board's decision we are not deeply concerned about, because we think that some service to the State has been rendered and that possibly some lives have been saved by reason of our training.

Soldiers of Civilian Duty. Who was responsible?

Complaint has been made in these columns recently by 'One of the Victims' regarding the action of some authorities in detailing A.I.F. Army Medical Corp men from the hospital ship 'Karoola' for work at the Exhibition. The writer pointed out that practically all the men were from New South Wales, and wished to return home.

Mr. Holmes, secretary of the Board of Health announced today that he had arranged for these men to be relieved of their duties, and to be replaced by discharged members of the Victorian A.I.F., A.M.C. Mr. Holmes added that he did not know why the 'Karoola' men were sent to the Exhibition. The first intimation he had of the matter was when he received a list from the Defence Department of the 36 men detailed for the work.

'LOONGANA' Still Idle- Crew not yet available.

Though it was stated today by the Shipping Controller that the prospects of an early settlement of the dispute with the seamen regarding the influenza bonus were good, up to a late hour this afternoon no crew had been procured for the 'Loongana.'

Several communications were received yesterday to the effect that the men were likely to accede to the owner's terms, but no official communication from the Seamen's Union on the matter is yet to hand. If the ships in Queensland and New South Wales are manned, a crew for the 'Loongana' will probably be forthcoming.

If a settlement is not effected by Feb 26, the stranded Queenslanders will probably be carried north in the 'Karoola', at present being prepared to freight – carrying in dry dock. Mr. A.H. Gibson, secretary of the Victorian branch of the Federated Seamen's Union, said today that in view of the fact that the seamen were greatly dissatisfied with the quarters on the 'Loongana' he had suggested that a portion of the second-class should be allowed to the crew, but the suggestion had not been adopted by the steamship owners.

Referring to the statement that seamen would be paid for periods of detention in quarantine, Mr. Gilson said the members of the crew of the 'Boonah', a Commonwealth – owned vessel, had not so far received a penny for the time they had spent in quarantine in West Australia, although application had been made.

Steamers 'Kanowna' and 'Karoola'

The former Australian hospital ship 'Karoola', which has been altered at Melbourne from the regulation hospital ship to an ordinary transport in accordance with Admiralty instructions, is to be recommissioned today for a voyage overseas.

The vessel was signing on crew yesterday.

The 'Kanowna', the second hospital ship, controlled by the Commonwealth authority, was due at Adelaide yesterday afternoon, where she is to coal before coming on to Melbourne.

Taken from a menu of Mess Dinner of Army Pay Corp Egypt by S/Sgt. S.L. Leslie.

The little grey house had a lonely look,
    There wasn't a soul around,
But we saw as we crossed the shallow brook,
    That the slip-rails lay on the ground,
We rode in up to the kitchen door,
    For the stock might take the track,
But a woman said with a weary smile,
    "My boys are absent many a mile,
And we'll leave the panels down awhile,
    To wait till the lads come back".

And over our Southern sunny Land,
    The same great thoughts hold true,
From the timbered hills, to the parching sand,
    And the wide green stretches too,
All the boys whore' done their bit,
    Though many a pal we'll lack,
Whether they're come from bush or town,
    We'll know they'll find the panels down,
To hearts they left – and love will crown,
    The day that the lads gets back.
Life. 1 Sept. 1916.

'If nature put not forth her power,
    About the opening of the flower,
Who is it that could live a single hour?'

Knowledge is now no more a fountain sealed
    Drink deep, until the habit of the slave
The sins of emptiness, gossip and spite
    And slander die. Better not be at all
Than NOT BE NOBLE.

End Diary 4.

The Close Gate Salisbury

Salisbury Cathedral

'Karoola', WWI. No.1 Australian Hospital Ship

Diary Five

APRIL, 1919

Monday 28th

Up early and found breakfast waiting. Caught 8.18 train for Launceston. Snowed heavily during the night. Fields simply a pure white and great banks of snow drifted up against the hedges, blown there by the wind. In same compartment as a young lady and gent on a walking tour. Had done most of peninsula from North to South, but owing to weather were training part of their journey. Amongst certain class of people this is a popular form of pastime and certainly a healthy, educational and profitable one. With packs neatly strapped to their backs and looking fit and rosy, these two looked ready for any emergency.

Arrived Launceston 9.45, and started my walk by short route to Trewarlet, first having a look over the pleasure grounds once again. These are at the hill, and the town reservoir nearby. Snow and hail very thick here. One can see for miles round from this place. Dartmoor was a large white sheet. Rained a good bit, but managed to keep dry. Arranged with Wise's on whom I called, to call and have tea on my way back to Station, for I intend going to London again for remainder of leave. Reach Dobbin's Cott and while waiting for dinner, and after telling Miss Husband all news from Padstow, go for a jaunt through the Duke of Cornwall's property, on hills opposite, by lane and road which leads to Callington. Hoped to have a couple of hours fishing, for trout are plentiful. Miss Husband has the latest designs in hooks and apparatus for catching them. Wanted to try my luck, but found after all, time would not permit.

Had dinner and started out. I intended to call at Trecarrel on my way and have a look at the old hall there, the Church etc. Began to drizzle again, but Miss Husband would come with me. Trecarrel is now a single farm, farmed not many years ago by Miss Husband's father. There is a large field in front and another at rear of house. 'History of Launceston' has it, that King Charles I camped in these fields with his army, when invading Cornwall. It is from here too, that Sir Trecarrel whom the same book says was a great astronomer. Says he predicted by aid of stars that his wife was to bear him a son, what the son should be etc. However, the baby was drowned in its bath and the father, having already begun building a huge mansion of Red Devon granite for the man to be, had this pulled down and carted to Launceston, of which the Church of St. Magdalene is built, previously described. Another building was started, but the old chap dying at the time, was abandoned, and later fell into pieces. However, the huge, cleverly cut masses of granite are still there, but a wood is growing over the remains. Some years ago, a society which pays attention to repair and renovation of old historical buildings, landmarks etc., promoted the idea of rebuilding this place with the same stone, which is as yet in perfect condition. This idea fell through however, owing to the key-stone of the whole missing. Miss Husband admitted to me that she had it herself at her house. I had seen it, but up to now had taken not much notice of it.

Obtained farmers permission to go into the hall, which is just at the rear of the house. This was built for banquets and dances by Trecarrel. A huge place, with beams and rafter of solid oak, and carvings of the same material. Walls of granite and two feet thick. Used now as storage depot for onions, potatoes, chaff etc. Had a look at the tiny, but substantially built church for those employed on the estate in those days. Society mentioned have repaired this. On either side of the place where the alter was, is a hole in the wall, where sacrament was passed out to lepers and others who owing to disease were not allowed admittance. Roof and carving also of oak. Miss Husband now walked as far as Trebullet with me, and we parted company, not without feelings of regret on either side. I do not know if I shall see this good, kind and charitable body again, but I do feel glad that I have had the good fortune to meet and know such a good Christian soul. Her little home of Dobbin' Cott, amongst those beautiful trees, babbling river, old mill and lovely fields, I consider a little heaven in itself. I should love a clear month to ramble about here.

Went to Wises and after a short time with them, was about to prepare for the road to Launceston, but Mr Wise would not hear of my walking, and insisted on driving me. Caught the 7.12pm. L. & S.W. train, having already purchased a ticket through to London from Padstow. Changed at Okehampton and had to wait for train from Plymouth. Travelled with soldiers of the Tommy Army of occupation on the Rhine. Had to change at Exeter to G.W. Both Coy's at same station viz St. Davids. Had an hour to wait, so caught a tram for the city and had a stroll up and down the High Street and about the Cathedral. Caught 10.25 for London, but when near Taunton heard from the guard that this train went on loop-line and not through Bath for a little while, so took his advice and got out at Taunton to wait for the next train at 2.30am in the morning. The S.M. fixed me up in waiting room, where I had a snooze and arranged to call me on arrival of train.

Tuesday 29th

Found it pretty cool on that old station and was well awake when the train arrived, but it was nice and warm in the train, for besides being crowded, they are heated through exhaust steam from the engines, running through pipes under seats etc. Had a nap and badly needed it, for besides being on the go a good deal of late, anticipated a big day today. When nearing Bath, kept awake so as not to go on in error. A lady ticket collector called out 'Bristol change for Wales!' Thought must be getting pretty close now, and knew we had not already passed through Bath. Next station was Swindon and then I knew something was wrong. No railway maps in my carriage and nobody else seemed to know, but after train had started found we had not gone to Bath at all, but coming over a loop line had passed it long ago. Now had to wait until train stopped at Reading a long run from last stop and only about 40 miles from London. I do not remember when I felt so perplexed as to what to do now. My time without any waste of time like this, was already fully booked in London. Anyhow I was determined not be beaten, so got out of the train to catch the next back to Bath. But here a fresh difficulty arose, the ticket collector insisted on my giving up my thro' ticket to London if I got off here, in spite of the fact that I offered to pay my own fare to Bath return. Now this was no joke, for having no half fare warrants left, I had to pay full civilian fare which is old rates plus 50%. Had a stiff argument with this fellow who tried to make out all the time that it was my own fault.

To finish up caught a train a few minutes later, the 6.18am. Vexed enough to determine not to buy a ticket back to Reading or to London either, seeing that I had already paid it. The country on either side very pretty indeed, and a long tunnel is gone through just before reaching Bath Station. Have heard so much about Bath, and its wonderful healing springs and old Roman Baths, that I could not resist a glimpse of it. Saw the inspector on Station, re my ticket for return journey, but he advised me to go to Provost Sgt. stationed at Police Stn, and arrange with him for it. Went straight there passing the museum on the right and Cathedral on the left. Had just turned o-clock and the Cathedral clock struck up on bells a familiar old tune which I think was 'For Britons never shall be slaves'. At least I think it was, anyhow I have heard that tune from bells of other clocks in England. Provost staff not yet arrived, so went for a walk, first having a look at the river, its weir and bridge, which is supposed to be only one of its kind in England, in that it has shops and houses etc on it. Went as far as Art Gallery and turning back returned through a park to the Police Stn. The Provost staff of about six had their office in one of the cells. Their duty is to watch for strays and ask to see leave passes of all Australians on leave from a camp near Bristol. Asked me to come back when ready.

Made straight for the Roman Baths. The first I saw was a small one in the middle of the road, but covered with a wall round it. Admission 6d. I think it was called the 'Cross Bath' being at junction of 4 roads. Hear wonderful testimony of healing powers of the springs (see pamphlet which gives a full account). Next went to Cathedral and had a look through. Roof a wonderful piece of work and supported by pillars which amaze me. Then sought out the Royal Baths, so called because royalty used to patronize them. One enters by a door in what is called the Grand Pump-room, and a 6d ticket admits one to the old Roman Baths now not in use. The halls and passages leading from the pump room are magnificent and entirely of marble. There are reading rooms, concert hall and all the rest of it where people attending the baths for treatment may sit, smoke or read. A splendid orchestra was rehearsing and if one is able to form any idea from pictures and paintings one so often sees of old Roman life, this just the thing, for the music sounding through those beautiful rooms and marble halls, puts one in mind of it. There are many glass cases containing relics found in excavations and from the old Roman Baths, which are intensely interesting.

Then went down stairs to the old excavations. Find too many things there to record. Statuary, bronze figures and stones with many inscriptions. The baths are not very deep, called the Great Bath. The water is warm and steam rises from the surface. Gold fish live in it. One notices the old leaden and clay pipes which at one time conveyed the water from the spring to this bath. Much of the old stone work is now exactly as it was, especially the bases of old pillars, which have not been interfered with. The Romans were great builders, and wonderfully industrious. The place is full of relics. Through window on the way through a passage, one sees what is known as the 'king's bath'. Is inside a stone wall in the middle of this building. In the centre of this bath is what appears to be a caldron, apparently right over the top of a spring, for steam gushes out from the centre of it and curls up into the atmosphere. (small drawing of same). 2d admits one to the pump room. People were collecting here, and I understand there is to be an orchestral concert. Everybody goes to a counter, and a couple of maids in neat attire of black dresses, white cap and cuffs, hands each a glass, containing nearly a pint, of spring water, right from a 4 tapped fountain, quite warm 120 deg, which is running all the time. Took a seat like the rest and started to take stock. The water has a most peculiar taste.

Next to me was a lady who had travelled the world a bit and knows Australia well. Soon fell into conversation. It seems persons suffering from diseases, mostly rheumatism and gout, lumbago, attend here for treatment. This was verified, for I noticed all sorts of people coming in, some with aid of sticks and crutches. People of rank too I could see and a sprinkling of Military Officers from Lt. Cols. downwards. Each went to the fountain for his or her glass of water, which after drinking, went to their baths, either to the large open one, or to private baths, which have railings, steps and tiled. Both about as large as a fair sized household bath. Celebrated pictures on the walls and much guilt, quite a top-notch room. Many of the old ladies gossip, and one in particular I noticed with tortoise handled spectacles viewing and taking note of everybody who entered. Kept her quite busy, for she was continually raising and lowering them. The orchestra now came in and rendered delightful music. I reckon this a grand experience for me, for it seemed such strange company. One by one people went to their baths. Heard about a wonderful old Sedan chair and began to walk around to find it. Stood in a corner. Queen

Elizabeth used this in her attendance at the Baths. Asked an old gentleman sitting near it, to tell me all about it. This accidently led to a conversation with his wife, who by the way, seemed to me to be one of the most charming women I have ever met. As the music was still in progress, I felt content, so we talked away and about many different things. My impressions of England so far etc., social conditions in Australia as compared to theirs etc. Seemed to feel that they were people 'well up'. Afterwards told me he was a barrister, just on a visit to Bath, but living at their sea-side home at Sidmouth for the present. Practises at Exeter and was pleased of my impressions of that city. I liked him for his unassuming attitude and broad-mindedness in all topics spoken of. Cherishes the thought that Colonies will be closer in union to Mother country since the War, and gives me his ideal for abolishing all petty misunderstandings and discrepancies.

Felt loath to leave these good folk. Outside I found many invalid's chairs had collected. These are hired out to sufferers requiring them and pushed by the owners. All rules for hired vehicles apply and they have their proper licensed stand. A fountain similar to one inside is in the middle of the street for use of general public free of charge. Heard that if I ascended the hill on the opposite side of the town could get a wonderful panoramic view, so accordingly caught a Combe Down tram. Hill very steep. Got off about a mile the other side of hill and walked back another way, over an old Roman Road which leads to Wells. Some very fine houses about this part. Climbed another hill, over which is a public garden, and reaching the top found myself on a terrace. The back gates of dwellings were contained in a stone wall, separating the dwellings from the garden. Seats are provided up here, and one of the finest views of a town I have ever seen was from here. One can pick out every part of the town and the surrounding hills and valleys, with their various shades of trees are indeed magnificent. Bath people boast of this and I think justifiably.

While one is in the streets one is impressed with the cleanliness of the place, but from here the whole town seems so beautifully laid out, and buildings all of one colour and grey looking, it looks doubly so. No smoke to speak of. Right at the back of the town and higher on the hill (Bath being partially built in a valley and partially on side of a hill) is a large allotment of buildings built in form of a crescent. Supposed to be finest crescent in the world, called Royal Crescent, masterpiece of its architect John Wood. In these buildings many distinguished Englishmen have lived. Sir Isaac Pitman, and others. Scene of midnight incident described by Chas Dickens in 'Pickwick Papers', when Mr Winkle and Mrs Dowler come before the screen.

Now strolled about the streets and looked in the shops generally, also had a look through museum. Many old Roman relics of interest there. Now went to the Police Stn. Found they had arrested an Aust. Corporal and had him in one of the cells. Went to the station and asked for Inspector, found another relieving him. Provost man introduced me and I stated my case. Said collector at Reading had no right to take my ticket, also that train had missed out Bath that morning. Spoke to guard on the train, and he with all courtesy, said 'Right ho! My boy, I'll look after you', and he did sure enough, found me a seat in the already crowded train. I had the number of my old ticket, but he did not want it, saying that he trusted me, so got a ride to London without extra fare at all. At end of journey felt I ought to offer him something but he refused it, saying the pleasure was his and he should like same if stuck in Aust. We Australians have always to be thankful to these railway men, London police, and bus conductors, they are wonderfully patient and good tempered and nothing seems too much trouble for them.

Arrived Paddington about 7 o'clock. Caught underground for Victoria, saw my lady friends of Y.W.C.A. Enquiry Bureau, then bus to Leicester Square and saw 'Maid of the Mountains'. Standing room only, but I enjoyed it immensely and felt no tiredness after a big day, and little sleep of late. Then walked to 'Lonsdale'. Found Mrs Hearne, but Mrs White stying at Chiswick owing to house decorators in. Mrs Hearne says she posted a book which I had been trying hard to get, but in vain, to Plymouth. No room at

Lonsdale, so went along to my old favourite, the Shakespeare Hut. Plenty of beds vacant and slept like a toff. Arranged to be called @ 7am in the morning, for I have plenty to do. Getting to feel that I know my way about London a bit better now, and can often take short cuts instead of walking long distances round and about.

Wednesday 30th

Up at 7, and having promised that I would go and see Mrs. Cann-Sargent in Stepney in the East End, caught a bus straight away, for hearing that she is a very busy woman and doing war-work, nursing etc., wished to get out there early. Her late husband – a brother to Dr. Wn of Padstow. Went past Royal Exchange and down Threadneedle St. through Aldgate and Whitechapel, where the traffic across junction of four roads is immense. Got out just prior to reaching Stepney Stn. Only about 8 o'clock then, and began to think this an unreasonable hour to call, so knowing I could not be far from the India Docks, enquired my way thence.

Went to South West India docks and soon found myself amongst a sea of masts and funnels. Quite close to the Thames. Walked long with a sailor just signed on for a voyage to Newcastle. Engineer in one of the Standard Ships. What huge cargo sheds and how many different of ships were there. Many undergoing repair, and changing their war paint for old colour, and others being converted from troop-ships to their original state. In the dock were several large ships taken over from Germany since the Armistice terms. On the sides of these were painted the words in English and German WAFFENSTILLSTAND – ARMISTICE. These were the 'LUCIE WOERMANN', 'WINDHUR' and another. I inspected one. The saloon panelling, table tops, shelves and pillars were all of white marble, but all told lacked the 'housiness' and comfy-home on the sea, as it were, that is found in our ships, and this an up-to-date ship. Chief Steward told me, that in a terribly dirty, neglected state when taken over, but now they are getting things ship-shape. Hear from several that the largest ship afloat viz the 'IMPERATOR' (550,000 tons) is to arrive at the docks on opposite side of river in three days time. By jove, I should like to see her. The German Navy taken over is in a rotten condition and the latest is that Britain wants to scrap them, ships as being not worth keeping. Go to the Thames front and simply lined with tiny docks for tugs and barges. Quite imagine how Dickens could find such a good spot for his tale of our "Mutual Friend".

Now wended my way back through the slums, which they tell me have improved during the war, owing to plenteous work for all, to the tram line and finally to Newark St., just rear of the great London Hospital. Imagine my disappointment on finding that Mrs Sargent had just left 20 minutes earlier, now only 10am. Supposed to be back at 12.30 for dinner, but I could not wait, so went back to London. Got off the bus at Billiter Squ, and enquired at Mc Ilwraiths office for letters and date of sailing of ship. Supposed to be next Tuesday. Then went to Royal Exchange which centre of London proper. It is here that London merchants dispose of merchandise, and weal the weeks prices. On the walls round the court are very fine paintings of large size, showing the earliest epoch of trading in England to foreign countries and other important incidents in the development of the same throughout the world till now. The latest picture is of Sir Doug Haig, his chief of Gen Staff, Prince of Wales and Gen Birdwood, leader of Anzacs at Gallipoli. Shown around by an old attendant wearing a beaver hat and long black robes.

Next had a look at Lloyds. Before the office door is an old gun brought up from an old wreck, a Naval ship carrying treasure of something like ¼ (or 114) million in gold, when this treasure salvaged many years later. Then went to Stock exchange near Bank of England, but not allowed in. Many wielders of the world shares entering and coming out and all wearing their silk-bell-topper hats. Know a thing or two some of these men I guess. Then had a look through Bank of England which is disappointing and not nearly approaches the style of our own Banking Chambers in Aust. Everything is plain and ordinary. Visited the clearing house, Public Institution deposits, and private banking dept for Companies etc. Seems cramped and tellers boxes very tiny and altogether not equal to our country branches apartments. But what about the Bank itself, the Great Bank of the world! How much money is handled in this place. The most interesting thing was the coin sorting machine, which picks out the particular class of coin and counts it. Many girls going in and coming out from most parts of the building and usually employed in the printing dept. Attendants dressed in old style similar to those of the Royal Exchange. Many temporary clerks employed, one, a broken down Baron, amongst them. Work of such dimensions during the war, that offices opened up all over the city and staff have been working till 10pm every night for months. Sand bags on roof, anti-aircraft, now taken down. Intentioned going to St. Bartholomew's Hospital to make certain enquiries, but being informed out of city a considerable distance, gave up idea, to my regret, so I found afterwards.

Then walked past Church of St. Pauls to Australia House in Aldwych. Thought I would have a decent look through the building while I had a chance. Five stories high, and all timber used being Australian. The staircases are wonderful, have never seen any other after style of these. In main entrance hall, tremendously enlarged photographs of Australian scenery and rural life. At end of this fine large hall most beautifully decorated. In basement, rooms and lounges for Australian Soldiers. Offices mostly taken by Military branches of one kind or another. Ground floor Commonwealth Bank for soldiers. Each of the 5 States represented by a counter for transacting business. The large windows facing Aldwych are filled with samples of wool, cereals, fruits etc., and many pictures showing growing of these. 'Emigrants with a little capital needed in Australian land settlement etc.,' are the notices. 'John Bull' has had a word or two to say about this and is justified I think, for plenty of colour and advertising, if not overestimating the wonderful opportunities in Aust certainly make the idea of emigration a most luring temptation.

Then walked to Lonsdale Hotel and had dinner with Mrs Hearne. Afterwards visited H.Q. again re transfer, but 'found' Col. Millard (D.G.M.S.) out. However as I was coming out, ran into our O.C. and Adjutant, who too, were going to see him. Told them the state of affairs, and they promised to do their best for me tomorrow, when they would come in again. Walking down Horseferry Rd, met Sister Macklin. It was a great little meeting. Heard nothing of her since her departure from Keswick just before me. Says that just a moment or two before left Str. Stacey. We three were in No. 7 ward (surgical) at Keswick. Having a little time to spare, thought I would take a run out to Stepney again. Found nobody home, and was about to come away, when a lady and a girl whom I noticed had just come out of a large church at back of the Hospital. Came and spoke to me, introduced herself as Mrs Vatcher, the vicars wife, and asked if she could deliver any message to Mrs Sargent seeing that she was absent. Showed me through a garden, of which her husband had planted, garden used by the nurses during their hours off. Wished to show me through the hospital (a good opportunity which I should have liked) but time did not permit.

Anyhow walked through the building to street in front for the tram. This was a most charming lady and wished to do lots and lots for me in various ways. She assists Mrs Sargent in her work, so I suppose felt interested in me. Had tea and walked to Haymarket and attended 'Chou-Chin-Chou,' London's favourite and now in its fourth year, and still exceedingly popular. Book ahead for days to get a seat. Got my ticket from American Y.M.C.A, Eagle Hut in the Strand. Madame Melba who is in London for Peace Day celebrations, occupied the Royal Box. Collected my traps from the hotel, caught tube at Museum for Paddington. Only had 10 minutes to catch train, so had to get a wriggle on. As it was uncertain that the train stopped at Paddington, changed at Oxford Circus for one direct. London was still well awake under the earth about 90ft down anyhow. Crowds of people were pushing about in masses from one platform to another waiting for their train home Seems almost uncanny this underworld, but is a very different affair to the real 'underworld of London' as we hear it spoken of. One can hear the trains rumbling during their approach in the dark tunnels, then a sudden stop as she pulls up sharply, calling of officials, clanging of gates and doors, a rush of the crowd, a whistle and like a flash, she has dived into darkness again. I was fearfully annoyed though on changing the trains. Oxford Circus is a labyrinth, and having been mis-directed was chasing about from passage to passage, upstairs, downstairs, round corners etc, and finding myself back in the same place, and trains all the time dashing to and away from those platforms to various parts of this great city. Gave up all hope of catching my train, but eventually got the right one. Trust I was not rude to a chap on whom I rushed and almost breathless asked him the correct platform for Paddington. After keeping me waiting for a reply for about ½ minute, which seemed like an hour to me, for I felt extraordinarily impatient, he slowly and doggedly said. 'Me no speak a-da-Engleez', and this with his forefinger to his lips. Poor beggar how does he find his way about London. Left him in great haste, for I felt like bursting, I was properly 'wet' and perplexed. Anyhow caught train, the moving staircase saved ½ minute, but thanks to the guard, voluntarily delayed the train till another official had purchased my ticket for me. Wonderful chaps these and an important train too. Would do this in Australia I do not think.

MAY, 1919

Thursday 1st

Went to Millbay docks where I left the ship, but not finding her there, informed that she now at No. 7 coaling berth, at the Admiralty Dockyard at Davenport. This a nuisance, for if I had known, could have stayed in train and got out at Davenport, instead of changing at North Road for Plymouth. So three miles now to join the ship.

Caught a train for Davenport and walked to the North Yard. Now I find this just suits me, for I have been wondering how I could get a pass to come through this dockyard to see the 'RESOLUTION', and others which I hear are here. And sure enough as I was wandering around looking for our red-funnel, pass ships, the size of which I have never before seen (i.e. war ships). Here in dry dock is the 'BENBOW', just off of our ship are the 'RESOLUTION' and 'REVENGE', and right opposite in the stream at junction of Lynher and Tamar rivers is the 'RAMILLES' at anchor, all these vessels the same class and the very latest in battle ships, being all built since the war, and oil fuelled. Countless other ships of all classes and sizes in dry dock, and afloat but in the yard. Compressed air hammers rattling, big cranes working, and activity of a very busy dock-yard. Intend to see all this later. Reported at ship by 9.

Went on top and surveyed the docks. Every building, wharf and dock presents the picture of solidarity, being entirely of a greyish granite. All 'heads' absent from the ship, and but for the guard, entirely deserted. Later in the afternoon, Cpl. Mallinger, Chick King and self, go to have a look over the 'RESOLUTION'. Found chap only too ready to show us over. Well, even the things I did happen to understand, I am afraid I could not describe here, and as for all that complicated machinery and wonderful devices of every kind, which to quote Chick Kings words, were 'too d------ human and uncanny, makes ones head ache!' Just let me say that the inside of one of her 15" gun turrets is a sight worth coming all the way from Aust. to see. I feel unable to give an adequate description of one of these even, for automatic clocks, double controls, hydraulic machinery which moves everything in a way 'too human'. The sides of the ship underwater are 'blistered', said to be a safe-guard against submarine attack. Went to 'brains of the ship' crammed full of devices, master compasses and the rest.

Also went up to fire control station, a dizzy height. From here the actual firing of the guns below, is carried out and strange to say, the man at the gun in the turret, does not see the object, or have any idea where she is, and is not aware of the firing of his gun, until it actually records. I have never seen such a mass of wires, pipes, compasses and most delicate instruments as are here to be seen and yet if this whole concern were shot away, four systems remain whereby the control of everything can be carried out just as efficiently. The search lights too are a revelation, and are not worked by a man standing immediately behind them as most are, but the controller and observer both, are well below decks, in fact not a man is to be seen anywhere when this ship is in action. In control tower a very small instrument finds exactly the position of an enemy vessel. This instrument automatically produces a similar result on gun below and the gunner moves his gun accordingly, then by a wonderful system of coloured lights, the man in the tower knows exactly when and as each and everything is done and made ready for it to be fired. When all lighting is complete, (and it is impossible by a method they have) for one thing to be left undone, without the other men knowing when doing his part of the job to the gun, he can ignite the charge and so fire the gun by means of just pressing an electric switch.

Had a look down the engine-room, which to give it its due, takes ones breath away. The engines are the turbine class and capable of driving at a speed of 25 knots. The 15 guns can and are sometimes fired @ 8 rounds in 3 minutes and every shell brought right from bottom of ship. Being the flagship of her squadron, a large clock dial is placed on top of tower. By this firing is directed, and other ships by looking at it may know what altitude etc., her guns are firing at. Another thing that may be worth mentioning is that these 5 ships of this class, during target practice, do not use the expensive old time target, which is only wasted, but during the war at any rate, actually fired at real 'live' ships. So accurate are the instruments etc., that orders are given to fire 100 yds astern of the object, and even up to 50 yds have been known. Only one accident had occurred.

Targets took too long to prepare, and besides thousands would be required if all ships in Navy went in for target practice during war when time was precious. The men are very proud of their Navy and own ship in particular. Fine fellows, manly in thought and gentlemanly in action, they think a lot of we Aust. I have heard that England's best men are in the Navy, and now that I am told seem to realize it. Our ship is supposed to leave @ 7 and anchor in Plymouth Sound. Nothing doing however, go off again in search of submarines, which I hear are in the docks. Found two of the British L. Class, real beauties. Had no difficulty in getting over the L8. The usual breezy, honest old Jack Tar came to my aid saying 'I don't see why you shouldn't, the war is over.' This is another marvel, in fact one cannot at all realize what is to be seen in the Royal Navy, until occasions crop up like these. Go down a man-hole, and at once, one is struck by the tidiness, nattiness, and system of the place as arranged under water.

At the bow are four torpedo tubes, and in the same compartment turn-cocks for flushing tanks with water. Also an instrument used for ascertaining exact position of enemy submarines, (an invention since the war). Middle compartment comprised of Officers cabins, and crews quarters. All cooking, boiling of water etc., done by electricity. Although space is limited, everything is so neatly arranged and in perfect order, that a 'place for everything, and everything in its place' gives the maximum amount of room. But the wonders are to come. The engines, 2 sets of 12 cylinders, one of the engineers joy and pride I should imagine. These when working automatically generate electricity, and when ship submerged, the electrics are used. Talk about switches, wires etc., these under-water craft are crammed full of machinery. Mice (some white and yellow) are kept in a cage. As the gas, sometimes give off a very harmful gas, even when stopped underwater, these mice fall the first victims, and accordingly give warning to the crew. By air purifiers the ship can if necessity arises, stay on the bottom of the ocean for weeks. Also have a device for morsing other craft under water, large disc arrangements can be seen on outer sides for this purpose. The chaps reckon life is good and sometimes exciting. This ship being overhauled for China Station. Guard (a windy one) @ 9pm.

Friday 2nd

Off guard at 9am. Most of boys back on ship now. As Rundle's ancestors came from Tavistock, thought he would like to have a look at the place. Train left Triary Stn. L.&S.W. Railway @ 1.22, so having plenty of time to spare, I took him round to 'Mayflower' wharf, fish market and other places I had previously seen. Train goes under the Saltash Bridge and runs along the left bank of the Tamar for some little distance, crossing over tributaries on the way. I had often wondered how I could get to Callington by rail, return by motor to Saltash or from Caldstock to Plymouth by boat.

Anyhow we decided to go to Callington, then Tavistock together and put in a good day. Have heard that scenery from Bere Alston to Callington is as good and almost similar to that of Switzerland, and I was keen to see it. Changed at Bere Alston and caught a light railway for Callington. Train was waiting. We were fully rewarded for all pains, for scenery of fir-woods, and landscapes were simply grand. Many tin mines up this way, and on either side we could see them. The country is very steep and progress was slow, so much so that judging by the groans and pains of the engine, one more carriage would have been too much for her. Pass over Caldstock Bridge, up to which excursion steamers from Plymouth come on certain days of the week. This is over the Tamar, and we are once more in Cornwall. Talking things over with a fellow passenger we decided that if we were to go to Tavistock that day, to get out at Gunnislake and walk there, a distance of 5 miles.

Gunnislake is only a small village and kept going probably by a couple of tin mines close handy. At one of these, the ore is carried by a flying-fox arrangement, a distance of about 3 miles to a crushing plant near the village. On the road come to the Tamar again, and cross over an ivy covered bridge, of a different structure to any yet that I have seen in England, water 50-60ft below. Up the next hill, a steep one, we aspire a number of rooks nests at the top of tall fir and pine trees, behind a high embankment wall, and on side of the road. Young Rundle thought that it a good idea to climb one of the trees and feel the nests and so did I. Feeling young and in good spirits we climbed over the fence, but found only one tree anything like decent to scale. Rundle stripped his tunic and leggings and soon began the school-boy trick. It was a long way to the first branch, but thanks to strong thick ivy growing up the trunk of the tree, proved a great help in reaching it. The rooks meantime were cow-cowing round the top of the tree, and becoming quite angry. He reached the top alright and reported 5 eggs in the first nest. This was good, but how to get them down was a difficulty. Resorted to 'blowing' them where he was and dropping the shells to me. A trifle larger than a pigeons egg, of pale blue colour, with light brown spots. Had just blown the 4th and was, by arrangement, putting the 5th in his mouth to bring down whole, with the idea of putting it into my lab incubator and hatching it for the fun of the thing, when a voice like the bellows of a bull, roared out, 'Hey! You young devil, what you be doing up there, come down out o'that, or I'll shoot'e'. Rundle a bit hard of hearing, and thinking I was speaking to him having a tremendous voice all his own, yelled out 'Ay!' Could be heard back in Gunnislake I believe. This annoyed our unwelcome visitor and he burst through the hedge exclaiming 'I'll teach'e to say ay to me, you young scoundrel, come down and with me to the village'. At that moment he caught sight of me for the first time and said in surprise 'Oh, it's you is it!' 'Yes', I replied,' how do you do', for to state the truth, I was greatly enjoying this pantomime to my heart's content. 'How am I, you blackguards' says he. 'What the, how the, devil the, why the, do you know you are trespassing! I'll take you in for this! Come down you young devil you, what do you mean by coming to my rookery and stealing my rook's eggs, come along with me, and I'll make you know all about this', and he raved, sputtered, spoke vehemently with rage. 'Look here old chap' says I, 'you're not good company for us, and we are not going anywhere with you. You cannot very well push or drag us into places we have not a mind to go!' Then he began to whine about his rooks, but I smiled at him all the time. Really it was tickling. I think I replied suitably when he called us fools etc., and I think I was rather a puzzle to him. 'Now look here' says I again. 'In Australia we call these blessed old things, or birds much like them Crows, and being a curse we're glad to get rid of them, in fact, those affected by them think we are jolly good fellows to either take the trouble to shoot, poison or pillage the nests, but if we have caused you any material loss, will pay you for it'. 'Pay! Pay! Poo-ay!' said he disgustedly. 'Here I breed rooks for a certain purpose and you rob them, how would you like me to come and take your canaries'. This was too funny. He looked in habit and dress, a real old Lord of the Manor. Had a walking stick, wore leather leggings, and gloves, and a sort of shooting coat, and had a dog with him. 'What are your names'. 'Mine is Marsten' said I. 'And his?' asked he pointing to Rundle just sliding down the tree. 'Smith' said I. Went over to help Rundle land to earth and whispered in his ear. 'Your name is Smith'. At the moment however Rundle was making an awful face, and without aiding his good looks had scratched his face and over his eye pretty well. Nodded his head at my remark and made signs that he wanted to spit into my hand. Held mine out and he spat what was once a rooks egg into it. Had bitten right into it, in his haste and excitement coming down. That spoiled our experiment. Meanwhile farmer Giles was looking on, so after Rundle had finished spluttering and spitting asked him his name. 'Howard' said he and my heart went into my mouth, but he finished 'Howard Smith'. He seemed satisfied, but couldn't resist giving a little lesson on trespassing. I told him laws in Aust. must be different, to which he replied we were not in Australia now. 'I have a son in Australia 10 years' he said and oh! heavens, must suddenly have remembered the fact, for he actually smiled and left us. My sides ached with laughing after he had gone, for I reckon this an experience worth having, and probably thought myself lucky these were not the old days, when for a similar offence men were exiled as convicts for life many to the very country which we so proudly represent today.

Rundle donned his apparel again and we made off on high road again for Tavistock. Noticed a prosperous looking farm and homestead near-by the rookery, so presume this where the squire dwells. The roads were a bit wet and muddy. A little further we passed a young lady whom I noticed was wearing a rising sun brooch at her neck. That proved she had met 'Aussies' before. Came to an old slate roofed light blue painted hotel called the 'Welcome Home' or 'Home, sweet, home" or some such name as that, quite odd anyhow. Now we wanted to get hold of some Devonshire cream, world famed it seems and we went into this wayside hotel to try and purchase some, for they had cows in the yard. Looking back, I noticed that the young lady had stopped and looked at us. Called out and asked her if it were possible to get cream anywhere round about. She then nodded her head and beckoned to us to come back. Tells us it would be difficult to get it from the farms today, for being Tavistock market day, all cream sent to market. However, advised us to go to Canon's Restaurant when we got there. Had an interesting chat with this girl. Told us that she had trained as nurse in London, but was now at home, keeping house for her dad. Told her the incident re the rooks. Said the owners name was Perkins, a very nice old man, and kind hearted chap, kept these rooks for the shooting season when he invited his friends, and kept up the sport in good old English style, by making pies of them. I confess I felt a bit sorry – half regretted our actions. She consented to tend our apologies and regrets to him, as they lived next farm.

Had just walked in from the town – had a basket full of days shopping in groceries etc. Consented to have her likeness taken photo of Devon roadside scene. Asked us, if we had the chance, to come for several days and stay with them in an empty cottage, but fully furnished nearby their own house and belonging to her father. This is typical of the western English people. Says she knows other 'Aussies' and would like us to come. Very kind of her I thought, especially not knowing what or who we might be. They are so trusting these people. A good 'stamp' of a Devonshire lass. Reached Tavistock, passing the Catholic church which has a notice in the ground to the effect that 'Trespasses will be prosecuted'. Something unusual we thought, not far from main door either. Turning to the right, come to a large bronze statue of Drake. Over the other side of river Rundle makes enquiries of people of his own name.

Walk to the town through main Street, Tavistock is a clean little place, proud of its substantial buildings and splendid shops. In Drake St., found Canons Restaurant. Everything here was scrupulously clean, neat and well arranged. Marble tops on everything and milk contained in large basins, jugs and dishes of pure white china. Rundle drank to his heart's content, but we could not get any cream.

Went for a walk around the town, across the river, and along the road to G.W.R. Station. Town half in valley, half on hill, but the river is delightful, by jove! I took a fancy to this place. That soft, mellow sort of scenery everywhere. Had a snack at another restaurant and I shall never forget the way in which these people, an old lady, man and wife and a maid, laughed, roared, and held their sides when we told them the tree act. It seemed almost ridiculous to me, but their enjoyment seemed genuine enough. The younger lady, a tall woman with auburn hair, especially seemed to think it a most remarkable and wonderful joke. Talk about a gabble, dear me, I think probably they may have frightened customers away. Believed they would have kept us talking all night but we '?pshied'. Looked over the Guild Hall, a fine old building, the market now nearby deserted and around the Town Hall.

Then another walk past down the Bedford Hotel (another nice building). This is a splendid street and called Bedford Place I think. Homes here were tip top class. Reaching the bridge where we first came, walked back along the river. Here, were men fishing for trout. Saw some, a fine fish with darkish and yellow spots and altogether a dark hue. It seems a licence has to be obtained from the Duke of Bedford to fish on this river. Last year the fish greatly decreased owing to a mine working higher up. Acids and chemicals found their way to the river, so the Duke had the mines closed and fresh spawn put in the river. This same gent owns a lot of inherited property round here. Some of his cottages let @ 1/6d per week, but when his constituency turned him down during an election, up went his rents immediately. A new law, or one of comparatively recent date prevents this, so the Duke came a thud. Below a fine old bridge which leads to the G.W.R. is a weir and at the side of it a series of steps, called a Salmon ladder. This enables the cunning fish to, as it were, climb up the water rushing in a big volume from step to step and so enable them to negotiate the river above the weir which is about 6ft high. The rear of the Bedford Hotel faces this and is surrounded by a high wall with a watch tower on top, much resembling those about castles. A fine English church in the town, but the highest steeple is that belonging to Scots Church. The old noisy lady at the restaurant gave us a very loud, vivid, account of how an Australian, a heavy-weight lifter by profession, led a mob in attack against a crowd of conscientious objectors to Military Service from Dartmoor prison, where they have been housed during the war. Both parties made this house their H.Q., but the latter took shelter in it. All in this house, seemed to think all Australians were dare-devils and worthy chaps, with strong arms and stalwart frame, by their terms of admiration.

Caught 9.30 train from L. & S.W., which station being right at top of the hill, looks over every nook and corner of Tavistock. To my mind, no doubt this is the prettiest little town in England I have yet seen. Well worth another visit, especially when those sycamore trees which line the banks of the river are out in full leaf. Had been given to understand that ship would move to the Sound today, but arriving in Plymouth, a steward told us, she had moored to a berth still higher in Devonport docks. This a jolly nuisance, for could have alighted at St.Budeaux St, and been not far from her. Now had to walk 3 miles as no trains running after 10pm and arrived at the ship, which we had difficulty in finding @ 1am, but felt satisfied that we had had a good day.

Saturday 3rd

Local leave granted. At Millbray Stn, meet a party of Yanks, looking at a map and wondering where and how to spend the day. I personally, intend going to Princetown and having a look at the old Dartmoor and Prison. Ask me for a suggestion and I make one and propose to go to Marsh Mills with them, and later advise them to go to Tavistock and put them on to the Canons Restaurant. Catch a train and from Plympton walk over to Marsh Mills a distance of about 1½ miles. They were keen on oranges and bought oranges @ 4d each, a huge price I thought, as we get 1 doz. for that amount in Aust.

Walked about for an hour. The country is typical of the English landscapes we see in paintings. Hear from them, that they belong to a ship carrying provisions to Germany. Germans treat them with kindness and appreciation (naturally) seeing that the populace are starving. Also that the crews of 16 British vessels, refused to take their cargoes of food into German ports, when they heard that their own people at home still short of food and paying dearly for it. Left them at Yelverton and changed to a train of one carriage 1st and third class and guard's van all compact. In company with two Jack-tars. One from the 'NEW ZEALAND' and been in all stunts with her. Hear from him all old sailors taken off her, owing to unpopularity of Jellicoe, and that new crew refused to take him from Bombay to Aust. Beatty seems to be the man of the hour in the Navy. Soon night on the moor. Snow still lying banked up against mounds of any sort. A cold, bleak, half-starved looking stretch. The line zig-zags and takes turns almost at right angles in places. Train would form a good letter U if long enough. No hedges, but short, stumpy grass and heather grows everywhere. Steel grey granite in huge blocks lying about everywhere, and small shaggy, long tailed moor ponies feeding in places. Look poor specimens to me. Reach Princetown. Could see at a glance that this only a small town. Every building is built of that grey moor-granite, which at once gives it the appearance of being cold, and a dreary desolate look.

Walked out of the town a bit, in order to get a good view of the prison. My word, how my thoughts run back over the stories and tales of prison life in this awful goal, when in olden days this place was a by-word and feared by all. Came back and had a very pleasant little snack over a neat table neatly set, in company of 4 other people. A good fire blazed and quite different to the cheerlessness outside. Ham and coffee and cake, constituted my fare and was good enough for me. If time had permitted intended walking back to meet the line from Brent to Plymouth and catching a train, but very suddenly a fearful dense fog set in and drizzly rain. Went to station, where I found a sociable S.M. over a good coal fire, to ask what trains to catch or place to walk for train. No more trains from Princetown that day, and he advised me strongly not to attempt walking over 14 miles of moor to Brent line, over which experienced men have before lost their way and caught in the bogs which abound on the way. Thought I would go to Tavistock, in fact had thought of doing this before.

Went down to the prison, passing a few shops in what may be called a street, and came to houses, inhabited by guards, warders etc, of the prison. Of two storeys and arranged in the block style. Went to prison gate and entered a courtyard under a huge arch with the French inscription on it. Came to gate, but locked of course, a strong iron barred structure. Found a warder in the guard room and being invited in, had a yarn with him for an hour and a half. A sociable old fellow, with 27 yrs service to his credit. The warm fire made me rudely sleepy I am afraid. Told me of some of his experiences of goal life as a warder, and not a little about the conscientious objectors who until very recently had inhabited the place. Convicts at the time were transported to Portland Bill prison the place I have before mentioned, when we called there for a pilot on our last trip. Convicts now back in their 'old home' and for several weeks are to be kept busy cleaning up and straightening things throughout after the previous occupants. Notice the huge key he used to unlock the gate when allowing other warders to pass in or out. Not allowed to go through, except by special permit from London. Ask him the direction, so that I may have a look at the burial grounds of the French and American prisoners who died at the prison. Had to walk round by the outer wall, through blocks of cheerless looking buildings, mostly built by these prisoners I believe. Found them behind the prison, and in front of open fields. Contained in two separate enclosures, the lane dividing them. There is a sort of obelisk erected in the centre of what may in proper time be a lawn (small hand drawing of same) and on each are written the simple words 'To the memory of the French (or American as in the case of American obelisk) prisoners who died in Dartmoor prison in the years 1809-1814'. Am told that many American have visited this spot. Went back to the town to try and get a book giving an authentic historical a/c of the founders, but could not purchase one from the bookstall there. Seen from a distance the prison appears to have three main blocks or wings of buildings. (detailed hand drawing of prison complex.)

Now a little after 7pm, so if to catch 9.30 train from Tavistock which is the last, have to look sharp, for 7 miles to go. Pass the goal again and for about 3 miles, walking is fairly easy, and between low walls of granite on either side. Many pine forests on the way and notices indicate that for this distance I am still amongst prison property. But oh what a fog. I have never seen its equal. Could hear sheep bleating and ponies scampering about but could not see them. Just had to follow the telegraph posts in case I should take a wrong turning. Suddenly find myself going downhill and after crossing over a bridge find I am in front of the half-way house. Near here are quarries worked by the convicts. But still what a fog. I resembled a phantom for my great-coat was white with hoar-frost. This is the sort of weather many a poor convict has attempted to escape.

Had a drink of moor water further back. It is clear, sweet and crisp. Then a long steep climb and down again towards Tavistock. Seemed to get below fog a bit here, and as the country round about Tavistock came into view, seemed to know where I was. Went through a tiny village a mile or so out and reached the town, main street, as clock was striking nine. Went into old restaurant for a drink and as soon as I put my head inside the door, and although many other people were there, the old lady caught sight of me, pointed her finger and bawled out. 'Come here, or I shoot'e'. She had to tell others about it and I was the subject of a seven days wonder. Younger woman said it had caused amusement to them all that day. Fancy! As I was going out, a young chap seated in the corner said 'I know you Aussie, you will find us home any time you like to come'. He was the brother or someone of the young lady we had met on the road yesterday. This old lady by mentioning the rook incident had given me away, and I presume this young lady had told him about it, so two and two made four to him by calculation.

Caught 9.30 train. Many rowdy, musical, song-loving footballers on board. Got out at St. Budeaux this time and soon reached the boat. Found 36 or so reinforcements to the staff had arrived from Forent? A.A.M.C. details Camp or Corp?

Sunday 4th
No more leave is the order of the day, although O.C. had asked permission from Embarkation Officer. Moved to our old position at No. 7 coaling berth. Later were granted leave to have a look round the docks only, and no passes required. Did not mention previously that the large steamer 'PERSIE' of the White Star Line in dock. Had been badly torpedoed, but now nearly fixed up. Also the P&O 'HIMALAYA' being refitted after war service. Had another look at the battle ship 'AJAX'. Shall always remember her, for the huge bow she has. Then saw the piles of 12" and 15" guns not far from the gun mounting wharf, the England's latest destroyers of 45 knots and depth charge apparatus, also two German boats given over since the Armistice. Just finished inspecting these (couldn't go below, manholes being locked) when I met one of our sergeants sent out to inform those of us about the dock, that leave had been granted till

midnight from 3pm. If I had been off earlier, fully intended going up Tamar by boat to Calstock, as I saw the trip advertised, and leaving 4pm. Had to rush back to the ship, and caught tram from gates, (over which Police protection very strict) caught car, alighted at St. Budeaux and walked to Saltash, hoping to catch boat as she called there. No luck however, as I found the trip had been cancelled.

Caught Maurice Sq. tram for Plymouth, and spent the very pleasant afternoon as it was, walking about the Hoe, with ships electrician, and 4th engineer. The flower gardens near the citadel on the Hoe are very fine, being prettily arranged, exhibiting a wonderful show of bloom. Crowds of people along the Hoe, a very fine parade indeed, overlooking the Sound and sea for miles. Went to Regimental Band concert on the pier, a fine structure and housed in. A good performance and much enjoyed.

Walked back with a Jack-tar to Davenport, knowing this to be absolutely my last walk in England, for how long. Goodness only knows, for the ship may not be required to return. Hear our delay in getting away now is because difficulty experienced in getting enough cases to fill us. Every Hospital in England, Tommy and otherwise searched for Australians. This sounds good, as many Austs. being shifted every month now, 10,000 from Davenport last month.

Monday 5th

Left berth at 2pm, only to hang on right in front of 'RESOLUTION's' bows, for about an hour. The old 'PERSIC' practically a new ship now, comes out from dock and goes to berth in the stream for coaling. Passed many war ships, one the 'COLLINGWOOD' anchored in mid-stream. English and American monitors, dozens of torpedo boats and light cruisers. Headed for Millbay and coo-eed by members of ships crews. A fine little nest of war-boats this inlet where the sea, Lynher and Tamar waters meet. Quite hidden from the sea. Several large steamers in the Sound. Passing between the fort and the breakwater, we have our last view of the Hoe and with aid of glasses can see old Drake looking out at us, but not playing bowls this time. Outside the point, dropped our pilot at the point, off a little town, first doing a complete circle in our own length in order to wait for his sailing boat to come up. The fields, nicely ploughed, are red in colour and look O.K. Probably this is why Devon is referred to as 'Red Devon by the sea'. Now quite close to the Eddystone light-house. Bound for Southampton again to pick up our patients. All busy preparing the wards. Later in the afternoon meet an old Pirie friend, Gordon Henry, now Warrant Officer, and attached to this staff for his return home. A glorious day and sun shining brightly. A great pity it was not like this, instead of so much rainy, and cold weather during our stay. However, it seems to be very good to feel the throb of the engines, and be @ sea.

Tuesday 6th

Arrived at Southampton early, and tied to a berth in front of 'KAISER-E-HIND' @ P.O. She was embarking troops of the Aust Flying Corp. When she had finished, the town Mayor in his robes gave them a farewell address. A band played good music from a cargo shed, for it was raining. Our patients had not yet arrived, so hearing that this boat going to Aust. through Suez Canal route, wrote Mother a hurried letter and gave it to one of the lads to post for me on arrival. Reckon she will reach home about a fortnight before us. A faster vessel besides. A big crowd assembled to see them off. By this act, I was able to run over and have a glimpse at the 'OLYMPIC'. Painted in a new coat now, and dispensed with her elaborate camouflage. A beautiful vessel.

Our patients had arrived, and with R.A.M.C. as stretcher bearers, began to put them in their wards in fine style. Surprised to find however, so many cot cases. General Birdwood, with two of his staff inspected our ship, and former shook hands with each man as he

ENGLAND

Pricetown prison

Amputees aboard ship

Goods from Tavistock Market

Young woman and Rex Sargent at Tavistock

Rex Sargent and friend travelling

Dr William Gostwyck Sargent and Mrs Agnes Hilda Sargent

'Hoe' from Plymouth Sound and Light House

was brought or walked up the gangway. Recognised by their colour-patches, all their units, wished them a bon voyage, safe return, and speedy recovery, ending with the words in nearly every case. 'She is a good ship, a splendid hospital'. He then went down to the 'KAISER-E-HIND' which had not yet gone, and watched the lads off there. Seems a decent, unconventional sort. Particularly friendly to all Anzacs identified. Certainly the Austs. made him what he is today. Took charge of 5th English Army in France. The other boat left, so we naturally expected the Mayor, band and crowd to come down to us, which they began to do, but as we were still embarking the police kept them back. It then began to shower, and although they waited for a good while, gradually dwindled away. Band gave one tune then left. Should like our lads to have a send-off, for to my mind even more deserved it than the troopship, all fit men, whereas our deck lined with armless and legless men. Piles of crutches and artificial limbs, were brought aboard for them. Get away about 9 o'clock still being light. Went down to the Solent and anchored for the night. How pleased at the prospect of getting home these poor lads are, and already delighted, and expressed it, with the good appearance, homeliness of the staff and feeling throughout.

Wednesday 7th

Reveille 5.30am and grind starts once again. New staff grumble at so early an hour. Got out in time to find ourselves just passing the Three Needles. We had come from our anchorage between the mainland and the Isle of Wight this time. The Needles adjoining the corner of the Isle is treacherous place for shipping. Water quite smooth as we passed quite closely by, but a dense fog had set in. A strong tide and current sweeps through this passage, and one can see it rushing past the buoys and over the rocks. A light-house at the Needle (3 large rocks). A weird sounding siren, much like a fog-horn, but with three notes at once, sounds loudly at frequent intervals from the light-house. Now I think as we leave it behind in the fog, which closes round, 'this may be my last glimpse of good old England'. A bit later and we stop in order that our mine sweeping gear may be put out, for there are still drifting mines about. The crew's galley cook is suddenly taken ill and put into hospital. I have been detailed to assist in D1 Ward for the voyage.

Thursday 8th

Hear that one of the patients in E4 Ward, wants to see me. Go down and find old Arthur Nelson with a broken leg. An old Keswick boy, and a school mate with me at Woodville. Says he had received a letter from Percy Barber just recently. We have a pay corps on board, sent for the purpose of auditing pay books and getting home at the same time. There are between 20 and 30 face cases from a special hospital in England run by Col. Newland our Adelaide surgeon. Some had had their faces completely blown, other the nose, palate, jaw or part of face. Wonderful how some of these pulled through, but thanks to the surgeons ability, flesh, cartilage and skin have been grafted from other parts of the body, in such a way as to render them presentable, poor lads. Many operations are necessary, as can only be done by stages. After leave in Aust, are to come to Adelaide, where Newland will treat them at his own hospital, for he intends returning to Aust. himself shortly. Plenty of work in the laboratory. Patients say they will be glad when we are in the warm zone.

Saturday 10th

We have a lot of jolly bad cases, and one sees more of them, now things have settled a bit. Several lads with both legs amputated, but they are very cheery and quite independent, refusing help, getting up the stairs by swinging up the hand-rails three steps at a time, and 'hobbling' over the door steps in a way, one would think would hurt them. To wash, climb right on top of wash stands and put their stumps either side of basin, manage in first class style. Wonderful chaps our Australians.

Note from diary Louis Schaeffer AWM

One mental patient upset the applecart again today, he had a bad fit, but was quite o.k. again within ½ hour, distressed other patients terribly, but is blissfully unaware of the acute attacks he experiences.

With us we have some shocking cases, there were thirty dressings done by Sister during the day, ghastly wounds.

Sunday 11th

A perfect day today and a treat to feel the good old sun. Passed between Santa Cruz and La Palma @ 6pm. Quite close to the former, but out of the sight of the latter. Could see distinctly the masts of ships, and later the lights of Tenerife. A fairly long island at one end is the town and @ the Southern the high peak of Mt. Tenerife. Our Chief Steward once lived on this island for 3 months and says that for living, is wonderful place. All kinds of fruit, fare cheap and lodgings very reasonable, good climate. Says that Nelson's flag of Trafalgar, in one of the oldest Cathedrals in the world there. Peak of the mount hidden in the clouds. For the first time in the history of the staff, a Red Cross Comfort issue to members today. Authority given by the Head, who came to see the ship at Southampton. Says that this should have been done right through the piece. T.B. patient died in E4 ward tonight. As I was going to bed, called to attend a P.Mortem and kept busy till midnight. Sea water a smoky-brown colour, almost resembling fresh river water, and suggestive that we may be off a river, as we are not very far from the coast of the Continent.

Tuesday 12th

Burial today. Another death in the afternoon, also a T.B. case, **(note from Diary of Louis Schaeffer AWM. One of these men was George Thomas Dunn, Boilermaker, who died from Pulmonary T.B)**. At burial today, the seamen turned out in Navy-blue and attended the funeral conducted by the C. of E. Padre. Only a few Military detailed to attend. The deceased was a seaman, at one time under our present boatswain on the "KATOOMBA'. Took ill while on an English ship and put into hospital. Strange that he should be embarked for his home on the sister to his old ship, along with his old boss.
Capt. White, a patient offers to deliver a series of lectures. Gave one tonight to a good audience on 'Britain Sea-power', not forgetting to mention Drake and the Hoe incident of course. A good lecture and interesting. Record speed today, 351 miles.

Wednesday 13th

2nd Lecture by Capt. White. Port side of promenade near O.C.'s cabin to be reserved for the purpose.

Thursday 14th

See land ahead during the afternoon and reach Sierra Leone (Freetown) at 6pm. A little distance from the shore is a wreck. A lovely looking vessel of about size of this. Looks exactly as if comfortably at anchor, but unfortunately lies fast on a coral reef, which runs out from shore, and forms a semi circle. The ship seems in a good state of repair, and paintwork is good, but so far all attempts to refloat her, have been in vain. Breakers over the reef show up distinctly. A light-house on the Point of the harbour. Slow down in speed. At the light-house is a large white bungalow and behind it, numbers of native huts, but on piles, appearing as if two storied. Thatched roofs, and nestled amongst a wealth of tropical vegetation. Go through a boom in a long mine net, and keep close to shore all the way along. The tropical growth is beautiful, palms and mango trees in abundance. See many natives working on vegetable gardens of deep red soil. Opposite to a block of low huts, which look like very large tents close to the shore. Hear this is a leper station. Very high hills at the back of the town, which now comes into view. (small hand drawing as described above). Can also see the Forts and barracks at the top of a small hill. The hills are covered with green, and altogether look very nice indeed.

Now opposite the town and built on a slope towards the harbour, can see the red roads, appears to be earth or ground. Grass growing on them except in the bare track, which suggests they may be natural and not made roads. The sea front is composed of warehouses of fair size and cleanliness, and a few small wharves for small boats, some of which were in them and consisted of sailing craft. We dropped anchor near two other vessels the 'WAR PALACE', and 'GAMBIA'. A strong tide coming in and not long before we swing round to it and faced the way we had come. Not very long before the Harbour-master, and police came off from shore to us in rowing boats, followed by a good many 'bum-boats', with vendors of fruit such as oranges, mangoes, pineapples and bananas, coconut skins which they called deer skins, bangles and other trinkets and baskets. They began selling, briskly too, at enormous profit. I took a fancy to mangoes, I like the pine-taste in them. There were also boys seated in tiny shells of canoes, who were out to dive for coins. In one or two, two were seated, and it was marvellous to watch them dive from the canoe and get back into it, without upsetting their frail craft. Propelled by short paddle by strokes from one side and then the other, which makes them skim like fish over the water. Sg. Biggs at his favourite sport in 'sharking', and caught a beauty, 11ft. in length. Took some effort to raise it to the well deck aft and caused amusement to onlookers. Severed its head, for its jaws sake, which will be bleached in the sun and varnished. Two others got off his line. We are now in the tropics and those who previously complained about the cold wish themselves back in the Arctic regions again. Luckily however, a nice breeze from the sea blew up tonight.

Friday 15th

Vendors out early to the ship, but not before the O.C. and Quartermaster, who had been ashore yesterday, instructed the N.C.O. to inform the patients, that they had made arrangements ashore for other good and reliable vendors of fruit to supply it at a fixed price. So some who came early, their old boats full for a good 'takings' harvest, came a thud. Obvious to the most casual observer, that those chaps a fine, solidly built, stamp of a man. Whereas the 'dinkum' old Negro tho, possessing the short, course curly hair, thick lips and yellow coloured palms and soles of feet. The latter looked very funny when they were diving, as when for the instant, two yellow soles only to be seen above water. Most of them could speak English, some very well indeed. Some became a bit cheeky and were pelted with spuds from the ship, when they would make off in their boats, shaking their fist and uttering loud exclamations the while, when spuds went over in showers. To see these chaps try to dodge them, some of which were deadly accurate, making awful faces in anticipation of injury, as they saw the missile approaching, and others covering their heads with their baskets, off the spuds would bounce with a wonderful recoil, and others again be on their stomachs at the bottom of the boat and had their heads out of sight under the seats, after the fashion of an old Ostrich, leaving their own seats exposed to the enemy bullets, which by the way often found their billet, by the fact, that a wriggle would follow, and a squirm for greater cover. The poor fellow with the paddle meantime, bore the full brunt of the assault, for what with ducking, dodging, side-stepping, and taking a stroke in between, made very little headway against a strong tide. Showed his white teeth and muttered curses (in his own lingo I bet). But like most natives, quite plucky when out of range eventually, all got up and laughed and began throwing the potatoes back which had fallen into the bottom of their boat. Of course the chaps here replied to the salvo, which to say the least was a good one.

However, just at that moment, big Barney Allen? the Chief Steward who is called 'The lord who provides', came along and caught them in the act of wasting his stores.

Slammed the cases together, looked very angry and growled, then said gruffly 'If you want to throw, go and throw coal into the ship, more use in that! Quite true, so the game was given up. Couldn't help laughing at a big boy on a canoe who kept saying, in 'Broken English'. 'Now come on, throw a coin, and see Lord Jellicoe catch'em, I'm Lord Jellicoe. Yus I am', this last, by slapping himself on the back and chest. Found the vendors very anxious to obtain shirts and trousers. These were bartered for their wares. Dug up an old tunic of mine. From where I was standing a chap on the water boat caught sight of it and offered a beautiful basket in exchange. Couldn't leave the sterilizer just then, so got Roberts to take it down for me. Said he would, but thought him a long time in returning. Found when I went to dinner that he had not made the exchange, because he wanted two for it (one for himself). Said he was going to try his luck after dinner, but I wanted no more waiting, and reckoned myself lucky to the offer of one for it.

Went on deck and was offered a deer skin, but not wanting it, a little later was offered another basket. At that very moment, a coal boy came up and wanted to know how much money I would take for it, and at that very moment Capt. Shields the pathologist came to me and wished my advice about the housing of a monkey he was thinking of buying. Only spoke to him for about ½ minute, and having handed the nigger the tunic just beforehand to look at, turned round to ask for it and found the boy with it had vanished. I raced round but could find no trace of him. I blessed him (without lay on of hands) – kept a vigilant look out, but sometime afterwards heard that a lad seen jumping into a boat with a Military tunic and making off to shore. Suppose his fortune had been made. Missed another basket. If only Roberts had done what he promised and more. Certainly, but no use of crying over spilt milk now. The kid after all deserved it for his alacrity in the disappearing trick. Wondered what else I could pawn, for I was bent on a basket, which would make a good work-basket for home. Dug out an old suit of pyjamas and old pair of shorts and got one this time. Negro told me if I put shorts with them, he would bless me. If he did, did it to himself, but not in the way I blessed his fellow countryman when my coat disappeared I hope.

This youngster had a companion, both were bright lads, so I brought them up on monkey deck to barter, (get the word, fancy I'm an old slave trader now). One started off, by getting hold of the remainder of my cigar, and finishing it off, simply stating he was quite fond of cigars, this in a very cool and collected manner. Said I hoped he enjoyed it, but couldn't find anymore butts to give away. His mate had a lovely set of teeth. Dental mechanic took an impression. Poor kid thought we wanted to take his teeth out, but we reassured him. 'I very much fear' says he. But he was delighted when he was given his model in plaster, and watched the process of its making with very great interest. Huge mouths these chaps have, our ordinary wax shields, were not nearly broad enough. Could see a couple of churches ashore, and am informed a very good mission also. I judge this because the name of one boat is 'John Wesley', another 'God is the best', and so on. Told by those of the crew who could get ashore, that Negroes, were mostly dressed 'to kill' and were great swells! Many had stiff white collars to the ears almost, pink shirts, white trouser etc. All sorts of stuff bartered on the ship today. Night baker had bought a basket for me, but being too large disposed of it. Finished coaling (coal in bags) and watering just before dark, and expect to get away tomorrow morning early. Officers and Sisters granted leave by shore authorities, but O.C. would not permit them to go, unless rank and file were able to go also.

Saturday 16th

As I gaze out over the town at any early hour this morning, the thought comes. 'If this ship had not called here on the last occasion, I should not be on board here now attached to the staff, for it was then that several of the old staff got Malarial fever and on her return to Aust. we ten S. Austr's were sent for.' Leave @ 7am, and for some distance head straight out to sea, then turn southwards for Cape Town. Some of the new staff not at all keen on the work and say that it is too constant, being never away from the job, others say that they have never worked so hard, made a great deal worse by the hot weather. Heavy tropical showers.

Tuesday 19th
Lecture by Corporal Mortimer on 'How to read faces, and determine character'. The man from Iron-Bark slow as usual. Am afraid I did not agree in a good many cases. Too many exceptions anyhow. If Col. Wilson and Matron Cooper, could only see what was going on, on promenade tonight, I think they would have died on the spot from apoplexy, for here were Sisters, and the present Matron herself, dancing with the diggers and staff. Cluster lights and pianist for the occasion. Some were used to shilling 'ops' I pretty well guess. First thing of this sort in ship's history as a hospital. Previously there was a fine looming out for the man and a rebuke for the Sister, if seen speaking to each other only.

Wednesday 20th
Renie's birthday *(his sister)*. Have something for her when I get home. Lecture by Capt. White on 'Joan of Arc'. He knows his subject, and proved intensely interesting. I took notes as it was so good. Three operations today, which I attended.

Thursday 21st
Three more operations today. Concert in evening.

Friday 22nd
Lecture on 'The making of Germany', and 'France Prussian War'. Bismark figures conspicuously.

Saturday 23rd
Lecture 'Making of Italy'. Alezzini? and especially Garibaldi are prominent characters. Audience improving more and more, a good sign.

Wednesday 27th
We have heard by wireless from the 'CERAMIC' that Cape Town an open port, so in anticipation of leave being granted by the shore authorities, O.C. has allowed patients access to their kits, for boots and clothing. Alongside our old berth by 3.30pm, and thanks to the O.C., leave was shortly after arranged and granted. Staff divided into sections. I myself on leave and went into the town with Henry and Frank Shearing. Good to be able to stretch one's legs again. Notice the very fine, temporary triumphal arch at entrance to Adderly St. Of pure white colour, with S.African coat of arms on it. Town gaily decorated with flags and bunting of all sorts, in readiness for welcoming back of troops expected by the 'SAXON' tomorrow. Same ship whose patients we took to Sydney from Melbourne, last trip. There is now an Anzac Buffet of very fine apartments, consisting of lounge, luncheon, reading, billiard and cloak rooms. Nice obliging staff of Sth. African girls with Austr. Secretaries run this show, for the purpose of entertaining Austr. soldiers returning this way. Did a little shopping and made enquiries as to trip etc. for tomorrow in case we should get off.

Went to a show in the evening, but it was very poor, the best item being the 'Sylva Trio', who were very good instrumentalists. Piano, violin and cello. The guard who went ashore on piquet duty on different posts in the town, to watch hotels, prohibited areas etc, had a very unpleasant time with drunken men on crutches, and crippled others. Some of the additional staff, thro' all their experiences say they have never seen anything so disgusting or one which shocked them such as this. Not a very nice thing for Australians on the whole, for Australians altogether have not been too popular here in Cape Town since the Boer War and civilians talk about and take great notice of happenings of this deplorable character. A nice fuss at ship's gangway when this crowd arrived. In spite ones admiration of our countrymen as soldiers, one feels a tinge of shame for them on these occasions. Hotels previously closed against us, but reopened now on trial to see how things go. This will about cook it. Coal and water already put into the ship, in fact brought alongside very shortly after our arrival. First seals we have seen were plentiful in Table Bay as we came in.

Thursday 28th

Detailed for a town piquet today. In charge of Capt. O'Brien marched to the Castle in the city. The Aust. Provost Corp, recently sent here, are quartered at this place. Also a chap from H.Q. London. Jolly fine times and billets some of these men get nowadays. Left in the barrack square, while a few arrangements were being made. Left to ourselves while the first piquet went out. The Officer got out of harm's way himself, and no arrangements being made for relief, dinner or tea, soon found this stunt consisted of red tape only. Supposed to wait until some Officer the X.Y.Z. came to his office about 11 o'clock before we were to know what to do. However, after having a drink and a bun at the canteen and look round the buildings which resembles an old fort very much, having its forage, grocery and other stores, magazine etc., got a bit jack of waiting. More than that the 'SAXON' soldiers were due in the Street @ 11am and we wished to see the procession, so with the Sgt. who was also desirous in this direction, we passed out of the Castle, which felt too much like a prison for me and escaped the guard on the gates, reaching fresh air again and space.

Went to the open grounds opposite the City Hall, where were a good number of ladies dressed in white and wearing badges, having large baskets of flowers in readiness for the boys procession. Had a yarn with two or three of these. We then went into Adderly St, and waited amongst crowds of people who had lined the streets and manned the buildings. The mounted police with their kaki topees, and navy blue uniforms and fine bay horses look particularly smart. While waiting, ran into the Standard Bank of South Africa to see the Assnt. Acct, Mr. Moffitt, whom I met here last time, but owing to sickness of his wife, cannot extend the invitation this time. He is a very nice fellow and both he and his wife are South Australians.

Procession of 1700 men now arrived marching under the Triumphal Arch and being cheered by the 'Diggers' from the balcony of the Anzac Buffet, just behind it. As they came into the crowd were cheered to the echo and clapped by everybody. Many relations espying their loved ones ran from the crowd and marched along with them. The buildings were decorated in great style. All men were marched to the City Hall for civic reception by the Mayor and others. Many Jacks in kilts were amongst the returned and were particularly popular with the Australians. Having promised Jack Treloar a long time ago to buy a feather boa for his wife should I come Cape Town again. Did so at a wholesale manufacturers recommended by the Y.M.C.A. Got one for Mother, but not the kind I wanted, having none in stock. Told by him that Carnarvon Lodge night tonight and recommended it, so let some of staff and ships people know. Lunched at the Y.M. then having seen a boa I really wanted for Mother, bought it. Some of the lads had gone over Rhode's estate by motor trip from Buffet, so my mate not having seen the place, chose going out there by tram in preference to invitation to a lady's home for afternoon and dinner in the evening. On tram met a lady showing three of our lads about and bound for the same place, so joined them.

FREETOWN

Fancy dress

A crocodile and friend seller

Crossing equator

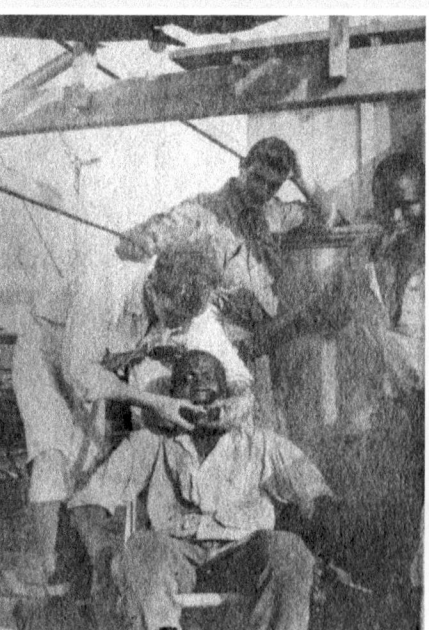
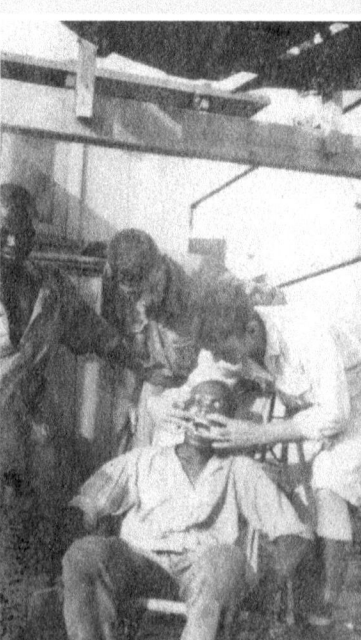

Fancy dress

Taking an impression

A good set (teeth)

Went to monument, and Rhodes seat, left then and walked to Rondebosch, his house. Have described all this on a previous occasion. It is a beautiful as ever. Hope to reach the house in time to meet the other boys and have a look through having heard much about the wonders of its interior. Found the other party had been and gone. At the back of the grand old Dutch house, is a beautiful garden of flags built in terraces, each terrace being bricked in, and having a pathway right through the centre, steps also of brick. Had a look through alright, filled with old Dutch furniture and curious of which Rhodes seems to have been keen. All ceilings and panelling of teak wood. French cabinet bought for 25 pounds, now insured for 3,000 pounds, Dutch wardrobe with secret drawers a novelty and ingenious arrangement, both of granite and massage bench of marble beats an Egyptian sarcophagus into a cocked hat. Tapestries are beautiful, while the beautiful Spanish leather on sitting room wall, exceeds anything I have seen in this way, being patterned in gilt. One library consists entirely of books dealing with Africa, of which Rhodes was very fond. Another one of books in general. One set in leather binding, translated from the Greek and type written cost 6,000 pounds. This old male servant showing us round knowing Rhodes personally and hear a few of deceased's qualities and peculiarities. The house presented to the ? for the use of its Premier during Parliament sittings, during which time he would have to be in town.

Gen. Botha now Premier, is away in France where doing wonderful work as a soldier, is now a member of the Peace Conference. Walked to railway stn, and caught train for the city. Did a little more shopping and went along to Roeland St. Met four others belonging to staff and ship there, and we had a most glorious evg indeed. Everything from start to finish and in every capacity, serious or joviality was perfect. Never enjoyed such a meeting more.

Walked back to railway with a gentleman from Rhodesia, who was most keen to make an appointment for the morrow, but our uncertainty in most things, prevented me from doing so. I was to have today off until 4.30pm, and then to do duty in wards till 9am. However, the O.C. on looking round the ship was not at all satisfied with the state or condition of the wards, so ordered cessation of leave until this was done. This casts a reflection on the thoroughness of the staff, and is the first time such a thing has happened. Personally I regret this, but I suppose one has to consider that the new additional staff who are only here to work their passage home, cannot be expected to take some interest in the work as the old staff or those permanently attached to the ship. The town piquet had already gone off @ 9am, and now a good many more hearing the latest, absented themselves and took their own leave, fearing none at all otherwise. This left much more work for those who remained. This was discovered by the W.O. who at 1.30, called a muster-roll, taking names of those present on parade and promising that they should have the whole day off tomorrow, while the absentees should remain and do the necessary work on the ship. Present parade divided into two parts until 9pm. I got the 2-6.30 leave. Knowing too well from past experience that tomorrows promise may come to naught, make a bee-line for the railway station, having a peep through the native fish market on the way. Large boats with huge Snook had just arrived and fishermen were landing them on the beach between the market stalls and the big town pier. Received a message that W.O. Henry was catching the 3.7 train for Muizenberg, precisely the destination I was bound for. Found him on the train with the lady and three other Australians whom we had met yesterday, having made their acquaintance quite accidentally. Muizenberg is on the north side of the peninsular and we had a pleasant little journey together. It possesses a wonderful long surf-bathing beach, which is quite safe for swimmers.

Went first to the bathing house, when on a slightly raised balcony, one may sit, have refreshments and watch bathers just in front. Mostly girls and women partaking of this healthy exercise and pastime today, and most were using the surfing boards and with skill too. A goodly number of these folk were Jewesses. A nice white sandy beach and many bathing and dressing houses built close to the water's edge are to be seen. Just at the back of the town the high and rugged hills, practically bare and stony, the Muizenberg Mountains give a good set-off, and right opposite the wide bay on the right, the town of Simon Town, a British Naval Base. The docks can be seen with aid of glasses, but the town seems small and fairly straggly. This kind lady now desired us to come to her sister's house to tea.

Crossed over the station and walked along the esplanade sea front towards Kalk Bay. This is a fine esplanade, and new up-to-date, pure white and red tiled houses line it. Those that are perched high up on the hills, must have taken some building, for to many it is a sheer climb to them from the road by steps built up. One of these paths built of steps is called 'Jacobs Ladder' a fitting name too and quite appropriate. Most of the houses are new and modern, but it is about half way to Kalk Bay (well known for its Jewish inhabitants and their quantity) that the old Dutch seaside cottage of the late Cecil Rhodes stands. It was here he took ill and died. One can see the window which was placed in the wall to admit off more light and air to his sick room. Died 1906. Still a dwelling house, for people inhabit it. Pass many motorists, for this is a favourite road, and motorists take the round run from Cape Town, returning via rear of Table Mountains and Hout Bay. Came to the little township of St. James, where there is a nice little railway stn, and tennis courts. The sea here is walled back, but with large rocks in places, reminds one very much of Port Elliot in S.A.

Reached the house we were bound for, high up on the hills. Were made very welcome indeed. A lovely view from the veranda over the whole harbour. Had tea and have never tasted such beautiful scones. One of the daughters provided music, but I had to cut my share short, as having to report back by 6.30pm, and also wishing to walk back to Muizenberg instead of catching train at St. James, for the sake of having another look about en route, on my own, started out. I will never forget that walk, or more particularly that effect of the beautiful sunset on the waters of that beautiful, tranquil bay. Reminded me of the sunset at Tripoli in Syria, but the like of which I have never really seen since. In my compartment of the train were three young English ladies and gentlemen returning from a holiday outing at the beach for today is a public holiday.

Kept the train ride one of entertainment and were what we should call back in Aust 'hard nuts'. One gent is a son of Devon, mining engineer in Rhodes on his own account. Doing well, but says mining in Rhod—seems to have slackened during war, and many miners given up and gone to Johannesburg. Duty in D1 ward til 9.30pm and hear of the terrible accident which happened to one of our poor, unfortunate patients in the city last night. This poor boy had been bed ridden for 7 months owing to spinal injury. Was brought aboard in England as a stretcher case, but good food, good attention and sea air had worked wonders in him, for very shortly afterwards, made such rapid strides, that he was able to get up and gradually got about, until on arrival here, felt so well was allowed leave on shore. Last night struck by an electric tram, and mutilated horribly. I know the facts but will not relate here. Removed to Wynberg Military Hospital, but not yet gained consciousness. Doctors there absolutely hold no hope for his recovery. What news for his poor mother when so near home, and already news by wireless has been notified re his return.

Saturday 30th

What I half predicted had happened, for orders came out that the staff would be granted no leave. Evidently the O.C. a bit annoyed over yesterday's events. Patients granted leave till 12.30, and ship leaves at 3pm. An unwise policy on O.C.'s part for we have learned before what it means to allow leave till nearly sailing time. Luckily however, orders came down that staff who were present on parade yesterday, could go ashore on piquet duty. Told that this would be all that could be done for us, accompanied by a very broad, but veiled hint, that we could practically please ourselves what we did once we got on shore.

In fact no Officer took charge of us, and N.C.O.'s not bothering, took Gharry for city. A party of us from D1 had made up our minds to go for a motor trip round the mountain, a trip highly spoken of and highly recommended. Trips are run there now by the Troops Welcome Committee at Feathers Market, by Charabancs, fare 3/- return. Booked a passage there yesterday in consideration of promise for today, but as they do not return until 3pm, had to cancel it. Got a large Wolseley car from the stand and made tracks with a party of 6 of us fare 11/- ea. Usually a bit lower, but another troopship with S. Africans having arrived, price up a bit.

Went to Sea Point, and Camp's Bay first, and one of our party drove. From Camp Bay a long twining road, hilly and with many sharp turns brings us to a high peak on the sea coast, which, leaving it in the right and proceeding inland, brings us to Hout Bay. On road just mentioned caught up and passed a good many pedestrians, evidently members of the mountaineering clubs. On approaching these people thought the females were girls of about 15 or 16, for wearing, what we men might call, if worn on ourselves, knickerbockers, to the knee, of dark hue and 'elastically' tight at the bottom end, and short skirts quite 3 or 4 inches above the bottom of the 'knickers'. Good strong boots and stockings in addition. But on passing and looking back, discovered them to be women of 30 and over, I'll wager. This seems preposterous to our unsophisticated minds of course, but I suppose the old saying would come true if we lived here and saw them often, viz 'familiarity breeds contempt' and we should take no notice of them. Anyhow for mountaineering work, this dress would be for more comfortable than the tight skirt, or other cumbersome outfit. The descent to Hout Bay Hotel is steep and in the valley are many small Dutch vegetable and cereal farms. The Hotel is a fine building, and nicely appointed place, nestled among avenues of large Oak trees.

A change seemed to be working up and mists began to settle on the mountain forming the old familiar tablecloth. It was thus hidden from view, and being 5,000ft above sea level, the marvellous fact is, that when the mists drift there, they stay, and form a dense cloud. The driving mists which escaped the mountain, went wherever the elements chose to take them. This could be plainly noticed. The road to Wynberg is steep and as suddenly descends. Oak and silver trees are in abundance, while large and extensive vineyards on either hand, add beauty to the general landscape. Muizenberg can be seen from the heights, but disappear on descending to Wynberg. Now we come to Oak trees properly. Pass the Wynberg Military Hospital, the place from where our patients from East Africa, Mesopotamia came, on our first trip to England. Stands well back amongst a cluster of trees. Many wealthy miners from Rhodesia live in this suburb, and consequently many fine houses are to be seen. Turn from the main road and turn up, passing thro' portion of Cecil Rhode's Estate and amongst forests of Oaks now. Hear that they are so plentiful as to be used as firewood. Had a bit of a race into the city with another car.

Arrived a little after midday, and found after our most enjoyable trip (40 miles) that we would not be required to report ship till 2pm, in meantime to remind any stragglers they should be back, parade the streets, and see if any in hotels etc. One Sgt. received a lusty kick of the shin-bone for his trouble in caring for one a bit muddled. However, I still had a bit of shopping to do for various people on the boat, which I did. Arriving back to the ship, almost penniless, a new experience for me, found a great shib-oo at the gangway caused by a few cantankerous drunks, who refused to go on board, or those who did, by coming back on wharf again, arguing, remonstrating etc. One or two Officers not a very good example to the men by their own incapacity. O.C.'s sister who came down to ship to see him, succeeded in quelling a disturbance near the road around two motor cars. Some of these fellows only really showing off, especially those walking on and off the ship, and needed somebody to give them a shake. S/Sgt. the masseur, a big hefty chap placed on gangway and when remonstrating with him to get off, he ordered them to stay on and implied his meaning by pushing as easily as possible two or three of them backwards, like so many straws. Made them wonder what they had struck and the trouble ended. Got away at 4pm. A small crowd of ladies had collected to see us off. As usual a good old swell on, which causes us to pitch a bit. Sea still smoky brown just here, owing to big drifts of sea-weed, the variety from which iodine is manufactured (1700 tons of coal taken in).

Sunday 31st

And now we are on our last, long lap for Australia and my jove, for the sake of getting my letters from home, hope we do a record run to Fremantle and all my missing ones turn up.

JUNE, 1919

Monday 1st

Evg lecture by Capt. White on 'Historical connection between England and America'.

Tuesday 2nd

Pretty cool nowadays and no sunshine about. Lecture on 'Freedom of Parliament in Eng' and Review of Jas 1st and Chas 1st reign.

Wednesday 3rd

Dance by Sisters, staff and patients on prom-deck.

Thursday 4th

Notice appears on board as follows, showing some difference to old regime to that of nowadays.

Commander W.C.?. Morgan, Gray Nicholls O.C., Officers, staff and convalescent, Matron and Sisters heartily invite the 'Diggers' of all ranks and Staff to a fancy dress ball to be held on boat deck 7.30 - 9.30pm. on evg. of the 6th instant.

First prize to
   Best male character
   Best female character
   Best Sustained character
   Best Most Original character

Friday 5th

Get the good news by wireless from a steamer somewhere in the vicinity that Influenza epidemic eased off a good deal in Aust, and that most ports open. This relieves one's mind, for after hearing of the terrible scourge wrought in Cape Town by this dread disease, and not having heard from home for months, goodness only knows what may have, or may happen to those at home.

Saturday 6th

Hear for the first time that we are far higher north than our usual run. Skipper wishes to dodge bad weather further south. Receive many applications for aniline dyes and colours for make-ups for tonight's fun. Everybody trooped up on the boat deck punctually to await procession of the masquerades. Visited all the wards prior to coming up, to allow cot cases to see them. About 30 in the procession and the cleverness of the disguise and adaptability to use such as at hand, and with such effect, causes one to admire, for with the material likely to be found on a ship in this capacity is very limited indeed. Rope, sheets, kemp, flags, and many other things common to a ship were greatly in evidence, and no doubt used to a very creditable attainment indeed. The T.B. patients were allowed use of the monkey deck, which overlooks the boat deck.

The entertainment began by a procession again and dancing. All sorts of dresses were representative of various National dress and costume. Greece, Egypt, Spain, Italian, French and the rest. Mr. Marwood was particularly fine in his higher class Egyptian dress and acted accordingly and without reserve for his rank. Rundle as 'Charlie Chaplin' and maintained the character well, also Pens, as a naughty baby. Some of the boys as Nurses and V.A.D's, and to do them credit, while no disrespect to the Sisters, looked jolly sight better than many of them, in fact some of the Sisters themselves, not prepared, were deceived by them. One lad as he was sitting down, had the embarrassing experience of having a plump little Sister (done up in Spanish dancer style, with Tambourine, short skirts and ribboned legs etc), sitting or rather reclining on his lap, just after a dance, stating that she felt tired. Replied of course, but Sister was also embarrassed on hearing a man's voice and quickly shifted 'her quarters'. Prizes to be decided by ballot. Just an inkling of an idea that our last masked ball on the Cape Town trip was a slight degree better all round, probably because, being entirely the boys turn-out, the units wags could go their hardest.

Prizes:-
Best sustained - Pens
Most original - Ad. Nelson (a patient).
Best female -   Sister Liddy.

Sunday 7th
Wireless from passing ship bound from Sydney – Durban that position regarding epidemic in Aust. much improved the day they left ?May. Also news of the Aust. flyer, Hawker, re his ill fated attempt to cross Atlantic to England, and fresh labour troubles in Melbourne, causing 30,000 idle. Ad.Nelson, winner of most original, has actually lost an eye and an arm poor fellow, and used his misfortune to advantage, on this occasion.

Tuesday 9th
Another TB patient 'gone west' last night and burial service held @ 1pm. today. Fairly busy with experiments in the lab. Capt. O'Brien and I dissecting a brain during evening. He and I read to each other as we proceeded. Another 2,000 miles to go before 'Aussie' is reached and then ?- Another Officer joined Capt. White in giving lectures. Is a professional lecturer, and his subject was 'Life in Germany in pre-war days.' Studied some years there himself.

Wednesday 10th
Notice given out re serious water shortage. Ship very high and feeling a rather big side swell rather much. 'Prussianising of Germany' by Lt. Chisholm. No wireless owing to severity of 'atmospherics'.

Friday 12th
Getting more empty every day, and now have a horrible list to star-board. Towards evening a strong south wind comes up, with rain and intense cold. Audience at lecture 'Life of Napoleon' had to move to sheltered side of deck. This lecture being taken in three parts. As crowd dispersing O.C. came from his cabin and read out a wireless just received from Skipper, requiring to know from Fremantle if any infectious cases of

influenza been on board. A declaration needed from N.C.O's in this respect. This order necessary, so that leave could be arranged for our troops, and would not be given until two hours before sailing time. However, to be subject to State Commandants sanitation and bona-fides certificate of Quarantine Officer. Gave a message to Chief Wireless Operator for transmission and coming up on deck afterwards to the lab, hear the dot and the dash spitting out into the bleak, starless, miserable night, to their destiny over a 1,000 miles away, while we still plod and labour on towards it, rolling and straining of the good old ship surrounded by seemingly endless expanse of 'white horses' crashing and breaking themselves against her with their cruel fury, as if they would only be too pleased to suck us into their depths. Seems strange on reflection, this mystical, silent, wonderful 'hand across the sea' communication. One feels almost in touch with our own civilization now, but feel so weird, remembering our present surroundings, and state of the elements. Bar for the company of a few Albatross which now follow us, there is a certain sense of isolation. One has difficulty to retain one's seat here in the laboratory. Am simply itching for my letters and a word from my loved ones. Another TB patient Sieving, died last night, was buried by R.C. Padre today. 'Life of Napoleon' part 2 by Capt. White.

Saturday 13th

In E3, most interesting lecture yet, by Lt. Chisholm on 'Latin Civilisation'. Part 3 of Napoleon by Capt. White. O.C. tended a vote of thanks on behalf of regular audiences. Capt. White replied suitably, stating that he was a teacher but History always his pet subject, and recommended it to all as one of absorbing interest helping one as it does, to view theology, religion, human weaknesses and character, and progress or decline in the ages, worlds expansion of civilisation and commerce.

Sunday 14th

352 miles to go from mid-day today, and O.C. has been notified by wireless that if ship arrives after 3.30pm, no leave can possibly be granted to the troops. All the lads very keen now on seeing 'Aussie'.

Note from diary Louis Schaeffer AWM

Young W. Aust lad died as ship rounded the headwater entering harbour at Freemantle. Sister and I wept.

Monday 15th

Rottnest sighted @ 12 mid-day and reached the anchorage at 2.30. All on board had to undergo the usual medical inspection by shore doctor. Pulled into wharf a little after 6 and disembarkation of W.A. patients immediately commenced. A good brass band present on the wharf to render popular airs. Troops granted leave from 7-11pm, staff to be halved 2 hrs each. Uncle Dave and Will Toms on wharf waiting for me. Get away as quickly as I can, meet them and they hurry me off to the tram, all bound to Will's place, where Aunt Emily is and where we are to spend the evening. Met Uncle Jim there also and had a most pleasant time, and to aid things, a nice, nice dinner which Winnie had been keeping hot for us. Hear from them confirmation re the unrest and shortage of food in the west owing to Melbourne trouble. Rioting had occurred and resulted in one death and a few injuries to others. Hear from Wireless operator that we are to sail at 7am. in the morning for Adelaide, which does me down to the ground, so get Will to wire Mother in the morning as to our latest movements. Will is a very energetic chap and his home does him great credit, for he has made vast improvements even since I was there last. Hear of Rollo's return, and inability to settle down to work yet. Has gone away camping in the country with some of his pals.

Being time to leave, walked with Aunt and Uncle to their house. This is a great old spot and can boast of numerous huge gum trees, which every real Australian can admire. Looked at Uncles improvements and stayed for a short time, then caught tram for High Street. Called at the yard to see Uncle Charley for a few minutes. Found him retiring to bed, having waited in vain for me. Many of the troops did not come back to ship until midnight. Coal scarce and only taking 250 tons.

Tuesday 16th
Left at 7. Not many people about. Fruit, cake and papers from all States are plentiful being brought last night by the kind Red Cross women of Fremantle for distribution. My mail of 18 letters brought to me. Soon finish my job in hand and make provision for a quiet hour to myself in the lab, so that I can digest it. Delighted to hear that all are well in spite of numerous cases of pneumonia influenza in Finsbury. Blessed if two or three of Mother's letters are not missing now, but glad to hear that the missing mail from home to me when at Melbourne, had been returned to them. Splendid letters from Jimmy Smith and Mitch, telling me of their experiences at Serviceton, during their 7 days quarantine prior to proceeding to Adelaide. Both now discharged and taking to their civilian duties O.K. Received a paper cutting from Smithy, re Sgt. Peter Hamilton's death by accident at his house in Scotland. (This cutting pasted at back of this diary). This is an old friend of Mitcham and one whom we took to England last trip (from Alexandria), it will be remembered. Hear also of young Redding's death during the Egypt riots. Both jolly fine chaps, whose loss, being more than unfortunate, regrettable are to be lamented. Nice interesting letter from S/Sgt. Gray stating he may go on land in irrigation areas for soldiers. Hear too of their fun with Col. Mar- as a 'digger' amongst them during their quarantine over N.S.W. border. Believe there is a movement on foot to try and spare we few S. Australians at Adelaide and to allow us to get off there.

Thursday 18th
Called by Mr. Mc Hugh to Orderly room with other S.A. lads and asked if we should care to get off in Adelaide, as he thinks sufficient staff would be left to carry on. Rundle and I agree to accept the offer. Notice up to crew, that Directors of their Coy, wish to grant a gratuity to all ships Officers, Engineers, Firemen, Stokers and Stewards who have been on service on the ship for 12 mths, gratuity to be proportionate to length of service over that. State they in this way, desire to show their appreciation of their (crew) help to Nation during the war.

Friday 19th
Am told that if I should care to go East, with the view of having a little trip to finish up with, can do so. Certainly very tempting – should like to see the good old ship to a finish now, but if I can be done without, my first duty lies at home, for I know they are waiting anxiously for me. Anyhow Sydney would be nothing startling at this time of the year. Winter, and everything at a standstill owing to increase of epidemic, and running the risk of catching quarantine from Sydney to Melbourne, and from Melbourne to Adelaide. The news that we had to proceed to Brisbane, seems to have fallen flat. Ship to pick up fitting in Melb, and for 6 weeks to undergo repair in Sydney and put in state to go on Aust. Coast, until 'KATOOMBA' from England relieves her and then she to go to builders for thorough overhaul, and fitted up as of old. This is as far as we know now.

Saturday 20th
Sighted Troubridge 11am, also Kangaroo Is. A bit before Semaphore, Largs etc. lights @ 8.30. Pilot alongside from Semaphore, followed his launch for a little way and dropped anchor. All kit ready for early morning. Patients to have early breakfast. Have a stroll on

boat deck with Robbo, and it is with mixed feeling that I realise this may be my very last quiet ¼ hr on the good old ship which has carried us safely so many thousands of miles. By kindness of chief wireless operator, listen to Horsey Stn. in Wales sending out news. Wonderful to think one is in touch with England, from which we have been travelling over 6 weeks. Hornsey using an 'arc' set (whistling signals) and speaking to Cairo. Hope delay of ship from Fremantle has not inconvenienced Mother and caused her to come to harbour today for nothing at all. A heavy land swell on aft K.I. Poor old Finney, crew's cook died during night. Came in with flag at half-mast.

Sunday 21st

Early breakfast for patients, and hurried medical inspection. At wharf Outer Harbour 10am, where altho' so early a nice little crowd had gathered. I espied Mother, Ada, Vere, Colin, (*younger sisters and brother*) Aunt's son and others, Mitch and Smithy amongst them. Semaphore messages over to Mitch. A lovely day. Soon told by W.O. to make my way off. Had all kit ready, so lost no time. Having a good many parcels, got all busy. Caught a later train, but met all others at Glanville. Having perambulator at station and found this conveyance very useful indeed. Took Father, Renie, Ralph and Vere (*younger sisters and brother*) later in the afternoon to Outer Harbour to see over the good old ship, which they much enjoyed. Poor old ship, I feel almost loath to part company. Had excellent fun and enjoyment exhibiting my wares and presents to all at home during the evening. Manifest pleasure to all and I was satisfied. It is lovely to be home again, but somehow one feels like a duck out of water, being suddenly thrown from a busy life into one in which I am to be able to do and go as I please for awhile at any rate, but I expect it will wear off as things become more settled.

Monday 22nd

Father and I enjoy a long walk about the paddocks, an experience I have often craved for of late.

Tuesday 23rd

Public holiday. Father and I go to Zoological gardens and to Aunties.

Wednesday 24th

Reported S.O.I's office Keswick Barracks for discharge and there met Pens, who had missed the ship on Saturday night, 'KAROOLA' sailed 12.30am. that Sunday morning. Had to wait for awhile for examining board, who were at Outer Harbour to meet 'BORDA' on arrival, so went over to Hospital to see if any old friends about. Found some of old Home Service crowd. Boarded @ 1pm and try new system of 'hurry up' tho' one finds oneself in one half hour practically a civilian again. A good deal of bungling though and shoving one from place to place, and often a 'Karoolian' finds himself in a mix up with a 'BELTANA' or 'BORDA' or vessel of some other name. Strange to say our old M.O. of A.A.M.C. at Mitcham put me through my final medical examination. Capt. Arnold remarked that he should know my papers well enough. A civvies 30/- suit thrown at me, signed a declaration undertaking to return my overcoat, received an application form to enable me to procure a train ticket at 1st class travelling free during my term of leave, to any part of the State. Five troopships in today, the old 'ZEALANDIA', being one of them, and still retains her tiger-striped camouflage. Having fixed up business at pay office North Terrace, thought I may as well go into the Office and see the heads and so report myself and find what my duties are to be and where I stand. However, just as I was standing outside, speaking to Smithy, met the Manager now Mudie, who asked me earnestly enough to come back to the Bank immediately and help them, as they were short handed and had been working at night for the last 4 weeks, the balance was behind, through shipping strike, and consequent shortage of coal, trams stopped after 7pm, and trains @ 8.35, and electric light was curtailed to a large extent, making the balance exceedingly difficult and awkward to run. Made out he could do with all extra help possible.

This very awkward for me, so went to Mr. Craigie for further particulars. This proposal of Mr. Mudie's seems unreasonable to me, and certainly they should have had to do without me should I have gone on to Sydney. Anyhow Mr. Craigie confirms it, but says if I should see my way clear to come back, which he hoped would not interfere with any arrangement I may have made, if I did so, my leave would be given me at a later date and when work was over. Gets me thinking, and advised by all bank chaps not to come back, but take all leave I wanted before returning at all. Go home and with Father think it well over. Decide although in a good many respects all the time blaming myself for doing so, to go back by end of month. It may have some advantages later on in way of good weather conditions and so on. My railway pass I find can be used anytime before December. Take a trip to Mt. Barker for weekend and to see old friends. Had a nice little time, but very disappointed indeed to find that the Bishop family have moved from Mt. Barker and gone to Grenfell in N.S.W. Received a letter from Mrs. Bishop later. Began work on July 1st. Have had no time hitherto to order a new suit, but Bank say they will be glad if I do have to work in my uniform.

(later) Work seems queer at first and am given duties on the ledgers to do. Confess that I feel a little indisposed to this sort of work for a bit, and am not at all settled. Fresh air and beautiful sunshine outside makes me feel restless and desire to be out in it roving about. 10 minutes only allowed for lunch with further ½ hour from 3.30-4pm. Pretty busy. Several days after advised by Mr. Mudie that Trustees have granted increase in Salary of 10 pounds, and that both he and Mr. Craigie admire and appreciate my actions etc. My birthday on 8th July, and my dear Mother and sister Bob give me another beautiful cake, similar to the one I received in Melbourne last trip. A real beauty. Get permission from Bank to have evg. off. A nice little gathering had been arranged and my old pals Jimmie, Mitch and Smith came along. All trains cut out after 8.30pm. owing to shortage of coal consequent upon the shipping strike, but they managed with cycles. Had a most pleasant evening thanks to the efforts of Mother and the girls. Made the recipient of a nice silver watch from all my home-folk, bless their thoughtfulness, a thing I greatly need since my last was stolen at Southampton.

During this week received my discharge 'a clean sheet', from H.Q. Keswick, and a little later all monies due to me up to and including day of discharge the 17th July. Approached by Mc Craigie and asked to take charge of new accounts dept, to be in absolute control and in no 'perfunctory manner'. Inspectors are going to country Branches and state their willingness to have me with them, one to Pt. Pirie and the other to Mt. Gambier, but owing to this job am not allowed. Two other lads just back from Palestine came in a week later than I, and also forego their leave until a later date. Balance is over and I am asked if I should like to go on leave now, but decide on Sept. 1st, as probably strike will be over, weather good, and train service resumes to old order of things. Probably go to Pirie for a few days, Mt. Gambier a day or so, Melb. about 3 days and remainder Broken Hill. Father trying to arrange his holidays in Sept. also.

Met G. Justice now Master 'S.S. CONQUEROR' and Supt, Subsidiary lights. Tells me he will be going for a trip to various parts of Spencer Gulf beginning of Sept, and says I may go too if I wish. May be away about a fortnight, but I think it will be grand to be on the old sea again for a reminder and touch of the past. Attend a 'welcome back' at Woodville church.

AUGUST, 1919

Sunday 3rd

Crofty is on 'ORMONDE'. Went to Harbour to meet her, but owing to tides (abnormal) were not allowed in that night. Hear since that he is to go to Sydney, and will be back in Adelaide in 2 or 3 weeks time. Waiting to hear latest news from him.

How I wished I were in England now, although quite settled and looking out for a good road for my future career, often feel that I wish my application had been granted for transfer. Would have only meant a little longer away from home and see by recent paper, all Australians expected to be away from England by end of Sept.

Met Sgt. Biggs who went round to Sydney with the good old ship. Says labourers working on every part of her, old fittings being taken out and replaced by those taken on at Melb. My microscope and laboratory at their mercy, and he predicts that some things there will have been stolen.

Received a letter from Mr. Mc Hugh stating had ship been recommissioned again, would have asked all S.A. boys to come back with him, but says she has now finished and will be put on coast until 'KATOOMBA' comes back from England and when she may probably go to Belfast for complete overhauling.

Thus have both the good old ship and myself finished with the Military and Admiralty, perhaps forever.

'Karoola' at Sea

MARCH, 1919

Tuesday 18th

My darling Mother,

I trust you received my letter OK from the West. Since writing that, I have been on shore at Fremantle and seen some of the folk. (*His Uncle and their families.*)

Arrived there with still a day and a half to go before our quarantine term expired. We were thoroughly examined in the 'Roads' before allowed to proceed to our usual berth in the river. (*Examined for symptoms of Spanish Flu.*)

Began coaling operations, but this work was necessarily slow, no labourers being allowed on board, so the 600 tons of coal had to be put into the bunkers from the hulks, by means of chutes, through the sides of the ship.

When the day and a half had gone our coaling was not finished, so we were given the night off. Went straight round to Charleys, because he has complained that I have never given him a chance to talk about our travels. The travellers from India and the sick nurse went ashore, but the former on our boat.

It was while we were nearing the wharf that I think to myself a funny little incident happened, which perhaps may not be out of the way to tell you.

Relatives and friends had gathered to meet the boys, making quite a nice little few altogether.

When we were still about 50 yards or so away, a young lady espied her worthy spouse amongst the crowd on board. She immediately had hysterics on the spot, clapped her hands, and did the Devils dance, or something like the latest modification of a corroboree. She soon made clear a little space on the edge of the wharf, backing her horse and cart about as she did with as good an effect as a policeman's horse might when put backwards into a crowd.

We gradually got a bit closer, and she began to scream out, calling him by name, 'Here you are! Come along! Quickly! Hurry! Hurray!' etc, and after each exclamation looking down at her feet and the clear space she had made, as if she expected him to jump, (and I have no doubt that she did). I did not blame the poor fellow for not doing so however, seeing that we were a good thirty feet away at this time and as far, almost, below the top for it was low water and tide out. I am afraid such a crowd being attracted, and our chaps sniggering as they did, I did not envy the young chap, who seemed a bit bashful. That is the price they must pay for such company as they reckon they enjoy, I suppose.

I am glad that it was he and not I anyhow.

The prettiest girls of England are supposed to be those of Devon. Having heard this on several occasions, make up my mind to look for myself on passing through. They're not bad at all. Might bring you one home this time my dear. I am sure you would not object and as for the girls, they would appreciate somebody from the old country. English youngsters are so much better than our Australian you know.

Well old Unc. Charley and I jumped into a tram and made for Point Walter, a nice little summer resort on the Swan. Spent a couple of pleasant hours there in peace and quietness on the lawns. When we were about to leave, a couple of boat loads of excursionists from Perth came down and began at once to play social evening games on the ground. They were a very homely lot.

Went along to Unc. Daves. They were just retiring to bed. I wished to leave them, but they would not hear of it. Had to stop for the rest of the evening.

Uncle has made two flower-pot stands from a rough piece of jarrah, with the simple aid of a knife and file. He is as proud of them as can be and they are certainly alright. Is more and more infatuated with their new home daily. It is certainly a bonny little place, and in pleasant locality and pleasantly situated. He is still very desirous in having you over there for a holiday, and if you have not gone over by the time I settle down again, I shall certainly bundle you off pack and baggage. So beware of my threat duck. Should like to have seen Winnie and Bill Toms, but time did not permit.

During that same morning, 200 cases of apples were sent alongside in a barge. When the first sling came up and momentarily poised in the air prior to lowering on the deck, one box became loose, fell out, and the remainder soon followed. The cases were broken, and as you may guess, there was a scatter of apples which rolled about all over the deck in their neat little tissue paper wrappings.

As you may further guess, there was also a rush and scramble for them by lookers on. Your worthy being one of the number, joined in, clearly satisfied of course that this could not be classed as 'pilfering'.

The Unit had to carry away about 200 cases to the bridge, where they were to be stowed until required for use. Well on two previous occasions, just the same quantity of this fruit, has been allowed to bake and decay in the hot tropical sun, and all thrown over board as they were, in their cases, and not one has been issued to us. Yet in the saloon Officers and Sisters have their ice-cream, grapes, pears, oranges, and apples fresh from the freezer every day. Anyhow I came off considerably well in this deal, and it was peculiar to notice that for every trip to the bridge by everybody carrying, their jumpers swelled more and more. Must have been apples I think? May as well eat them while they are good and while we have the chance, is our motto.

We got away at 7 o'clock the next morning and have had pretty good weather since. Have had one or two sharp tropical showers, and we find it pretty warm working below decks. On top however, we have had a nice steady breeze all through and fairly cool. We passed over the line a couple of days ago.

Yesterday we sighted land for the first time since leaving the West. This was the Malabar Coast of Southern India. Passed by quite close and could see a large steamer lying off a small port.

At the same time today we passed what is known as Pigeon Island. You may find it on the map. The 4th Officer pointed the route out to me today by the chart. At the present moment we are off land again and passing small sailing vessels which resemble Ceylon tea-ships somewhat, they are known as 'Dhows'. Sailing craft on the Nile are similarly rigged and go by that name.

A bit of anxiety was felt the other day by those responsible for our ships supply of meat etc.

The freezers went bung, and the keeping qualities of about 5,000 pounds worth of meat being in the balance.

The engineers worked night and day at the breakage and happy to relate, although a very tough job indeed, set things in order again.

We expect to arrive at Bombay tomorrow night, and I hope we soon get on shore, as they fooled us round for about 2 days last time.

I have quite a lot to do there this time, for those chaps from India have put me wise to a few things, about things just outside Bombay.

We get no wireless news of any kind nowadays. We received the intimation from Colombo radio that all news had been officially censored.

This is usually done when any serious trouble breaks out. I hope this is not so in this case, for I think everybody is anxious that the war will end alright. Just now though, industrial unrest in England promises to be serious, and I am afraid the Bolshevik movement in Europe will not improve things, nor the I.W.W. or O.B.U. in Australia either, for that matter. These organizations set one thinking, so far I am anything but favourably impressed for though admitting their claims may be just, their methods of attaining them are not to my mind justifiable at this stage of other troubles. I wish these extremists would be patient for a while longer, till things are set a bit in ship shape order. Ireland is inclined to give more bother, while America is forging ahead, improving and making good all the time. Beating us in everything hands down, getting experience from our troubles, and putting it to good use. The I.W.W. is kicked out and kept down in Chicago, their Head Quarters, and consequently they come to Aust., where they know they can play old Harry, without being molested.

There will be a lot of bad and bitter feeling amongst all classes I am afraid. For my own part, I intend to leave the riotous blighters to themselves, myself well apart. I don't agree with either parties. They disgust me, and it all amounts to greed and envy, no matter how you look at it. I live peaceably and intend to, and this world is good enough for me. If other, but the envious class hatred methods, were adopted, would be a different thing. Rome wasn't built in a day. Most returning soldiers have no time for this sort of thing, having had enough trouble and fighting of their own. Seems strange that most of these people making so much trouble and ado at home, have done nothing for their country in this crisis, and their attempted efforts to make things so very much better in such a very short time for themselves could not have been possible had Germany won this War. Through our soldier's efforts they have been able to remain at home and get busy stirring up strife, yet they have no time for a soldier. I have been told myself by one of them, a real fanatic. Anyhow I hope the R.S.A., stick close, immune from the poisonous lies these wretches tell them when they return, and preference given to returned soldiers, in spite of what the others say, for my goodness they deserve it.

I have seen so much, just how this one ship has been fooled, and wasted by these confounded rotters who come on here to work when ashore. They disgust everybody and I'm sure I am properly 'fed up' with the whole crowd. They steal everything they can lay hands on, and take the very boots off your feet if you didn't keep awake. Many times in Melb., I have been asked for mine by coalies, (and yet they have no time for a soldier). They get 2/6d per hour and double time for Sat and Sundays, also time and a half anything over 8 hours. Yet we get 6/- day for day of 15 hours, and lives risked into the bargain.

Anyhow dear this is meant more for poor old daddy than yourself, and is only by the way. These are the sort of things which confront a young man as he begins to ask how and why, as he grows up, and finds a world about him. I am however convinced that politics are rotten and instead of the uplifting of the masses as these few extremists make out, only ends in a real class warfare of jealousy and hatred, making a few notorious, puts money in their pockets and leaves the working man in the same place, with much more to suffer and decidedly betrayed.

When he gets his feet again, somebody else, a great leader rises out of the ashes and so on over again.

I deplore the trivial excuses put forward by these one eyed gunners. I wonder Tom Price doesn't rise from his grave.

Our new O.C. held his inspection of the hospital yesterday, which is just ready for incoming patients.

He expressed himself as being, to use his own words, 'Very much pleased and satisfied, and the work was very, very nice indeed'. He said he would give us the afternoon off as a sign of his appreciation and free use of the boat deck. Also said we had a handsome reputation, and trusted it would be kept up, under his care, for he intended all future promotions to come from this staff when we are reinforced in England. Wants 2 Sgts and four Corporals, but I do not intend putting in at all, and I know I stand a good chance. Would not accept promotion, if offered to me now, for various reasons.

I hope that Mitch and Smithy have received their discharge ere this. I used often to wonder when a youngster, as I stood on the sea beach, whether any of those little waves, which continually kept bubbling and lapping up on the sand, ever saw, or touched some poor wandering, lonely old ship, right out at sea somewhere.

They almost used to say something to me, I remember being much impressed when Alva Perkins went to sea. At Pt. Melb. I liked to listen to these wavelets. I think sometimes it is a wonder I did not go to sea. Those same little harmless, whispering chaps are very different to their big boisterous brothers is mid ocean.

Yesterday the sea was very calm, and resembled glass for all the world. It was beautiful to watch the ship's bows turning the water over. The wave this caused seemed too lazy to break into foam, but rolled over, just like a fold of velvet instead.

I still feel I could bump the heads of those people responsible for detaining my letters from you at Melbourne.

I wanted nothing else, for I had a fit of the blues in Melb. I think. Should like to have had Ada's likeness, for in England I was particularly requested to bring or send photographs of my folk at home, and this would have been something to show.

I hope you get this letter in better condition than you received my last from Bombay. You remember it.

Well dear, I must close this now having told you all for this time I think.

Give my fondest love to Daddy, Ada, Bobs, Renie, Ralphie, and little Colin. He must be a little man now. I sincerely hope that Ralphie is quite better again and doing splendidly.

Accept my love for your lovely self, wishing you all, happiness and health. Quite well myself. Your loving son Rex.

P.S. Do not trouble to write regularly dear, so long as I get all the news, I'll be satisfied. Do not make it a tie upon yourself to write every Sunday. Still address letters C/- 'Karoola' No. 1 Austr.. H.S. C/- Transport Office, Melbourne.

Sincerely trust you received my diary posted to you from Fremantle. R.

MARCH, 1919

Sunday 30

My darling Mother,

We passed through the Gates of Babel-Mandels, into the Red Sea at 5pm today, and Aden at 8 o'clock this morning. I am becoming quite a familiar traveller to these parts now.

There is quite a lot really, to tell you this time after our visit to Bombay, this is, if I told you of every little incident, but I suppose that will hardly be necessary.

In my last I think I left you one day out from Bombay. At midday on the next we reached the Bombay floating lights. This is a small boat with a light on it and a bell whose tongue swings with every movement of the boat caused by the waves. At first you would think we were going right on past it, but suddenly we take a turn at right angles and pass closely to it, en route for Bombay. This is about 20 miles from the place. Behind us was a large steamer following, which we had passed earlier in the day. Reached Bombay at about 2 o'clock and contrary to last time, when we tied up in the anchorage for a day and a half, went straight up to the wharf and tied to a place called the Mahawl. This is at the entrance to the dock gate of the Alexandra Docks, and a large sorting P.O. for inward and outward mails by steamer, is opposite.

Coming through the anchorage we passed close to the HMS 'NEW ZEALAND', the ship in which Jellico is making his trip to Australia and New Zealand. The crew were busily at work painting the sides and giving her a spruce up, for she was to be thrown open for inspection in a few days hence.

I made up my mind to have a look over if opportunity offered, altho' the dates were really after the time we should be here.

Leave was granted the first night, also a change from last time, but by arrangement I was put on guard, for having a fairly lengthy and busy programme on hand, I wished to get this done and have a free hand afterwards, without hindrances like these. Amongst these outings I wished to take a run into the country to Poonah and Nasik. The latter place is a great spot for the purchase of brass, for the people there specialize in the manufacture of brass ornaments and things.

I had not left any stone unturned to get right to business, one of the boys going on shore had made enquiries from the Railway Station re the daily trains to this place for me.

I noticed coming in, that a three funnelled cruiser was lying at the Naval docks. Later on somebody told me that the old "TOPAZE" was at Bombay, so I presumed it was she. I was glad of this, for I wished to go on board and make a few enquiries about Dr. Shone Sargent, *(relative),* who was Fleet Surgeon on her, who taking ill in the Red Sea and put in hospital at Aden, was subsequently taken on to Bombay, where he died. It transpires that he died just 3 or 4 days before we were here on the last occasion. All his people have heard is that he received a sun-stroke while on duty in the Persian Gulf.

I promised them that if ever I went to Bombay again, I would visit his grave etc. I have not only done that at a place called Sewri Cemetery, 7 miles out, but visited and had a look over the ship, found that his Principal Medical Officer and a great friend of his, lived at the Hotel Majestic, a large fashionable place in Bombay.

Ascertained a good deal of news from him and met others who knew him, also the Captain of the ship who is a local preacher. Met him at the Cooperidge Camp Y.M.C.A. Hut. A jolly fine chap too, in fact they all are.

Dr. Shone was only 25, only child of Dr. Wm. Sargent of Padstow, Cornwall, and is a descendant of a brother to grandfather Amos, and of same generation as myself.

Seems to have been very much admired, esteemed and respected by all the ships company, who still mourn his loss. Got news too of the luggage and deceased's gear, part of which had gone astray. Mrs. Sargent was greatly upset about this, and complained to the Admiralty about it. It appears that Staff Surgeon Egan, his Chief, had had it all packed and nailed down securely, and despatched it to England by via of Teranto in Italy. Italians are bounders in robbing luggage on railways, and this is what befell this, proved by the fact that his mother on opening the box discovered that suits of clothes had been dragged and pulled about in the dirt. All his medical books and a pair of binoculars had disappeared. They will be very pleased to know what I have to tell them. Of course this 'getting news' extended over the whole time nearly, we had in Bombay, and was done a bit at a time, altho' I made good headway the very first day. This is a coincidence is it not? At Lezant, are the fishing rods, guns etc of the poor boy, for he was a great sport.

His father and he, as well as some of his uncles collected together with their wives every year on one of the farms of the Sargents called 'Dobbin's Cott' and spent their holidays there. They have shooting licences of the farms round about, and have a good old time. Went shooting myself from 'Trewarlett', after pheasants and other game. Lovely country there. However this is only by the way, the whole makes a nice little story which I must not spoil before I come home again.

One night went for a motor drive to Malabar Hill through various parts of Bombay and along the beach to a place known as Colabar, where there is a large English Military Hospital. One of them accompanied me to the markets one afternoon, and assisted in making purchases for me, (you would like to know what they are wouldn't you?) Hired a Gharry for the occasion and it was real fun, said she felt honoured on a/c of my letting her choose the articles (I had a big say all the same). I believe I could fill a small book of the many things seen and done, but of course I can only give you a very crude account here. I seemed to know my way about as well as if I had lived there for months. Miss Cowdrey is the Y.W.C.A. Secretary of Bombay branch. Things are run on a large scale and she has assistants, all of whom are highly educated and persons of gentle birth. Her father is a doctor in America. A young Sydney lady arrived for 5 years work for the Y.W. the week before our arrival, in the 'ORONTES'. We passed this vessel coming out of harbour as we were going in. She with two other gents, Y.M.C.A. Secs accompanied us on the motor trip.

Last time I was here she, (Miss Cowdrey) gave me a little ivory lucky dog. This has been all over the place with me and I returned it to her. She reckoned it quite a novel idea. With her, she has English ladies too, and they all live in a large flat at the top of a six storey building, just at the rear of the famous Taj-Mahal Hotel, and a place well known as 'Greens'. From their window a lovely view of the harbour and all vessels coming in or going out can be had. The 'NEW ZEALAND' lies right opposite in the harbour, and one can see her quite distinctly.

Went to see the Walkers, (Supt of Bombay police) and spent a very pleasant evening with them. Wanted to know what had become of Mitchell, as the Cowdreys had of Nankivell.

There are only 3 S.A. lads left now, and young Rundle usually accompanies me on my excursions.

The poor kid was troubled with boils though, on this trip unfortunately. When he was well enough to get about, we went to look up a friend of his at the Freeman Thomas Hospital, an Australian Nurse. Most hospitals in India are staffed with Australian Sisters, though there are no Austr. hospitals in the country. Outside the Thomas hospital are Turkish field guns and pontoons used by Johnny Turk in his attack on the Suez Canal. These things were captured by the Indians.

I saw the place in Bombay, where hundreds of tons of timber had been stacked at the time of the influenza epidemic. Hindus cremate their deceased and as thousands were dying every day, you may guess the stokers had plenty of work to do.

As we passed sparks were flying up higher than the high iron fence which surrounded the place. Another body on the grill I suppose.

If you peep into my diary for the beginning of July last year, you will find there an account of how the bodies of Parsees are disposed of. Vultures do the business at their towers at Malabar Hill.

Such pretty little birds, but much nicer at a distance, or a bit further away than when they alight on ones shoulder, and scratch round ones head in an inquisitive sort of way, to see whether one is dead or not. A bit too highly trained for my liking and certainly a familiarity which is revolting. I rather like to hear their chirp and whistle. If not so overgrown would make excellent canaries, but would be scarcely safe to drop off to sleep when they were about. Might wake up to find joey calmly enjoying a leg or contemplating a feed on some other part of your anatomy.

Time simply flew in Bombay, and partly owing to being otherwise busy, Rundle laid up, and the trains not quite suiting the time we got off in the morning, after all, was unable to get into the country.

This was very disappointing, the more so as that since we find it could have been done if a certain officer on board had been sport enough. It appears that the O.C. told him at the beginning, that if any one of the staff wished to go into the country, he was to be given extended leave to do so, providing no other duties had been detailed him.

Nothing was said to us of this, and consequently all were ignorant of the facts, until the O.C. asked one of our N.C.Os if any had gone up the line. On being told that all had to report to the ship each night, he was very vexed and said he would require the reason why this concession had not been granted.

Anyhow it is all over now, but it stung at first. The Officer concerned is the Adjutant now that Capt Southwood has left us, so does pretty well as he pleases. There is no love lost between us however, for I have given him and his crowd of satellites, fellows who crawl after him for stripes, to understand what I think of them and their methods. Over same thing that happened in Melbourne last, satisfied me with him, and another matter in Bombay, in which I had fully made up my mind to interview the O.C. on behalf of everybody concerned, until fortunately I was spared the trouble by our Warrant Officer using his influence and setting things right. Not worth the space to mention here, but it is remarkable what some fellows will do if they think nobody will say anything or probably not notice it.

This chap is a Pomey and has the hide of a rhinoceros, and he and his crowd (only created since our good old officers left and taking advantage of new O.C.s inexperience so far) have no love for me. They know I tumble through their games, and being nothing to me, and never hoping to see them for life again after this, I am in the happy position of being independent and able to put the others up to the dodge. Not that you would notice it, you know, they are aware that I can afford to say what I like, being right, but on the other hand, happily content, friendly, and of good feeling respect with the rest of the unit, I refuse to have these others on my mind.

I can put up with swearers, and roughies, so long as they are straight and have a good heart, but I abhor the cringing, sneaky, snaky, back-scratching crawler, the man who sinks his own personality and individuality to gain a thing he requires, makes out to people he is a jolly good fellow himself, but all the time pulling, pulling cautiously and stealthily some wire, by which through some chance he may luckily have got hold of. Father knows the kind of reptile well. Marvellous the kind of individual one can meet sometimes. As soon as ever I discover anything like this in a man, I break off without any hesitation whatsoever, any relations or intimacy previously existing, the same as I believe Father would do in similar circumstances.

We had to work all day Sunday, for we were to embark next day. Leave was given at four o'clock, but I was due for guard duty again. However one of the other boys intimating that he did not intend going on shore, asked him to do duty for me, which he accordingly did.

Never catch me loafing round here, if by any chance there is an opportunity of looking a bit about on land.

Went ashore with a chap named Roberts, since christened 'Earl' after the renowned Earl Roberts.

Went down to the Taj Mahal pier, to try and get out to the 'NEW ZEALAND' by rowing a sailing boat.

Was not really inspection day, but we intended risking our chances on that. But these natives of India are the biggest rogues in business that it is possible to imagine, and consequently boat here was very high, one native wanted 5 rupees to take us across (1 rupee = 1/4d English). Could not get him down any lower either, for the beggar knew that people would give anything to get over on inspection days to come, and they always take we Australians down if they can, thinking we have plenty of money and can afford anything. I asked several Englishmen if this price was correct and they said it would be absurd to pay it. I was determined to get across, and the fellow wouldn't come down a single anna, so hit upon the plan of going across in the boat and when on board the 'NEW ZEALAND' ask the Blue jackets what they usually paid to come ashore, and pay the fellow accordingly and let him bark for the rest.

When we went to his boat, found a lady waiting there with her little boy. She intended going for a sail only, but when she learned that we were bound for the war-ship, at once fell in with the idea and decided to come with us.

When we reached the ship, I made due enquiries and found the correct price to be 2 rupees return for two.

We paid him 2 for the three single, and as he started to argue the point as they always do, we put the money into his hand and a big Jack-tar put his foot against the bow and gave it a mighty shove. The owner was obliged to go where his boat went, so of course went with it. As for our part we went peacefully on our way. Finding no difficulty in going just where we wished to. A boy was sent to us to show round the ship. She is indeed a beauty. About her are inscriptions on brass, as 'Fear God, honour the King', and so on, as well as dates showing the different engagements of which she had been a participant, as Heligoland, Dogger Bank and others. In front of the 1st funnel is to be seen a huge piece of armour plate torn by one of the enemy shells, from the base of one of the 12" gun turrets. She has 8 guns of this size and many others of smaller calibre.

How many ladders of all descriptions we had to climb, I really do not know, but the English lady who was rather reserved at first, came from behind her barricade in these manoeuvres. We were really a happy party, and were given much amusement by an English Johnny who had joined us. He was one of those excitable sort, and very inquisitive. Asked the lad the most ridiculous questions, and one followed the other before the first had been properly answered. I must tell you about these things in my 'lecture'. To notice and see the funny side of human mannerisms, not only gives amusement at times but interesting study as well.

We lost him however, and the last I heard of him was that he was seen up the mast examining the wireless apparatus.

In the heads dining room is a beautiful silver model of the HMS 'Iron Duke" presented to Lady Jellico by the crew of that ship, when her husband was Admiral of the Navy and used this as his flagship. Saw also the sitting room or lounge as well as part of the apartments set aside for these two people. Did not see them however, as they were at the time, at Delhi.

Amongst the ships treasures is a quantity of beautiful silver-plate presented by New Zealand people, and silver shields won by the gunners in target practice.

She is to take a run up to Karachi (in the Punjab District) before Jellico joins her for his trip to Fremantle.

The ship was presented by the New Zealand Govt. to the Royal Navy in 1913, and is a sister ship to the 'AUSTRALIA' presented by the Commonwealth. Both are battle cruisers.

It was dark by the time we had finished our inspection. The crew is one picked from men who have been on service in the North Sea, as well as reserves from Devonport, a British Naval Base just near Plymouth, both places which I visited when in England. The boatswain is a good chap, a Devonite from Plymouth. One of those rolling, rollicking, breezy, easy, red-faced sea dogs.

A steamer came alongside with Officers from the ship, who had returned from a joy excursion given by people on shore. It was fun getting the lady on to this boat from the warship through the rails and other obstacles, and altho' probably undignified, she went at it like a brick. I was invited to stay the night on the cruiser, but of course had to get back. We landed at the Naval dock (having the ride 'baksheesh') just astern of the 'TOPAZE". My word what a difference in the living conditions of the men in these two vessels. Fine healthy stalwart men go to pieces and return with ruined health in vessels in this Indian squadron. Shone (Welsh for John) Sargent detested the life from the very first, and I believe did heaps of good for the men in his untiring attendance on them, when for weeks they had to live on bread and fat in the Red Sea, under a hot tropical sun and without enough water for a decent wash. My word they have to live it these men, for I saw the ship, our quarters are a paradise to theirs.

The lady, whose husband is in the Indian Civil Service, is staying at the 'Hotel-Majestic' too, until 8th of April, when her ship arrives to take them to England.

Invited us to dinner at the 'Majestic'. Could not do that, so asked us to lunch on the morrow, but that was also impossible, as we were to sail at noon.

Went round to the Cooperidge Hut as I told you and interviewed Capt. Woods R.N.

Reported at the ship at 10 o'clock, and took over from the lad who had relieved me. There had been a continuous guard over the 210 cases of apples we had taken on board at Fremantle ever since we came here. It was my turn to go up on the bridge where they are stacked with two others, to look after them. This has been brought about by the theft of a few while at sea, by members of the crew and others, but I'll guarantee more have disappeared since we took over the charge of them, than all the trip put together, not having tasted one since leaving Austr.

The Southern Cross can be plainly seen from Bombay, but it is getting lower and lower now that we are travelling northwards through the Red Sea.

The very first night we arrived, we heard the rumour that we were to carry in addition to patients, about 60 wives and 40 children of Officers and men in the Indian Army. Quite an army of natives and dock workers arrived the very next day to fix up bunks for them and cork the decks of the ship.

Our main surgical ward is now used by the 1st Class women passengers, and a lower medical, for the second. We started our embarkation at 9 o'clock on the Monday, at a new berth to which we had shifted for the purpose. Right opposite, a large shed decorated with flags etc. and fitted up generally for the welcoming back of Indian troops from France and Mesopotamia.

It is very pitiable in a way to think we are to be turned into a passenger ship at last. I was detailed for duty at the gangway and I expected some joy out of this, my duty for a time being to prevent the passengers from bringing on more than a minimum amount of luggage, or that which only required for immediate use to be taken with them, the remainder to go down the ships hold, to be available later on. Knowing what a jolly nuisance English Officers are in this regard myself, and the Sergeant with me, expected to have a lively time, especially with the women thrown in. Anticipated from the very jump, these people would look upon we common soldiers, as mere earth, for in India, native servants by the score wait upon them hand and foot, do everything at their bidding, and such it was, by a few of them. Patients as well as troops loaded with their rifles and accoutrement (mostly Gordon Highlanders came on in fine style) but in the middle of it, the foolish embarkation officer began sending the women and children on with their luggage and bungalows from various parts of India, for I am sure they brought everything they possessed with them. This began to mess things up and interfere with order of routine in a grand style, and was soon noticed by the Warrant Officer, who reported it to the O.C. He soon stopped it, then the Embarkation Officer on shore went off and gave his mind about our interference and so on. A real picnic for me and no little amusement. A Captain and his wife, brought a lot with them, carried by Coolies. We pulled them up, but the woman, tried to take no notice. We insisted however, for she was pulling and tugging a bit, nearly sending the poor Coolie off his feet. Finding it was no good, although her husband was pushing from the other end, she began to stamp her feet, screaming like a cockatoo that she would have it, and behaved most unseemingly for a lady. You know these people think we are as easily bluffed as the poor Tommies, and were greatly insulted and felt their dignity rubbed by being pulled up by mere lower ranks. However we were equally determined that she should not, but the noise she made! Only a young couple too. The Sgt. told the Officer he should be ashamed of himself, and that sobered him, he demanded his wife to stop her noise, which to give her credit, accordingly did, and at length we got our own way.

The old Embark – Officer when appealed to, said wringing his hands, 'I cannot help it lady, you are travelling by an Austr. ship and you know what THEY are!' Dreadful people I suppose he thought, but I added that this was a Military ship and not a glorious P.& O. liner specially fitted up for passengers. All women in India now are classified as to their state of health for a change from the country, just the same as our soldiers booked for return to Aust are, as C1, C2, & C3 and so on. Having waited in vain a long time for a ship to take them to England, they were mighty glad to come along with us, on the clear understanding however, that they accepted the best we had to offer.

Following these people, other ladies came, but they used different tactics altogether. Altho' really having too much gear to go to their quarters with, I daresay they thought diplomacy in this instance, the better part of valour. Said their night attire was in this box, children's clothes in that etc., but asked very nicely and ladylike, so let them pass. I suppose they thought I was a greeney and easily smoodged over, but nothing of the sort, I did it to impart an object lesson to the other folk, who did look when they saw what might have happened if they had been a bit more decent about it. I cannot tell you all, for other funny things followed, but will some day. I think most of them forgot that in reality some poor Tommy was deprived from going home, who had been out here, 4 years or more, and with legitimate claims, because they, through their position, had secured the passage which really belongs to him. In no other parts except Egypt are Officers allowed to take their wives and families with them, a jolly big concession I reckon.

Talk about piles and piles of luggage, you would think that England would sink into the sea when we put it on the Island.

Have never met such fussers over luggage as the women, kept running back to have a look at it, getting into little knots and arguing about it, gabbling all the while to the natives. Just imagine how this would have disturbed embarkation and held up the troops coming up the gangway, if we had not prohibited it at the beginning.

However things were set right at last, and things ready for 'letting go'. Just at this moment, hundreds of Indian troops just arrived by a troopship, and under English and Indian Officers, came marching along the dock road to this huge shed for their welcome and feast. Their band meantime rendered airs for our benefit such as 'Old-langsyne' etc. Well they played too, being all wind instruments. Then they played marches for the Indians, who fell into step and my word, didn't they throw their chests out and carry themselves erect.

It looked grand and inspiring. I was delighted at this opportunity of seeing them. You trust I was high up on the monkey deck.

Things have gone smoothly up to date, but plenty of clauses have appeared in orders, informing our passengers they must not do this or that. Quite reasonable, and has the effect of preventing the idea that they run the ship. Will be well disciplined by the time we get them home. At any rate they have found their place amongst we Australians.

It seems so strange to see noisy, racing, romping children tearing about the decks, and women promenading or sitting about. Some of the children are babes in arms.

Who ever would have thought we should come to this, but it is a novelty and quite an experience.

I have discovered that a number of the women smoke and drink spirits. Indeed takes no finding out, for some are as brazen as brass. The life in the East spoils a good many I am afraid. Fancy mothers smoking before their children. I can scarcely believe my eyes. I wonder if the youngsters when they think of it when grown up, would be ashamed. However some classes of society do not bother about scruples of this kind.

It is nothing to wake up in the middle of the night when sleeping on deck, to find that some youngster crying, has been the cause of disturbance of your slumbers. I do duty for part of the day in an Offices ward. I must confess they are very nice to me. Several are Doctors of the Indian Medical Service and I have had some most interesting chats with them.

Come up here to the lab sometimes. I am sorry to state that one was suspected of tuberculosis and I had to make an examination. I hoped he was not, for he has always told me that he had tried hard to escape it since he had double pneumonia and lung troubles and thought he had succeeded, and was practising exercises every morning to ward any infection of the kind off. However, I took great pains and made a careful microscopic test today.

The result leaves no room for doubt. He has to be isolated tonight in a small ward where an Officer, his wife and three small children are berthed. They will have to move from there and other provisions made. This poor chap is a clever Doctor and has his wife on board. He approached me several times today, requiring to know if the result was positive or otherwise, but I could not tell him. He seemed very anxious, so I put it in the Majors hands to inform him. Must be a dreadful thing after climbing up in life as he has done, spent much money on education and established himself, to contract this dread disease at last. We struck quite a friendship for I have been able to do little things for him in lots of ways since he came on board. I will visit him as opportunity offers, for I have the run of the ship, quite a privilege.

Another Officer belongs to the famous Gurkhas (you have heard of them). He is in the civil service of India, a consulting-engineer in the Ganges canals and locks. Lent by the Govt. to the Military. He has had wide experiences in big game hunting in the jungles of India. Have very interesting chats with him. Went down the hold especially to get a book of photographs of hunting etc., to show me. I am much fascinated by the accounts he has given me. We have a Politics Officer, another name for a British magistrate, only holding honorary Military rank, an Excise Officer, a naval commander and others, so you see one does, by chatting to them, learn quite a good bit, about things and places in general from where they come, the life there etc. Amongst the troops we have Bucks, Queens, Gordons, Devons and others, quite a number of English regiments represented.

1st. April. Just at this moment we are passing a large steamer going same way as ourselves. Saw her smoke early this morning and have been all day before catching up.

Only tonight I was reading over one of your old letters in which you mention the dilapidated state in which you received my last letter from Bombay, that the letter containing some photographs I had mentioned, had not arrived yet. Have you received them since? You also said that you could not resist reading the letter, although a fairly lengthy one, in the midst of your washing, which had consequently made you late for the day. Realising the above number I think you had probably better take a day off for this may also delay you if you receive it on a Monday.

However this is all the pleasure I can give you while away, so may as well tell you everything to give you a general idea how things are progressing.

The other night a concert was held amongst the first class passengers on the boat deck. Could see the proceedings from my position here. Went off alright and several good performers took part. There is a good lady violinist amongst them.

2nd Apl. Tonight one is to be given by the children, organised by a girl of 13. A very clever youngster. She saw the ships printer about the programme. Arranged with the carpenter for erection of platform, the Chief Steward about refreshments for performers, and the O.C. for the free use of boat deck for rehearsals. She arranged one of the plays herself I believe. See programme enclosed.

Today we received news by wireless of the rumpus in Egypt and Syria, by Bedouins. Have seen many of these chaps when in Palestine. Fine, tall, handsome fellows, real sons of the desert, of which they are masters, nevertheless they are as treacherous and as treasonable a race as ever existed. I could tell you stories of their doings up that way, the Arabs are not in it with them.

I see the Europeans are being moved from Egypt, we will soon be at Port Said now, so wonder if we will be delayed or whether we will have anything to do with moving these fugitives. Would rather get off the ship and see the game for myself than be fooling about, in fact I half hope that our O.C. will be asked to share some men for the occasion. Would be a change to be in a flare up wouldn't it?

Yesterday was April fool's day, and some of the Officers passed the time away playing artful tricks on the ladies.

I thought of you, you old scamp, and those silly old tricks which used to catch me napping.

We are not sure of the port of call in England, but hear we may disembark these people at Southampton, and discharge our cargo in London. The latter would do me admirably well.

I am reminded that in a fortnight from today will be Bob's birthday. (*Sister*). Bless the dear kid, she is no youngster now. I am sorry I cannot be home for the occasion, but I hope she makes herself as nice a cake as she made for me. Would like to send her something, but do not care to risk it, the way things are situated in Egypt. Mail arrangements are sure to be upset and I have had enough punishment, through mail services, to please me.

I have seen the O.C. re transfer to new duties in England, and he has willingly promised to recommend it, but at the same time, does not hold much hope, as he thinks all remaining vacancies are filled and various staffs cut down greatly in strength, all through the peace there.

I was much amused this morning by hearing that a Major (a Dr) in my ward, who is a real hard case, and who has struck up a rather friendly acquaintance with a newly married French lady on board, (who uses a perfume which pervades the atmosphere for miles) is now forbidden by his wife to talk to her. One of the other Officers said to him as he was dressing, 'Major there is a lady outside wishing to see you, says she did not see you at all last evening'. With rather a guilty red face, with eyes open wide and in a whisper somewhat, said 'Who is it, my wife?' I thought that very funny, but I think it was only a 'stall' put up by this other Officer, there being no lady in reality outside at all. Anyhow the Major said 'I'm very busy dressing just now', so did not see for himself.

Well dear, I must leave you now, the mail closes very soon and I still have lots to write.

I have written on one side of paper only as I am tired of scratching on the back of pages.

Give my very fondest love to dear old Daddy, Ada, Bobs', Renie, Ralph and little Colin and accept all for yourself you darling.

I hope and trust you are all quite well and happy as this at present leaves me.

Trust that Ralphie is now quite better.

Your loving Son Rex.

P.S. Re the ladies perfume, I hear that a ship sent out a wireless message requiring to know if any other ship in the vicinity of the Red Sea had caught fire, or if any assistance was required. She proved to be 40 miles distant. Do you believe it?

The carpenters are erecting a stage now for tonight's concert. I may mention that this little girl organiser, made it plainly understood that she was not going to pay for all these things, such as printing and refreshments etc. Of course those concerned couldn't refuse her. Admission 1/-, 6d. and 3d.

APRIL, 1919

13th Sunday

My darling Mother,

Just another little note before we reach England. I trust you received alright, my last, posted from Suez.

We came through the canal after staying at this place for a few hours only, in order to have the searchlight fixed to the bow. The light is a very brilliant one, and is used during the passage through the canal at night, for it must be remembered that the channel is not much more than a chain wide and being 58 miles long, and ships speed not to exceed more than 4 miles per hour, a journey overnight is necessary.

Before reaching Suez, we had received news from day to day re the trouble in Egypt, and I daresay you have read of it in the newspapers ere this. Where previously an Australian Camp had been, and other smaller ones here and there, are now to be seen hundreds of tents, mostly of Indians, in case of any trouble this way. Egypt is now picqueted all over like this. I have seen many Bedouins and know a bit about them, but it is mostly the educated or higher class of Egyptian, who is the real cause of trouble and has used these people for his own ends.

A native gets a very swollen head, and wishes to cast off all show of dependence, when he acquires education, as a rule. Further, he likes to have his own way with his own more unfortunate countryman, to keep him down, tax him and so on, and live on the fat of the land. British during their occupation have stopped this and the 'bully' or 'top-dog' wishes to be rid of them to gain their own ends. There are so many classes and creeds and so much ignorance, that I am afraid the poor, untaught and unseeing natives, is exploited in many ways. In countries like these, one class has not much sympathy for the other. It has since quietened down, but in todays wireless further trouble has taken place. Ungrateful dogs to Great Brittain, these people I speak of. You should see the country to realise that for it is wonderful what can be done with the land, and hundreds of other ways, giving employment to countless thousands, which could never possibly be, but for the British.

Troops who were booked to go home to England and Australia, have now to stay. This is not good for one's temper and patience, so that the soldiers will be all there to deal pretty sternly if necessity arises. A few hours brings us to Ismalia on the Great Bitter Lake. We had to anchor here to wait for a steamer coming from the other way in the Canal.

It was great to see her old searchlight gleaming ahead and peering into the darkness, when still a very long distance from us.

At 5.30 reveille in the morning, just rose in time to see ourselves entering Pt. Said. Many larger ships were in port, as this is our important coaling station. Saw the old 'CALEDONIAN' (still a good old ship) the P.& O. 'MALWA', and several other very large vessels. Took up our usual berth and soon began coaling and watering operations. After we had been there a bit, a large three decked beautiful looking passenger ship came into port. This ship was previously owned by Austrian shippers, but being captured during the war, the Italians took her over for their own use. A few Italian troops were on board.

The first class passengers, i.e., Officers and their women folk were granted shore leave until 3pm, but it was compulsory for the Officers to wear revolvers at their belts. Along the Canal we had noticed this. There had been trouble at Port Said and no risks were being taken. A few revolutionaries had been shot. Immediate action is the only way to convince a fanatic mind. Women carried hat-pins for their self protection.

The number 14 Australian General Hospital has now been removed to Cairo, so did not see old friends of Keswick, as we did last voyage.

We left at sundown. The air was crisp, biting and fresh.

Have made friends with one or two Officers, who are jolly fine fellows indeed. It is wonderful the amount of interest these people take in Australians and anything Australian. Some wish to come and settle out here.

I should have mentioned that we took on about 40 more patients at Pt. Said. Just a few were cot cases and the rest convalescent. My word, they were glad to get on board, for they felt the need of change of food and living very much.

One chap, a staff Sergeant, was in Mesopotamia, worked his way to Bagdad and thence to Aleppo, meeting our forces who were chasing the retreating Turks along the Syrian Coast, just at the time we were up there.

Only one of these chaps I have met. Had a most interesting chat. Also travelled India in quest of remounts for the forces. Says that lately he had to shoot 450 beautiful draught horses, between the age of 6 and 8 years. Same horses are bringing between 60 and 80 pounds in England at the present time. Freight charges are too high to send them to England. Doesn't it seem a shame, after all their useful and faithful service. Afraid it would not do to let father witness thousands of these, God's beasts and most beautiful animals being destroyed. I am told our Austr. boys were very much put out at having to part with their good four-footed pals for this purpose in Palestine. Arab horses are however, sold to the Arabs and other desert wanderers at a very high figure. There seems no end of waste in war.

Things have been going along smoothly enough in the Mediterranean. It is a lovely old sea this you know. Off Malta it seems to be nearly always angry about something, but afterwards it is smooth, the days have been good, the atmosphere crisp and sparkling (especially at reveille, 5.30 in the morning), plenty of moonshine at night, and nice sunshine by day.

Our old Aust. Southern Cross disappeared the last night out from Suez, but we see some jolly fine stars here in the Northern Hemisphere.

Two days out from Port Said, we passed a huge heavily armoured man-of-war, quite closely. Had two funnels and looked a very majestic monster indeed. The ships 3rd Officer told me that this was the 'CENTURIAN' one of the very latest super-dreadnoughts.

We have passed many steamers lately either proceeding same way, or opposite direction to ourselves for we are in the trade route here.

A day from Gibraltar we received wireless instructions to stop there to pick up a few more patients from Navy and Garrison, for England.

The old Rock is a wonderful looking thing, when we first noticed it this time, it appeared quite white in the morning light. On rising could plainly see the coast of Morocco on our left and that of Spain on our right, so knew we could not be far off.

We anchored outside the breakwater and waited according to instructions from the Signal Station.

Small boats came off from shore laden with oranges, lemons, tobacco, cigars and preserves, such as raisons and figs.

These fellows were Spaniards and real crooks. Oranges, real scimps of things sold at 1/- doz, and cigars which correctly should have been 6/- per hundred, sold at 10/- for 50.

I could not suppress a laugh, when I saw two or three fellows who had sampled the oranges they purchased, begin throwing them one by one with great accuracy back to the vendors, filling their boat with smashed oranges and skin pieces. Of course the Spaniards put on an injured air, which he used to extravagance (naturally I suppose), but it was overdone, so he got a few more, sent over by the 'next lift'. No more sale for that day I am thinking.

The harbour was simply packed with ships, with just a sprinkling of war craft.

The old Rock appears to the human eye to be impregnable, so monstrous and grim and unsalable does it look.

Before very long a small steamer came out to us with about 8 patients, 4 of these being cot cases, and naval men, also 4 nurses from the Barracks Hospital, being returned to England. The boat went away and came back with a German prisoner, but the O.C. refused to take him without a guard being sent over him, so he was taken back.

Now this was a God-send to several soldiers who had been waiting for weeks for a ship home. All other ships before us had been crammed full. Ten or twelve of these were sent along with this chap, mostly N.C.O's. Seemed absurd to have so many, but it was a good excuse for the Port Authorities to send them and the O.C. did not object.

They sleep in a few spare bunks in our quarters.

The Hun by the way, is a fat, squat little chap, wearing the typical German Uniform. Seems he had been taken to Alexandria and was on the way to England, when he was taken sick with appendicitis and put ashore here for operation and treatment.

We got away at 1pm in the afternoon, and in good time to see Ceuta and Tangiers on the Moroccan Coast. A large two funnelled French ship left shortly after, but taking a shorter cut than we, has left us behind long ago.

All the passengers are dreading the famous old Bay of Biscay which we enter tomorrow.

Some of them are not very good sailors, a fact proved during the little kick-up off Malta.

14th. Entered the old Bay this morning, and still nice and easy going, but this afternoon, the wind is blowing cold and hard, the waves rise a bit, and we find ourselves, doing a little gambling, by way of pitch and toss, and an occasional roll. Further proof of some passengers 'unseaworthiness'.

Things a bit quieter than usual, and some of our boys think it a treat, thereby getting rid of the rowdy youngsters now and again.

The other evening a concert was held, having been previously postponed owing to the weather. Passengers, Officers and troops took part, and the whole thing was a great success. The favourite song was 'I must get a cup of co-hoa-co before the ca-han-teen sha-huts'.

Troops are always ready for nonsense like this.

I attended an operation for removal of glands this afternoon, (not in an official capacity though). I can see these whenever I like.

Seeing some of the sufferers with surplus bile in sta-ma-harks (sea-sickness) reminds me of that old yarn re the steward, who going up on deck one day, asked a lady (who by the way had on anaemic looking gentleman lying half across her, with his head on her lap, and resting there as if they were the closest relations that could be). 'Yes Madam, yours is a beef tea, and what can I get for your husband'. Said she. 'Please ask him, he is not my husband!' Ha-ha, what-what?

It is raining like mad now, and the jolly water is coming through these closed windows, and running all over my bench and dripping on my legs. There is a dry spot about a foot square, and I have the writing block on that, but as the aqua drops in, it splashes over my letter, and I have to cover with a piece of blotting paper as I go along.

Excuse this terrible scrawl, I have a very bad pen, and more water in the ink than is necessary, and to make matters worse, this place being the highest on the ship, shakes like a leaf, causing everything to rattle most weirdly, for with every roll, and toss, the propellers give it what-ho-she bumps. One moment I am reaching for the line and another leaning almost heavily on the pen as she comes back, and right over top of the paper. Never mind she is a good ship, and like this by way of a change, wouldn't care if she stood on her stern. I am a real soldier sailor now.

We are bound for Southampton, which we expect to reach day after tomorrow. There is some talk that after we disembark our cargo of 'souls,' we have to proceed to London to discharge the cargo of material. That would do me first class, for it would be handy to the great metropolis.

Received two letters from Suez, one from Mrs MacKinnon re land and the others from Cornwall which I enclose.

Do not know how I will get on re transfer, but it would be wonderful thing to get off for a short while.

I must still ask you to keep this to yourself and not allow it to get outside the family circle yet.

Something has just fallen with a crash next door, in the dental workshop, and I hear the event being greeted with a few kind words of endearment by the chap working in there.

Everything not securely fixed, will move if one is not on the lookout.

Have just had a peep outside. The wind is howling through the rigging and while we are trying to pursue a course say this ----- we are going ^^^^^either the stern or the bow twisting round as the waves catch her. Nothing but big white horses on this desolate waste of water, for as far as the eye can reach.

I see a young lady walking (or trying to) along the boat deck with two gents. At every lean over or reel of the ship, she grabs them both, even the slightest provocation suffices, but judging by her looks, the action of the ship is not really provoking her at all.

I suppose in years to come I will long for another day like this one, under such another circumstance. No doubt the old sea has a calling, quite its own, and I have experienced it. As you say, when the time comes to leave the ship, one will feel the parting company.

We have been paid today. I was stony broke when we left Bombay, but having drawn no money since leaving home, am now afloat once again. I always leave my pay in the Orderly Room in case of emergency and I have found this a wise policy on more than one occasion.

A beautiful wave has just splashed against the ship and the spray came right up and over here. What a force in them, just push the ship one side, as if it were only a match-box.

(Later just before going to bed) It is now after 10 o'clock. I have been doing a little sewing and darning, so as to be quite ready and up to date when we get leave in England. The old adage that a stitch in time saves nine, is a very true one I find.

Water is till running off my bench, as if a tap were let over it. The wind is stronger still now, and amounts to something like a shriek. The good old ship is behaving well under the circumstances. It is perhaps as well that we are not going the other way, or we should know all about it. The wind is very icy, but on our quarter. Passed a steamer towing a ship, probably one in distress. No easy, comfy job I guess in this sea.

Just a little while ago, another passed us quite closely. A poor old tramp, and I watched her through my glasses.

All I could see of her at times was her funnel just above the level of the water, when she would bob up very suddenly and be lost to view again in the trough of the sea.

They are getting a lively time of it, I know. I saw one huge wave rush along her whole length, seemingly to engulf the poor old beggar. This sort of weather must be pretty rough on sailing ships. Just as I wrote that last few words a wave hit us causing the ship to heel over quickly, and as suddenly overbalancing me and my stool, also a big chair I have here. I am getting used to it by spreading my legs out and trying to act the tripod trick with only two stilts. We have an old naval Officer on board who told me tonight that this was one of the best sea boats he had ever travelled in, proved by a sea such as this.

Now I must go and shave before turning in (ah, there's a good yun). Too wet to sleep out tonight, will be first time missed since leaving Australia. Have written to your cousin, stating I am on my way to visit her.

How very different these angry, foaming, lashing, huge waves, to those little dreamy, whispering, murmuring wavelets at Melb beach, I told you of, or that velvety, lazy, blue, smiling ocean of the tropics, when no typhoon about. This is grey and vexed looking and a dangerous customer, seems at war with the elements that cause it.

You in your still, quiet cots, with perhaps the door ajar to admit a little air, probably cannot conceive the difference as this is. It's fun though. 15th. Well dear I found a spot on the well deck after all to sleep on, and dreamt the dreams of the just.

This morning however the wind came up with more fury than ever, and has kept so all day. There is now quite a gale on and waves are continually splashing up over the decks, even sometimes sending the spray right over this house.

Caught up to a poor old tramp this morning, but she had given the sea best and was 'hove to'. We however are still plunging and running straight into it. A little later we came up to a little sailing vessel, no larger than one of those ketches at Port Adelaide. She had only a storm jib up and was running before the wind, and appeared to be doing splendidly. She was completely lost to view at times.

There have been many smashes owing to extreme rolling of the ship. You should have seen the state of things here in the lab when I came up this morning. A valuable electric incubator suffered damage through falling to the floor from a good height. Have had heavy rain and hail today. One would think these windows which are facing the weather, would break through the force of the hail against them.

Ugh! How she shivers and trembles, I have to hold tight to my bench as I write this, with knees hard up against, underneath. We will reach the English Channel tomorrow and are to encounter easterly winds. Talk about foam and waves lashing themselves to pieces, you should see this, but I say again, she is a good old ship. The old lab floor is awash, but it will drain away some day I suppose. It would be absurd to try and tidy, wash or straighten anything till this is over. Officer's luggage rolls about the ward floor as if every trunk and package were on wheels.

16th. Well darling, the sea was much calmer this morning. Later in the day I noticed that the water was greeny coloured, seeming to indicate that we were in the English Channel. Sighted land, the Isle of Wight @ 4pm, and when Ventnor was reached, turned and proceeded along the shore, and later turned towards Portsmouth. The Isle looks lovely, and I was fortunate enough to catch the sun setting behind the hills, and shining through the tall trees which lined the top.

Many steam and sailing ships about. A good fog on last time we were here, but quite clear tonight. A pilot joined us, and we are now anchored off St. Helen's, in what is known as the 'Southampton Waters'.

The clock goes on 1 hour tonight, in order to conform with the daylight saving scheme in England. Already late as I have been tidying and straightening up tonight, and will lose an hours rest as it is.

One of the poor little youngsters is down sick with diphtheria today. Hard luck just as he is almost ready to go off. I am endeavouring to grow the causal germ on blood-serum agar media, ready for the morning, but the smash yesterday has upset my incubator, and I have a temporary arrangement going. Expect to go in to Port tomorrow early and disembark. Noticed the topmast of a wrecked vessel as we were coming in, (just above water).

One of the Sgts fell down yesterday, heavily upon a rail, when the ship gave a sudden, very violent lurch. He cut his face a good deal, and is disfigured for a week or so, hard luck also, if he wished at all to look OK to meet his lady here.

17th. Went in very early and found the port full of ships, took up our old berth, into which two very powerful tugs quickly placed us. While we were at the anchorage, an American lake steamer laden with Tommies came in, and another, a British vessel with good old Australians from France, who coo-ee-ed and waved to us.

Many of them, know the good old 'Karoola' I guess.

No crowd congregated to meet us. The troops were taken off and sent by train before the Officers and passengers.

I had a lively time helping some of the Officers with their luggage. I do not know how they would have got on otherwise, seem to have too much even for themselves to look after.

They have been very good to me, for I have kept them strictly in their place all through. All had an early breakfast, and were keen on making me a present of some sort as a token of their appreciation, which I thought was decent enough.

To make a long story short, all were got rid of, and the ship cleared by 1pm., but now word came, that owing to the dock labourer's refusal to discharge the cargo till after Easter holidays, we have to proceed to Devonport @ 4pm to unload there. This is a big naval base, and only a mile or so from Plymouth. I have been here before and much enjoyed myself during my stay. It is also only a couple of hours by train from Launceston which is handy, although further away from London, where I wanted to go first of all.

Left punctually @ 4pm, and coming down the Southampton Water again, see many ships at the anchorage waiting to go up to port. About a dozen peculiarly built naval ships too, and all the afternoon and right up to time of writing, ships, ships all around and about us, either going from or coming to Southampton for it is a very important shipping port indeed. We are now off the Isle of Wight. A good many lighthouses mark the way along its coast. It seems to be good, to have the ship clear of the crowd once again. The O.C. and Adjutant have gone to London Headquarters to make arrangements re leave etc., and peace and quietness reigns supreme.

Everything such as bedding and ward utensils have already been stowed and cleared away.

Well darling, I will close this now, with perhaps an abrupt conclusion, for Plymouth being a port of call for inward and outward mail steamers bound from and to Australia, I may catch an early post with this, for we arrive first thing in the morning. We have already slowed down, so as not to reach there too early before daybreak.

I daresay the folk who came home with us, will soon be at their own homes, and will be glad of the change, for many have not been to England for a good number of years.

I sincerely trust all are quite well and happy at home, I long for a letter from you now.

My fondest love to my dear father, Ada, Bobs, Renie, Ralphie and little Colin. We had a youngster on board very much like that young tinker. Love for yourself you darling, and God bless you is my sincerest wish.

Your loving Son, Rex.

P.S. Hear rumours of serious trouble in Bombay and in other parts of India. Seem fortunate to have got away when we did. I hope the murder of a few European women and children is not a true report.

www.ingramcontent.com/pod-product-compliance
Lightning Source LLC
Chambersburg PA
CBHW041238240426
43661CB00070B/2915